HUMAN RIGHTS
Towards a Global Values System

Dr. Denise R. Ames

Published in 2016 by Center for Global Awareness

Text copyright © 2016 by Dr. Denise R. Ames
Images are copyright © the respective owners as noted in each credit and are used under
    one of the following licenses:
Creative Commons License 3.0 *http://creativecommons.org/licenses/by-sa/3.0/*
GNU Free Documentation License
Uncredited images are, to the best of the author's knowledge, in the public domain.

All rights reserved. No portion of this book may be reproduced, stored in a retrieval system, or transmitted in any form or by any means—mechanical, electronic, photocopying, recording, or otherwise—without written permission from the publisher.

ISBN: 978-1-943841-04-2

Book and cover design by Jeanine McGann
Graphic images on cover designed by Freepik.com

The principal text of this book was composed in Minion Pro

The Center for Global Awareness
Albuquerque, New Mexico, USA
www.global-awareness.org

Acknowledgments

I would like to thank several people in helping to bring this human rights book project to fruition. First and foremost, as always, a special thanks to Nancy W. Harmon, my partner and board of directors member at the Center for Global Awareness. Her crisp editing, countless suggestions and unfailing support have helped to make this book possible. Second, I would like to extend a special thanks to Jeanine McGann for her excellent work in formatting, editing, and getting the book ready for market. Her thorough work for the Center for Global Awareness is certainly appreciated and without her efforts, CGA would cease to operate efficiently. Also, thanks to Sarah Sheesely, the CGA program manager. Her suggestions and review of the book has been appreciated. A special thanks to two reviewers: Francisco Gomes de Matos, Ph.D., a peace linguist and human rights educator from Recife, Brazil and Jacque Brown Williams a secondary school teacher for 40 years, folk tales collector, and human rights activist in her local area of North Carolina.

Contents

Acknowledgments..iii
Preface...vii

Chapter 1. Human Rights: An Introduction
An Introduction to Human Rights..2
Definitions of Human Rights..3
Categories of Human Rights...4
    Three Generations of Rights..4
    Six Families of Rights..5
Universal Declaration of Human Rights (UDHR)...................................6
Other Human Rights Documents...7
Human Rights: Ten Characteristics...8
Why Human Rights?..10
    Two Worldviews: Eastern and Western...11
A History and Philosophy of Human Rights..12
    Ethic of Reciprocity or the Golden Rule..12
    Indigenous People..13
    Ubuntu..14
    Mesopotamia and Hammurabi's Code..16
    Judeo-Christian Tradition..17
    Persian Empire: The Cyrus the Cyclinder..17
    Buddhism..18
    Confucianism...20
    Ancient Greek Philosophers...21
    Stoics...22
    Maurya Empire of Ancient India...22
    Christianity and St. Thomas Aquinas..23
    Islam..24
    England in the Middle Ages and the Magna Carta..........................26
    European Renaissance and Humanism...27
    The Western Enlightenment...27
    The 19th and 20th Centuries..29

Chapter 2. Social Movements & Human Rights
What are Social Movements?...32
    Social Movements: A Definition..32
    Types of Social Movements..34
    Life Cycle of a Social Movement..34
    Social Movement Tactics..35
    The Rise of Social Movements...36
Early Social Movements...36
    The Abolitionist Social Movement..36
    Public Education as a Social Movement...38
    The Women's Suffrage Movement...40
    The Environmental Movement..41
    The Labor Movement..43
    Child Rights and Labor Movement...44
Social Movements: The Modern Era 1945 to 1990................................45
    The American Civil Rights Movement...45
    The Women's Movement..47

    The Modern Environmental Movement...48
    LGBT Social Movement..50
Global Social Movements: 1990 Onward..51
    Global Justice Movements..52
    Rights of Corporations...53
    Anti-Consumerism Movement..54
    Environmental Movement...56
    Rights of Indigenous Peoples...56
    The LGBT Movement...59
    Human Rights for People with Disabilities..59
    Children's Rights..60

Chapter 3. Human Rights Violations
Introduction to Human Rights Violations..64
    The Rome Statute of the International Criminal Court.....................................64
The Crime of Aggression..65
    The 2003 Invasion of Iraq...66
War Crimes...67
    My Lai Massacre..68
Crimes Against Humanity..68
    The Trail of Tears...68
    The Crimes of Charles Taylor..69
Genocide...71
    Ralph Lemkin..71
    The What, Why, Who, How and When, and Where of Genocide......................73
        The What of Genocide..73
        The Why of Genocide...75
        The Who of Genocide..75
        The How and When of Genocide...76
        The Where of Genocide..76
Genocide in History: Five Case Studies..77
    The Biblical Old Testament...77
    Rome..78
    Christians...78
    The Mongols..79
    Indigenous Peoples of North and South America..79
Twentieth Century Genocides..80
    The Holocaust...80
        Liberation...85
        The Story of Anne Frank: A Holocaust Victim..85
    Rwanda..87

Chapter 4. Case Studies of Human Rights Abuses
The Zulu of South Africa...96
The Democratic Republic of the Congo...98
Armenia..104
Ukraine...106
Cambodia...108
Guatemala..110
Bosnia and Kosovo...112
The Taliban...117
The Crisis in Darfur...122

Chapter 5. Human Rights Activists
An Introduction to Human Rights Activists...128
Wangari Maathai, Kenya..128
Shirin Ebadi, Iran...133
Aung San Suu Kyi, Burma..139
Rigoberta Menchu, Guatemala..143
Muhammad Yunus, Bangladesh..149
His Holiness The Dali Llama, Tibet..154

Chapter 6. Human Rights Today
The Role of the United Nations in Protecting Human Rights....................................162
    The United Nations Human Rights Treaties...163
    United Nations Human Rights Agencies..164
Regional Human Rights Organizations...166
    1. The European Convention for the Protection of Human Rights....................166
    2. The Inter-American Commission on Human Rights.......................................166
    3. African Commission on Human and Peoples' Rights......................................166
    4. The Arab Charter on Human Rights...167
    5. The ASEAN Intergovernmental Commission on Human Rights....................168
Promotion of Human Rights by States...168
Non-Governmental Organizations..169
    Amnesty International..170
    The Carter Center...172
    Freedom House...174
    Human Rights First...175
    Human Rights Watch..177
    International Committee of the Red Cross...180
    Oxfam...182
    Robert F. Kennedy Center for Justice and Human Rights...................................185
Local Human Rights Organizations..187
    The Albuquerque Center for Peace and Justice...187
The Focus of Human Rights in the Future...188
    1. Euthanasia..188
    2. Animal Rights..189
    3. Right to Life...189
    4. Human Rights and Multi-National Corporations...190
    5. Human Rights and the Environment..190
Concluding Insights: The Future of Human Rights...190

Endnotes..192
Glossary...202
Index..210
About the Author..215

Bibliography - http://global-awareness.org/resources/rightsdocs/biblio.pdf
Additional Resources - http://global-awareness.org/resources/humanrights.html

PREFACE

The book, *Human Rights: Towards a Global Values System*, has taken many interesting twists and turns on its path to completion. By all counts, it should not have been written or completed, but I have finished the book and I am very happy to share it with you.

It started in the summer of 2008. I just finished teaching my last class on world history at the community college in Albuquerque, and I was ready for a new venture. Although I loved teaching and I would miss interacting with students, I was ready to move on. I just didn't know quite yet what that move was going to be. I decided a good start was to send out letters of inquiry to educational publishers about publishing a global issues series and my holistic world history book.

I got a quick response from a well-known and long established educational publisher about writing a series of four books called the Global Skills series for secondary school students. My world history book, which was already mostly completed, would be worked into the line-up the next year. I was ecstatic!

The Global Skills book series was to be about the subjects of Terrorism, Immigration, Globalization, and Human Rights. Infused through the content of the books would be global skills that I and the publisher thought were necessary for secondary students to know. I was thrilled with the prospect and the challenge of writing the books and quickly agreed to take on the project.

My first decision was deciding on what would be my first book. I mulled over my choices. I rightly thought that terrorism, immigration, and the global economy were such "hot button" issues that they would be the most difficult to explain in an even-handed way. Also, the topics were complex, and it would take some thought and research to convey them in a simplified yet interesting way for secondary students. I thought that the human rights topic was one that most people agreed with and supported and it would be easier to write than the other three topics. Also, I was very interested in human rights!

My second big decision was to consider which global skills for students would be woven throughout the book. The publisher suggested some traditional skills that students learn in social studies classes, such as geographic literacy, writing skills, examining primary source documents, citizenship, and critical thinking. I thought these were good, but I wanted to incorporate what I think are other important global skills, such as systems thinking and cross-cultural awareness, into the mix as well. It didn't take much persuading to get the publisher on board with my suggestion for two more important global skills.

I dove into the project with gusto! I found that the story of human rights takes us on a wild ride of extreme emotions. One minute we are confronted with the evil of human depravity as the Holocaust unfolds and the next minute the butchery of the Rwanda genocide is told. Yet, the spirit of human compassion and love is voiced through the work of human rights activists at every level, from the wonderful work of noted environmentalist Wangari Maathai to the dedication of rank-and-file workers that I interviewed at organizations such as Freedom House, Robert F. Kennedy Center or the Carter Center. As a reader of this human rights book, it is best to prepare to be taken on an emotional roller-coaster ride.

As 2008 came to a close, I had the go ahead for the outline of the four book series, and I had also completed chapter one of the human rights book. I submitted the first draft of the chapter, the editor replied that it needed some editing, but the ideas were good and to go ahead with the other chapters. I asked again about the contract that was supposed to be forthcoming, and I got another vague promise that the board of directors hadn't convened to approve the contract yet, but there were no problems—just be patient. I had an uneasy feeling that something was going on behind the scenes and it wouldn't be beneficial to me.

I continued the project, but not with the gusto that I had before. I began to supplement my work on the human rights book with edits and rewrites of my holistic world history book. I also started to do preliminary research into the global economy. The financial crisis was now full-blown, and discussion about the economy was an interesting and incendiary topic. In the fall of 2009, over a year after I took on the project, I got the news.

The publisher that had been around for over 50 years and a mainstay of social studies resources was being merged with a bigger publisher. The publisher was yet another victim of the corporatization of the publishing industry and the global economy that makes it difficult for small, family-owned businesses to survive. Although I had seen the writing on wall for the past 6 months, I was still disappointed. But out of that disappointment, another path emerged that has actually been more in alignment with my professional and personal goals.

I had started a small organization in June 2003 called the Center for Global Awareness (CGA). The goal of CGA was to conduct workshops and professional development services for educators about the topics of a holistic world history, the global economy and global awareness. I was the main person at CGA, while others might join me in a particular project or event. I thoroughly enjoyed the work and particularly liked the freedom to create materials on topics I thought were important and share them with others. CGA stayed small, since I continued my adjunct teaching as well. With the end of my publishing project, I decided to turn to making CGA a larger and more influential organization.

As luck would have it, I reconnected in the summer of 2009 with a friend whom I first met in 2002, Nancy Harmon. We first met at a study group on the global economy in 2002. It was a wonderful experience, and I liked Nancy immediately. We were able to laugh despite the serious topic we were studying. In fact, the discussion group inspired me to form my infant organization, CGA. In 2009, Nancy and I were serving on the board of directors of a nonprofit called Peace Pals. We enjoyed our work on the board and the hard-working and inspiring president of the organization, Sarah Wilkerson.

Nancy was retiring from teaching at the end of 2009, but was interested in staying connected to the educational field. I told her about my work at CGA and that I wanted to expand it and make it a nonprofit. She was interested in joining me as a partner and board of director's member. I was thrilled and immediately agreed. In 2010 we applied for nonprofit status through the IRS.

We decided that CGA would develop global topic materials from a holistic approach and global perspective. We would target the 9-university educational audience. Our first order of business was to get some materials ready to market and create a new website for our organization. Nancy is an excellent editor and edited my holistic world history book and an educator's handbook for teaching world history. The human rights book, although not forgotten, was suddenly thrust onto the back burner, as the goal of getting CGA ready as a nonprofit organization was top priority.

From 2010 onwards, other books quickly followed: the global economy, financial literacy, a brief edition of the global economy, and a second edition of the holistic world history. Countless blogs, lesson plans, and consulting work for other educational organizations took precedence over the human rights book. But it was not forgotten, and finally in 2015 I decided to finish writing and filling in the research gaps of the book. I am a better starter than finisher, and finishing the book seemed like a daunting task. But once I got re-involved in the book I became as enthusiastic as I was in the summer of 2009.

One of the ideas that I did want to emphasize in this book that was not as apparent to me in 2009 is the fact that human rights is not universally accepted as a values system throughout the world. In fact, generally speaking, I think the indifference to human rights is currently more pronounced than it was in 2009. The world, to me and to other commentators, appears to be getting more authoritarian with strong ideologies that deny followers the freedom of open-mindedness and compassion, the cornerstones of human rights. To me, human rights is a viable global values system and I have argued for this case in the book.

Hopefully, with lots of dedication and forbearance, supporters can promote human rights as a global values system that can be the foundation for the ethical and moral code of our interdependent world. This book is dedicated to that prospect.

Please visit the website at http://global-awareness.org/resources/humanrights.html to access the FREE resources for this book.

Please note that the bold terms throughout the text are in the glossary located on page 202.

CHAPTER ONE

HUMAN RIGHTS: AN INTRODUCTION

"...recognition of the inherent dignity and of the equal and inalienable rights of all members of the human family is the foundation of freedom, justice and peace in the world."

— *Preamble to the Universal Declaration of Human Rights, 1948*

AN INTRODUCTION TO HUMAN RIGHTS

Malin... *"When Malin was 14, she was exchanged for 15 heads of cattle. She was to be married in an arranged marriage and pulled out of school in order to prepare for the wedding. Although she had dreamed about becoming a health worker, her father refused to allow her to continue schooling and eventually sent her mother away since she also disagreed with the marriage. According to her father, her education was not a priority compared to 15 heads of cattle. Determined to return to school and prevent the marriage, Malin wrote to a local council member in Kenya asking for help.*

When the media became involved, officials arrested her father-in-law. Afterwards, Malin says, "That was the happiest moment in the whole drama because it meant that I had won, and it was possible to go against tradition." Besides arranged marriages, girls are prevented from attending school because of the obligation to siblings and household chores."

Helen... *"In Costa Rica, Helen, although only 11, stays home to clean the house, unable to afford school. "I'm only in second grade because whenever I go to school, they take me out," she says. "The first time it was because my brother Ricardo was born, and I had to take care of him. Later, it was because my mom didn't have the money to keep us all in school."* [1]

These heart-wrenching stories have a common thread: they are about human rights. These stories touch many of us emotionally—we may feel compassion for the victims and want to help their situation. Although emotional responses are certainly valid reactions to human rights abuses, I will expand the story of human rights in this book to include a wide range of explanations, institutions, organizations, laws, treaties, documents, philosophies, history, case studies, dedicated individuals, emotional reactions, and changes in attitudes.

The purpose of this book is to provide a general overview of critical human rights debates and issues today and in the past. It is also to argue for the implementation and acceptance of human rights as a global values system. Just imagine that I put a question mark in the title of this book: *Human Rights: Towards a Global Values System?* This questions mark shows that I am questioning whether human rights are actually accepted globally as universal human values. Although I live in the United States and Western values, such as freedom of speech, expression, religion, the press and the dignity of all humans, are deeply imbedded in my outlook of life, I realize that many people in other parts of the world do not hold these values. Either they are not part of their cultural foundation, or their governments or other authorities restrict their exercising of these values. My aim in this book is to explain, encourage and support an expanded notion of human rights as a universal values system for all global citizens to embrace. This expanded notion of human rights is not just a modern or Western concept; it has broad and deep historical roots that span diverse cultures, societies, and nations throughout the world. With this expanded notion, human rights can be a universal values system for all to uphold. This book is designed to help global citizens acquire knowledge, attitudes, and skills to become better informed about the complex issue of human rights and more actively engaged in working for change.

Most of us probably understand that the individual stories above are violations of human rights, but wonder why humans can be so violent at times and so compassionate at other times. This is a dilemma that has confused people for thousands of years. Religious scholar and writer Karen Armstrong has put forth a simple, yet intriguing, explanation for this dilemma in her book *Fields of Blood: Religion and the History of Violence*. Each person has basically three parts to his/her brain she writes. In our "old brain" or **reptilian brain** that we have inherited from the reptiles 500 million years ago, our self-centered survival behaviors—feed, fight, flee, and reproduce—direct us with no altruistic impulses. About 120 million years ago after mammals appeared, our **limbic system** formed over the core brain and stimulated new behaviors, such as protecting others, nurturing the young, and sharing with other humans for survival—in other words, empathy. About 20,000-40,000 years ago, humans evolved the **neocortex**, home of reasoning powers and self-awareness. Thus, humans today struggle with the conflicting impulses of their three distinct parts of the brain.[2] States, governments, empires or those in power, by their very nature, use violence and abuse our human rights to maintain power and perpetuate the state. Every state in history has done this. I know my country, the United States, is guilty of many abuses, even though it has advanced human rights and instituted many mechanisms to check abuses and power. I have found in my research of human rights that the old, reptilian brain violently asserts itself much too frequently through history. When triggers of scarce resources, territorial infringement, or threats to power structures are present, the reptilian brain takes over and overshadows the two other parts of the brain. But human rights as a universal values system draw from the limbic and neocortex brain, which offers a compassionate counter to our innately violent reptilian behaviors.

There is a lot more to human rights than we may think. Here are a few of the many questions that this book addresses: what are human rights, who possesses human rights, what happens to those who violate human rights, how many human rights are there, what is the history of human rights, should they be narrowly or broadly interpreted, who protects human rights, what happens when human rights are violated, why do we need human rights? But before we delve into our study of real human rights issues, let's step back and get a foundation for the subject. In this introductory chapter we will first define the issue (not as easy as you may think), discuss the characteristics of human rights, give a brief history, and examine several important documents that have helped shape the human rights issue. I invite you to join with me in this intriguing, somber, and inspiring exploration of the fascinating subject of human rights.

DEFINITIONS OF HUMAN RIGHTS

Human rights are difficult to define. Diverse cultures, people, nations, and institutions can interpret what seems like a simple concept, quite differently. When the media typically uses the term, it often means protection from random jailing, all forms of torture, retribution for speaking out or protesting against a government. However, the meaning of human rights is broader and more complex and, therefore, a wide range of definitions is given. Let's look at six different definitions.

Human rights ...
1. ... "are basic moral guarantees that people in all countries and cultures [supposedly] have simply because they are people. Calling these guarantees "rights" suggests that all individuals have them, they are of high priority ...and they are held to be universal." (James Nickel, *Making Sense of Human Rights*)
2. ... "are universal rights [that] belong to individuals by virtue of their being human, encompassing civil, political, economic, social, and cultural rights and freedoms, and based on the notion of personal dignity and worth." (*Columbia Electronic Encyclopedia*)

3. ...require three interlocking qualities: Rights must be natural (inherent in human beings), equal (same for everyone), and universal (applicable everywhere). All humans...possess them equally... because they are human beings. (Lynn Hunt, *America.gov*)

4. ... "are a special sort of inalienable moral right. They attach to all persons equally, by virtue of their humanity, irrespective of race, nationality, or membership of any particular social group. They specify the minimum conditions for human dignity and a tolerable life." (Peter Burnell, *Ask Answer*)

5. ... "are the basic rights and freedoms to which all humans are entitled; ...including the right to life and liberty, freedom of thought and expression, and equality before the law." (*American Heritage Dictionary*)

6. ... "include international norms (standards) that help to protect all people everywhere from severe political, legal, and social abuses." James Nickel (*Plato*, Stanford University)

Questions to Consider
1. Which of these definitions do you think is the best? Why?

CATEGORIES OF HUMAN RIGHTS

Different groupings of human rights help us remember and better understand them. Below are two groupings of human rights—three generations of rights and six families of rights.

THREE GENERATIONS OF RIGHTS

A handy way of studying human rights is to see how they have evolved and expanded historically. This grouping of human rights outlines three generations of rights.

1. First Generation of Human Rights: Political and Civil Rights

First generation of human rights limits what others, including the government, can do to an individual and include the most recognized ones of life, liberty, right of peaceful assembly, and freedom of thought, religion (worship), and speech. Every citizen shall have the right to take part freely in the activities of his/her government, either directly or through freely chosen representatives. They also include freedom of movement, freedom from torture, and the right to own property. A majority of the world community of nations accepts these rights. Political and civil rights expanded during the European Enlightenment period in the 17th and 18th centuries, but also have a long history in many other traditions (see history section). During the Enlightenment, philosophers created well-known documents that gradually put human rights into national and international law codes.

2. Second Generation Rights: Social, Economic, and Cultural Rights

Second generation rights evolved after the passage of civil and political rights. They grew out of the harsh economic conditions in the mid-1800s, when many people's livelihoods fluctuated with the ups and downs of the marketplace. Many lost their wages to crooked employers or worked under unclean and unsafe conditions. These rights include equality and nondiscrimination for women and minorities, the right to work, fair pay, safe and healthy working conditions, the right to form trade unions, social security, and sufficient food, clothing, housing, health care, and education.

3. Third Generation Rights: Group Rights and the Environment

Third generation rights include rights for women, minorities, and indigenous peoples. These rights are of special interest today, as they are still being debated and defined. Freedom from discrimination is important in the United Nation's (UN) Universal Declaration of Rights and is also included in later treaties. The UN's Civil and Political Covenant, for example, calls upon participating states to respect and protect their people's rights "without distinction of any kind, such as race, color, sex, language, political or other opinion, national or social origin, property, birth, or social status."³ Minority groups are often targets of violence, ranging from name calling to actual bodily abuse. Thus, human rights documents include rights that refer to minorities clearly and give them special protections. Several standard individual rights are especially important to ethnic (national or cultural) and religious minorities, such as the right to freedom of association, assembly, religion, and freedom from discrimination. Article 27 of the Civil and Political Covenant says ethnic or religious minorities "shall not be denied the right … to enjoy their own culture, to profess and practice their own religion, or use their own language."

Environmental rights are rights of nature. You may question whether these are actually human rights since the rights' holders are not human, but this is an example in which human rights are viewed broadly. This right establishes a minimal environmental standard which gives all people the right to a clean, healthy, and safe environment. But environmental protection is very expensive and difficult to carry out. Many governments are unable to adequately protect the environment, since they must meet their citizens most basic needs first. The important point is that the goal of environmental protection may not be immediately met—rather it is stated as a high-priority and steps are taken to eventually reach this goal.

Since the writing and passage of the Declaration of Human Rights in 1948, new human rights have been added. However, when thinking about adding new rights to the document, it is important to realize that if no new resources or money are available to help put into action the particular right, it may be difficult to get new rights enacted. Rights do not just magically get enacted without sufficient resources.⁴

SIX FAMILIES OF RIGHTS[5]

The following are **six families of rights**:
1. Security rights…protect against crimes such as murder, massacre, torture, and rape.
2. Due process rights…protect against legal abuses such as imprisonment without trial, secret trials, and excessive punishments.
3. Liberty rights…protect freedoms such as belief, expression, association, assembly, and movement.
4. Political rights…protect individual participation in politics such as communicating, assembling, protesting, voting, and serving in public office.
5. Equality rights…guarantee equal citizenship, equality before the law, and nondiscrimination.
6. Social or welfare rights…require that government provide education for all children and protect them against severe poverty and starvation.

The Universal Declaration does not include group rights, but later treaties do. **Group rights** protect ethnic groups from genocide and support ownership of their national territories and resources.

Our Rights[6]

Freedom of thought, conscience and religion
Freedom of opinion and expression
Right to life, liberty and security
Freedom of peaceful assembly and association
Freedom from slavery
Prohibition of torture
Prevention of cruel, inhuman or degrading treatment
Right to an education
Recognition before the law
Prevention of arbitrary arrest, detention or exile
Right to a fair and public hearing
Right to freedom of movement
Right to a nationality
Right to ownership of property
Right to work and join trade unions
Right to rest and leisure
Right to an adequate standard of living
Right to marry, with free and full consent of both people

Universal Declaration of Human Rights (UDHR)

After the end of World War II in 1945, many people looked back at the horrors unleashed by the war and wondered what happened to our sense of humanity, morals and ethics. The shock of the terrible Holocaust, the dropping of the atomic bomb by the U.S., killing thousands of Japanese civilians, and the death and suffering of millions around the world (the Chinese had the most deaths with an estimated 25 million). This cruelty affected many concerned citizens who decided they could no longer look the other way while tyrants jailed, tortured, and killed their fellow citizens. They took steps to found an international organization called the **United Nations** (UN) in 1945. The stated purpose of the UN is to set up a framework for national cooperation in the areas of international law and security, economic development, social progress, human rights, and world peace. Today the UN is located on international territory in New York City and has 193 member states.

One of the main accomplishments of the UN is the passage of the **Universal Declaration of Human Rights** (UDHR) in 1948. Former First Lady Eleanor Roosevelt, wife of former U.S. President Franklin Roosevelt and noted humanitarian, served as President and Chair of the UN Commission on Human Rights from 1946-1952. Under her able and dedicated

Eleanor Roosevelt holding the Spanish version of the Universal Declaration of Human Rights.

leadership, member states passed over two dozen human rights laws. International human rights' experts researched and wrote the UDHR, including representatives from all continents and all major religions, and drawing on contributions from peace leaders around the world, such as Mahatma Gandhi of India. Civil, political, economic, social and cultural rights were included as inseparable, basic human rights. The countries that signed the document pledged to respect and protect the dignity and rights of all humans across the globe.

United Nations Declaration of Human Rights 1948[7]
Preamble

Whereas recognition of the inherent dignity and of the equal and inalienable rights of all members of the human family is the foundation of freedom, justice and peace in the world,

Whereas disregard and contempt for human rights have resulted in barbarous acts which have outraged the conscience of mankind, and the advent of a world in which human beings shall enjoy freedom of speech and belief and freedom from fear and want has been proclaimed as the highest aspiration of the common people,

Whereas it is essential, if man is not to be compelled to have recourse, as a last resort, to rebellion against tyranny and oppression, that human rights should be protected by the rule of law,

Whereas it is essential to promote the development of friendly relations between nations,

Whereas the peoples of the United Nations have in the Charter reaffirmed their faith in fundamental human rights, in the dignity and worth of the human person and in the equal rights of men and women and have determined to promote social progress and better standards of life in larger freedom,

Whereas Member States have pledged themselves to achieve, in co-operation with the United Nations, the promotion of universal respect for and observance of human rights and fundamental freedoms,

Whereas a common understanding of these rights and freedoms is of the greatest importance for the full realization of this pledge,

Now, Therefore THE GENERAL ASSEMBLY proclaims THIS UNIVERSAL DECLARATION OF HUMAN RIGHTS as a common standard of achievement for all peoples and all nations, to the end that every individual and every organ of society, keeping this Declaration constantly in mind, shall strive by teaching and education to promote respect for these rights and freedoms and by progressive measures, national and international, to secure their universal and effective recognition and observance, both among the peoples of Member States themselves and among the peoples of territories under their jurisdiction.

OTHER HUMAN RIGHTS DOCUMENTS

International laws guarantee human rights. They explain the ways governments should promote and protect human rights and fundamental freedoms of individuals or groups. Although the Universal Declaration of Human Rights document carries the most weight, many other significant documents such as international treaties, national laws, and general principles, have been drawn upon to form today's human rights program. The following 10 documents are a few of the many significant contributions added to the body of human rights policies since the end of World War II.

1. **Genocide Convention**, the United Nations Convention on the Prevention and Punishment of the Crime of Genocide (CPPCG), was adopted by the UN General Assembly in 1948, and by 2009 140 countries have ratified the convention. Article 2 of the convention states that **genocide** is "acts committed with intent to destroy, in whole or in part, a national, ethnical, racial or religious group: killing members of the group; causing serious bodily or mental harm to members of the group; deliberately inflicting on the group conditions of life, calculated to bring about its physical destruction in whole or in part; imposing measures intended to prevent births within the group; [and] forcibly transferring children of the group to another group." Ideally, all participating countries should prevent and punish actions of genocide in war and peacetime.

2. **European Social Charter**, adopted in 1961 and revised significantly in 1996 guarantees rights and freedoms which affect the daily lives of all individuals. The basic rights include housing, health, education, employment, social and legal protection, free movement of persons and non discrimination.

3. The **International Convention on the Elimination of All Forms of Racial Discrimination** (ICERD), adopted and signed by the UN General Assembly on December 21, 1965, became effective on January 4, 1969. The ICERD promotes second-generation human rights in which signature-nations commit to do away with racial discrimination.

4. **United Nation's International Covenant on Economic, Social, and Cultural Rights** is a treaty adopted and signed by the UN General Assembly in 1966 and has been effective since 1976. Delegates work toward enjoyment of economic, social, and cultural rights (ESCR), including labor,

health, education, and an adequate standard of living.

5. **The Convention on the Elimination of All Forms of Discrimination Against Women** (CEDAW), adopted in 1979 by the UN General Assembly, is often described as an international bill of rights for women. It consists of a preamble and 30 articles, defines discrimination against women and establishes a plan of action to end it.

6. **The African Charter on Human and Peoples' Rights** (also known as the Banjul Charter, 1981) promotes and protects human rights and basic freedoms for Africans. In addition to recognizing the basic individual rights, the Charter supports collective or group rights, also called people rights. The Charter recognizes group rights more than Western human rights documents, which tend to promote individual rights. It also formally spoke out against apartheid in South Africa and colonialism.

30th-aniversary of the Banjul Charter

7. **The United Nations Convention Against Torture and Other Cruel, Inhuman or Degrading Treatment or Punishment**, adopted by the UN General Assembly in 1984, aims to prevent torture worldwide, requires states to take measures to prevent torture within their national borders, and prevents states from returning those to their home country who may face torture.

8. **Convention on the Rights of the Child**, adopted in 1989, fully extends human rights to children, more so than any other legal document up to that point. The Convention's preamble states: "The child, by reason of his physical and mental immaturity, needs special safeguards and care, including appropriate legal protection, before as well as after birth." All UN members have signed the convention; however, all but three countries have yet to ratify it: Somalia, South Sudan and the U.S. Currently, President Barack Obama has supported ratification but Republicans in the Senate have not brought the treaty to a vote.

9. **The Convention on the Rights of All Migrant Workers**, adopted in 1990, defines a migrant worker as a person who is…"engaged in a remunerated [paid] activity in a State of which he or she is not a national." The document legally ensures protection and respect for the human rights of all migrants.

10. **The Vienna Declaration and Program of Action** (VDPA) is a declaration adopted by consensus at the World Conference on Human Rights in 1993 in Vienna, Austria. The VDPA considers the promotion and protection of human rights a matter of high priority for the international community and repeats the universality of human rights as a standard for conduct. It emphasizes that all human rights are of equal importance, seeking to end the debate about which rights—civil, political, economic, social, or cultural—are more important. VDPA also draws attention to women's rights and the rights of the "girl-child."

Human Rights: Ten Characteristics

The next step in building upon our basic understanding of human rights is to describe it more fully. I like to describe human rights as a big umbrella term in which many different characteristics and explanations are sheltered underneath the umbrella's expanse. The following are 10 characteristics of human rights:

1. Human rights involve both rights and obligations. In agreement with international law, individual nations must respect, protect and carry out human rights in their particular country and governments must guard individuals and groups against human rights abuses.

2. Human rights are political standards guiding governments in respectful treatment of their people. But they do not apply to individual conduct such as a ban on lying or shoplifting.

3. Human rights are numerous (several dozen) rather than few.

4. Human rights are minimal standards that focus on eliminating the worst actions rather than achieving the best actions. They outline satisfactory lives for all people rather than promote great hopes and lofty ideals.

5. Human rights are international norms (standards) covering all countries and all people. Some people use the term universal to describe human rights, but recognize that certain people because of special circumstances do not hold some rights. For example, only adult citizens have the right to vote, and freedom of movement does not apply to those in prison.

6. Human rights are inalienable or indivisible. Thomas Jefferson wrote about **inalienable rights** in the U.S. Declaration of Independence. The government cannot take away these rights, except in special situations and according to due process. They are difficult to lose. For example, the government may take away the right to liberty if it finds a person guilty of a crime in a court of law and is imprisoned.

7. Human rights have a **rightholder**, the person possessing the particular rights. Broadly speaking, rightholders are all people living today. They have expanded over the years to include people who were and are more likely to be discriminated against, such as women, children, racial and religious minorities and indigenous peoples. The right to freedom of speech, for example, means a rightholder has the freedom to speak up against his/her government without fear of punishment.

8. Rightholders have **addresses** that have duties and responsibilities. When a person has his/her human rights violated, the UN does not take up the case; instead, the violated person addresses his/her own government. For example, if the Mexican government denies a Mexican citizen the legal right to assembly for a discriminatory reason, the citizen may address the Mexican government for violation of his/her civil rights. International agencies and governments of countries other than one's own are backup addresses and provide encouragement, assistance, and sometimes disapproval to the addressed state in order to assist it in fulfilling its human rights responsibilities.

9. Human rights are high-priority norms and their violations are a serious offense.

10. Human rights are moral and/or legal rights. In the U.S, human rights are often called civil or constitutional rights, which are considered to be both moral and legal rights. Let's look at the difference.

Legal rights refer to existing legal codes and the law recognizes and protects them. For example, education laws in the U.S. guarantee an individual's legal right to receive a satisfactory education. But s/he does not have a legal right to an education in India. In contrast, **moral rights** exist apart from legal rights. Moral rights are not dependent upon the actions of jurists and legislators. These rights include the sense of decency and justice that each person has simply because they are human. For example, many people said that the black majority in apartheid South Africa possessed a moral right to full political participation, even though no such legal right existed in the country. Those opposing the apartheid government said it was a moral rights issue that the government denied moral rights to the majority of its black inhabitants. Many African-American citizens made the same argument in the Civil Rights movement in the 1950s and 1960s. Human rights often start off as moral rights, but the goal is to receive legal recognition and become legal rights.[8]

Why Human Rights?[9]

An important question still remains: How did we get our human rights? Or, put another way: Why do we have human rights? To answer these questions we will look historically at three justifications for human rights: God-given, human morality, and evolution of laws.

1. God-given or Innate Rights

Thomas Jefferson famously claimed in the U.S. Declaration of Independence in 1776 that people "are endowed by their Creator with certain inalienable rights that among these are "life, liberty, and the pursuit of happiness." Those that support God-given rights wish to put less emphasis on human decisions and legal action, and instead they argue that humans are born with rights that God gave to them. In this view, God is the supreme lawmaker and he passed on basic human rights to his subjects.

God-given rights must be very general, such as life, liberty, and freedom, so that they can be applied across thousands of years of human history, not just recent history. However, the most recent human rights are numerous and specific, such as freedom of religion or right to a fair trial. Even if people are born with God-given rights, an explanation of how we moved from general rights to specific rights is needed. Also billions of people throughout the world do not believe in the sort of God that gives rights to humans, such as the justice-wielding God found in Christianity, Islam, and Judaism. Thus, a God-given reason for human rights does not necessarily appeal to them.

2. Inborn Human Morality

Human groups have sets of **morals**, which are important norms of behavior for that group to follow. These moral codes contain specific norms, such as a prohibition against the intentional murder of an innocent person and specific values, such as placing a value on human life. If most human groups forbid murder, these norms can make up a human right: the right to life. If this reasoning is used, human rights are basic moral norms that all humans groups share.

This line of reasoning seems sensible but contains some problems. First, it seems unlikely that all human groups are against torture, discrimination, or unfair trials. Nations and cultures hold different views on these topics. Human rights laws are supposed to change existing norms that do not support human rights, not just describe the existing moral situation. Second, not all societies and/or cultures support individual rights; many consider group rights as more important. Third, human rights are mainly about the obligations of governments, which have not historically considered these rights as important. Think of the arbitrary rule of the Roman emperors, Genghis Khan, or Nazi Germany.

3. Evolved as Norms of National and International Law

The third way in which human rights have come about is through a steady and continual

13th Amendment to the U.S. Constitution, Abolishes Slavery

building of norms of acceptable human behavior and actions that have evolved into national and international law. At the international level, according to this view, human rights norms exist because governments have turned treaties into international law. Human rights norms exist at the national level because legislatures have passed laws, judges have decided cases, or laws have been enacted through customs, such as English Common Law in the U.S. and UK. For example, in the U.S. the 13th Amendment to the Constitution declared slavery illegal. Different countries passed similar restrictions against slavery. The human right prohibiting slavery exists in both national and international laws. Human rights have progressed through a sometimes painstakingly slow process into our international awareness.

Two Worldviews: Eastern and Western

Many people do not consider group rights, such as the dignity and right to exist of indigenous peoples, as important as individual civil and political rights. Why were individual rights preferred over group rights in 1948? It depends, of course, on the preferences of those who drafted the document, and they were primarily from the West (U.S. and Western Europe) where individualism was valued over group rights.

When studying human rights it is beneficial to look at the issue from two perspectives or what I call worldviews. One is a Western worldview, and the other is the view that has traditionally been more important to people from Asia, Africa, and indigenous peoples that I will call an Eastern worldview. Both worldviews go back thousands of years. Although this is a simplification of a complex topic, it is important to understand that there is a difference between the two worldviews.

The **Western worldview** emphasizes individualism: individual accomplishment and responsibility, thinking of oneself as separate from one's family or others. An individual is a separate and independent being with distinct desires, goals, needs, talents, personality, intellect, and desires. An individual is rewarded for accomplishments because s/he is a self-starter or hard-worker. Likewise, failure is the individual's fault for being lazy, undisciplined, or not talented. An individual stands on his/her own two feet, separate and apart from others. Since individualism is of utmost importance in this worldview, global political bodies believe each person should be granted individual rights.

The **Eastern worldview** has traditionally emphasized the collective or group as more important than the individual. The significance of the family, group, clan, tribe, or nation overshadows individual achievements, desires, goals, or dreams. The Eastern worldview emphasizes an individual's responsibility to the well-being and stability of the family, group, or nation, rather than to his/her own individual rights.

At the time of the writing of the Declaration of Human Rights in 1948, the Western worldview was especially dominant. The influence of the West through imperialism and trade had spread throughout the world and Westerners were eager to make their values the norm for the rest of the world to follow. They have been somewhat, but not completely, successful in this crusade. A country such as India, which traditionally has held to the Eastern worldview, has accepted some Western values and blended them into their own unique traditions, such as a democracy. The same can be said for China, Africa, and the Middle East. Yet, the Western worldview has not wiped out the Eastern worldview; it continues around the world. The addition of the third generation of rights is recognition of the importance of group rights, which figure so notably in the Eastern worldview. Some people argue that the emphasis on individual rights has gone too far, and responsibility for the family, community, and global commons has been ignored. One of the consequences of the Western worldview is the worsening environment which is the result of encouraging the individual to amass consumer goods to reward successes and satisfy individual desires.

Questions to Consider
1. Which worldview appeals most to you? Explain.
2. What worldview influences your own beliefs and behaviors more?

A History and Philosophy of Human Rights

"Every religion emphasizes human improvement, love, respect for others, sharing other people's suffering. On these lines every religion had more or less the same viewpoint and the same goal."

–Dali Lama (Tibetan Buddhism)

Ethic of Reciprocity or the Golden Rule

At this point you may think that the concept of human rights is a great idea, and you are happy that human rights rules protect you and your fellow citizens. Yet, you may be wondering why practically the whole world accepts the principles of human rights. Despite the diversity of beliefs, there is a growing agreement that all humans are equal and all should enjoy basic human rights. Why is this happening? One answer is the **Ethic of Reciprocity**, better known as the **Golden Rule**. It is a worldwide ethical code that states that one has a right to just treatment, and a responsibility to ensure justice for others. In other words, one must treat others as one would like to be treated.

The Golden Rule or the Ethic of Reciprocity has its roots in almost all world cultures, religions, ethical systems, and philosophies. A key element of the Golden Rule is that a person treats all people, not just members of his/her in-group, with consideration. Almost all societies have passages in their oral traditions, holy texts, philosophies, or writings of their leaders that promote this ethic. The Golden Rule is in the philosophies and oral traditions of ancient India, Africa, Greece, Europe, the Middle East, the Americas, China, and indigenous peoples. Philosophers and religious figures have stated it in different ways, but it is basically the same moral message. One example familiar in North America is the Golden Rule of Christianity attributed to Jesus of Nazareth in the Biblical book of Luke which says "Do onto others as you would wish them do onto you."

The Ethic of Reciprocity is an important moral truth. It essentially says that people share inborn human rights, simply because they are human. The Ethic is a basis for the modern concept of human rights. Since world citizens share a common world ethic—the Universal Declaration of Human Rights—they are able to directly connect with core beliefs and values of other people around the world. In 1993, the Parliament of the World's Religions enshrined the Ethic of Reciprocity in the "Declaration toward a Global Ethic."

The development of human rights is based upon religious, cultural, philosophical and legal teachings through history. Traditions from indigenous people, ancient documents, religious traditions, and philosophical writings have all contributed to the body of human rights. This history section expands on the idea that there is a global ethic of human rights that holds the same basic meaning. Therefore, the concept of human rights comes from many different traditions; it draws on the neocortex part of the human brain. Let us turn to finding out how diverse traditions from around the world have created and carried out what we call human rights today, and how diverse contributions have blended together to create this concept. I have arranged the categories of contributors in a loose chronological order.

Indigenous People

The history of human rights starts with **indigenous peoples**, after all, their way of life has a very long history. For thousands and even millions of years humans have lived as hunters and gatherers (foragers), much longer than our modern way of life! Did they have human rights? They did not as we think of them today; in fact, their emphasis was on group rights rather than individual rights. But they needed to share with each other in order to survive, and this emphasis on sharing shaped their political, economic, religious, and social values and beliefs.

Many indigenous societies had ways of living to insure that all members of their group got along and lived long and productive lives. In order for them to accomplish this, they promoted two key values: cooperation and sharing. Parents have told their children to share toys and play nicely for many years, but indigenous peoples knew that they must get along and share in order to survive. They had no other choice. Therefore, their thinking about human rights was to make sure that they all shared on a fairly equal basis.

Indigenous people did not want any one individual to stand out from the rest, even though everyone has different abilities and talents. For example, all the young men in an indigenous camping group were not equal hunters; some were better than others. Just like today, there are star basketball or football players. But the group had to make sure that the young man who was the best hunter didn't get a "big head" or an inflated ego. If he did, this could cause the other young male hunters to get angry at him for his prideful ways and fights would break out. Conflict would cloud their otherwise friendly relations.

The elders, the leaders of most indigenous groups of people, would know from their experience that they needed to tamp down the young man's prideful ways, and they knew how to do it. For instance, they would not praise the young man if he killed a meaty deer. In fact, they might ridicule him instead. They might say, "Why did you bring that pitiful looking animal to our camp, it is hardly worth butchering. You call yourself a hunter?" Thus, the group leaders did not reward or praise individual talents and skills. The young man would quickly realize that his smug behavior had been out of line with the norms of the group and he had to change his behavior or risk further shame or even punishment from the elders. The young hunter would not get to eat all of the deer that he bagged; instead, he would be required to share his catch with other group members. He would automatically share his catch with those who could not hunt, such as small children and the elderly.

!Kung Village, Botswana, Africa

This true story of an indigenous group of people, the !Kung of southwestern Africa, shows that they did not think of individual human rights as a value but rather thought of human rights as keeping the group together so all could survive. Their high priority values were sharing, cooperation, and devaluing the individual in favor of the group; all were necessary for the continuation of their way of life. Thus, the Western notion of individual, civil, political, and economic human rights would be completely foreign to them. They more closely identified with group rights.

UBUNTU

The African philosophy of **Ubuntu** (humanness) contributes to modern human rights ideas. Ubuntu (pronounced as uu-Boon-too) is a cultural view of what it is to be human and focuses on people's commitment and relationship with each other. The Ubuntu philosophy encourages respect, sharing, helpfulness, caring, unselfishness, and serving the community. The word has its roots in the Bantu languages of Africa, which spread throughout sub-Saharan Africa beginning around 3,000-2,500 BCE and continues today, especially in the southern part of Africa. Ubuntu forms the basis of the African philosophy of life, which is played out in daily life experiences. It is used everyday to settle different levels of disagreements and conflicts. According to Ubuntu, there is a common bond between us all, and it is through this bond that we discover our own humanity.[10]

Archbishop Desmond Tutu

Tutu (b. 1934) was awarded the Nobel Peace Prize in 1984 for speaking out against apartheid in South Africa. He movingly describes the philosophy of Ubuntu ...

"One of the sayings in our country is Ubuntu—the essence of being human. Ubuntu speaks about the fact that you can't exist as a human being in isolation. It speaks about our interconnectedness, about wholeness. You can't be human all by yourself, and when you have this quality—Ubuntu—you are known for your generosity. We think of ourselves far too

Desmond Tutu at the UN

frequently as just individuals, separated from one another, whereas we are all connected and what each one of us does affects the whole world. When we do well, it spreads out to the whole of humanity. A person with Ubuntu is open, compassionate, hospitable, warm, and available to others, affirming of others, does not feel threatened that others are able and good, for he or she has a proper self-assurance that comes from knowing that he or she belongs in a greater whole and is diminished when others are humiliated or diminished, when others are tortured or oppressed."[11]

The concept of Ubuntu defines the individual in terms of his/her multiple relationships with others. It follows the Zulu (a tribe in southern Africa) saying "A person is a person through (other) persons." This means that a person who acts with humanity towards all will eventually be an ancestor worthy of respect and admiration. Those who uphold the belief of Ubuntu throughout their lives will, in death, achieve a connection with those still living.[12] The three sayings on the left form the practice of Ubuntu and are deeply rooted in traditional African political philosophy.

Visitors have a special place in the hearts of Africans. According to their tradition, they

Traditional Ubuntu Sayings[13]
1. To be human is to uphold one's humanity by recognizing the humanity of others.
2. If and when one is faced with a choice between wealth and the safeguarding of the life of another, then one should [choose] the preservation of life.
3. The king owes all his powers to the will of the people under him.

do not need to burden themselves with carrying belongings as they travel. It is part of the African custom to make every individual visitor as comfortable as possible. Nelson Mandela, the first black president of South Africa, explained, "When a traveler through a country would stop at a village, he didn't have to ask for food or for water. Once he stops, the people give him food and entertain him."[14]

In the African nation of Zimbabwe, when individuals follow Ubuntu rules they do not call elderly people by their given name; instead, they are called by their family name. The purpose of this tradition is to reject individualism. The individual identity is replaced with the larger group identity that encircles a person. Family identification is extended to include a bond with the village, region, nation, and beyond. Ubuntu encourages individuals to behave in an unselfish manner and give up their individual identity for their community. It strives for harmony and the spirit of sharing. For example, those who believe in Ubuntu will never allow orphans to live alone in the community. The roles of mother and father are not just tied to a single child, but all children are considered part of their family.

The concept of Ubuntu in southern Africa is quite different from some Western ideas and laws. Under the Ubuntu system of law, crimes committed by one individual against another go far beyond the two individuals involved to even include their families. Ubuntu law tends to support solutions and punishments that bring people together instead of keep them apart. For instance, a crime of murder might lead to the creation of a bond of marriage between the victim's family and the accused's family. But this does not mean that the individual accused of the crime is not punished; instead, the person who committed the crime is punished twice, both inside and outside the family and social circles. The punishment for the crime can be quite severe, as the accused may have to pay a huge fine and undergo social disgrace and humiliation. It may take years of demonstrating Ubuntu before the victim's family pardons the accused individual and wholly accepts him/her back into the community.

There is no one above the law in the Ubuntu belief system. A leader who follows Ubuntu is selfless, talks widely with others, and listens deeply to those s/he rules. The leader does not adopt a lifestyle that is more lavish than the others in the group and shares what s/he owns with them. A leader cannot impose his/her will on those s/he rules, but allows the people to lead themselves. Royal power springs from the people. Thus, all laws made by the leader express the will of the people who must respect and obey them. African law is positive, not negative. It does not say: "Thou shalt not," but "Thou shalt." Laws direct how individuals and communities should behave towards each other and how punishment is meted out. The ultimate goal is to create balance and harmony in the community.[15]

Ubuntu has a strong religious meaning, which is important for many southern Africans who have different traditions. Many Africans believe that ancestors continue to exist amongst the living in the form of spirits, and each individual has a link to that spirit. If you are in need, you can call on your ancestors' spirits and they will get involved on your behalf. Therefore, it is important not only to honor your ancestors, but for you to later become an ancestor worthy of respect. For this to happen you agree to value your community's rules, connect with current community members and respect those that have passed on. You promise to carry out Ubuntu beliefs during your lifetime.[16]

Today, many southern African rulers, for many reasons, are guilty of corruption and severe rule. This has created a wide gap between the values of most African people and their rulers, and violent conflict has often resulted. In order for peace to triumph, some African activists call for a new beginning, in which the people of Africa are able to reject conflict, ideas of superiority and dominance, and bring about a culture of peace, inclusiveness, and security for all. This change draws on the cultural heritage of Ubuntu.

> **Questions to Consider**
> 1. What is your opinion about Ubuntu? Do you think it could work in your country?

MESOPOTAMIA AND HAMMURABI'S CODE

Some humans began to move from villages to form cities around 3500 BCE (before the Common Era) in Mesopotamia (now the area of Iraq). This movement to cities occurred at different times and places around the world and resulted in more people living together in closer quarters. The rules for people living together in hunting and gathering groups or small villages were no longer meeting the needs of people living in cities, who might not be related to each other or even know their neighbors. Thus, city dwellers began to create different rules that fit their new living conditions. Instead of passing on rules orally, the new invention of writing meant that scribes could write rules, often etched in stone to show their permanence. The early law codes show the rules for city dwellers to live by.

The earliest known written legal code is the Code of Ur-Nammu that dates to 2050 BCE. However, one of the most famous examples of a legal code is **Hammurabi's Code**, named after King Hammurabi of Babylon (Iraq and Syria today), which was etched onto a seven foot slab of basalt stone in 1780 BCE. Hammurabi believed that the gods ordered him to deliver the law to his people. The code spelled out rules and punishments for breaking particular rules. However, the punishments did not always fit the crime, and some are quite harsh by today's standards. Although these laws are hardly human rights of today, it does show the process of codifying laws that eventually evolved into human rights. The following are a few of Hammurabi's 282 rules in the language of the day:

The Code of Hummurabi

22 If anyone is committing a robbery and is caught, then he shall be put to death.

138 If a man wishes to separate from his wife who has borne him no children, he shall give her the amount of her purchase money and the dowry which she brought from her father's house, and let her go.

148 If a man take a wife, and she be seized by disease, if he then desire to take a second wife he shall not put away his wife, who has been attacked by disease, but he shall keep her in the house which he has built and support her so long as she lives.

195 If a son strike his father, his hands shall be hewn off.

196 If a man put out the eye of another man, his eye shall be put out.

205 If the slave of a freed man strike the body of a freed man, his ear shall be cut off.

209/210 If a man strike a free-born woman so that she lose her unborn child, he shall pay ten shekels for her loss. If the woman dies, his daughter shall be put to death.

229/230 If a Builder builds a house for someone, and does not construct it properly, and the house which he built falls in and kills its owner, then that builder shall be put to death. If it kill the son of the owner the son of that builder shall be put to death.

Hammurabi's Code on clay tablets

JUDEO-CHRISTIAN TRADITION

Judaism is a religious tradition that has contributed to the body of human rights. The three monotheistic religions—Judaism, Christianity, and Islam—believe that only one God exists. The early followers of Judaism believed that each person can have a personal relationship with God and that he is both merciful and loving, as well as metes out punishment to those who disobey his commands. Also important is the idea of individual worth, which is different from the emphasis on the group. The concept of individualism, important in the West, had its roots in the Judeo-Christian tradition.

Obedience to the law of God became a key element of Judaic beliefs. Although each person had the ability to choose between good and evil, no person could devise his/her own ethical and moral standards. People had to follow certain standards. According to the Judeo-Christian tradition, God made known his commandments, his ideals of right behavior, to Moses on Mount Sinai around 1380 BCE. The Ten Commandments, according to tradition, were etched onto two stone tablets to show their unchanging nature. They are a list of religious and moral rules that Judeo-Christians accept as God's ethical standards; if not then punishment and suffering will follow. Judaism and Christianity accept the Ten Commandments as their moral foundation, and they are important to Islam as well. Various religious groups translate and divide the Ten Commandments differently; the version in the box above is the Catholic/Lutheran shortened version.[17]

The Ten Commandments

1. I am the Lord your God, You shall have no other gods before me.
2. You shall not make wrongful use of the name of your God.
3. Remember the Sabbath and keep it holy.
4. Honor your father and mother.
5. You shall not murder (kill).
6. You shall not commit adultery.
7. You shall not steal.
8. You shall not bear false witness against your neighbor.
9. You shall not covet your neighbor's wife.
10. You shall not covet anything that belongs to your neighbor.

THE PERSIAN EMPIRE: THE CYRUS CYLINDER

Following the Persian conquest of Babylon in 539 BCE, the Persian emperor Cyrus the Great (600-530 BCE) issued a document written on a clay cylinder called the **Cyrus Cylinder**. The writing on the cylinder describes how Cyrus had improved the lives of the citizens of Babylonia, sent home lost peoples and rebuilt temples and religious shrines. At the time, the victors in battle massacred the defeated people and looted their homes. Cyrus broke with this cruel tradition and treated his newly conquered subjects with tolerance, moderation and generosity, although self-interest may certainly have influenced his peace-making policy. As stated on the cylinder and in the Bible, one of Cyrus' acts of tolerance was that he allowed some Jews living in Babylon to return to their

The Cyrus Cylinder

homeland. He also financed the rebuilding of the Jewish temple in Jerusalem.

Some modern scholars call the Cyrus cylinder "the world's first declaration of human rights."[18] Iranian scholar Reza Shabani reasons that the cylinder "discusses human rights in a way unique for the era, dealing with ways to protect the honor, prestige, and religious beliefs of all the nations dependent to Iran in those days."[19] The Cyrus Cylinder contributed to the body of ideas that helped create our modern concepts of human rights.

BUDDHISM

Buddhism currently has about 365 million followers and is the world's 4th largest religion after Christianity, Islam and Hinduism. Little is known of the founder's, Siddhartha Gautama (563-460 BCE), early life and no scribe wrote his biography during his lifetime. According to tradition, Siddhartha was born a prince in Kalinga, India. As in the case with other religious leaders, miraculous stories described his birth to his mother, Maya, and father, the king of the Śākyas clan. In one legend, he emerged from his mother's side without causing her any pain. In another legend, the earth shook at his birth and as a newborn, he was showered with water. His family named him Siddhartha, the "one who has achieved his aim," and Gautama was his clan name.

The Three Trainings or Practices of Buddhism

1. **Sila**: Virtue, good conduct, and morality are based on two principles: equality, all living entities are equal, and reciprocity, to do onto others as you would wish them to do onto you.
2. **Samadhi**: Concentration and meditation develops the mind and is the path to wisdom, which in turn leads to personal freedom, and is essential in maintaining good conduct.
3. **Prajna**: Judgment, insight, wisdom, and enlightenment are the real heart of Buddhism. Wisdom will emerge if the mind is pure and calm.

Raised as a Hindu, Siddhartha's parents thought he would follow in his father's footsteps as king. But his parents were deeply troubled by a prediction from a fortune teller, who said at his birth that he would either become a great monarch or a monk and a great religious teacher. They wanted Siddhartha to follow into the kingship rather than into the life of a monk, so his parents raised him in a state of comfort and encouraged him to attach to earthly desires and pleasure. At the age of 16, he married his wife Yaśodharā and at the age of 29 they had their first son. Shortly after his son's birth, Siddhartha fell into an intensely troubled state when he spotted a helpless, elderly man suffering from advanced disease and a grieving family carrying the dead body of a family member to a cremation site. He reflected deeply upon the suffering brought about by old age,

The Four Noble Truths of Buddhism

1. Suffering is real and has many causes, such as loss, sickness, pain, failure, rejection, the impermanence of pleasure, and unsatisfied desires.
2. The cause of suffering is the desire to have and control things and takes many forms, such as craving sensual pleasures, desire for fame, and desire to avoid unpleasant sensations, like fear, anger or jealousy.
3. There is an end to suffering which stops with final enlightenment. The mind experiences complete freedom, and lets go of any desire or craving.
4. In order to end suffering, one must follow the Eightfold Path.

illness, and death and had a vision of a religious monk who led a calm life of meditation. These visions pushed him to follow the path of a monk and seek a spiritual solution to life's problems brought about by human suffering. He left his wife, child, luxurious lifestyle, and future role as king in order to seek truth. It was not an unusual practice at the time for some men to leave their families and lead the life of a monk.

He first tried meditation, and learned this valuable skill. However, meditation did not last forever. He then joined a group of other monks in a forest where he practiced breath control and fasted intensely for six years. He skirted the edge of death by only eating a few grains of rice each day, but after suffering great physical pain, he abandoned this path. He realized that neither of the extremes he experienced would lead to enlightenment. Instead, he found the path to enlightenment—a state of freedom and release from suffering—was to pursue a middle way. For him, practicing moderation and meditation was the middle way. One night, while seated underneath a large Bodhi tree, he experienced major spiritual breakthroughs and attained enlightenment—now he was known as "The Buddha" (the Awakened One). For seven days after his enlightenment he puzzled over his future: whether to withdraw from the world and live a life of isolation or whether to reenter the world and teach his Middle Way. He decided to share his teachings with others. He wandered through Northeast India for decades, teaching all who would listen, eventually drawing tens of thousands of followers. He later established an order of monks and nuns. His wife Yaśodharā became the first nun. In his late 70s, his health began to fail. After 45 years of teaching, he died of natural causes in a small town, Kuśinagara, at the age of 80.[20]

Buddhism is a collection of beliefs and practices. This brief overview gives a few of the Buddhist traditions—ethical conduct, morality, behaviors, practices, and traditions—that are closely tied to human rights. Buddhism has organized many of its ethical and moral teachings into numbered groups.

The five precepts (teachings) are Buddhist ethical practice. Scholars often compare them with the Ten Commandments of Christianity; however, the precepts are different in that they are to be taken as recommendations, not commandments. This means the individual is encouraged to use his/her own intelligence to apply these rules in the best possible way instead of commanding behavior. The five precepts are rules to live by; like

The Eightfold Path

1. Right Understanding of the Four Noble Truths.
2. Right Thinking: following the right path in life.
3. Right Speech: no lying, criticism, condemning, gossip, harsh language.
4. Right Conduct (see the Five Precepts below).
5. Right Livelihood; support yourself without harming others.
6. Right Effort: promote good thoughts; conquer evil thoughts.
7. Right Mindfulness: become aware of your body, mind and feelings.
8. Right Concentration: meditate to achieve a higher state of consciousness.

Five Precepts in Buddhism

1. Avoid harming living beings (practice non-violence)
2. Avoid taking things not freely given (not committing theft
3. Avoid sensual (sexual) misconduct
4. Avoid lying (speaking truth always)
5. Avoid intoxicating drinks, drugs, which lead to loss of mindfulness

training rules that if followed they can help a person live a life of happiness, helpfulness, and meditation.

From this brief description, we can see that Buddhism focuses less attention on individualism and more emphasis on others. But the Dalai Lama (Tibetan Buddhism) feels that human rights are in harmony with the moral values of traditional Buddhism and provides a useful way for expressing Buddhist views on today's political and social issues.

> **Questions to Consider**
> 1. Do you think Buddhism has made a contribution to the body of human rights today? Explain.

CONFUCIANISM

Based on the teachings of the Chinese philosopher Confucius (551–479 BCE), **Confucianism** is a Chinese ethical and philosophical system that focuses on human morality and wrong action. Confucius lived during the Chou dynasty in China, an era known for its moral slackness. His parents died when he was a child, leaving him alone in the world. Later in life, he wandered through China, giving advice to the rulers. A small band of dedicated students followed him during this time. He spent the last years of his life teaching and died around the age of 72.

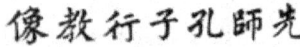

Confucius

During Confucius' lifetime, China was in a constant state of upheaval and wars. Confucius believed that at this time China needed a strict set of rules and standards to guide people in proper behavior. He stated that the ideal person needed to exhibit good moral character, and respect his leader, ancestors and father. He also thought the ideal person needed to think for himself in order to discover what was right and wrong. Confucius directed his teachings to males; females were not important to him. He encouraged the leaders of China to live their lives in a good, moral manner, and to set a good example as role models for their people. He believed the country would run much more smoothly if it followed his teachings.

Confucius, like Socrates, did not write down his teachings, but the second generation of Confucius followers collected his teachings into the *Analects*, the most honored of his texts. His writings dealt primarily with individual morality and ethics, and the proper use of political power by the rulers. It is a complex system of moral, social, political, philosophical, and somewhat religious thought that has influenced the culture and history of East Asia. The Confucian version of the Ethic of Reciprocity, or the Golden Rule was: "What you do not wish for yourself, do not do to others."

Confucius never stated whether man was born good or evil, noting that "by nature men are similar; by practice men are wide apart." Therefore, they must study and practice the right values: Li, respectability and good manners; Hsiao, love within the family, love of parents and parental love for their children; Yi, righteousness; Xin, honesty and trust; Jen, compassion, humaneness (the highest Confucian value); and Chung, loyalty to the state.

The basic teachings of Confucianism stressed the importance of an individual's moral education so that moral principles would govern the state rather than harsh laws. Social harmony was the greatest goal of Confucianism; every individual needed to know his or her place in the social order. If the teaching of good behaviors is strong enough, it will completely influence the individual, and thus, each person will behave properly to avoid shame and "losing face."

Confucius also helped establish a school that taught government rulers to have a strong sense of duty to the state. He promoted the idea of meritocracy, in which leadership is based on ability and talent rather than on class privilege or wealth. This contributed to the introduction of the imperial examination system in China that allowed anyone, including poor peasants, to become a government officer, a position which brought wealth and honor to the whole family. But the male student (no females) must first pass a rigorous written examination that took years of study, and only a few passed. The Chinese imperial examination system started around 165 BCE and grew over the centuries until it officially ended in 1905.

Another concept in Confucianism is tolerance towards others. In fact, many people who practice Confucianism are also Buddhist, Taoist, Muslim, or Christian. The idea was that all religions have something important to say. No one specific religion can be completely correct and know everything, and thus, everyone can learn from another's point of view. In his lifetime, Confucius lived a simple life and never knew the impact of his teachings. It wasn't until years after his death that China and East Asia began to adopt Confucianism. Even today, Confucian teachings are influential in China and East Asia.

ANCIENT GREEK PHILOSOPHERS

"I am not an Athenian or a Greek, but a citizen of the world." – Socrates

During the time period 470-322 BCE, the philosophers in ancient Greece—in particular Socrates, Plato, and Aristotle—began to articulate the concept of human rights that we know today. Instead of using the term human rights, however, many Greek philosophers used the term natural rights; these were rights they said came from natural law. According to the Greek tradition, natural law reflected the natural order of the universe. These philosophers thought that nature set natural law and was everywhere. This natural order provided the basis for rational systems of justice and universal principles in order for humans to evaluate the moral authority of man-made laws. The Greek philosophers believed that these universal principles came from humans' inborn sense of right and wrong, rather than governmental laws which were secondary in importance.

Natural law is the theory or belief that certain rights exist independently of any government's granting of those rights. It was superior to laws passed by governments because man-made laws could be different in every society and carried out at the whim of rulers. Plato, Aristotle and others favored natural law and said that morality is not man-made but natural. All people must obey natural laws, whether or not government enacts them. Aristotle believed that natural law is the same truth everywhere, it was universal. It was the belief at the time that governments could apply general laws of nature as a system of justice for all societies, regardless of their culture or customs. This natural, moral law surpassed local legal codes.[21] For example, the reasoning leading to the formation of the Bill of Rights in England and the U.S. drew on the theory of natural law. Whenever a group rebels against their government and asserts rights that the government hasn't granted them, they are claiming natural law. Those who drafted the Universal Declaration of Human Rights used the theory of natural law to justify their endeavors.

The concept of natural law was vague enough to keep philosophers busy trying to refine the idea for over 2,000 years. Ancient Greeks began to put natural laws into their law codes. They are remembered for their valuable contribution to the concept of human rights. The idea of natural law is very similar to the concept of human rights today and is considered valid for all humans around the world. Natural law is also superior to national or local laws when those laws overturn human rights laws.

Stoics

The Stoic philosophers drew upon the classical Greeks, while adding their own insights. **Stoicism** was founded by the philosopher Zeno (333-263 BCE) in Athens, Greece. The Stoics expanded upon the work of the Greek philosophers in the area of natural law and provided a complete explanation of natural law. The Stoics argued that the universe is governed by reason, or a rational principle sometimes called God, mind, or fate. They said that all humans have reason, and they can know and obey its law. The Stoics believed that to live morally meant to live in accord with one's nature or according to right reason. They thought passion and emotion were foolish; thus, the wise individual should seek to live a rational life. All human beings have the ability to make choices (a free will). However, even with that ability, they will not necessarily obey natural law. But if they act with reason, they will be "following nature."

Stoics said it was most important for humans to live a rational life. They presented their philosophy as a way of life, and they thought that the best sign of an individual's philosophy was not what a person said but how s/he behaved. The Stoics thought the best goal in life was to live in harmony with Nature, which meant living in harmony with natural law.

Stoics celebrated three universal ideals: individual worth, moral duty, and the universal brotherhood of all humanity. They believed in the natural equality of all human beings and were noted for their compassionate treatment of slaves. Seneca, a Stoic philosopher from Rome, said, "Kindly remember that he whom you call your slave sprang from the same stock, is smiled upon by the same skies, is on equal terms with yourself and breathes, lives, and dies."[2]

The Roman author Cicero (106–43 B.C.E.), was a Stoic philosopher and orator during the time of the Roman Republic (509-27BCE). He extended the principle of natural law to include the idea of equality of justice for all humans. Cicero spelled out the principle that people have a duty to protect justice for all humans, regardless of their nationality or ethnicity. He defined natural law: "True law is right reason in agreement with Nature; it is of universal application, unchanging and everlasting. . . . There will not be different laws at Rome and at Athens, or different laws now and in the future, but one eternal and unchangeable law will be valid for all nations and for all times."[23]

Stoicism was a popular and enduring philosophy, with a large following throughout Greece and the Roman Empire. Their ideas influenced Enlightenment philosophers in the 17th and 18th centuries and contributed to the body of human rights that continues today.

Maurya Empire of Ancient India

The **Maurya Empire** (321-185 BCE) was an extensive and powerful empire in ancient India. This empire established unmatched principles of civil rights in the 3rd century BCE under one of its most famous rulers, Ashoka the Great (ruled from 272-231 BCE).

Ashoka in his youth was rude and disobedient but also very smart and he possessed outstanding warrior skills. He excelled at deadly sword fighting and, according to legend, he killed a lion with only a wooden rod. Ashoka's grandfather was a Mauryan emperor, and Ashoka, because of his keen intellect, was his grandfather's favorite. His grandfather willingly gave up the glory of ruling to follow a simple life, in keeping with the nonviolent tradition of India. Although the grandfather threw away his sword, Ashoka seized the sword and kept it, in spite of his grandfather's warnings that violence was not the right way. Ashoka turned into a fearsome warrior and a heartless general. He was known as "the cruel one" because of his constant wars and brutal slaughters.

Ashoka

But Ashoka had a change of heart. After witnessing the horrifying deaths and untold suffering of 110,000 people during his conquest of Kalinga (northern India) in 265 BCE, which he himself had directed, he felt great sorrow for what he had done. As a result, he made a dramatic change in his life and rejected violence and adopted Buddhism. From then on he came to be known as "the pious Ashoka."

During his rule, he pursued a policy of ahimsa (nonviolence in Sanskrit, an ancient Indian language) and the protection of human rights. His chief concern was the happiness and well-being of his subjects, whom he treated equally regardless of their religion, politics, or social class. This collection of beliefs is called the Edicts of Ashoka, a set of 33 writings on pillars, boulders, and cave walls scattered throughout northern India. The edicts spell out social and moral principles that today we would call human rights. For example, he immediately stopped the unnecessary slaughter or injury to animals, such as sport hunting and branding. He also showed mercy to those imprisoned. He offered common citizens free education at universities and built free hospitals for both humans and animals. Ashoka defined the main principles of nonviolence as tolerance of all groups and opinions, obedience to parents, respect for teachers and priests, generosity towards all, and humane treatment of servants. Ashoka is known as an emperor for all ages.[24]

CHRISTIANITY AND ST. THOMAS AQUINAS

Jesus of Nazareth, the central figure of **Christianity**, rebelled against the state control of the Roman Empire. For punishment of his acts of defiance and preaching of a more peaceful world, the Roman state crucified him on the cross. But Christianity did not end with Jesus' death; for example, Christian philosophers found that the natural law principles of the Stoics were in line with their own beliefs. They connected the idea of natural law with the law of God. **St. Thomas Aquinas** (1223-1274 CE) is an admired Christian philosopher who expanded upon the idea of natural law. In his writings, Aquinas called the rational guidance of creation by God the "Eternal Law." For Aquinas, natural law is part of God's eternal law which humans understand because of their powers of reason. Since humans are rational creatures, they can direct their own good actions and guide the good actions of others. To Aquinas this participation in the Eternal Law by rational creatures is called the Natural Law. Thus, it was possible to distinguish good from evil by the "natural light of reason."

Jesus, Byzantine style

Aquinas understood that reason and freedom guided human nature; it is the human ability to reason and to make free choices that sets humans apart from animals. He went on to explain that objects and animals without free will act by nature as God wills them to do, but humans may choose either to play a part in God's plan or not. Reason can tell us what this plan is; we can discover our purpose. But with freedom comes the responsibility to do as God made us to do. Christians in Europe over the centuries agreed with Aquinas' Eternal Law and the belief in the existence of a universal moral community.

Christianity has contributed to the concepts of human rights that we take for granted today. The teaching of Jesus, in Matthew 22:21, for example, is often cited as the origin of the separation of church and state when Jesus preaches to render to Caesar what belongs to Caesar and to God what belongs to God. Not only does this separation help prevent the excesses of a theocratic state, but it also gives origin to the concept of limited government by advancing the concept that state power has limits and must respect the integrity of each person.

Christianity promotes human dignity, the foundational concept of human rights. Christian teachings call for respecting those who are poor and downtrodden. Jesus' teachings transformed values in which the last and poorest became first, and values of discrimination once scorned came to represent the loftiest human ideals. For example, the Beatitudes—a new set of Christian ideals focusing on a spirit of love and humility—were preached by Jesus and are known as the Sermon on the Mount. They echo Jesus' highest ideals on mercy, spirituality, and compassion. Probably the most recited is the first beatitude: "Blessed are the poor in spirit: for theirs is the kingdom of Heaven."

Christians have placed a high importance on marriage and the family. Family life changed from subordination by the state to an elevated status through the sacrament of marriage. Christianity introduced the concept of consent by both spouses as being a prerequisite of marriage, a vital instrument in promoting equality and preventing people being pressured into marriage against their will. Christian teachings of mutual love and charity contributed to institutions such as hospitals and orphanages.

Politically, Christian leaders, who consider themselves as servants of others, has provided the basis for political and social accountability. The political leader, the merchant, and the priest are called upon to serve people by attending to their needs. Through its defense of human dignity, Christianity inspired campaigns to end slavery, achieve democracy and promote self-government, as well as the first attempts to formulate a doctrine of human rights. Many modern formulations of human rights owe a lot to Christianity. The Universal Declaration of Human Rights adopted by the United Nations in 1948 is based on the premise that all human lives have worth and that all lives count equally.

ISLAM

Islam is one of the three monotheistic religions, along with Christianity and Judaism that trace their roots to the patriarch Abraham. The religion is based on the teachings found in the Qur'an (Koran), believed by followers to be the exact words of Allah (God) as revealed to the Arab prophet **Muhammad** (570-632 CE) through a messenger, the angel Gabriel. Muhammad did not write the Qur'an, but his companions reportedly wrote down his recitations while he was alive. Qur'an, meaning recitation, is divided into 114 suras or chapters and contains 6,236 verses. The earlier suras are primarily concerned with ethical and spiritual topics, while the later suras mostly discuss social and moral issues important to the Muslim community. The Qur'an is more concerned with moral guidance than legal teachings, and believers look to it as the sourcebook of Islamic principles and values. A follower of Islam is a Muslim, meaning "one who submits" to God.

Islam is the fastest growing religion in the world today with 1.3 billion followers and a growth rate of 1.84 percent per year. It is the second largest religion in the world, after Christianity.[25] The Five Pillars of Islam found in the Qur'an represent the core practices that each member of the faith follows.

The Qur'an, like many of the religious texts before it, does not directly address human rights. Rather, it calls attention to the fact that all rights come from God through the prophets. Therefore, human rights in Islam are clearly rights that God has granted; they are not necessarily rights granted by the government.

Five Pillars of Islam

1. Faith, recited as "There is no God but Allah; Muhammad is His prophet."
2. Pray five times daily facing Mecca (a city in Saudi Arabia).
3. Almsgiving, or giving to the poor.
4. Fasting during the holy month of Ramadan.
5. Pilgrimage to Mecca, if possible, once a lifetime.

The Constitution of Medina, drafted by Muhammad in 622, was an early document that set out rights for Muhammad's community. It was a formal agreement between Muhammad and the city of Medina, including Muslims, Jews, and those who practiced indigenous religions. Muhammad drew up the document to bring an end to the bitter fighting between tribes. It spelled out a number of rights and responsibilities for the different religious communities of Medina in order to bring them within the fold of one community. One of the significant rights was that the community would protect freedom of religion, and Medina would serve as a sacred place, barring all violence and weapons.[26]

In the field of human rights, early Islamic judges introduced a number of legal concepts before the 12th century that helped shape the field of human rights known today. These included charity, brotherhood, human self-respect, the dignity of labor; the notion of an ideal law; the condemnation of antisocial behavior, the presumption of innocence, fair contracts, freedom from usury (interest on loans), women's rights, privacy, individual freedom, equality before the law, legal representation, supremacy of the law, independence of judges, tolerance, and democratic participation. The life and property of all citizens in an Islamic state are sacred, whether a person is Muslim or not. Islam also protects honor, so in Islam, insulting others or making fun of them is prohibited.

Early Islamic law promoted the concept of inalienable rights, which prohibited a ruler from taking away certain rights from his subjects. Islamic judges also said the rule of law should be equal for all classes. No person was above the law, and the law did not allow discrimination on the grounds of religion, race, color, or kinship. The law recognized two sets of human rights. In addition to the category of civil rights and political rights, Islamic law also recognized an additional category: social, economic and cultural rights, which was not recognized in the Western legal tradition until the International Covenant on Economic, Social and Cultural Rights in 1966. The right of privacy, which the Western legal traditions did not recognize until modern times, was part of Islamic law since its beginning.

Symbol of Islam

Early Islamic law introduced the concepts of welfare and pension as forms of charity or almsgiving, one of the Five Pillars of Islam. Islamic governments collected taxes which they used to provide income for the needy, including the poor, elderly, orphans, widows, and the disabled. Historians consider these to be one of the earliest welfare states. A famous Islamic jurist Al-Ghazali (1058-1111), said the government should store up food supplies for the needy in every region in case a disaster or famine occurred.

The institution of slavery has existed in past Islamic societies. But Islam has outlined five ways to free slaves, severely condemned those who enslave free people, and regulated the slave trade. Slaves, arguably, had more rights under Islam than Christianity, since an owner could not mistreat them and laws said slaves should be treated as equals. Owners freed many slaves after a certain period of time.

Women generally had more legal rights, such as the right to own property, under Islamic law than they did under Western laws until changes in the 19th and 20th centuries. Islamic law gave women legal status, which directly affected the areas important to women at the time: marriage, divorce, and inheritance. For example, under Islamic law the dowry, which for many years traditions had regarded as a brideprice paid to the father by the groom's family, became a gift retained by the wife as part of her personal property. Islamic law viewed marriage as a contract, in which the woman's consent was necessary. Islamic societies gave women inheritance rights; this right of inheritance had previously been restricted to male relatives. In fact, Muhammad's wife Khadijah was 15 years his senior and a wealthy merchant in her own right. They had a monogamous marriage (one spouse at a time) until her death 25 years after their marriage. After this time, Muhammad took four wives, according to tradition. Apparently, Muhammad improved the lives of women legally and in the area of family life, marriage, education, and economic rights.

Most countries of the Middle East and North Africa today continue a dual system of secular (non-religious) and religious courts; the religious courts mainly regulate marriage and inheritance, while secular courts decide legal matters. At the time of this writing, Saudi Arabia and Iran keep religious courts for all aspects of jurisprudence.

ENGLAND IN THE MIDDLE AGES: THE MAGNA CARTA

The **Magna Carta** is often cited as contributing to the development of human rights and the rule of constitutional law. It was an English charter first issued in 1215 and written because of a disagreement about the rights of the king, the Catholic Church, and wealthy English landowners. In a bold move, the Magna Carta required the king to give up certain rights and abide by the law that would bind his actions. It also protected certain rights of the people and enumerated what later came to be thought of as human rights. Among them was the right of the church to be free from governmental interference and the rights of all free citizens to own and inherit property and to be protected from excessive taxes. It established the right of widows who owned property to choose not to remarry, and established principles of due process and equality before the law. It also contained provisions forbidding bribery and official misconduct.[27]

The Magna Carta influenced the development of English Common Law and many constitutional documents, such as the United States Constitution and Bill of Rights. Common Law refers to the legal system developed through decisions of courts called case law, rather than through laws passed by legislatures or by executive action. Judges create and fine-tune common law over the years. The Magna Carta has become an important foundation for the freedom of the individual against arbitrary authority.

Questions to Consider
1. Do you think the Magna Carta actually contributed to human rights today, or is its significance overstated? Explain.

EUROPEAN RENAISSANCE AND HUMANISM

Humanism started in Europe during the Renaissance in the 14th century. Influenced by ancient Greek and Roman philosophy, **humanism** is an educational and philosophical outlook that emphasizes the personal worth of the individual and the central importance of human values, as opposed to only religious belief. There were and still are both Christian humanists and secular (non-religious) humanists. It began as an educational program called the humanities that were in keeping with Christian teachings. By the middle of the 16th century, humanism had won wide acceptance as a popular educational system.

Symbol of Humanism

The idea of humanism eventually developed into the belief of the dignity of humanity. For humanists, humans are unique in God's creation and they have a special relationship to God. From its beginnings, the purpose of the humanist education program was to prepare students to participate in public life for the common good. Out of educational humanism came a strain of humanism called civic humanism. The civic humanists emphasized political science and political action, while educational humanists emphasized grammar, rhetoric, and logic. According to civic humanists, citizens should be responsible for one another and should define themselves primarily in relation to their duties to their family and their government. This idea glorified participation in public affairs.

THE WESTERN ENLIGHTENMENT

In Europe during the 17th and 18th centuries, a philosophical movement called the **Enlightenment** started to question the power of the kings and queens. The Enlightenment philosophers suggested that there should be a "social contract" between the rulers and the ruled a concept of rights similar to today's idea of human rights. Over the centuries, these ideas have taken hold and extended across the world.

During the Enlightenment era, ideals such as natural rights, morality, liberty, human dignity and equality provided a foundation for building a more equal political system. These ideals sparked shattering political disorder throughout the 18th century. For example, in France angry revolutionaries paraded King Louis IV and his unpopular wife Marie Antoinette through the streets to the guillotine for their public beheading. Revolutionaries overthrew or replaced some very powerful kings with leaders who protected and promoted these new ideals of freedom and liberty. New documents such as the United States' Declaration of Independence and the French National Assembly's Declaration of the Rights of Man and Citizen resulted from these struggles.

John Locke (1632–1704), one of the most famous Enlightenment philosophers, contributed to the concept of natural rights, the notion that people are naturally free and equal. His ideas were important in the development of the modern idea of rights. Locke's central argument claimed that individuals possess natural rights, no matter if the state recognized these rights. Locke went on to say that natural rights flowed from natural law and natural laws came from God. Locke said there are three natural rights—life, everyone is entitled to live; liberty, everyone is entitled to do anything they want to so long as it doesn't conflict with the first right; and property, people are entitled to own all they create or gain so long as it doesn't conflict with the first two rights. At the root of Locke's ideas was that each of us must be free from threats to our life, liberty, and personal property. Locke thought the main purpose of government was to protect an individual's basic natural rights.

Governments existed to serve the interests of the people, and not a king or ruling elite. He went so far as to say that if a ruler went against natural law and failed in his/her duty to protect the natural rights of his/her citizens—life, liberty, and property—then the people have the moral authority to take up arms against their government and create a new one.

For those of us living in the United States, John Locke is most noteworthy because he influenced our founding fathers, especially our third president, Thomas Jefferson. Jefferson agreed with John Locke's ideas of natural rights and famously included them in The Declaration of Independence, signed on July 4, 1776. The document declared the desire of some (not all) American colonists to be independent from Great Britain and to set up their own separate nation. In the declaration Jefferson stated his most famous words on the subject of individual rights—"We hold these truths to be self-evident, that all men are created equal, that they are endowed by their Creator with certain unalienable Rights that among these are Life, Liberty, and the Pursuit of Happiness." In the United States Declaration of Independence Thomas Jefferson differed from Locke in that he substituted "pursuit of happiness" in place of "property."

Immanuel Kant (1724-1804), an 18th century German philosopher, provided a foundation of moral reasoning for human rights that did not necessarily require that these rights come from God. The central themes of his moral philosophy are important in contemporary human rights: the ideals of equality and the moral independence of rational human beings. Kant said that the best reason for human rights is because of the human ability to reason, and these principles of reason should be applied equally to all rational persons. For him, acting in pursuit of one's own interests or desires is not right action; right action is acting in agreement with the principles that all rational individuals accept. For Kant, the capacity to reason was the distinguishing characteristic of humanity and the basis for human dignity. Although difficult to understand, Kant's philosophy is important in the historical development of human rights.

As we have seen, men have contributed to all the ideas about human rights! One notable Enlightenment philosopher who expanded upon the concept of individual rights was **Mary Wollstonecraft** (1759-1797). She wrote the Vindication of the Rights of Women (1792), in which she argued that women are not naturally inferior to men but appear to be only because they lack education. She thought that society should treat both men and women as rational beings, and she imagined a social order founded on reason. She worked to extend political suffrage to women who had been denied political and civil rights.

Mary Wollstonecraft

Thomas Paine (1731–1809) was an important Enlightenment philosopher in the U.S. In his influential book Rights of Man (1791), he emphasized that laws alone cannot grant natural rights because this would legally mean that the government could take these rights away under certain circumstances.

Three important documents in the 17th and 18th centuries helped to establish the concept of human rights as they were put into law codes: England, the English Bill of Rights (1689); the United States, the Declaration of Independence (1776), the Bill of Rights and the Constitution (1789); and France, the Declaration of the Rights of Man and Citizen (1789). These documents provide a comparison of the agreement among many of the Enlightenment philosophers about the importance of basic natural rights.

THE 19TH AND 20TH CENTURIES

Many social and political movements spearheaded the drive for human rights in the 19th and 20th centuries. A few are covered below and Chapter 2 will cover them in more depth.

In 1831, William Lloyd Garrison, an American abolitionist against slavery, urged newspaper readers to join him in "the great cause of human rights." It looks as though the term human rights probably came into use between Paine's book *The Rights of Man* and Garrison's newspaper article. In 1849, Henry David Thoreau wrote about human rights in his essay On the Duty of Civil Disobedience, which influenced later human rights and civil rights thinkers. **Civil disobedience** is the active, professed refusal to obey certain laws, demands, and commands of a government, or of an occupying international power. The U.S. Supreme Court Justice David Davis, appointed by President Abraham Lincoln, wrote in 1867 that "in the protection of the law, human rights are secured; withdraw that protection and they are at the mercy of wicked rulers or the clamor of an excited people."[28]

The concept of human rights expanded in the 19th and 20th centuries. In Western Europe and North America, labor unions brought about laws granting workers the right to strike, establishing minimum work conditions and stopping or regulating child labor. Abolitionists fought hard and succeeded in abolishing slavery and the slave trade. For instance, Abraham Lincoln's Emancipation Proclamation abolished slavery in the rebel states in 1862, and Brazil abolished slavery in 1889. The women's rights movement struggled for many years to gain the right to vote (suffrage) for women. Success in gaining women's suffrage came about at different dates in the 20th century, although New Zealand was the first nation to grant women the right to vote in 1893. The U.S. passed the 19th amendment to its constitution which made it legal for women to vote in 1920, even though the territory of Wyoming granted suffrage to women years earlier in 1869. The newly created modern nation of Turkey granted women voting rights in 1926. France, a center of Enlightenment thinking in the 18th century, only granted women voting rights in 1944, although the government abolished slavery in 1794. The adoption of the Universal Declaration of Human Rights Voting Rights for Women, as stated in Article 21, passed into international law in 1948.

Between World War I and World War II (1919-1939) the world community of nations established a number of

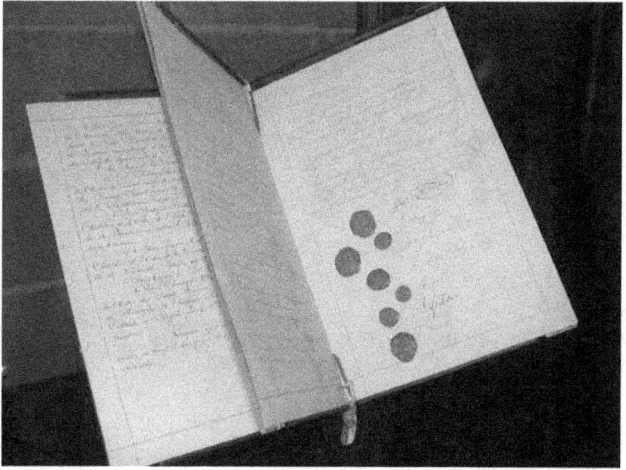

Original Geneva Conventions 1864

organizations to ensure peace and stability throughout the world. The most notable was the League of Nations in 1919, following the end of the devastating World War I. The League's goals included disarmament, preventing future wars, and settling disputes between countries through negotiation and diplomacy. Part of its charter was an order to promote many of the rights which were later included into the Universal Declaration of Human Rights.

The Geneva Conventions consist of four treaties that came into being between 1864 and 1949. It was in large part a direct result of efforts by the Red Cross. Although the four treaties are chiefly concerned with the treatment of the wounded, civilians shipwrecked and prisoners of war, it was at the forefront of the international community's first attempt to define laws of war.

After the horrors of another even more deadly war, World War II (1939–1945), a renewed commitment to protect basic principles of human rights was generally accepted around the world. There was general recognition of the idea that the human rights practices of individual countries toward their own citizens are matters of international concern. The 1945 United Nations Charter included a commitment to respect human rights, but it was the Universal Declaration of Human Rights that provided the basic statement of widely accepted international human rights standards.

Questions to Consider

1. Which traditions discussed in this section do you think has had the greatest impact in shaping the concept of human rights today? Explain.

As we have seen, human rights have a long historical heritage. Underlying the principal of human rights is a belief in the existence of a form of justice valid for all peoples, everywhere. The doctrine of human rights has come to occupy center stage in world affairs. It has become central to our understanding of how human beings should treat one another and how national and international political organizations should treat humanity. Human rights are best thought of as moral guarantees for each human being to lead a minimally good life. The case for human rights remains a morally powerful one. Perhaps the most convincing reason for the importance of human rights may rest upon our imagination. Try imagining a world without human rights!

Let's next turn to how human rights have expanded in the last 200 years through the efforts of activists involved in social movements.

CHAPTER TWO

SOCIAL MOVEMENTS AND HUMAN RIGHTS

"Major social movements eventually fade into the landscape not because they have diminished but because they have become a permanent part of our perceptions and experience."

— *Freda Adler*

WHAT ARE SOCIAL MOVEMENTS?

Rosa Parks and the Civil Rights Movement

Rosa Parks in jail

"I was arrested on December 1st, 1955 for refusing to stand up on the orders of the bus driver, after the white seats had been occupied in the front....I took a seat that was just back of where the white people were sitting, in fact, the last seat. A man was next to the window, and I took an aisle seat and there were two women across. We went on undisturbed until about the third stop when some white people boarded the bus and left one man standing. And when the driver noticed him standing, he told us to stand up and let him have those front seats. And when the other three people—after some hesitancy—stood up, he wanted to know if I was going to stand up, and I was not. And he told me he would have me arrested. And I told him he may do that. And of course, he did.

I was arrested on a Thursday evening, and on Friday evening they had the meeting at the Dexter Avenue Baptist Church, where Dr. Martin Luther King was the pastor. A number of citizens came and I told them the story and then it became news about my being arrested. My trial was December 5th, when they found me guilty. ...We set a meeting at the Holt Street Baptist Church on the evening of December 5th, because [that] was the day the people ... did not ride the bus. In fact, most of the buses were just about empty. It came to a vote, and unanimously it was decided that they would not ride the buses anymore until changes for the better were made."[1]

Rosa Parks (1913-2005) is credited with starting the American civil rights movement. At her death the U.S. Congress praised her achievements and called her the "Mother of the Modern-Day Civil Rights Movement." For many years Parks was portrayed as an innocent bystander who was merely tired after a long day of work and instantly decided to refuse to give up her bus seat to a white person. However, Rosa Parks was actually very active in civil rights and served as the secretary of the Montgomery, Alabama chapter of the National Association for the Advancement of Colored People (NAACP). She took action because, as she put it, "she was tired of giving in" to white authority.

Many African Americans over the years have displayed acts of defiance against discrimination and segregation but it was Rosa Parks' act of rebellion that sparked a national movement. In fact, many consider the civil rights movement to be the most significant social movement of the 20th century. In this chapter we will look at the expansion of human rights through the efforts of various social movements. Most of the social movements we will study have taken place in the U.S., but actually social movements have taken place all over the world. First we will historically examine American social movements and look at a few world-wide movements. Why have social movements started and ended, who joins them, what are their goals, and how do they get attention? Next, we will investigate social movements in three different historical eras—early era (1800-1945), modern era (1945-1990), and contemporary era (1990-present). Particular social movements will be examined in all three eras, and others in just one or two eras.

SOCIAL MOVEMENTS: A DEFINITION

A **social movement** is about changing mainstream ideas, laws, policies, attitudes, and beliefs about a particular issue and, thus, expanding the civil rights of the discriminated group. Social movements are a type of group action in which a large number of people sharing a similar interest work together to achieve a common goal. These large informal groups of individuals and/or organizations focus on changing specific political, social, economic, cultural or environmental issues. Their actions are usually coordinated and formed to carry out, resist, or undo what they think is a social wrong. Those involved in social movements actively work to change the course of history by their collective action and do not passively accept the status quo. Although some social movements have failed in their goals, others have brought about social changes—some minor and some far-reaching. Social movements may last for several years or even decades. Those in social movements have a shared belief or philosophy that provides a reason to condemn existing social conditions, an understanding of the movement's purpose, a distinction between "us" and "them," and a plan of action. To have a social movement, there needs to be polarizing differences between groups of people (us and them).

Social movements are usually loosely organized and spontaneous and do not follow rigid rules and procedures. They collectively support a social goal, typically a change in society's structure or values and introduce new ways of thinking about issues. They range in size from small, local groups to large worldwide movements. Sometimes movements may suffer from divisions over goals and tactics, which may cause the movement to split apart. If some of the goals are reached, as was the case with the civil rights movement, it may take away some of the movement's energy. According to sociologist, Charles Tilly, social movements are campaigns by which ordinary people can participate in public politics. He sees that social movements follow certain strategies to gather public awareness of

Social Movement Definitions

1. Sidney Tarrow defines social movements as collective challenges to elites, opponents, authorities, established groups or cultural values by people with common purposes and unity. He distinguishes social movements from political parties and interest groups.[3]
2. Herbert Blumer defines social movements as collective projects to establish a new order of life. They develop because of a condition of unrest, and get their motivation, on one hand, from dissatisfaction with the current form of life, and on the other hand, from wishes and hopes for a new way of living.[4]
3. Luther Gerlach and Virginia Hine identify five key factors for a social movement to take off: an organization held together by personal beliefs; face-to-face recruitment by committed individuals; personal commitment by an individual or an experience which separates them in some way from the established order; a belief which provides a foundation for a vision of change; and real or imagined opposition from society at large.[5]
4. William Kornhauser defines social movements as mass movements that mobilize people who are alienated from mainstream society, who do not believe in the authority of the established order, and who are ready to engage in efforts to destroy it. The greatest numbers of people involved in social movements are those who have the fewest ties to the mainstream social order.
5. Ralph H. Turner and Lewis M. Killian define a social movement as a collection of people promoting or resisting a change in society or the organization of which they are a part. Group membership fluctuates, and leadership is determined more by informal membership response than by formal procedures.[6]

their campaign: creation of special-purpose associations, public meetings, vigils, solemn processions, rallies, demonstrations, petition drives, statements to public media, and pamphleteering.[2]

Questions to Consider
1. Which definition do you think is the best? How would you define a social movement?

TYPES OF SOCIAL MOVEMENTS

There are several different types of social movements, and each movement may include different types as well.[7]

1. **Reform movements** are committed to changing some norms, usually legal ones. For example, a trade union has a goal of increasing workers' rights, a green movement wants a set of ecological laws, those against capital punishment want to do away with it, or pro-life advocates work to make abortion illegal.

2. **Radical movements** are more committed to fundamentally changing a society; more so than reform movements. For example, the Weathermen in the 1960s wanted to overthrow capitalism in the U.S.

3. **Conservative movements** want to defend existing norms, values, and attitudes. For example, the slow food movement is opposed to the spread of genetically modified foods, an anti-immigration movement seeks to stop illegal immigration into the U.S. and to preserve the country's "original" character.

4. **Peace movements** use a non-violent approach and civil disobedience as a way to draw attention to their goals. The American Civil Rights movement led by Martin Luther King and the Indian national independence movement led by Mohandas Gandhi would fall into this category.

Black Panther logo

5. **Violent social movements** use tactics that include violence, rebellion, or revolution to achieve their goals. For example, the American Civil Rights movement took a violent turn when the Black Panthers in the 1960s advocated violence and separation from white, mainstream America.

6. **Group-focused movements** strive to change groups or society in general. For example, those in the climate change movement work to get everyone to adopt greener ways of living in order to avert future environmental catastrophe for everyone on the planet.

7. **Individual-focused movements** work to safeguard individuals, not necessarily society at large; religious movements would fall in this category. For example, those in the pro-life movement campaign to save the life of the unborn.

LIFE CYCLE OF A SOCIAL MOVEMENT

Social movements do not last forever. They have a life cycle during which they start, grow, achieve their goals or fail, and eventually end. They are more likely to start when the times are responsive to their message, such as today's climate change movements that draw on scientific evidence to support their claims. A social movement needs a particular event to spark a chain of reactions leading to its birth.[8] For example, the Polish Solidarity movement in the 1980s eventually toppled the communist regimes of Eastern Europe, but it started when a trade union activist was fired from her job. A problem facing a developing social movement is getting the message out to a wider audience.

Many social movements unite around a charismatic leader. This person is often active in recruiting members and in making sure the movement succeeds. After the social movement is underway, there are two likely phases in recruiting new members: the first phase draws together people interested in the ideals of the movement and the second phase comes after the movement is better known or trendy. People who join in the second phase will likely be the first to leave when the movement suffers setbacks.[9]

Social movements lose momentum and eventually end. As a social movement grows, the once loosely organized groups shift to more formalized interest groups staffed by officials. As media interest declines, so does public interest and funding. Efforts to rejuvenate the movement may lead to bitter infighting. The leaders may "burn out" or take related positions in government. Some movement leaders may even move on to work in businesses they were previously trying to change.

To avoid the fate of stagnation or ending, the social movement's organization needs to be decentralized and flexible rather than a highly centralized bureaucracy. Diversity is the key in keeping a social movement going, which means drawing on various groups as participants. Social movements range from multi-million dollar professionally-led operations staffed by experts, to neighborhood associations organized by concerned citizens in response to local issues.[10] No two social organizations are alike.

SOCIAL MOVEMENT TACTICS

Social activists use a variety of tactics to reach their goals. One common tactic is **protest**, which is an objection, complaint or disapproval of something. Protests are reactions to events or situations, sometimes in favor, but most likely opposed. Protesters wish to make their opinions heard in an attempt to influence public opinion or government policy using disruptive, confrontational, and direct action. Groups find that protest activities increase awareness and are more successful in achieving their goals than other means. They have found that "rude and crude" confrontation is far more effective than "polite protest".[11]

Lobbying is the practice of influencing decisions made by governmental legislators or officials for the benefit of its citizens. A lobbyist, legislator, citizen, or organized group explains the goals of the organizations s/he represents. Lobbying takes money; therefore, organizations that hire lobbyists are usually well-funded. Lobbyists represent corporate or business interests, foreign governments, and non-profit organizations, such as the Public Broadcasting Station (PBS). Many lobbyists have offices on the legendary K Street in Washington D.C. **Litigation** or lawsuits are

Forms of Direct Action

protest march
picketing
street protest
lock-downs
protest songs
chanting/cheerleading
petitions
letter writing
sit-ins
riots
public suicide
hunger strike
occupation
strike
walk-out
boycott
teach-in

legal proceedings used to settle a dispute. For example, many indigenous peoples have brought cases of land ownership through litigation in the courts and have been able to reclaim some of their ancestral lands.

The Rise of Social Movements

Particular events, beliefs, circumstances, and technological changes have created social movements in the last 200 years. The indirect and direct purpose of these social movements has expanded human rights to individuals and groups marginalized by mainstream society and the worldview of the powerful. I have divided the social movements into three eras: early (1800-1945), modern (1945-1990), and global (1990-present). I have selected social movements that I think will be of most interest to you.

Early Social Movements: 1800-1945

The term social movement did not exist before the 19th century. Nonetheless, they first appeared in Britain and North America around 1800. These early movements focused on extending human rights to include people without wealth or property. Reformers were concerned about extreme poverty and wealth gaps and fought for specific under-privileged groups, such as slaves, the working class, and children. They worked on goals, such as improving individuals' standard of living or freeing slaves from bondage.

The rise of social movements in the early era grew out of modern conditions. Mass education, economic well-being, communication technologies, and democratic principles, such as freedom of thought, speech and expression, inspired activists to collectively press for change for those on the margins of society. The thriving Western economies gave rise to a well-educated, affluent middle class, who had the means to launch or be active in social movements and to financially support them. The ravages of early industrialization and the dreadful overcrowding conditions in cities spurred the formation of many social movements. Unregulated industrialization led to worker abuse by employers, which helped spawn child rights movements, while labor groups demanded fair wages, a shorter working day and the right to organize. Other movements worked to expand suffrage to all citizens, women's rights campaigns, temperance crusades, public education for all, humane treatment for the mentally ill, rights of religious minorities, and expanded education. The abuses of European imperialistic conquests led to social movements to oppose this exploitation. Urbanization helped make it possible for social movements to organize large numbers of people in small areas. Thus, cities were the site of early organizing.

The Abolitionist Social Movement

The British abolitionist movement around 1800 was most likely the first documented social movement. Its goal was to end slavery and the Atlantic slave trade that transported slaves primarily from Africa to the Americas. Black resistance, Christian humanitarianism, and the intellectual current of the Enlightenment era all contributed to the appeal of the **abolitionist movement**. However, slaveholders and their supporters powerfully resisted ending human bondage. Greater public awareness about the brutality of slavery and the Atlantic slave trade played a role in the start of the abolitionist movement. Slaves suffered under brutal conditions as the transporters chained, branded, and crowded them into the hold of disease-ridden slave ships. The ship's crew merely tossed those who died over-board. Upon arrival in the Western hemisphere, the owners demanded they perform back-breaking labor for the rest of their lives.

In the early years, Great Britain had the strongest abolitionist movement. The first to condemn slavery were the Quakers, who believed that all people, regardless, of race, were equal in the eyes of God. They took the first steps against slavery by establishing the first antislavery society in 1783. Some Evangelical Christians joined the Quakers. Led by Evangelical William Wilberforce, a member of the British Parliament, and Thomas Clarkson, a Quaker, the society started petition drives, education efforts, and lobbying in an attempt to end British involvement in slave trading. Although opposed by many, the society achieved its goal in 1807, when the British Parliament abolished the slave trade. Wilberforce's story gained international attention with the release of the film *Amazing Grace* in 2007, which coincided with the 200th anniversary of the date on which Parliament voted to ban the slave trade.

Official medallion of the British Anti-Slavery Society, 1795

During the 19th century British abolitionism became more radical and demanded the immediate emancipation of slaves. Finally the British Parliament passed the Emancipation Act in 1833. By 1838, all slaves in the British Empire were free. Thereafter, British abolitionism fragmented into various efforts against the illegal slave trade, slavery in Africa and slavery in the United States.

The ideals of the American Revolution contributed to the start of the abolitionist movement in the U.S., since it became difficult for many white Americans, who were fighting for independence in the name of liberty and universal natural rights, to support the continuation of slavery. These ideas of liberty and freedom motivated Congress to ban slavery in the Northwest Territory in 1787, and during this time many slaveholders in Maryland and Virginia freed their slaves. Despite these early successes, by the mid-1780s the abolitionist movement in the U.S. was in decline. The South resisted the movement, since the growth of the cotton industry fueled by the invention of Eli Whitney's cotton gin in 1793 made slavery an even more profitable business. With so much money invested in slaves, an ideology developed that said blacks were biologically, morally, and intellectually inferior to whites and should be enslaved.

A spirit of evangelical religious revival spread in the North. Evangelicals believed that America was in need of moral renewal, and as dedicated Christians, they would carry out a series of reforms to eliminate social evils. These reforms included women's rights, temperance, educational improvements, humane treatment for the mentally ill, and the abolition of slavery. They took up these causes with fervor.

The leading abolitionist of the day was a white New Englander, William Lloyd Garrison. In 1831, he began publishing a weekly abolitionist newspaper called *The Liberator*. Convinced that slavery was a sin, he and other like-minded abolitionists formed the American Anti-Slavery Society (AASS). Its goal was to emancipate slaves and award them equal rights. Numbering 250,000 members by 1838, the AASS spread rapidly across the North and employed fire-brand speakers, sent petitions to Congress, and even mailed abolitionist information to Southerners. Their activities produced an angry reaction in the North and especially the South, where Southern postmasters refused to deliver antislavery literature.

Abolitionist efforts intensified through the 1840s and 1850s. One of the most notable efforts was *Uncle Tom's Cabin*, written by Harriet Beecher Stowe in 1852. She wrote, "For, so inconsistent is human nature, especially in the ideal, that not to undertake a thing at all seems better than to undertake and come short." The book showed the reality of slavery and humanized the sufferings of the main character, the slave Uncle Tom. It was the best-selling book in the 19th century and helped fuel the abolitionist cause.

Abolitionist pressured Lincoln to sign the **Emancipation Proclamation**, which declared slaves free within the bounds of the Confederacy, in January 1863. The eventual Northern victory and continuing abolitionist pressure led in 1865 to the ratification of the 13th Amendment to the Constitution, which banned involuntary servitude throughout the country. After these achievements, the American abolitionist movements came to an end. Even though the shackles of slavery had been lifted, the majority of black southerners remained poor agricultural farmers well into the 20th century.

Brazil, which had 1.5 million slaves in 1870, was the remaining slaveholding nation in the Western hemisphere. In Brazil politically powerful sugar and coffee planters steadfastly defended slave labor. Finally, unrest on plantations and the refusal of the army to step in to halt the flight of slaves from their masters resulted in the total abolition of slavery in Brazil in 1888. Although slavery disappeared from the Western hemisphere, it lingered in Africa into the 20th century.

Questions to Consider
1. If you were an abolitionist in the 1800s, what tactics would you have used to advance your cause?

Public Education as a Social Movement

Public education, a significant social movement of the 19th century, was dedicated to extending the human right of free, public education to all people regardless of social class. A basic form of public education started in the 1600s in the New England colonies of the U.S., but the reason for education at the time was for children to be versed in Puritan and Congregationalist religious doctrine. By the middle of the 18th century, private schooling, not public, had become the norm. Thomas Jefferson spearheaded the creation of public schools, and his ideas influenced educational policies into the 19th century. He believed the government should direct education, it should be free from religious biases, and it should be for all. A national system of formal education would not develop until the 19th century. Early on the public education system was highly localized, with public school students attending classes for only a few weeks each winter, often in rudimentary schoolhouses and taught by untrained teachers. A quality education was available only to wealthy students at private schools. Reformers fought for the education of all children.

Horace Mann (1769-1859), a leading reformer from Massachusetts, turned his attention toward public schools in 1837, starting a social movement that he was involved in for the rest of his life. Mann established the state board of education in Massachusetts and served as the board's first secretary. He used his position to enact major educational reforms to ensure every child would receive an education funded by local taxes. He fought for ways to improve public schools and equalize educational opportunity by calling for teacher-training institutes, increasing the school year to six months, and gaining funds for teacher salaries, books and school construction. He thought that all children should learn in "common" schools, yet he did not take a stand against school segregation in his own city of Boston.[12]

Mann and other reformers argued that public education would help shape good citizens, unite society around common goals and prevent crime and poverty. He often framed public education in economic terms, saying that public education would increase the wealth of individuals, communities, the state and the country as a whole while teaching respect for private property. His influence soon spread beyond Massachusetts as more states took up the idea of universal schooling. As a result, by the end of the 19th century free public education at the elementary level was available for all American children.

Mann lived at a time of tremendous social change when immigrants poured into the Northeastern states, farmers left rural areas to work in factories, and cities grew rapidly with crime and poverty on the rise. Some historians make the case that the turmoil alarmed Mann and other middle class reformers, and they encouraged public education as a way to bring order and discipline

Horace Mann

to the working class. Threatened by the growing population of urban poor, reformers placed a major emphasis on "moral training," standardization and classroom drill. But most historians see Mann's legacy as positive, citing his overall contributions to a more egalitarian and democratic society. He believed political stability and social harmony depended on education: a basic level of literacy and teaching common public ideals. He saw public schooling as central to good citizenship, democratic participation and societal well-being.

Booker T. Washington (1856-1915), a promoter of education, was born into slavery. He founded the Tuskegee Institute in Alabama, and he became a leading voice for the educational and economic improvement of African Americans. Drawing on his philosophy of racial solidarity, self-help and working with whites, he saw vocational education as a way to teach manual skills to African Americans that would help them work their way up the social and economic ladder. Washington spoke on the lecture circuit about the educational needs of African Americans. His popular lectures championed the values of hard work, determination and self-discipline. He forged the Tuskegee Institute into a leader in vocational training and character-building. African-American educator W.E.B. Dubois disagreed with Washington's approach to education and said that African Americans needed a "real education" that would teach children "to know, to think and to aspire."[13] The public hotly debated the two approaches to education at the beginning of the 20th century, and the debate continues today.

By the early 20th century, reformers had reached their goal of providing public education for all. Yet, another educational movement would arise at this time: progressive education. **John Dewey** (1859-1952) led this movement and is arguably the most influential educator in U.S. history. A noted philosopher, he is most remembered for his educational theories that broke new ground and continue to wield influence. As an alternative to the drill-and-recitation methods that were the exclusive approach to education in the 19th century, Dewey said education should be grounded in experience. The child's psychological and physical development should guide educational practices, inside and outside the classroom. The ideas of child-centered learning formed the basis of progressive education, enjoying continued popularity even today.

> **Questions to Consider**
> 1. How are the ideas of educational reformers through the last two centuries reflected in the debate about school reform today?

THE WOMEN'S SUFFRAGE MOVEMENT

Starting in 1848 in Seneca Falls, New York, the American **woman's suffrage movement** supported the human rights goal of gaining suffrage for women 21 years and over. It was a long struggle. Not until 1920, with the passage of the 19th amendment, were women finally able to vote in their first national election. It took over 70 years of consistent organizing and lobbying for woman's suffrage to become law. Many notable reformers dedicated their lives to the cause.

Elizabeth Cady Stanton (1815-1902) co-organized the 1848 Seneca Falls convention, credited as the beginning of the American woman's suffrage movement. She presented the Declaration of Sentiments at the convention, regarded as a foundational document in the movement; it followed the format of the Declaration of Independence, except it focused on woman's rights. Stanton and other organizers saw the event as a step in the continuing effort to gain greater social, civil and moral rights for women. They promoted the event as the first time that women and men gathered together to demand women's right to vote. Over 300 attended the convention including Frederick Douglass, a well-known black abolitionist, who spoke at the convention and lent his support to its goals. Abolitionist William Lloyd Garrison also attended. Many activists were involved in both the woman's suffrage and the abolitionist movement.

During and after the Civil War, little was heard of the woman's movement, but in 1869 Susan B. Anthony (1820-1906) and Stanton formed the all-female National Woman Suffrage Association (NWSA). Anthony, born a Quaker, dedicated her life to the cause. For 45 years she traveled the U.S. and Europe giving 75 to 100 speeches every year on women's rights. Their aim was to pass an amendment that gave women the right to vote in all elections.

Lucy Stone (1818-1893) organized another suffrage group in 1869, the much larger and more moderate American Woman Suffrage Association (AWSA), which included both men and women. AWSA supported the 15th Amendment as written, arguing that it was acceptable for black men to vote before moving forward with voting rights for women. In 1890, the two splintered women's rights organizations united to form the National American Woman Suffrage Association (NAWSA) with Anthony serving as president from 1890 to 1900. Lobbying hard to get the right to vote for women, the organization had a hearing before every Congress every year from 1869 to 1919.

The U.S. entered World War I in 1917, which provided the final push for the realization of woman's suffrage in America. President Woodrow Wilson announced that World War I was a war for democracy, even though women did not have the vote in the U.S. Women suffragists were outraged and held up banners saying that the U.S. was not a democracy. Finally, the embarrassed President gave his support and Congress passed the 19th Amendment to the Constitution. Women, finally, had the right to vote.

With their goal accomplished, the women's suffrage movement broke up. Some of its leaders, such as Alice Paul (1885-1977), shifted the cause to equal rights for women. She wrote an Equal Rights Amendment but it failed to gain any significant momentum. With the Depression in the

1930s, the focus for most women shifted to merely surviving and feeding their families. Equal rights were not a priority at the time. It would not be until the 1950s that the women's movement championed different goals.

THE ENVIRONMENTAL MOVEMENT

The environmental movement is a social movement that has continued from the 19th century onward. Since we are viewing human rights from a broad context in this book, preserving our planet for future generations is a vital human rights issue. Although the focus has changed in each of the eras, I will include the movement in three phases since I believe it is one of the most pressing issues of our time.

A budding conservation movement developed in the 19th century with the United States, along with British India and other European countries, playing a leading role worldwide. During the 19th century, many Americans developed a deep and long-lasting passion for nature. Tales of the untamed wilderness and the raw-boned West told of spectacular landscapes unspoiled by urbanization and industrialization. Nature was the romanticized subject of countless paintings by artists who showed sweeping vistas and boundless opportunities for expansion. However, in the late 19th century, the demands of industry and urban consumption were devouring the unspoiled gifts of nature in order to harvest its valuable natural resources. Destructive practices in open-pit mining, overgrazing of cattle and sheep, and clear-cutting timber were changing the landscape of a scenic American wilderness to an American wasteland.

Conservation groups responded to industry's exploitation of nature by forming a social movement. They sought to protect natural resources, including plant and animal species and their habitat. Upper class white males who enjoyed outdoor activities such as hunting, fishing, and camping were the main leaders of the movement. Their disputes were mostly between those who wanted to leave the natural environment in a pristine state and those who viewed it as a place for recreation and pleasure. The U.S. Congress, in one of the first conservation acts, established Hot Springs Reservation in Arkansas in 1832, and it was made a national park in 1933. When Congress established Yellowstone as a national park in 1872, conservation shot into public awareness. During this era, many organizations formed that continue today, such as the National Audubon Society which opened chapters in 1896 and the Sierra Club.

As with all movements, there were different factions involved in the early stages, each voicing its particular viewpoint. Conservationists wanted to use natural resources wisely and assure their availability for future generations. The early conservation movement included fisheries and wildlife management, water and soil conservation and sustainable forestry. **Preservationists** wanted to protect resources in their natural state and did not believe that nature's purpose was to serve humans. Instead, they saw humans as part of nature enveloped in an interdependent web of life. This split between the two views continues. Portraying this split are three notable leaders who each held a different view about the environment: Henry David Thoreau and John Muir were preservationists and Theodore Roosevelt was a conservationist.

Henry David Thoreau (1817-1862) wrote *Walden*, a study of wildlife, simple living, and self-sufficiency, while living in a cabin on Walden Pond in Massachusetts. Thoreau lived what he called a "deliberate life." He was attuned to nature and did not get caught up in the drive to acquire material goods that he thought consumed many people's lives. He also wrote an essay, *Civil Disobedience*, in which he stated that acts of civil disobedience or individual resistance to civil government is a moral duty if the state is unjust. He believed that non-violent resistance or protest was a worthy reaction to unfair government actions. The essay influenced many peace activists in later years, including Mahatma Gandhi from India and Martin Luther King. Thoreau also supported the abolitionist movement.

John Muir (1838-1914), an American naturalist, scientifically studied plants and animals. His writings and philosophy strongly influenced the formation of the modern environmental movement. He was an early advocate of preservation of U.S. wilderness, and his letters, essays, and books tell of his adventures in nature, especially in the Sierra Nevada mountain range of California. They are still popular today. His direct activism helped to save the Yosemite Valley and Sequoia National Park in California and other wilderness areas from the ravages of clear-cut logging, dam building, urban development, and mining. He founded the Sierra Club in 1892 and became the first president. Sierra Club continues to be one of the largest conservationist organizations in the United States.

U.S. President Theodore Roosevelt and John Muir in Yosemite National Park, 1906

Theodore Roosevelt (1858-1919) loved nature and spent as much time as possible outdoors. He brought his love of nature to the presidency and was the first president to consider the environment as a national issue. As president (1901-1909) he permanently preserved some of America's most unique natural treasures. He placed under public protection national parks, national forests, game and bird preserves, and other federal reservations totaling approximately 230,000,000 acres; this was about 84,000 acres added every day. He designated five national parks—Crater Lake in Oregon, Wind Cave in South Dakota, Sullys Hill in North Dakota, Platt in Oklahoma, and Mesa Verde in Colorado. President Roosevelt declared the Grand Canyon a national monument in 1908 and it became a National Park in 1919. He authorized creating 150 national forests, 8 national monuments, and many other projects.[14] Roosevelt and Muir both admired each other very much, and the two nature lovers took a memorable three day camping trip together in Yosemite National Park.[15]

It was during the Roosevelt administration that the first divisions between the conservationists and preservationists emerged. The legendary split between Gifford Pinchot, the first Chief of the Forest Service and a conservationist, and John Muir, a preservationist, illustrated this division. Muir thought Pinchot's policies of management and efficient land use gave in too much to industry demands.[16] Pinchot thought that these were very practical policies for an economic system that required cheap natural resources for economic growth. This split continues today.

Questions to Consider
1. Are you a preservationist or conservationist? Why?

The Labor Movement

The **labor movement** is a broad term that refers to a social movement made up of workers, many of whom have organized themselves into collective associations called unions. **Unions** represent the interests of workers by campaigning for better treatment and benefits from employers and for governments to pass laws granting workers certain rights. These campaigns have improved human rights for workers. The labor movement has attracted workers in countries that have industrialized, such as European countries and the United States. Action by the labor movement has led to reforms for many workers, such as the 2-day weekend, minimum wages, paid holidays, and the 8-hour day.

The labor movement had its beginnings in reaction to the Industrial Revolution that started in late 18th century England, a major event in world history. A growing number of workers in the 19th century toiled in factories churning out mass-produced products such as textiles and machinery. The early factories were dirty, dangerous, and filled with misery for the workers. Employers, eager to make a profit, were intent on getting as much labor at the lowest possible cost from their workers. They skimped on safety devices, sanitation, and environmental protection and even locked workers in the factory to prevent them from leaving or taking "unnecessary" breaks. Some employers favored women and child workers, who labored for even less money than men and didn't protest about their poor working conditions.

Workers' Memorial Day poster, Mother Jones

Workers gradually banded together to form associations and then unions to try to collectively stop their exploitation and to put pressure on employers to improve their working conditions and pay. Organized in 1869, the **Knights of Labor** was the first successful national labor organization in the U.S. The Knights believed that by unifying all workers together, they would be able to accomplish their goals. After 1878, membership included women and African Americans but excluded bankers, doctors, lawyers, gamblers, stockholders, and liquor manufacturers because they considered them to be unproductive members of society. The labor union demanded an end to child and convict labor, equal pay for women, a progressive income tax, and cooperative employer-employee ownership of mines and factories. However, by 1900, the labor union ended because of mismanagement and other problems.

One of the memorable organizers for the Knights of Labor was the colorful Mary Harris Jones. Factory owners despised her, but union members and workers loved and respected her, bestowing upon her the nickname "Mother Jones," affectionately known as "The Miners' Angel." During her lifetime she helped recruit thousands of women members to the union. Despite tragedies, she persevered in her efforts to expand human rights for workers. Her clever declaration expressed her fierce determination: "Pray for the dead and fight like hell for the living." When she was denounced on the Senate floor as the "grandmother of all agitators," she replied: "I hope to live long enough to be the great-grandmother of all agitators."[17]

The Knights of Labor gave way to the **American Federation of Labor (AFL)**, which was the largest union in the U.S. for the first half of the 20th century. Samuel Gompers founded the organization in 1886 and served as president until his death in 1924. For the first 50 years, craft unions dominated the AFL. A craft union organized workers according to their particular skill or craft; for example, carpenters had a union. In 1934, mass production workers split from the AFL to form the **Congress of Industrial Organizations (CIO)**. Mass production is the repetitive manufacture of large amounts of standardized products on moving assembly lines. The AFL and CIO continued as separate unions during World War II but reunited in 1955. They succeeded in getting an 8-hour day, a 5-day work week, health and pension benefits, good wages, safer working conditions, and they eliminated child labor. In 1945, nearly one-third of all U.S. workers belonged to unions, which declined to 12.4 percent in 2008.[18] The AFL-CIO continues as one organization today. The unions contributed to establishing human rights for workers.

Child Rights and the Labor Movement

Today child labor is considered a human rights violation, but during early industrialization in the 1800s, children as young as four were working long hours in dangerous jobs for low wages. Poor families needed their wage contribution to their meager income pool. Over two million children worked for very low wages, often just pennies a day. Sometimes their work-week stretched to 70 hours. Agile boys worked as chimney sweeps; small children scrambled under machinery to retrieve cotton bobbins; and young boys crawled through tunnels too narrow and low for adults in coal mines.[19] Children working in factories suffered health problems, such as bronchitis and tuberculosis due to poor ventilation. Child coal miners began work at the age of 5 and often died before the age of 25. Most coal miners—children and adults—worked 16-hour days. They experienced damp, depressing, and dangerous conditions. Many of them had to transport the coal on their backs, which led to back problems, paralysis or death.[20] Some children undertook work as apprentices in trades, such as boys in construction or girls in domestic service. Working hours were long: builders worked 64 hours a week in summer and 52 hours in winter, while domestic servants regularly worked 80-hour weeks. Some children also worked as prostitutes.

Like Britain, the U.S. had child labor abuses. The British Parliament passed the Factory Acts in 1802 and 1819, in which they restricted the working hours of children in factories and cotton mills to 12 hours per day. Parliament postponed further reform until 1847 when both adults and children were limited to a 10-hour work day. The U.S. was slow to recognize human rights for children. In large cities in the 1800s, for example, orphans frequently had to find work to support themselves. Changes started in the mid-1800s with the Children's Rights Movement, when reformers organized "orphan trains" to transport orphans to homes in the Midwest.

Social reformers and unions lobbied for the abolishment of child labor. Jane Addams, for example, a dedicated reformer, started the Hull House in Chicago to help poor and immigrant children and their families. But it was not until 1916, that Congress passed the first child labor bill, the Keating-Owen Act, which banned the sale of any article produced by the labor of a child labor under the age of 14 in a factory, cannery, or mine, and it regulated the number of hours a child could work.[21] However, it took the Great Depression to end child labor nationwide; adults had become so desperate for jobs that they would work for the same wage as children. In 1938, President Franklin D. Roosevelt signed the Fair Labor Standards Act which, amongst other things, placed limits on many forms of child labor.

SOCIAL MOVEMENTS: THE MODERN ERA 1945-1990

After the end of World War II, the spread of democratic ideals unleashed after the atrocities of the war sparked modern Western social movements. Westerners vowed to never let happen again the wholesale discrimination against Jews, homosexuals, and other minorities by the fascist and communist countries.

Social activists took slow but determined steps to eliminate discrimination and genocide and to expand human rights. Modern social movements have also benefitted from the spread of mass education. Many movements started at universities, where mass education and freedom of expression were/are fertile grounds for social movements. Also, a liberal arts education was popular at this time, through which many people became aware of problems associated with modern society that have led to the desire for change. The close living quarters of students has also helped them to organize protests and discussion. For example, the protests against the Vietnam War in the 1960s and early 1970s had roots in universities. Women's rights or feminism, pro-choice and pro-life, gay rights, civil rights, anti-nuclear and peace, global justice and environmental protection were some of the significant movements that emerged during this era. Also, after the war the right of colonized countries to gain independence gathered momentum.

THE AMERICAN CIVIL RIGHTS MOVEMENT

From about 1950 to 1980, worldwide civil rights movements—amidst much civil unrest and popular rebellion—worked for political, social, and economic rights, such as equality before the law. In the late 1960s, the civil rights movement splintered, and a faction took a sharp turn to the radical left. This section concentrates mainly on the American Civil Rights movement.

From 1954-1968, the civil rights movement aimed at reforms such as abolishing racial discrimination and racism against African Americans, particularly egregious in the South. The movement highlighted the inequities and discrimination that governments, businesses, educational institutions, and communities imposed upon African Americans. Activists engaged in acts of nonviolent protest and civil disobedience that often resulted in clashes with government authorities. Forms of protest and civil disobedience included boycotts, such as the successful Montgomery bus boycott (1955–1956) in Montgomery, Alabama; "sit-ins," such as in Greensboro, North Carolina (1960); marches, such as the March on Washington (1963); and a wide range of other nonviolent acts. Rosa Parks sparked the American Civil Rights movement, but the Montgomery bus boycott following her arrest was beneficial in the long term. Many figures rose to prominence during the boycott, most notably **Martin Luther King Jr.**, whose leadership in the boycott catapulted him to national fame. It lasted for one year, and led to a Supreme Court decision declaring that Alabama and Montgomery laws segregating buses were unconstitutional.

On February 1, 1960, four African American college students staged a "sit-in" at a "white's only" lunch counter at a Woolworth's store in Greensboro, North Carolina. The lunch counter only had stools for whites, while blacks had to stand to eat. A waitress refused to serve them and she notified the store manager of the sit-in. The manager asked the students to leave, and when they didn't he called the police to have them removed. The following morning the four students, along with 27 others, showed up at Woolworth's to protest. As the days went on, more and more students participated in the sit-in.[22] Four days after the sit-in began, 300 students arrived at Woolworth's to peacefully protest the segregated lunch counter. Racial tensions mounted and the demonstrations grew more violent. A bomb scare forced the protesters out of Woolworth's, and the manager closed his store for over two weeks.

The impact of the **Greensboro sit-in** was significant. The idea spread to other North Carolina cities—Winston-Salem, Durham, Raleigh, and Charlotte—where students launched their own sit-ins. Other cities across the South like Lexington, Kentucky, Richmond, Virginia and Nashville and Chattanooga, Tennessee also saw protests. Although the majority of these protests were peaceful, in a few instances protests became violent, such as in Chattanooga, Tennessee, where fights broke out between blacks and whites. The sit-ins received significant national media and government attention which led to some positive results. President Dwight Eisenhower supported the students and expressed his sympathy for those fighting for their human and civil rights.

In Greensboro's Woolworth's store, the sit-in was successful; the lunch counter was desegregated several months after the first protests. In many cities, the sit-ins helped to achieve the desegregation of lunch counters and other public places. The media covered the desegregation issue nationwide, beginning with lunch counters and spreading to include transport facilities, art galleries, beaches, parks, swimming pools, libraries, and even museums around the South. The Civil Rights Act of 1964 required desegregation in all public accommodations.

Greensboro sit-in lunch counter

In 1993, a section of the Woolworth's lunch counter in Greensboro was donated to the Smithsonian Institution in Washington D.C., where it is on display.

From all over the nation streams of buses, trains, and cars made their way to the nation's capital on August 28, 1963 for the most memorable march of the civil rights era, the March on Washington. All told, more than 2,000 buses, 21 special trains, 10 chartered airliners, and uncounted cars delivered over 200,000 marchers to Washington D.C.[23] Estimates of the number of marchers varied from 200,000 (police) to over 300,000 (leaders of the march). About 80 percent of the marchers were African American. Civil rights leaders wanted to pressure the administration of President John F. Kennedy to draft a strong federal civil rights bill. The march is widely credited as helping to pass the Civil Rights Act (1964) and the National Voting Rights Act (1965). Marchers assembled at the Washington Monument to march the short distance to the Lincoln Memorial. Speakers included notable civil rights leaders, Catholic, Protestant, and Jewish religious leaders, labor leader Walter Reuther, and actress Josephine Baker, the only female speaker. Folk musicians Bob Dylan and Joan

Baez performed as well. But the most memorable event was Dr. Martin Luther King's mesmerizing delivery at the Lincoln Memorial of his historic "I Have a Dream" speech, advocating racial harmony and non-violent protest.

On April 4, 1968, in Memphis, Tennessee, an assassin's bullet silenced King's moderate voice. As early as 1966, a more radical voice had challenged King's non-violent approach, the Black Power movement—which lasted from about 1966 to 1975. The movement enlarged the aims of the civil rights movement to include racial dignity, economic and political self-sufficiency, and freedom from oppression. The Black Power movement was a worldwide movement for some people of African descent, but primarily included African Americans. The movement was popular among those who were impatient and critical of the nonviolent approach to confronting racism practiced by Martin Luther King, Jr., and other moderates. They also rejected desegregation as a primary goal of the movement.

The **Black Power** movement demands included defense against racial oppression and black separatism—the establishment of separate social institutions and a self-sufficient, separate economy. Often Black Power activists pushed for the open use of violence as a means to achieve their aims. Such positions were, for the most part, in direct conflict with the leaders of the mainstream movement; thus, the two movements were opposed to each other's goals. The movement highlighted racial pride, such as "Black is Beautiful." Members chastised black men and women who straightened their hair and lightened or bleached their skin in response to mainstream American culture, which commonly regarded black features as less attractive or desirable than white features. The movement encouraged the popular Afro hair style. Most importantly, it encouraged a generation of African Americans to feel pride about who they were and how they looked. The Black Power movement put forth the idea of "soul," which was a kind of identity for black individuals and groups.[24]

Probably the most famous of several highly charismatic Black Power leaders was Malcolm X (1925-1965). Born Malcolm Little, he was a self-taught Muslim minister, public speaker, and human rights activist. His admirers agreed with his harsh criticism of white America, and his detractors accused him of preaching racism, black supremacy, and violence. Malcolm X was assassinated under suspicious circumstances in 1965, leaving behind a wife and six daughters. Two leaders co-founded the Black Panther Party in 1966: Bobby Seale (b. 1936) and Huey P. Newton (1942-1989). Stokely Carmichael (1941-1998) was very active in the movement; the federal government closely monitored all four leaders.

THE WOMEN'S MOVEMENT

The woman's movement resurfaced in the 1960s, after largely disappearing from national awareness with the passage of the 19th amendment in 1920. **Betty Friedan** and her book, *The Feminine Mystique*, written in 1963, is often credited with igniting the second phase of the women's movement. Friedan concluded that many women found a general unease in their lives, resulting from the fact that they only had one identity—that of wife and mother; all other roles, such as careers, were closed. She also stated that society considered women's work as less meaningful and valuable than men's work.

Friedan went on to found the National Organization for Women (NOW) in 1966, which aimed to bring women "into the mainstream of American society now" in "fully equal partnership with men." She continued to be an active feminist leader in the 1960s, founding many organizations and championing many causes. Most people see her as the most important, visible, and influential feminist of the 1960s.

THE MODERN ENVIRONMENTAL MOVEMENT

The second era of the environmental movement got underway in 1945. The earlier movement emphasized the protection or efficient management of the natural environment, while modern environmentalism aimed to clean-up and control pollution. Also, the movement changed from top-down control by technicians and managers to bottom-up grassroots demands from individual citizens and citizen groups, as exemplified in the work of Rachel Carson. Another strain of the movement was a philosophical understanding of nature as an interdependent web, as exemplified in the work of Aldo Leopold.

Rachel Carson

Rachel Carson (1907-1964) wrote *Silent Spring* in 1962, and it is widely credited with helping to advance the modern environmental movement. Carson, a marine biologist, is known as the "godmother of modern environmentalism."[25] In the late 1950s, Carson turned her attention to conservation and the environmental problems caused by synthetic pesticides. A gifted writer, she documented in her book the harmful effects of pesticides on the environment, particularly on birds. Carson found that DDT caused thinner egg shells in birds, which resulted in reproductive problems and death. Most of the book described pesticides effect on natural ecosystems, but four chapters linked pesticides to cases of human illnesses, such as cancer. She accused the chemical industry of intentionally and irresponsibly spreading untrue information about pesticides, and public officials' uncritical acceptance of industry's claims.[26] Carson called into question the notion of scientific progress—an important American belief which places utmost confidence in scientific answers. The overriding theme of Silent Spring is the powerful and often negative effect humans have on the natural world.[27]

Carson's most direct legacy in the environmental movement was the campaign to ban the use of DDT in the U.S., and to ban or limit its use throughout the world. Ultimately the campaign led to a nationwide ban on DDT and other pesticides in 1972. Her environmental activism inspired a grassroots movement that helped create the Environmental Protection Agency in 1970. Carson had critics. They argued that restrictions placed on pesticides have caused needless deaths and hampered agriculture, and more generally that environmental regulation unnecessarily restricts economic freedom. Some declared that her scientific findings did not support her claims.[28]

Despite the critics, Rachel Carson's work has had a powerful impact on the American public's environmental concerns, such as pesticides and pollution, and her work was a rallying cry for the infant environmental movement in the 1960s. No one would be able to sell pollution as the necessary underside of progress so easily or uncritically anymore. She also inspired the later deep ecology movement, and the overall strength of the environmental movement going forward.[29] President Jimmy Carter posthumously awarded Carson the Presidential Medal of Freedom.'

Aldo Leopold (1887-1948), an American ecologist, forester, and environmentalist, helped launch a new direction in environmental thought with his book *A Sand County Almanac*, written in 1948 and published after his death. Leopold lived and taught in Madison, Wisconsin; he was influential in the development of modern environmental ethics and championed wilderness preservation. Leopold introduced a new term used into the environmental movement: ecology. **Ecology** is a branch of biology dealing with the study of living things, their environment, and the relation between the two. When used in a cultural sense, ecology means the study of the detrimental effects of modern civilization on the environment, with a view toward prevention or reversal through conservation.[30] In *Sand County Almanac*, Leopold spelled out the importance of ecology—meaning that all is connected—when studying the environment. He firmly believed that land is not a commodity (has a monetary value) to be possessed; rather, humans must have mutual respect for the earth in order not to destroy it. He also puts forth the idea that humans will never be free if they have no wild spaces in which to roam. One of the most memorable quotes in the book describes the idea of a "Land Ethic." He writes, "A thing is right when it tends to preserve the integrity, stability and beauty of the biotic community. It is wrong when it tends otherwise."

By the late 1960s, environmental activists linked the destruction of the natural environment to the interplay of new technology, industry, politics, and economic power held by giant corporations. A series of dramatic environmental catastrophes hit at this time to galvanize action. One was the 1969 combustion of a river along the industrial section of Cleveland, Ohio. Environmentalists responded to these events by demanding government protection from environmental pollution and destruction. With the support of the Nixon administration, Congress passed a series of environmental laws.

On April 22, 1970, the first Earth Day brought together over 22 million Americans to celebrate quality-of-life issues and environmental concerns. The idea of a clean and safe environment as a human right was gaining momentum. The environmental movement gained even more publicity, awareness, and impetus when a seemingly endless string of toxic chemical episodes occurred. One of the foremost examples was the Love Canal campaign, a tragedy that would be seared into public memory for decades.

The 1978 tragedy at Love Canal spurred individuals across the nation to get involved with grassroots campaigns. Love Canal, a housing development in Niagara Falls, New York, was built on a landfill operated by the Hooker Chemical Company, which had been dumping highly toxic industrial chemicals there for decades. In 1978, an Environmental Protection Agency (EPA) investigator warned that "even though some of these landfills have been closed down, they may stand like ticking time bombs." Just months later, Love Canal exploded. The EPA investigator found buried corroding waste-disposal drums that had broken through the soil and into people's backyards. Trees and gardens were turning black and dying. One neighborhood swimming pool had popped up from its foundation, afloat on a sea of chemicals. Puddles of noxious toxins were everywhere: some pooled in residents' yards, some festered in basements, and others poisoned school grounds. Everywhere the deadly air had a faint, choking smell. Children returned

Environmental Legislation and Date Passed

1963 Clean Air Act
1965 The Wilderness Act
1967 Air Quality Act
1968 National Trails Act
1968 Wild and Scenic Rivers Act
1969 National Environmental Policy Act, created the Environmental Protection Agency (EPA)
1970 Clean Air Act Extension
1970 April 22 First Earth Day
1972 Pesticides Act (DDT banned in U.S.)
1972 Water Pollution Control Act
1973 Endangered Species Act

from play outdoors coated with burns on their hands and faces. Pets lost their fur. Disturbingly high birth defects and miscarriages stalked the Love Canal neighborhood. One of the most common chemicals seeping through the ground and into homes was benzene—a known human carcinogen.[31] The public was outraged, as American taxpayers had to foot the bill for the toxic clean-up.

In the 1980s, President Ronald Reagan sparked a backlash against many environmental policies. To symbolically show his opposition to environmental issues, he removed the solar panels that his predecessor Jimmy Carter had installed on the White House roof. Environmental concerns were not foremost on people's minds in the 1980s; instead attention turned to making money and consuming material goods. The counterculture hippies of the 1960s and early 1970s turned into the Yuppies of the 1980s, who were intent on making a good living and spending it for their own pleasure.

Yet, the environmental movement was not silent. Well known environmental groups, such as the Sierra Club, Audubon Society, and Wilderness Society, continued an agenda to awaken public awareness about environmental issues, battling for the environment in courts and fighting the industrial lobbies in Congress. These well-established organizations with sizable budgets and capable staff performed a much needed function in the 1980s, when the environment was not everyone's main concern.

The LGBT Social Movement

Before the 1960s, the public had no common, non-derogatory words for non-heterosexuality. The closest such term, third gender, went back to the 1860s but never gained wide use in the U.S.

Stonewall Inn, 1969

Homosexual, the first widely used term, originally carried negative meaning and was generally replaced by homophile in the 1950s and 1960s, and then gay in the 1970s. As lesbians gained greater public awareness, the phrase "gay and lesbian" became more common. In the late 1970s and the early 1980s, some gays and lesbians became less tolerant of bisexual or transgender people. From about 1988, the initialism **LGBT** saw infrequent use in the U.S., not until the 1990s did those within the movement speak of gay, lesbian, bisexual and transgender people with equal respect.

Homosexual rights groups existed in the West prior to World War II, but following the war, new groups started to form or others revived in Britain, France, Germany, the Netherlands, the Scandinavian countries and U.S. Gays in the 1950s and 1960s faced a hostile legal system and widespread discrimination. These groups usually preferred the term homophile to homosexual, emphasizing love over sex. The movement began in the late 1950s and 1960s in the U.S. and other Western countries. These groups aimed to show that gay people could be assimilated into society, favoring non-confrontational policies and lobbying to influence politics. Any demonstrations they held were orderly and polite.

The last years of the 1960s ushered in many contentious, active social movements, such as the

Black Power movement, Women's Liberation, and the anti-Vietnam war movements, which inspired some LGBT activists to become more radical. The Gay Liberation movement emerged, partially in response to the Stonewall riots in 1969.

Very few establishments welcomed openly gay people in the 1950s and 1960s, with the exception of the Stonewall Inn located in New York City's Greenwich Village neighborhood. Owned by the Mafia, the bar catered to an assortment of patrons and was popular among the poorest and most marginalized gay people. Police raids on gay bars were routine in the 1960s, but during a raid at the **Stonewall Inn** in the early morning hours of June 28, 1969, officers quickly lost control of the situation when patrons resisted arrest. Tensions between the police and gay community of Greenwich Village flared up into a series of spontaneous, violent demonstrations the next evening and again several nights later. Within weeks, residents organized into groups with the goal of establishing places for gays and lesbians to be open about their sexual orientation without fear of harassment or arrest.

Inspired by the events at Stonewall Inn, organizers founded gay rights organizations across the U.S. and the world within a few years. In several other large cities on June 28, 1970, the first Gay Pride marches took place remembering the Stonewall anniversary. Today, organizers hold annual world-wide Gay Pride events at the end of June to mark the event. The Stonewall riots are considered to be the single most important event leading to the gay liberation movement and the modern fight for LGBT human rights in the U.S. A new era of the gay rights movement began in the 1980s with the emergence of AIDS (acquired immune deficiency syndrome). This era saw a resurgence of militancy with direct action groups like AIDS Coalition to Unleash Power (ACT UP), formed in 1987. There was an association between AIDS and homosexuality, resulting in higher levels of prejudice.

Questions to Consider
1. Imagine you are in the LGBT social movement. What tactics would you use to gain attention and create change for your cause?

Global Social Movements: 1990s Onward

Social movements continue to be a powerful influence on promoting, maintaining and expanding human rights at the local, regional, national and global levels. In the modern era, most social movements were local and national in scope. However, social movements today include those with a local and national scope, but many have expanded to a global reach. Many issues today have a global impact, such as climate change and other environmental issues, and just a local, regional or national movement cannot address these issues alone. From the printed pamphlets circulating in the 18th century to coffeehouse meetings and newspapers in the 19th and 20th centuries, to the Internet in the 21st century, these communication tools have become important factors in the growth of social movements. Global citizens' movements are emerging, where citizens around the world are committed to create a new type of society in which the notion of human rights is expanded to more people.

Although we see more global social government, many social movements remain at a grassroots, local level. They are based on local or regional issues and objectives, such as protecting a specific natural area, organizing to prevent building a Walmart in a neighborhood, protesting the demolition of a historic building, or organizing a soup kitchen or food pantry to feed the poor and hungry. But today's social movements have begun to focus on a broader range of human rights than in previous eras: the right to health care, clean water, housing, peace, democracy, and education; protection against starvation and poverty; recognition of indigenous rights; child protection; the right to enjoy healthy food and protection against industrial agriculture; the right to form unions and labor rights; the elimination of torture and capital punishment; pro and anti-abortion rights; the right to carry a gun and the right to control guns; and the list continues. Obviously, we won't be able to cover all these issues; therefore, I have selected several that I think are the most significant and far-reaching and that you will find interesting.

GLOBAL JUSTICE MOVEMENTS

Some activists at the end of the 1990s have joined a network of **global justice movements**, a loose collection of individuals and groups with the common theme of disapproval of the way that the world political-economy is functioning. This "movement of movements" encompasses various actions, such as anti-globalization, alter-globalization, and anti-corporate globalization. By and large, activists support a variety of causes: promote fair trade rules, advocate for greater social equality, back more equal economic distribution, criticize global institutions, such as the World Trade Organization, halt environmental degradation, and expand human rights to marginalized people. The mainstream media often calls the global justice movement the anti-globalization movement, but supporters say they are not anti-globalization. They claim that they support the globalization of communication and people but are against the global expansion of corporate power and neoliberalism. Alter-globalization is a social movement whose proponents support global cooperation and interaction but oppose what they describe as the negative effects of economic globalization, instead working for environmental and climate protection, economic justice, labor protection, protection of indigenous cultures, peace and civil liberties. They see themselves as an alternative to neoliberal globalization.

Many global justice activists are critical of the type of capitalism—neoliberalism—that the U.S. and some other Western countries promote. Often called corporate capitalism, laissez-faire capitalism, casino capitalism, free-trade or free-market capitalism, among other terms, I will use the term neoliberalism because it is used more frequently among academics and countries outside the U.S. Neoliberal capitalism is displacing managed capitalism (from 1930s to 1970s), which means the government has a hand in planning and running the economy. **Neoliberalism** seeks to privatize (owned by private companies) services that the government provides, such as prisons, schools, health care, social security, and the military. It supports the removal of regulations on corporate power and reduces government influence in businesses and personal lives. It pursues policies that help the wealthy, such as reduced taxes, so that they will have capital with which to create jobs; thus, neoliberal policies shift taxes to the lower and middle classes. They tap down wages for the working and middle classes in order to divert more of the profits to the elites. They also push "free" trade policies that remove tariffs from imported and exported goods and services. These policies took off in the 1980s and are continuing today.

Global justice protesters target "free trade" agreements as a major reason for the economic gap between rich and poor countries, and they pinpoint how this gap affects human rights. An example is how free trade agreements affect small farmers in both rich and poor countries. One free trade agreement passed in 1994 exemplifies this problem, the North American Free Trade Association (NAFTA), an agreement between Mexico, U.S. and Canada. With NAFTA, agricultural products are sold across national boundaries without tariffs (taxes) added to the product. In reality, many farmers, unable to make a living with the new rules, lost out, and many had to sell their land and farms. Thousands of farmers left their villages (often with their families) to go to the cities to find work to support their family. Many decided to immigrate to the U.S. to get jobs and then send money back to their families. Immigration from Mexico to the U.S. increased significantly since the passage of NAFTA. Activists point to NAFTA as a problem with the way the world economy works—it is unsustainable, increases poverty, concentrates wealth in the hands of the rich, and harms the environment.

Many activists agree that the present-day economic system is not a good one, but there is a wide variety of ideas about alternatives. Some believe they should overthrow the whole capitalist economic system with little thought about a system to replace it. Some believe that through higher taxes on the wealthy, more money should circulate to the poor. Others think that a more local economy is the answer. Others think that our government should regulate the economy more, such as breaking up the large financial banks that contributed to the economic crisis in 2008. Or the government should provide health care to all through a single payer system. Over the past years, activists are directing more attention to building grassroots alternatives to neoliberal globalization.

Thousands of organizations support global justice principles but are too numerous to list. However, a few of the important organizational pillars of the global justice movement include Via Campesina, the family farmers' international; Peoples' Global Action, a loose collection of youth groups; Jubilee 2000, a Christian-based movement working to relieve international debt; Friends of the Earth, an environmental group; and some think-tanks like Focus on the Global South and Third World Network, as well as some large transnational trade union organizations. The movement's largest and most visible campaigns are direct action and civil disobedience.

Questions to Consider
1. If you were (or are) in the global justice movement, what do you think should be the focus of your efforts? If you don't agree with the movement, what would you do to counter it?

Rights of Corporations

Many global justice activists say the global economy has taken a dangerous turn since the early 1980s, with large, unregulated multi-national corporations and giant financial institutions dominating the global economy and benefiting a small elite. An important question is: "Should corporations have rights afforded to humans, and if so which ones?" This is a sticky question that this brief section on corporate rights hopes to illuminate. Actually, the U.S. Supreme Court has already recognized that corporations, as associations of people, may exercise many of the rights of natural persons and has recognized that corporations are protected under the equal protection clause of the 14th Amendment as decided by the **Santa Clara County v. Southern Pacific Railroad** case in 1886. First some background information.

After the end of the Civil War in 1865, the wealthy railroad barons amassed great political power. To further their power, these barons schemed to get the courts to give corporations the rights held by individuals. Citing the 14th amendment, they repeatedly attempted to get the court to declare that they were persons. They finally got their chance in the famous 1886 Supreme Court case: *Santa Clara County v. Southern Pacific Railroad*. Even though the Supreme Court strongly objected to the railroad's corporate claim to human rights, the court's reporter, who was in cahoots with the railroad barons, secretly inserted into the Court Reporter's headnotes in the case the rule that railroad corporations were persons in the same category as humans. It ruled that, under the Constitution, a private corporation was a "natural person," entitled to all the rights and privileges of a human being. This single, tricky legal stroke changed the nature of corporations. Thereafter, based on the court reporter's headnotes and ignoring the actual court ruling, later courts have expanded the idea of corporate human rights.[32]

Activists cite many examples of how global corporations are violating people's human rights and harming the planet. Many believe that giant multi-national corporations undermine local and national economies. Walmart serves as an example to explain this concept. Walmart reigns as one of the largest corporations in the world, and it is everywhere. When Walmart comes into a community, many small, local businesses close because they cannot compete with Walmart's low prices. Because the prices are low, in the long run the store hurts the local community by driving out small businesses that employ local people at higher wages than Walmart. The money from local businesses—sales, profits, wages, and taxes—mostly stays and circulates in the local community, which creates a multiplier effect that increases the financial well-being of the whole community. In contrast, Walmart's profits go to its shareholders who live around the world, and to one of the wealthiest families in the world—the Walton's. Also, Chinese workers make most of Walmart's products, many of which were once made in the U.S., such as Rubbermaid. Companies have outsourced manufacturing to factories in China to take advantage of its cheap labor and lax environmental controls. The result is that well-paying manufacturing jobs where workers actually produced something have disappeared, leaving towns and workers that relied on these industries unemployed and often in a desperate situation.

Another problem that global justice activists cite is that corporations make deals with elites in poor countries to extract their natural resources at a favorable price and leave the poor to suffer the consequences, such as in Nigeria, Bolivia, and the Congo. Activists say that extractive corporations, such as oil companies, often cause permanent damage to a country's biodiversity and create terrible pollution. Those left to clean up the mess or suffer disease from toxic chemicals are the poor.

Many activists use different strategies to counter growing corporate power. The following is an example of activists in London using litigation against McDonalds, a multi-national corporation. McDonald's filed a lawsuit against environmental activists Helen Steel, a former postman, and David Morris, a gardener, over a pamphlet they wrote criticizing the company. Known as the McLibel Trial, it ran for two and a half years and became the longest trial in English history. A single judge, Justice Bell, heard the whole trial and delivered his verdict in June 1997. The judge ruled that McDonald's exploits and misleads children with their advertising, is responsible for cruelty to animals, is against unions and pays its workers low wages. But the judge said Steel and Morris failed to prove all their points and he ruled that they had libeled McDonald's and should pay 60,000 pounds in damages. They refused. Afraid of more bad publicity, McDonald's did not pursue the case. In March 1999, the Court of Appeal made further rulings that said it was fair comment to specify that McDonald's employees "do badly in terms of pay and conditions," and true that "if one eats enough McDonald's food, one's diet may well become high in fat, with the very real risk of heart disease." As a result of the court case, the anti-McDonald's campaign mushroomed, press coverage increased, a website was launched and a feature length documentary was broadcast.[33] The case showed that ordinary people can change the world.

Anti-Consumerism Movement

Anti-consumerism, a social movement that rejects certain kinds of consumerism, condemns modern corporations. You may think it is a stretch to say that this social movement affects human rights, but consumerism indirectly affects human rights and we need to be aware of its dire effects.

We all need to consume certain goods and products in order to live: food, shelter, clothing, and health care. In fact, most Americans pride themselves in having a "standard of living" that is materially comfortable. For example, we like to have running water, hot showers, a house that is comfortable and warm in the winter and cool in the summer, and more clothing than what we have on our backs. You might ask, Why are some people against this? Let's look at this issue in a little more depth.

People in the U.S. today consume goods and products way beyond their basic needs. **Consumerism** is consumption of particular material goods that support a specific life-style that society in general considers important. This life-style includes new model cars, large homes, home appliances, abundant food and clothing, jewelry, vacations, electronic products such as TVs, computers, smart phones, and thousands of other material goods. A **materialist** is a person for whom collecting material goods is an important priority, and more specifically, refers to a person who primarily pursues wealth and luxury. In American society materialism is promoted as an important goal that we all should pursue. Consumerism represents 70 percent of the total U.S. economy. The foundation of our whole economy and society revolves around consumerism. However, there are problems with consumerism; the consumption of consumer goods is not sustainable. The oil that drives our cars, or the paper used in our books, or the coal needed to drive our electric power plants all cause pollution and climate change, and their consumption cannot continue indefinitely. We are extracting the earth's resources to make consumer products faster than the earth can replenish them. This is where the anti-consumer social movement steps in.

Anti-consumerism Campaign

People in the anti-consumerism movement say that Americans consume too much. Americans make-up about 5 percent of the world's population but consume 30 percent of the world's resources.[34] The resources supporting our consumer way of life are quickly diminishing; two to three more earths are needed just to support America's consumer desires. And to make matters worse, other people around the world, such as the Chinese and Indians, are adopting consumption patterns like Americans. The earth is finite, yet our consumer desires are infinite. This cannot continue.

Anti-consumerists believe that advertising plays a huge role in influencing what a society decides are acceptable and important values. Advertisers claim that their products are the key to securing happiness and attaining wealth and recognition by others. Anti-consumerist claim that these ads are not harmless, but actually hurt a society because they tell consumers that accumulating more and more possessions will bring them more happiness, health, security, and popularity. Actually, studies show that the opposite happens. We are not happier, and we are certainly not healthier. In fact, impulsive consumption of a product with the illusion that it will satisfy a certain want or desire actually leaves us more depressed and unsatisfied.[35] Of course, this is exactly what advertisers have planned all along, since an unquenched want spurs consumption of more goods in an endless cycle of trying to achieve the pleasure that advertising assures us their product will provide and that we innately yearn for.

Adults are pawns to the advertising industry. Their sense of belonging and identity has shifted from identity with place to brands of consumer products. Identity has become reflective of 'lifestyles' that are closely associated with commercial brands and the products they label and include what we eat, wear, and consume.[36] The brands indicate one's particular income, class, and place. Although it appears that we freely choose these identities for ourselves, actually they show the influence of the commercial culture that surrounds every aspect of our daily lives. Advertisers happily promote this brand identification among consumers because it cuts across national and ethnic boundaries to mold a true globalization of identity. Consumers identify with the Nike swoosh from Chicago to Jakarta to Tokyo.

The anti-consumerism movement is educating Americans and other people around the world to a different way of life and different values. Social activists believe consumerism is connected to war, greed, loneliness, alienation, isolation, crime, environmental degradation, and general social discontent. They point out that the main responsibility of corporations is to answer only to shareholders, giving human rights and other issues almost no consideration. Activists believe that we do have the choice to reject the consumerist society and that different behaviors, choices and habits can support a sustainable community. For example, recycling or buying some products in thrift shops or at garage sales can help conserve resources. Buy locally produced products at farmer's markets, county fairs or locally owned stores can promote sustainability. Activists feel that promoting an attitude of stewardship for the next generation to emulate is a positive contribution to our mental and spiritual well-being.

Environmental Movement

In the third era, new citizen-based, grassroots environmental movements have emerged alongside the older, larger, and better-known organizations, such as the Sierra Club. The grassroots organizations believe in citizen participation in environmental decision-making. Many see the mainstream organizations as too accommodating to business, industry, and government. For example, the antitoxic campaign is a self-described "movement of housewives" that is led by politically inexperienced women. These activists are motivated by a desire to protect their families and communities from toxic contamination arising from waste dumps, incinerators, ground water contamination, and air pollution.[37]

Another hot topic today is climate change. Hundreds of organizations have formed to help solve the threat of climate change, such as the **Intergovernmental Panel on Climate Change** (IPCC). The very active 350.org organizes climate-focused campaigns, projects and actions led from the bottom-up by people in 188 countries, all connected through email. They have local groups throughout the world, and if there is none in your community, you are invited to start one. The winner of the 2007 Nobel Peace Prize, the IPCC is the leading body for the assessment of climate change established by the UN Environment Program (UNEP) and the World Meteorological Organization (WMO) to provide the world with the current state of climate change and its potential environmental and socio-economic consequences.

Rights of Indigenous Peoples

The term indigenous peoples can be used to describe any ethnic group of people who inhabit a geographic region with which they have the earliest known historical connection, alongside more recent immigrants who have populated the region and may be greater in number.[38] Other terms for indigenous peoples are used: native people, first people, First Nations, Indians (in the Americas), and aboriginals (Australia). They nurture 80 percent of the world's cultural and biological diversity and occupy 20 percent of the world's land surface. Indigenous peoples form a wide spectrum of humanity. They live in nearly all the countries on all the continents of the world and range from traditional hunter-gatherers and subsistence farmers to educated professionals. They form the majority of the population in some countries, such as Bolivia, while in others they constitute a small minority. Indigenous peoples are concerned with preserving land, protecting their language and promoting their culture. Some strive to preserve traditional ways of life, while others seek greater participation in modern society.[39] Regardless of their way of life, they all share a history of injustice. Indigenous peoples have been killed, tortured, enslaved, and in some cases victims of genocide. Those who have conquered and colonized them have treated them as inferior humans and tried to steal their dignity and identity. Conquerors have denied them the right to participate in their own governance and the fundamental right of self-determination.[40]

The United Nations General Assembly passed the **Declaration on the Rights of Indigenous Peoples** in 2007. Taking 22 years to finally come to a vote, the Declaration was favored by 142 countries, with four voting against, and 11 abstaining. The four member states that voted against the Declaration were Australia, Canada, New Zealand and the U.S., each of which have significant indigenous populations. Bolivia was the first country to approve the Declaration. Eva Morales, the first indigenous head of state in Bolivia since Spanish conquest, stated, "We are the first country to turn this declaration into a law and that is important." The UN describes the Declaration as setting "an important standard for the treatment of indigenous peoples that will undoubtedly be a significant tool towards eliminating human rights violations against the planet's 370 million indigenous people and assisting them in combating discrimination and marginalization." The Declaration sets out individual and collective rights of indigenous peoples, such as their rights to culture, identity, language, employment, health, and education. It prohibits discrimination and "promotes their full and effective participation in all matters that concern them and their right to remain distinct and to pursue their own visions of economic and social development."[41]

Indigenous peoples, nomadic Taureg peoples in southern Algeria

The impact of economic globalization on indigenous peoples is very powerful, as they often occupy the last "undeveloped" places on earth, where resources and genetic diversity are still abundant. Global corporations and state-run enterprises seek these natural resources for their industries. Many governments which rule native peoples have made trade and investment agreements with global corporations and state-enterprises, who then "open up" previously isolated territory occupied by native people for the removal of valuable natural resources. Also, many national governments have borrowed money from large financial banks, such as the World Bank, and are legally bound to sell these natural resources to whomever wants to buy them in order to pay back the loans. Most native communities are not consulted about these decisions but often it is their traditional lands that are being exploited. These circumstances have forced them to defend their homelands from the construction of big dams, mines, pipelines, roads, energy developments, or military invasions that all threaten their native lands and culture.

Another issue that is threatening indigenous peoples' way of life is that their land covers over 80 percent of the planet's biodiversity. This biodiversity is a treasure chest of planets that can potentially be used in the development of new medicines to cure diseases. Drug companies around the world are eager to get these rare plants that can then be made commercially available. The World Trade Organization (WTO) has passed rules on the patenting of genetic resources that have made it possible for large corporations to take these genetic materials from plants on native peoples land and then develop patented products. The drug companies make potentially enormous profits, while indigenous peoples are left out.

Indigenous peoples are fighting for their land, culture, livelihood, and survival. Here are a few examples of indigenous social movements from every continent except Antarctica: The Bayaka in Central African Republic, whose community is being destroyed by logging; the Dinka and Nuer in Sudan, whose lands are being taken over for oil reserves; the Wichí in Argentina, who are facing a major highway construction through their territory; gold mining on Miskito lands in Nicaragua; eco-tourism on Kuna land in Panama; mining on Australian aboriginal lands; the Jharkhand tribal community dislocation due to a mega-dam project in India; industrial plantations destroying tropical forests on which the Dayak people in Indonesia depend; export coffee plantations evicting Montangards from their homeland in Vietnam; uranium mining, and the resulting toxic waste contaminating the ecosystem on which the Dene and Cree in Canada rely; overfishing jeopardizing survival of Chukchi and Eskimo in Russia; and mining on North American Indian lands, including the Western Shoshone, Quechan Nation, Mohawk, and Zuni peoples.[42]

Today there are many activists who are working to preserve indigenous ways of life. Winona LaDuke, Green Party vice-presidential candidate in 1996 and 2000, traces her native roots to the Ojibwe from Minnesota. She now heads the White Earth Land Recovery Project in Minnesota and the Indigenous Women's Network. There are a number of active non-governmental organizations (NGOs) in the indigenous movement: Amazon Watch, Indigenous Environmental Network, International Indian Treaty Council, Project Underground, Oilwatch, Nicaragua Network, Survival International, Cultural Survival, World Rainforest Movement, MiningWatch in Canada, and the Tebtebba Foundation in the Philippines.[43]

Today, indigenous peoples face the challenges of extinction or survival and renewal. Globalization is not merely a question of marginalization for indigenous peoples; it is a multi-pronged attack on their existence, livelihoods and culture. For example, one short-lived movement in my home community of Albuquerque, New Mexico attempted to stop the construction of a major highway west of the city that would disrupt native petroglyph paintings done hundreds of years ago. Although the highway was built and the movement dissolved, it still was successful in drawing attention to the petroglyph paintings, arranging for their preservation, and recognizing the rights of native people. If indigenous communities are wiped out, they will take with them vast indigenous knowledge, rich cultural traditions, hope of preserving the natural world, and a simpler, more holistic way of life for future generations.

THE LGBT MOVEMENT

Since the 1990s, LBGT movements, a term that did not exist before 1990, have been achieving human rights for lesbian, gay, bisexual, transgender and transsexual people around the world. The LGBT movement advocates for the equalized acceptance of LGBT people in society. Although there is no overarching central organization that represents the interests of all LGBT people, many different LGBT rights organizations are active worldwide and promote political activism and cultural activity, including lobbying, street marches, social groups, media, art, and research. The 1990s saw a rapid push of the transgender movement. Today, same-sex marriage is one of the issues that has galvanized a great deal of momentum. The Netherlands was the first country to allow same-sex marriage in 2001, and the movement has spread worldwide. In the U.S., a growing number of states are recognizing same-sex marriage as legal. My home state of New Mexico is one of the many states that allow same-sex marriage.

Human Rights for the LGBT community expanded when the 1993 law forbidding homosexual people from serving openly in the United States military—"Don't ask, don't tell"—was repealed in 2010. This meant that gays and lesbians could now serve openly in the military without fear of discharge because of their sexual orientation. Also, in 2012, the U.S. Department of Housing and Urban Development's Office of Fair Housing and Equal Opportunity issued a regulation to prohibit discrimination in federally-assisted housing programs. The new regulations ensure that housing programs are open to all eligible persons, regardless of sexual orientation or gender identity.

A variety of individuals and organizations oppose the LGBT movements. They claim to have a personal, moral, political, or religious objection to LGBT people. Some social conservatives believe that sexual relationships should be between people of the opposite sex, and same-sex couples undermine the traditional family. Some people worry that gay rights may conflict with individuals' freedom of speech, religious freedoms in the workplace, and the ability to run churches, charitable organizations and other religious organizations that hold opposing social and cultural views to the LGBT community. Religious organizations are concerned that they may be required to accept and perform same-sex marriages or risk losing their tax-exempt status.

The Human Rights Campaign is the largest LGBT civil rights advocacy group and political lobbying organization in the U.S. According to the HRC, it has more than 1.5 million members and supporters. It is an umbrella group, one arm of which focuses on lobbying Congress and state and local officials for support of pro-LGBT bills, while the other arm mobilizes grassroots action amongst its members. The HRC also supports candidates promoting LGBT rights.

The United Nations Human Rights Council is an inter-governmental body whose 47 member states are responsible for promoting and protecting human rights around the world. In 2011, UNHRC passed its first resolution recognizing LGBT rights. A follow-up report documented violations of the human rights of LGBT people, including hate crimes, criminalization of homosexuality, and discrimination. The report urged all countries which had not yet done so to enact laws protecting basic LGBT rights.

HUMAN RIGHTS FOR PERSONS WITH DISABILITIES

The disability rights movement is relatively recent. **Disability** is the result of an impairment that may be physical, mental, sensory, emotional, developmental, or some combination of these. A disability may be present from birth or happen during a person's lifetime. The disability rights movement works to guarantee equal opportunities and equal rights for people with disabilities.

The goals of the movement are accessibility and safety in transportation and the physical environment, equal opportunities in independent living, employment, education, and housing, and freedom from abuse, neglect, and violations of patients' rights. Civil rights legislation is sought to secure these opportunities and rights.

The rights of individuals with disabilities are grounded in a human rights framework based on the United Nations Charter and other instruments. Persons with disabilities are entitled to exercise their civil, political, social, economic and cultural rights on an equal basis with others under all the international treaties. In order that the rights of persons with disabilities may be further realized, international law has encouraged all states to incorporate human rights standards into their national legislation. Although the means chosen to promote full realization of economic, social and cultural rights of persons with disabilities may differ among countries, there is no country exempt from the need for improved policies and laws for individuals with disabilities.[44]

International symbol of access

CHILDREN'S RIGHTS

There are many social movements today aimed at protecting the human rights of children. They cover a wide range of issues that adversely affect children: protecting against child marriage, outlawing child soldiers, preventing trafficking children, making child labor illegal, protecting against excessive advertising directed at children, addressing child poverty and homelessness, making education compulsory, plus many others. We will cover a few of these topics in this section.

The UN General Assembly passed the Convention on the Rights of the Child in 1989. The Convention has been ratified by 192 countries; all but two member countries have signed the Convention but have not yet ratified it as of this writing: the U.S. and Somalia. The Convention's preamble states that "the child, by reason of his physical and mental immaturity, needs special safeguards and care, including appropriate legal protection, before as well as after birth." The Convention defines a child as any human under the age of 18, unless a country's law recognizes an earlier age of majority.[45] Several international organizations advocate for children's human rights: Save the Children, Free the Children, and the Children's Defense Fund. The Child Rights Information Network, or CRIN, formed in 1983, is a group of 1,600 non-governmental organizations from around the world which work to ensure that the Convention is enforced.

One of the most egregious children's issues is child marriage. The practice continues to be disturbingly common, with more than 60 million women age 20-24 married before they turn 18. In some countries more than half of all girls are married before the age of 18: these include Niger and Mali, where the incidence of child marriage is a staggering 75 percent, Chad with 72 percent, Bangladesh with 64 percent, Guinea with 63 percent, Central African Republic with 61 percent, Mozambique with 56 percent, and Nepal with 51percent.[46] Child marriage does not benefit the young girls. They are more at risk for domestic violence, more likely to be uneducated, at a greater risk of contracting HIV/AIDS, and more likely to bear children before they are physically ready. In fact, early marriage is a death sentence for 70,000 young brides who die every year as a result of pregnancy or childbirth difficulties. Studies show that girls who give birth before the age of 15 are five times more likely to die in childbirth than women in their twenties. Also, the babies of child mothers are at a greater risk of dying.[47]

In the very poor country of Mali in Africa, where nearly 75 percent of women are married before the age of 18, child marriage has reached a crisis proportion. With so many young girls forced into early marriage and bearing children before they are physically mature, the corresponding rates of mother and child death is perilously high. While there has been a slight decrease in child marriage rates since 1987, when nearly 80 percent of Malian women married as children, the numbers are not dropping fast enough.

Child rights activists say child marriage is a neglected issue. To correct this problem, UNICEF in 2008 joined together with a local NGO, government agency, and media representatives to organize the first public awareness campaign in Mali to inform people about the dangers of early marriage. One community representative at the program said, "We were ignorant. We married girls at 9, 10, 11 or 12 years old. Now, we've seen the reality. We will no longer practice this."[48]

A 15-year-old girl told an Amnesty International representative that the Lord's Resistance Army (LRA), an armed opposition movement fighting the Ugandan government in central Africa, forcibly abducted her at night from her home. "I would like you to give a message. Please do your best to tell the world what is happening to us, the children, so that other children don't have to pass through this violence." The army forced her to kill a boy who tried to escape. She saw another boy being hacked to death for alarming authorities when a friend ran away. The army beat her when she dropped a water container and ran for cover under gunfire. She received 35 days of military training, and they sent her out to fight the government army.[49]

Over the last 10 years, hundreds of thousands of children have fought and died in conflicts around the world. They are frequently killed or injured in combat or when forced to lay mines or explosives. They receive little food and live under harsh conditions. Their captors

Poster against child and forced marriage

almost always treat them brutally, and they are subjected to beatings and humiliating treatment. Girl soldiers are particularly at risk of rape, sexual harassment and abuse, as well as being forced into combat. The problem is most critical in Africa, where children as young as nine have been involved in armed conflicts. Children are also used as soldiers in various Asian countries and in parts of Latin America, Europe and the Middle East. Most child soldiers are between 14 and 18 years old; while many enlist "voluntarily," it is actually a means of survival in war-torn regions or after seeing family members tortured or killed. Others join because of poverty and lack of work or educational opportunities. Many girls have reported enlisting to escape domestic servitude, violence and sexual abuse. Forcibly kidnapping children for military combat continues to occur in some countries. Children as young as nine have been abducted and forced into combat.

Child labor is still common in some parts of the world. According to UN Children's Fund

(UNICEF), there are an estimated 158 million children, aged 5 to 14, in child labor worldwide, excluding child domestic labor. Most of the world's 250 million working children are 11 to 14 years old, but as many as 60 million are between the ages of 5 and 11. The incidence of child labor is highest in Africa, where an estimated 41 percent of children 5 to 14 work, compared with Asia where 21 percent work, and Latin America where 17 percent work.[50] Only about 1 percent of children 5 to 14 work in the U.S., Canada, Europe, and other wealthier countries. Although many people assume that child labor means sweatshop labor, most labor is performed in the informal sector, such as agricultural work, helping in family businesses, having one's own business, such as selling items on the street, or doing odd jobs. Other children are forced to do tedious and repetitive jobs, such as assembling boxes, polishing shoes, stocking a store's products, or cleaning. They may work in factories, mining, quarrying, or prostitution. At least 1 million children a year are forced or enticed into prostitution, part of a huge network of exploitation that stretches from South Asia, to Russia, to Latin America. All the work is done for minimal pay.[51]

There have been many well-publicized investigations into child labor abuses. One of the most famous of these cases was in 1996 when Nike, an American shoe maker, was charged with employing Indonesian children under 16 years old to produce their athletic sneakers. A report confirmed that the children worked in sweatshops like "slaves." Factories were hiring 11 and 12 year-old girls to make sneakers for 22 cents an hour. It costs $5 to make high-end athletic shoes in Indonesia, which cost more than $125 in the U.S.[52] The bad publicity caused Nike to make changes in their overseas sweatshop operations.

Questions to Consider
1. What social movement do you think is the most compelling or urgent? Which one might you be drawn to participate in?

This chapter gives a broad sampling of social movements in the U.S. and worldwide. It is inspiring to read about the social movements that through their collective grassroots efforts have had a positive impact in expanding human rights for people who have been marginalized from mainstream society.

Next is an investigation of human rights violations: the crime of aggression, war crimes, crimes against humanity, and genocide.

CHAPTER THREE

Human Rights Violations

""First they came for the Communists, but I was not a Communist – so I said nothing. Then they came for the Social Democrats, but I was not a Social Democrats – so I did nothing. Then came the trade unionists, but I was not a trade unionists. And then they came for the Jews, but I was not a Jew – so I did little. Then when they came for me, there was no one left who could stand up for me."

— Martin Niemoeller. [1]

An Introduction to Human Rights Violations

Martin Nielmoeller wrote the powerful words on the preceding page about the Holocaust that took place during World War II. His point was that we all must be aware of atrocities that perpetrators direct against our fellow citizens. This means to be aware of violations that occur in our own backyards and on a global stage. Also, we must work to prevent violations from happening or escalating to horrific proportions. The first step is awareness. The point of this chapter is to focus on actual human rights violations and atrocities that have been committed in the past and are taking place today to heighten our awareness of the topic. If we are more aware, we are more likely to take a stand in preventing human rights abuses.

"No man is an island," wrote the English poet John Donne in the 17th century. We are all connected to a larger network of family, community, tribe, nation, and world. As members of this larger network, we are part of an invisible web of hundreds, if not thousands, of social rules. People today inherited behaviors from those who lived in small, homogenous groups with other similar individuals in hunting and gathering bands. Through our long human history, we evolved behaviors that signaled a protective distrust of others who were not like us. There was an inborn sense of in-group versus out-group. These social rules were necessary and ensured human survival; it was important to know who to trust, who to fear, and difference signaled suspicion. Sometimes distrust of others reached violent confrontation, and at other times, the veil of distrust was lifted and out-groups would get along.

Today is different. We no longer live in small homogenous bands of people; we live in a world community that exhibits a wide range of human differences: skin color, culture, history, worldviews, religions, political beliefs, gender, age, sexual orientation, and economic status. Whether our distrust and even hostility of others is innate or not, it does not serve us well in today's diverse world. Just a few years ago we changed from a majority of the world's people living in rural areas to a majority of the world's people living in cities with people of different racial, ethnic, and national identities. Living peacefully in these dense urban settings is necessary. It is vital that we adapt and understand global differences.

Distrust of others can have a dark side. Recognition of differences is natural and usually harmless, but sometimes it can turn destructive. Instead of just observing differences, a group may start to label the out-group as dirty, ignorant, dishonest, lazy, shiftless, sneaky, evil, and so on. When this occurs, groups remove or isolate those who are different. And in some cases, societies may commit atrocities against them or even decide to get rid of them altogether.[2] Perpetrators may call certain groups of people alien, subhuman, "cockroaches," or other demeaning terms and work to eliminate the enemy.

This chapter describes a range of human rights violations that have taken place in the world. Although these violations have occurred throughout human history, they have magnified in horror in the 20th century. After the end of the ghastly World War II, many people decided that these repulsive acts of inhumanity could not continue and took steps to stop them. One of these steps is the formation of the International Criminal Court.

The Rome Statute of the International Criminal Court

The Rome Statute of the International Criminal Court is the treaty that established the **International Criminal Court (ICC)**. The United Nations adopted the statute in Rome on July 17, 1998, by a vote of 120 to 7, with 21 countries not voting. The seven countries that voted against the treaty were Iraq, Israel, Libya, the People's Republic of China, Qatar, the United States, and Yemen. The court became official on July 1, 2002 and can only put on trial crimes committed on or after that date. The Court has 18 judges with the official seat in The Hague, Netherlands, but its trials may take place anywhere.

International Criminal Court logo

At the heart of the effort to establish the first international criminal court in history is the question of what crimes will be covered and how will they be defined. Once human rights norms are established internationally, the question arises about what should be done by way of punishment and accountability for political, military, and ethnic leaders who have organized and carried out severe human rights violations. One part of the statue emphasizes that the Court has authority over only "the most serious crimes of concern to the international community." The second part emphasizes that the Court is intended to balance, not replace, an individual nation's criminal justice system. For example, the Court would exercise its authority only in cases where nations do not exercise their national authority, or because they are unable or unwilling to do so. Most countries do not want the ICC to take over their authority.[3]

The ICC prosecutes individuals for the most serious crimes to our international community. Although a majority of nations have signed the treaty, a number of states, including China and the U.S. have not joined as of this writing.[4] In order for prosecutions to take place, the crimes must be clearly defined, a very difficult job. In this chapter all four categories of the crimes noted in the Rome Statute are outlined: the crime of aggression, war crimes, crimes against humanity, and genocide.

THE CRIME OF AGGRESSION

It is hard to find an acceptable definition of the **crime of aggression**. In 1974, the UN General Assembly said it was the act of one nation against another. Another UN Commission said that it should also hold individuals responsible for acts of aggression. They said that individuals in leadership positions, who planned, prepared, or waged aggression should be held responsible for their actions.[5] The definition of aggression should apply to a wide range of situations and clear enough for individuals to know what acts are prohibited. Those who want to include the crime of aggression under the Court's authority want to make sure that those individuals who commit such acts do not go unpunished. They hope that holding individuals responsible for the crime of aggression will be a clear warning to other would-be aggressors. They want to prevent aggression from reaching the more serious categories of war crimes, crimes against humanity, or

Acts of Aggression

- a State sending soldiers to carry out grave acts of armed force against another State
- the blockade of ports or coasts of a State
- bombardment by armed forces of a State against the territory of another State
- invasion or attachment by the armed forces of a State or the territory of another State
- military occupation, or annexation of territory by the use of force

genocide. The above (preceding page) is a list of what are considered to be acts of aggression.

THE 2003 INVASION OF IRAQ

Some people claim that the **2003 invasion of Iraq** is an example of the crime of aggression and another side just as passionately says it was not. The U.S. led the invasion, the UK played a secondary role, and several other nations lent their support. The invasion marked the beginning of the Iraq War which helped destabilize the Middle East. According to U.S. President George W. Bush, the invasion was "to disarm Iraq of weapons of mass destruction (WMD), to end Saddam Hussein's support for terrorism, and to free the Iraqi people."[6] Both houses of Congress overwhelmingly passed a resolution to authorize the use of military force against Iraq. However, the public was bitterly divided over the invasion.

U.S. army photo in front of the "Hands of Victory" monument at Baghdad's Ceremony Square in November 2003

Some long-time U.S. allies, including France, Germany, and Canada, strongly opposed the invasion. Their leaders argued that there was no evidence of weapons for mass destruction (WMD) and that invading Iraq was not justified. There were also many worldwide protests, including a rally of 3 million people in Rome, which is listed in the Guinness Book of Records as the largest anti-war rally in history. Estimates show that between January and April, 2003, 36 million people around the world took part in 3,000 protests against the Iraq War.[7] Nevertheless, the U.S. went ahead with the invasion. On May 1, 2003, the U.S. declared an end to major combat operations, ending the invasion and beginning the occupation period. Although destroying WMDs was one of the declared reasons for war, the Central Intelligence Agency (CIA) released a report in 2005 stating that no WMDs had been found in Iraq.[8]

As evidence of U.S. and British claims about Iraqi WMDs and links to terrorism weakened, some supporters of the invasion shifted their reasons for the war to the human rights violations of Iraqi president Saddam Hussein's government. But Human Rights Watch, a leading human rights organization, has argued that human rights concerns were never a central reason for the invasion. They did not believe that humanitarian reasons justified military intervention because "the killing in Iraq at the time was not of the exceptional nature that would justify such intervention."[9] However, many supporters of the invasion claimed that Saddam Hussein directed the killing or disappearance of over 200,000 Iraqis.[10] A debate continues today over the legality of the 2003 invasion of Iraq. The debate centers on the question of whether the invasion was an uncalled-for attack on an independent country that may have broken international law, or if the UN Security Council actually authorized the invasion.

Questions to Consider

1. Do you think the invasion of Iraq in 2003 was a crime of aggression or legally justified?

WAR CRIMES

War crimes are "violations of the laws or customs of war." The International Criminal Court (ICC) tries war crimes that are violations of the laws in international and non-international armed conflicts.

1. Special protections to certain persons: wounded and sick in armed forces, shipwrecked members of armed forces at sea, POWs (prisoners of war), and civilians during wartime. The ICC considers the following acts a serious violation: willful killing or causing great suffering, torture or inhuman treatment, extensive destruction of non-military cities, depriving a prisoner of war a fair trial, and taking or killing of hostages.

2. A selective list of war crimes includes: targeting civilians, targeting buildings devoted to art, science, or monuments; killing combatants who have surrendered; pillaging, rape, sexual slavery, enforced prostitution, enforced pregnancy, enforced sterilization, and other forms of sexual violence; using civilians to protect specific locations from military attack; intentional starvation of civilians; and using children under the age of 15 in armed forces.

War crimes, like all the human rights violations in this chapter, are a much debated topic. One person's opinion that an act is a war crime may not be the same as another person's opinion. Having a clear definition helps but does not always solve the problem. Another debated issue is that winners have received more favorable treatment than others. This is often called "victor's justice," which means that some believe (usually the losers) that the winning nation applies different rules to judge what is right or wrong. An example is when the U.S. and its allies bombed German and Japanese cities populated mainly by civilians during World War II. One target was the German city of Dresden, which was firebombed, killing 25,000 to 100,000 civilians in a fiery inferno.[11] Two other targets were the Japanese cities of Hiroshima and Nagasaki in World War II, where the U.S. dropped two deadly atomic bombs killing over 140,000 people, mostly civilians, with thousands more dying after the bomb's impact due to radiation poisoning. Also from 1961-1971, the U.S. military used an herbicide and defoliant with the code name of Agent Orange against civilian targets in the Vietnam War. According to the post-war Vietnamese government, 4.8 million Vietnamese people were exposed to Agent Orange, resulting in 400,000 deaths and disabilities, while 500,000 children were born with birth defects.[12]

Since the end of World War II (1945), the U.S. has been the most powerful nation in the world and the beacon of human rights support and democracy to millions. But all nations are susceptible to moral letdowns and policy abuses and the U.S. is no exception. Over the years, there have been many accusations of war crimes leveled against the U.S., including the genocide of Native Americans and the atomic bombings of the Japanese cities mentioned above. Unfortunately, there is no defined process in the U.S. for addressing war crimes accusations. Some people say that the U.S. has never committed war crimes, while others say that every act of aggression or war is a war crime. Looking at the reality of war, warfare, colonialism, and imperialism, and empire, the truth is probably somewhere in the middle. Not every event of mass killing is a war crime, but some are. In many cases, blinding nationalism interferes with the discussion. In truth, every society that engages in warfare has at some time committed an atrocity that probably is a war crime. Along with all the nations of the world, the U.S. is no exception.

Questions to Consider

1. Why do you think the U.S. has not joined the ICC?

MY LAI MASSACRE

On March 16, 1968, during the height of the Vietnam War (early 1960s-1973), the village of **My Lai** was the site of the mass murder of 347 to 504 villagers by a United States Army platoon. Almost all of those massacred were civilians, most of them women, children, and the elderly. Some of the victims were sexually abused, beaten, tortured, or maimed, and some of the bodies were found mutilated.[13] Courts charged 26 U.S. soldiers, including 14 officers, for their actions at My Lai and its cover-up. Only Lt. William Calley was convicted in 1971 of premeditated murder of 22 civilians in the massacre. Although the judge sentenced him to life in prison, he served only 3½ years under house arrest. Others were indicted but not convicted, and most of the charges were eventually dropped.

In 1969 the war crime became public and sparked widespread outrage around the world. The massacre also further reduced public support for the Vietnam War on the home front. Three U.S. servicemen who made an effort to halt the massacre and protect the wounded were sharply condemned by U.S. Congressmen. They received hate mail and death threats, and mutilated animals were dropped on their doorsteps. Their heroism was eventually honored 30 years after the event.[14] Investigators at the Defense Department uncovered documents showing that atrocities by U.S. forces during the Vietnam War were more extensive than had been officially recognized; the documents detailed 320 suspected incidents.

Questions to Consider
1. Do you think that the My Lai Massacre was a war crime? Explain your position.

CRIMES AGAINST HUMANITY

Crimes against humanity, as defined by the ICC, "are particularly odious offences in that they constitute a serious attack on human dignity or grave humiliation or a degradation of one or more human beings. They are not isolated or sporadic events, but are part either of a government policy or of a wide practice of atrocities tolerated or condoned by a government or a de facto [actual] authority."[15]

Isolated inhumane acts may be serious violations of human rights, or depending on the circumstances, war crimes, but may fall short of falling into the category of crimes against humanity. Perhaps the best way to understand crimes against humanity is to look at two case studies. The first one is the U.S. Indian Removal Act of 1830, also known as the Trial of Tears and the second is that of Charles Taylor, the former president of Liberia in Africa.

Crimes Against Humanity

- murder
- extermination
- enslavement
- deportation or forcible transfer of a population
- torture
- rape or other sexual abuse, enforced prostitution
- persecution against a group on political, racial, national, ethnic, cultural or religious grounds
- enforced disappearance of persons
- other inhumane acts causing serious injury to body or to mental or physical health
- detention, imprisonment or denial of liberty in violation of international law

THE TRAIL OF TEARS

On May 28, 1830, U.S. President Andrew Jackson authorized the Indian Removal Act that authorized the relocation of Native Americans from their homelands in the southeast to what was known as Indian Territory in present day Oklahoma in the west. The five Native American tribes were referred to as the Five Civilized Tribes—the Cherokee, Chickasaw, Choctaw, Creek, and Seminole. They lived as sovereign nations in the American South until the discovery of gold on Cherokee land in Georgia in 1828. With the enticement of gold along with American settlers clamoring for more land, the president and others found a way to strip all native peoples of their land east of the Mississippi River.

The American army forced native peoples to undertake the westward journey. Over 15,000 died of exposure, starvation, and disease on the journey, known as the **Trail of Tears**. Although the Trail of Tears is most closely associated with the Cherokee specifically, and the Southeast tribes more generally, approximately one-third to one-half of the 100,000 native people removed were from the Northeast.[16]

Elizabeth Brown Stephens (1903), a Cherokee Indian who walked the Trail of Tears in 1838

Ethnic cleansing refers to the maltreatment through imprisonment, removal, or killing of members of an ethnic minority by a local majority to achieve ethnic homogeneity in majority-controlled territory. Although the term ethnic cleansing was used frequently in the early 1990s to describe war events in the former Yugoslavia, it is a fitting term to describe the Trail of Tears in the 1830s in the U.S. as well.

THE CRIMES OF CHARLES TAYLOR

Diamond smuggling, gun-running, weapons trafficking, corruption, and murder—sounds like the subject of an action adventure film. And, indeed, it is. Two high-profile Hollywood films—*Blood Diamonds* (2006) starring Leonardo deCaprio and *Lord of War* (2005) starring Nicolas Cage—plus the award winning documentary *Pray the Devil Back to Hell* (2008) have chronicled human rights atrocities in neighboring west African countries of Sierra Leone and Liberia. Aside from Hollywood glamour, the atrocities in these countries were real. One of the masterminds of the real atrocities affecting both nations was the former president of Liberia, Charles Taylor. The ICC convicted him of war crime and crimes against humanity and in May 2012, Taylor was sentenced to 50 years in prison.

Charles Taylor was born in 1948 in Monrovia, Liberia, a country which former American slaves founded in the mid-19th century and an upper class of Americo-Liberians governed until 1980. As a young man he attended Bentley College in Massachusetts, earning a degree in economics in 1977. He returned to his native country and took a position as a purchaser of equipment for the Liberian government. His first brush with the law came in 1983 when he was fired from his job for embezzling almost $1,000,000 and sending the funds to an American bank account. He fled the country, only to be arrested in 1984 by two US Deputy Marshals in Massachusetts for embezzlement. He was jailed for his crimes.

On September 15, 1985, in a dramatic prison escape, Taylor and four other inmates sawed through a bar covering a window in an unused laundry room. They knotted a sheet to serve as their ladder, dropped 12 feet to the ground, and then climbed a security fence to escape their imprisonment. They met up with accomplices who drove them in a getaway car to Staten Island, New York. Taylor fled the U.S., and shortly thereafter traveled to Libya, a country in North Africa, where he underwent guerrilla training. Eventually he left Libya and used his training to instigate a civil war in Liberia.

In December 1989, Taylor launched a Libyan-funded armed uprising from Côte d'Ivoire (Ivory Coast) into Liberia with the intent of overthrowing the government. Under his command, his forces toppled and tortured to death the Liberian president. During the ensuing civil war, as many as seven factions fought for control of Liberia's valuable natural resources—iron ore, diamonds, timber, and rubber. After the official end of the civil war in 1996, Taylor became Liberia's president the next year. But peace did not come to Liberia after his election, and during his entire reign the civil war continued.

The international community has accused Taylor of numerous crimes since he took office in 1997, including assisting rebel forces in Sierra Leone with weapon sales in exchange for diamonds. He also was involved in acts of atrocities against civilians that have left thousands dead or mutilated, with an unknown number abducted and tortured. His widespread recruitment of children as soldiers in the war in Sierra Leone has been particularly heinous. In 2003, the UN issued a warrant for Taylor's arrest, charging him with war crimes. The UN said Taylor created and backed rebels in Sierra Leone, who committed a range of atrocities including the use of child soldiers.[17] Taylor also harbored members of the terrorist group Al-Qaeda, sought in connection with the 1998 bombings of U.S. embassies in Kenya and Tanzania.[18] In 2003, he announced his resignation and the following day handed over power to the vice-president. He then flew to Nigeria, where the Nigerian government provided housing for him and his associates.

In 2009, Charles Taylor testified at his ICC's war crimes trial in The Hague, Netherlands. Despite his proclamation of innocence, he was found guilty of arming and backing the rebels in Sierra Leone's 1991-2002 civil war from neighboring Liberia in order to seize control of Sierra Leone's diamond riches. The Special Court found Taylor guilty in April 2012 of all 11 war crime charges against him. The judge sentenced him to 50 years in prison, the first African head of state to be tried by an international tribunal.

The rebels backed by Taylor brought Sierra Leone to its knees. They are blamed for hacking off the arms and legs of civilians with machetes and eating the organs of civilians they had killed. An estimated 500,000 people were the victims of killings, mutilation and other atrocities during that war. Child soldiers committed some of the worst crimes; they were drugged to desensitize them to the horror of their actions.

Karman, Gbowee, and Sirleaf display their Nobel Peace Prize in 2011

Like other deposed leaders before him who faced judgment—Yugoslavia's Slobodan Milosevic and Iraq's Saddam Hussein—Taylor used his day in court to profess his devotion to his people and deny any wrongdoing. He denied sponsoring the rebel invasion of Sierra Leone, tolerating amputations, plotting the capture of the capital, Freetown, or trafficking illegally mined "blood diamonds."[19] Over 18 months, dozens of witnesses, some missing their hands, testified to the brutality of the rebel forces. Witnesses formerly associated with Taylor claimed to have passed weapons and messages to the rebels on Taylor's orders and transferred diamonds—sometimes in mayonnaise jars.

His appearance at the U.N.-backed Special Court for Sierra Leone was widely broadcast in West Africa, giving Liberians their first chance to hear him in court since he resigned in 2003 and went into exile in Nigeria. His trial had special meaning to a group of "market women" in Liberia led by Leymah Gbowee. They collectively pressured the warring factions in Liberia to attend peace talks and to end Liberia's 14-year civil war. Their amazing struggle for peace paved the way for the election of Ellen Johnson-Sirleaf as president of Liberia—the first democratically-elected female head of state in Africa. For their efforts, they were awarded the Nobel Peace Prize in 2011.

GENOCIDE

"If the killing of one Jew or one Pole is a crime, the killing of all the Jews and all the Poles is not a lesser crime."[20] — Ralph Lemkin

What is the first thing that comes to your mind when you think of genocide? Most people think of extraordinary violence. But history is full of bloody battles, murders, starvations, wars, bombings, and other violent acts. Genocide is different. The crucial difference is within the minds of those who commit genocide. They seek to destroy not just people, but entire cultures. Those committing genocide, called perpetrators, can destroy cultures by burning schools, libraries, and houses of worship; seizing homes and possessions; renaming streets; and paving over graveyards.

Genocide is both the gravest and greatest of human crimes. There is plenty of debate about the definition of genocide. In fact, it has become a word used to describe many different forms of direct and indirect killing. Actually it it is a very specific term that simply refers to violent crimes committed against groups with the intent to completely exterminate a selected group. The Genocide Convention further defines genocide as the intent to destroy, in whole or in part, a national, ethnical, racial or religious group.

The term genocide is a very recent word that did not exist before 1944. We owe a debt of gratitude to a very courageous individual, Ralph Lemkin, who fought tirelessly to bring the crime of genocide to the world's attention. Here is his story.

Genocide Includes:[21]

- Killing members of the group
- Causing serious bodily or mental harm to members of the group
- Deliberately inflicting on the group conditions to bring about its physical destruction
- Imposing measures intended to prevent births within the group
- Forcibly transferring children of the group to another group

RALPH LEMKIN

Ralph Lemkin (1900-1959) was born on a farm in eastern Poland, an area that is now part of the nation of Belarus. He grew up in a Jewish family dedicated to the arts. His father was a farmer and his intelligent mother was a painter, linguist, and philosopher with a large collection of books on literature and history. Even as a child he was horrified by the massacres of unarmed civilians that had taken place throughout history. He was especially fascinated with stories of the Roman Empire, in particular Emperor Nero. Nero threw Christians to the lions in gladiator shows in an attempt to wipe out their new religion. Ralph constantly questioned his mother: "How could such a thing happen? Why would people allow it? How could they cheer those bloody acts?" With his mother as an influence, he mastered ten languages by the age of 14, including French, Spanish, Hebrew, Yiddish, and Russian.

As a young man Lemkin turned to the study of law. He began to tackle the problem that would become his life's work: the fact that mass killing was not punishable by law. Using his language skills, he combed through books of law codes from modern and ancient civilizations in search of some law that prohibited the killing of one group by another. He found none; therefore, he began to write his own law. In 1933 he presented a draft of this law to an international conference of the League of Nations in Madrid, Spain. The conference did not take up his suggestion, in part because governments did not want the League to get involved in individual countries. But Lemkin did not give up.

The rise of Hitler and the Nazis in Germany during the 1930s alarmed Lemkin. He begged his parents and neighbors to flee Poland when the Nazis invaded in 1939, but they refused. He fled to Sweden, then to the U.S. in 1941, where he secured a teaching position at Duke University.

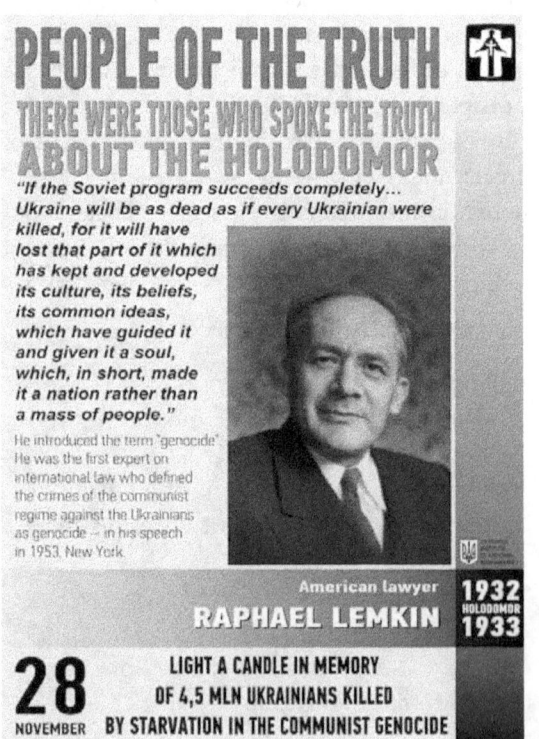

Ralph Lemkin spoke out against the Soviet Holodomor in Ukraine

Lemkin was struck by a speech made by British Prime Minister, Winston Churchill, when he described Nazi actions as a "crime without a name." Churchill's phrase stuck with him. Lemkin reasoned that people couldn't understand the Nazi actions because there was no word to explain it, so he decided to create his own word.

He wanted a word that was universal in its meaning. It would apply to all mass killings in history, not just what was currently happening in Europe to the Jews. He also wanted a word that would be clear-cut and carry moral authority. When people used this word, Lemkin reasoned, it should never be confused with anything else. After much thought, in 1944 he created the word "genocide" by combining geno-, from the Greek word for race or tribe, with -cide, from the Latin word to kill. A new word was born.

In 1946, soon after the end of World War II (1945) Lemkin traveled to Nuremberg, Germany, where he sadly learned that 49 of his 53 family members in Poland had died. He only found his older brother, sister-in-law and their two sons in Germany. His work to advance the concept of genocide would continue in Nuremberg. A war tribunal had set up a court in Nuremberg to try Nazi officials for war crimes. Hitler had committed suicide just days before the war ended, but other top Nazis had been captured, arrested, and charged with crimes. Lemkin hoped to get his newly coined term "genocide" into the vocabulary of international law. But Lemkin would be battling against a basic concept in international law, **sovereignty**. The modern world is organized into political units called nations. Each nation is recognized as being sovereign; each nation is independent and allowed to run its own affairs without direct interference from other nations. This is the bedrock of international law. As Lemkin was finding out, even if a country was murdering its own citizens, other nations could do little to legally stop it. Nations could do as they pleased, just like a father had the right to discipline his children or wife for what he considered wrongdoing. Lemkin wanted to change this idea.

Lemkin worked tirelessly, lobbying governments and diplomats to make genocide an internationally recognized crime. However, the judges convicted the Nazi war criminals of crimes against peace and humanity; the word genocide was not used. He called it "the blackest day" of his life, but he did not despair. Instead, he headed to New York where the UN was still in its infancy; he hoped to make an impact there. Lemkin found a more willing audience in New York than in Nuremberg. He was the driving force behind a resolution that condemned genocide, which passed the UN General Assembly on December 9, 1948 with all 55 delegates voting to approve the law. Although the law against genocide passed, it still had to be submitted and ratified by each country's government. Many governments did ratify the law, but one in particular did not—the United States. Some of you might be surprised that the U.S. Senate did not pass this law. However, some Americans were worried that the U.S. treatment of Native Americans could be punished under the genocide law and many Southern lawmakers were concerned that segregation laws and lynching of African Americans might be considered genocide as well. Others refused to give up American sovereignty. He would not live to see his country ratify the treaty. It was not until 1986, with President Ronald Reagan's support, that the U.S. Senate finally ratified the treaty, becoming the 98th nation to do so.

Laws Against Genocide Protect Four Groups:[21]

1. A national group is individuals whose identity is defined by a common country or national origin.
2. An ethnic group is defined by common cultural traditions, language or heritage.
3. A racial group means a set of individuals whose identity is defined by physical characteristics.
4. A religious group is individuals whose identity is defined by common religious creeds, beliefs, doctrines, practices, or rituals.

Lemkin was nominated seven times for the Nobel Peace Prize, but his work was largely unrecognized until after his death. He died in poverty in New York City on August 28, 1959.[22]

Questions to Consider
1. What obstacles did Ralph Lemkin face in his efforts to make known the atrocity of genocide?

THE WHAT, WHY, WHO, HOW AND WHEN, AND WHERE OF GENOCIDE

The story of Ralph Lemkin gives a background of how the word genocide came about. Let's next turn to a few nagging questions about the who, what, where, how and why of genocide. This background will provide greater understanding about genocide and help explain actual historical examples.

THE WHAT OF GENOCIDE

As Lemkin realized, genocide is a crime on a different scale from all other crimes against humanity. Further separating genocide from other crimes are two elements: intent and action. Statements or orders can directly prove intent, which is different from motive. Whatever the motive for the crime—seizure of land, national security, territorial boundaries—if perpetrators commit acts intended to destroy a group or event part of a group, it is genocide. The phrase "in whole or in part" is important because perpetrators need not intend to destroy the entire group; if only part of a group is destroyed, it is genocide.[23]

Genocide is a process that evolves in eight expected but not unstoppable stages. At each stage, preventive measures can stop it. The process does not follow all the stages in order.[25]

The Eight Stages of Genocide

1. Classification: All cultures have ethnic, race, religious, or national categories to divide people into "us and them." At this early stage, the main preventive measure is to develop institutions that go beyond ethnic or racial divisions and actively encourage tolerance and understanding. A search for common ground is vital to early prevention.

The Nazi flag

2. Symbols: Names are given to the classifications, such as "Jews" or "Gypsies", or distinguish them by colors or dress, and apply the symbols to group members. When combined with hatred, symbols may be forced upon unwilling members such as the yellow star for Jews under Nazi rule. Hate symbols, such as a swastika, and hate speech can be legally forbidden. Group markings like gang clothing or tribal scarring can be outlawed as well.

3. Dehumanization: One group denies the humanity of the other group, who are equated with animals, vermin, insects or diseases. It is easier to kill a cockroach than another human. At this stage, hate propaganda in print and on hate radios demonizes the victim group. Leaders should criticize hate speech, shut down hate radio stations, and ban hate propaganda. Hate crimes and violence should be punished.

4. Organization: The state organizes genocide. Trained and armed special army units or militias let states deny their responsibility. The state plans genocidal killings. To combat this stage, states should not allow membership in these militias. The UN should impose arms embargoes on citizens and countries involved in genocidal massacres, and investigate violations.

5. Polarization: The perpetrators' purpose is to drive the groups apart. Hate groups broadcast divisive propaganda. Laws may forbid intermarriage or social interaction. Moderates are targeted and frightened into silence. They are most able to stop genocide, so they are the first to be arrested and killed.

6. Preparation: The perpetrators identify and separate out victims because of their ethnic or religious identity, and force them to wear identifying symbols. The state draws up death lists, confiscates property, and segregates victims into ghettoes, deports them into concentration camps, or confines them to a famine-struck region where they are starved. At this stage, a Genocide Emergency must be declared.

7. Extermination begins, and can quickly become the mass killing called genocide. The killers do not believe their victims are fully human. When the state sponsors extermination, the armed forces often work with militias to do the killing.

8. Denial always follows genocide. The perpetrators dig up mass graves, burn bodies, cover up evidence, intimidate witnesses, deny any crimes and often blame the victims. They block investigations of the crimes, and continue to govern until driven from power, when they flee into exile. An International Criminal Court will arrest, prosecute and punish perpetrators.

THE WHY OF GENOCIDE

There are several different explanations for why genocide takes place. One **"evil man" theory** is often given as an explanation. And the most evil of all evil men is Adolph Hitler, the leader of Nazi Germany (1933-1945) and the main perpetrator of the Holocaust. Another evil man, more recently cited, is Saddam Hussein, who was guilty of massacring 50,000 to 200,000 Kurds in northern Iraq in 1988. Although these two men were the key decision makers in the crime of genocide, they did not carry it out alone. This theory is too simplistic and does not explain why accomplices are drawn into carrying out genocide.[26]

Second, in some cases governments or powerful groups want new settlers to take over the land of the people already living there. A government or corporation may want to take over an area that is rich in natural resources—like oil, land, gold, or timber—or set up a factory to take advantage of cheap labor and lax environmental laws. They may need to get rid of indigenous people living there to get the resources. A third reason is that a group or a government feels that there is a threat from "other" ethnic, political, or social groups and it wants to get rid of them. This happened in the Rwandan genocide in Africa where the majority Hutu tribe, who were in power, committed genocide against the minority Tutsi tribe.[27]

A fourth explanation for genocide is that a government may want to establish a "pure" or utopian society, where only people of a certain race, class, religion or sexual orientation will be allowed to live. Genocide leaders may claim they are "cleansing" or "purifying" their nation of impure influence. Hitler's treatment of Jews, homosexuals, Roma (gypsies), disabled and others during the Holocaust is an example. In the Cambodian genocide all those who were not of "pure" Cambodian ancestry were killed.[28]

THE WHO OF GENOCIDE

The who of genocide involves several categories of victims. Victims are usually vulnerable people in society and the perpetrators choose them because they appear to be a threat. They may be an elite minority, such as the Tutis, Jews, and educated Cambodians. Or they may be groups that oppose the genocide, such as the communists in Nazi Germany or moderate Hutus in Rwanda. The first victims are often the most well-known people in the community—political and religious leaders, intellectuals and teachers—since they are the most likely to have the ability to organize resistance to the perpetrators.[29]

Perpetrators often make clear distinctions between men and women and between boys and girls. Men are usually the first killed, because in most cultures men are still the leaders. They expect men to be more of a physical threat than women or young children. They want to isolate and kill them before they organize to resist the genocide. Men are more likely to do the killing, but women in certain situations have been just as brutal. Women may appear protected in some genocidal situations; in most cases they are not killed as quickly. But this is not always true. For instance, in the Nazi concentration camp of Auschwitz, pregnant women and women with young children were the first to be gassed. Single women and men, as long as they were healthy enough to work, sometimes survived a little longer.[30]

A great deal of planning and organization is necessary to carry out some genocides, while others are chaotic, as in the case of Rwanda. One of the first steps in planned genocides is to take away the targeted group's rights and physically isolate them from others. For example, Jews in Nazi Germany could not own their own businesses and in Poland the Nazis herded Jews into a Warsaw ghetto. Ultimately Nazis rounded up Jews and transported them to concentration camps that resulted in the deaths of millions.[31]

Who are the perpetrators? The **perpetrators** plan and recruit others to carry out the killings. They may be the government, government collaborators, an army, mercenaries (private army), a militia (a band of soldiers), or ordinary citizens. Since it is too big a job for just a few people, perpetrators must always enlist the help of others. Government armies commit most genocide, but private or corporate armies of mercenaries are often hired to assist with the killing. These "paramilitaries" are experienced, well-armed and more highly motivated than regular soldiers. They're also more familiar with killing. The Janjaweed militia in Darfur, Sudan is an example. Also there are those who are involved indirectly, such as businesspeople in charge of transporting victims to concentration camps in Nazi Germany.[32]

Perpetrators often use media to spread messages of hate and dis-information about the group they want to victimize. A talk radio station in Rwanda before the April 1994 genocide, referred to Tutsis as cockroaches, and played music that encouraged Hutus to kill Tutsis. Nazi Germany widely used books, newspapers and especially films to spread hatred against Jews, Roma and the disabled.[33]

Most people find killing to be morally and physically disgusting. According to genocide expert Jane Singer, the first question many people ask about genocide is, "How is it possible for human beings to kill other human beings so easily?"[34] Veteran soldiers admit that it gets easier each time they kill. Some people describe a "high" feeling when participating in a group killing. It is somewhat different when ordinary people kill. They realize that the perpetrators are all-powerful, and they are afraid that they must either "kill or be killed." When the killings are staged in daylight and in public, as often was the case in Rwanda, it implies that the act is lawful and acceptable, making it harder to take a stand against the genocide. There is also the need to "go along with the crowd," and to conform to one's own group or to patriotically support one's country. Another reason is that people often obey authority figures; they go along with someone who orders them or encourages them to torture and kill others.[35]

Psychologist Stanley Milgram conducted an experiment in the 1960s that showed people's willingness to obey authority. In his experiment, he instructed people to direct electric shocks of increasing harshness to staged "victims." The staged victims pleaded with those administering the shocks to stop. However, Milgram found that most people followed instructions, even if it hurt other people, as long as the order came from someone they saw as a legitimate authority. Milgram concluded that only a small percentage of people were able to resist the authority's instructions. Most people obeyed.[36]

Bystanders are the people or groups of people or even whole countries that see events take place and do nothing to stop them. Niemoller's quote at the beginning of this chapter showed that the bystanders' indifference and failure to act allowed genocide to take place and continue. But many people do not act even when they're not personally in danger. Perhaps the "us-them" propaganda (misinformation) has been successful in convincing them the victims are not really human or deserve their harsh treatment.

THE HOW AND WHEN OF GENOCIDE

In most societies, some people hate other people or want to have power over them. They may focus this hatred on people's characteristics, such as their race, ethnicity, class, religion, sexual orientation, or gender. In most cases, this hatred is not acted upon. But in some cases people develop elaborate explanations about their hatred and begin to act and encourage others to act against the targeted groups. When a large part of a society is caught up in acting upon—or ignoring others acting upon—these hatreds, the situation may evolve into genocide.[37]

Genocide often takes place during war, or under the cover of war. The Armenian genocide that took place in the Ottoman Empire during World War I and the Holocaust that Germany carried out during World War II are both examples. Some experts say wartime acts against civilian enemies should be considered genocide, such as the bombings of Hiroshima and Nagasaki during WWII. While many agree that these bombings were war crimes, the intent was not to destroy an entire group but to end a war.[38]

Genocide often takes place during a period of political or social upheaval. Genocide expert Helen Fein identifies possible candidates for genocide as countries that are moving from authoritarian rule to more democratic rule, a situation that frequently sets off a power struggle. Gregory Stanton of Genocide Watch says that genocides do not result from "state failure," but from "state success, from too much state power." He cites Nazi Germany, the Soviet Union in 1930s, and Cambodia in the 1970s as examples.[39]

THE WHERE OF GENOCIDE

Genocide can take place anywhere and everywhere. Those countries or societies where genocide is more likely to occur often glorify their own nation and despise others; it also occurs in nations that are not open to diversity of thought, religion and expression. For example, the breakup of the former Soviet Union, unleashed nationalistic sentiments in the nations forged out of the former Yugoslavia. Authoritarian leader Joseph Tito had tight control of the different ethnic groups but when he died in 1980, ethnic divisions and conflict grew and eventually erupted in a series of wars a decade after his death. The struggles between different nationalities, ethnicities, and religions created a storm of conflict.

Genocide is more likely to occur in a place where the perpetrators have themselves been victims of violence or genocide in the past. For example, the Hutus, perpetrators of genocide in Rwanda in the 1990s, had been victims of genocidal massacres by the Tutsis in neighboring Burundi in 1972.

GENOCIDE IN HISTORY: FIVE CASE STUDIES

"The word is new, the concept is ancient," wrote Leo Kuper in his study of genocide in 1981.[40] Genocide has frequently occurred through history. But determining which historical events are genocide and which are merely criminal or inhuman behavior is not a clear-cut matter. In nearly every case where claims of genocide have been made, various sides have fiercely disagreed. An accusation of genocide is not taken lightly and will almost always be controversial. The following case studies of genocides and alleged genocides should be understood in this way and cannot be regarded as the final word on this subject.

THE BIBLICAL OLD TESTAMENT

The Biblical Old Testament has examples of what we would define as genocide today. For example, in the Book of Genesis (6:17-19) God decides to "destroy all flesh in which is the breath of life from under heaven," with the exception of Noah and a small core of human and animal life. God's people are to be a holy people, kept apart, separated from the idol worshipping neighbors. In

1 Samuel 15: 2-3, the Lord declares: "I will punish the Amalekites for what they did in opposing the Israelites when they came up out of Egypt. Now go and attack Amalek and utterly destroy all that they have; do not spare them, but kill both man and woman, child and infant, ox and sheep, camel and donkey."[41] Apparently, the Amalekites disappeared from history.

The Book of Numbers 31 describes a genocide. All Medianite men are killed by the Israelites in accordance with God's command, but his order, transmitted by Moses, to kill all the women as well is not carried out, and God is angry. Moses berates the Israelites, whereupon they go out and kill all the women and all the male children; only virgin girls are left alive.[42]

ROME

The imperial city of Rome was very powerful and expanded its boundaries into a large state. It was constantly at war to keep or expand its territory. The Phoenician city of Carthage fought Rome in a series of three Punic wars. Rome's siege and eventual razing of Carthage at the close of the Third Punic War (149-146 BCE) is an example of early genocide. Rome sought to stem the supposed threat posed by Carthage (site of present day Tunis, Tunisia), but the Romans had other reasons to conquer Carthage. By the middle of the second century BCE the population of Rome was 400,000 and rising. Feeding the growing populace was a major challenge. The farmlands surrounding Carthage were the most productive and the easiest to access of all agricultural lands not yet under Roman control. Though the citizens of Carthage fought bravely, the crushing Roman military pushed them back. The Roman army killed and drove from their land at least 150,000 Carthaginians out of a population of 200,000-400,000. Although disputed by some historians, legend has it, ironically, that after the battle the Roman army sowed the surrounding countryside with salt to ensure that nothing would grow there again. Even if the Romans did not salt the earth, they were vicious in their extermination of the citizens of Carthage.[43]

CHRISTIANS

Among Rome's other victims during its imperial rule were the followers of Jesus. After his death in 33 CE, the Roman army subjected Jesus' followers to savage persecutions and mass murder. Emperor Nero (37-68 CE) provides the first documented case of imperially-supervised persecution of the Christians in the Roman Empire. In 64 CE (AD), a great fire broke out in Rome, destroying portions of the city and devastating the economy. According to Tacitus, a Roman historian, the population searched for a scapegoat and held Nero responsible. To deflect blame, Nero targeted Christians. Tacitus writes: "Accordingly, an arrest was first made of all who pleaded guilty; then, upon their information, an immense multitude was convicted, not so much of the crime of firing the city, as of hatred against

Persecution of Christians in the Roman Empire

mankind. Mockery of every sort was added to their deaths. Covered with the skins of beasts, they were torn by dogs and perished, or were nailed to crosses, or were doomed to the flames and burnt, to serve as a nightly illumination, when daylight had expired."[44]

Persecution of Christians continued from the 1st to the early 4th century until Constantine I legalized the Christian religion. From this moment, historians note that Christianity turned from a persecuted into a persecuting religion. From the 9th to 14th centuries CE, Christians carried out incidents of torture. During this time, the church launched the Crusades, religious campaigns against "unbelievers."[45] In the Holy Land, Jews and Muslims unsuccessfully fought together to defend Jerusalem from invasion by the Crusaders. On July 15, 1099 the Crusaders entered the city. They massacred Jewish and Muslim civilians and destroyed mosques and the city.[46] Three more crusades followed and massacres continued. In the last Crusade, European Crusaders detoured to Constantinople, a Christian city, and sacked and plundered it. In the end, the Christian Crusaders lost control of the Holy Land to the Muslims.

THE MONGOLS

In the 13th century, a million Mongol horsemen, under the leadership of Genghis Khan (Temüjin), surged out of the arid grasslands of East Asia to lay waste to vast territories extending to the gates of Western Europe. Historian Eric Margolis stated that "entire nations were exterminated, leaving behind nothing but rubble, fallow fields, and bones."[47] The Mongol Empire, at its most powerful in the 13th and 14th century, was the largest adjoining empire in human history. Astride their sturdy ponies, the Mongol armies could ride for days, even sleeping in their saddles. If on an important mission, instead of taking breaks to eat, they stuck a type of straw into their pony's neck and sucked their blood for nourishment. They were fearless, extremely well organized, and ruthless in their conquests. Many historians said the Mongols were genocidal killers. The death toll of their victims —through battle, massacre, flooding, and famine—is placed at 40 million. Many ancient sources described Genghis Khan's conquests as wholesale destruction on an unprecedented scale, causing terrifying death and a drastic decline in Asian populations. For example, from 1220 – 1260, the population of Persia may have dropped from 2,500,000 to 250,000 as a result of mass extermination and famine inflicted by the Mongols.[48]

INDIGENOUS PEOPLES OF NORTH AND SOUTH AMERICA

In 1492, a Spanish expedition headed by Christopher Columbus reached the Americas, after which European exploration and colonization rapidly expanded. As a result of European contact, the indigenous populations dropped dramatically over the next few decades. Europeans directly murdered thousands. Some died of starvation, some enslaved native laborers were simply worked to death, and most died as a result of diseases for which they had no resistance—mainly smallpox, influenza, and measles. In 1492, estimates of native populations in the Americas ranged widely from 8 to 140 million people, based on archaeological data and written European records. After contact, approximately 80 percent died.[49]

Whether the decimation of the indigenous population of North and South America after 1492 was a true genocide or not is open to debate. Historian David Stannard concludes that the indigenous peoples of America, including Hawaii, were the victims of a "Euro-American genocidal war." He calls the European conquest of the Americas "the most massive interrelated sequence of genocides in the history of the world." While conceding that the majority of the indigenous peoples

A 16th-century illustration depicting Spanish atrocities during the conquest of Cuba

fell victim to the ravages of European disease, he estimates that almost 100 million died in what he calls the American Holocaust.[50] Those in agreement state that European conquest was one of the most massive and longest lasting genocidal campaigns in human history. It continued until almost all American indigenous peoples died, along with much of their language, culture and religion.[51]

While the majority of historians agree that a small number of Europeans unjustly inflicted death and suffering upon millions of American natives, they mostly argue that genocide, which is a crime of intent, was not the intent of European colonizers. Genocide is defined (in part) as a crime "committed with intent to destroy, in whole or in part, a national, ethnic, racial or religious group." Therefore, nearly all mainstream scholars do not use the term genocide to describe the overall depopulation of American natives. However, instead of seeing the whole history of European colonization as one long act of genocide, there are a number of specific wars and campaigns which were arguably genocidal in intent and effect. One of them I described above, the Indian Removal Act of 1830 or the Trail of Tears.[52]

Questions to Consider
1. Which of the five case studies do you think was genocide? Explain.

TWENTIETH CENTURY GENOCIDES

Genocide has been a constant through history. However, the 20th century is considered one of the most horrific in our long human history. Perhaps it is because the mass killings are still fresh in our memory; we may actually know someone who survived genocide. In this next section I have selected two horrendous genocides to examine: the Holocaust and Rwanda.

THE HOLOCAUST

The **Holocaust** is the classic case of genocide. Few people would disagree. The mass killings of the Holocaust took place in Germany and Eastern Europe primarily during World War II (1939-1945). Although many individuals were involved in the atrocities, the main architect of the slaughter was the German leader Adolph Hitler. Most people associate the Holocaust with the mass extermination of Jewish people, but other less-known groups were targeted as well—Roma (Gypsies), Poles, Russians, mentally and physically disabled, socialists, communists, homosexuals, Afro-Germans, and Jehovah's Witnesses.

Adolph Hitler was born in 1889 in a small Austrian village just across the border from Germany. As a teenager, he was interested in German nationalism and believed that all Germans should be in one country. But Austria at the time was part of a large multiethnic Hapsburg Empire, with diverse people who spoke different languages and practiced different religions. The young Hitler settled in Vienna, capital of the empire, where he hoped to study art. Instead his passions turned to hating Jews. He commented: The more I saw them, "the more sharply they became distinguished in my eyes from the rest of humanity."[53] During World War I, the 25 year-old Hitler enthusiastically enlisted in the German army. He rose to the rank of corporal, but his service was cut short when a shell burst and caused a leg wound. During his recovery, the civilian unrest and complaints directed against the war angered him. Jews, he determined, caused the defeat of Germany.

The victorious World War I allies (U.S. Great Britain and France) forced the defeated Germany to accept total responsibility for the war and pay huge reparations (damages). This caused bitterness and economic unrest across Germany. The country printed so much paper money to pay for the reparations that the exchange rate at one point was 1 trillion marks (German currency) to the U.S. dollar. People needed a wheelbarrow full of marks to buy a loaf of bread. Outbreaks of violence rocked the nation as different groups, such as Communists, tried to seize control of the weak and ineffective democratic government. But the army was able to put down the rebellions. A gifted orator, Hitler delivered angry, passionate speeches to the soldiers, blaming Communists and Jews for Germany's defeat in the war. Many of the soldiers, seeking someone to blame for troubles in Germany, sided with Hitler.

In late 1919, Hitler joined a political party which supported a strong government that discriminated against Jews. In charge of recruitment, he rose to higher positions in the party, which at the time numbered only 3,000 members.[54] In 1920, Hitler chose the swastika as a symbol for the National Socialist German Workers' Party, and its members were called Nazis. The Nazis promoted the idea that the German blond-haired, blue-eyed Aryan "race" was superior and others, such as Jews and Slavic people (Russians, Serbs, and others), were inferior. They demanded that Germans needed more *Lebensraum* or "living space" for their people and a leader with absolute authority to carry this out.

The economic and political situation in Germany stabilized somewhat in the mid-1920s. Prices returned to a fairly normal range, businesses and factories reopened, and the German citizens were not as bitter. Since the economy improved, the Nazi party was not very popular, and Hitler's anti-Semitic ranting attracted little serious attention. But that changed with the economic collapse at the end of 1929.

The 1930s opened with a terrible depression that caused a downward slump in the world economy. The depression hit Germany, like the U.S., very hard, and millions of workers lost their jobs. Because Hitler had a simple answer to a complex problem—Jews, Communists, and a weak democracy were the cause of all problems—many people turned to him and his Nazi party to restore order. Hitler won increasing numbers of votes in German elections, and finally in 1933 maneuvered his way into the position of chancellor, the most powerful position in the German government.

With the Nazis firmly in control, Hitler began to suspend constitutional rights and freedoms—press, assembly, association—which also included a plan to eliminate the Jews. It started with a ban that stated Jews could not own property or work at professional jobs. Although anti-Semitism was not new in Europe, it took a much more vicious turn under the Nazis. Jewish schoolchildren were discriminated against, and, for example, a law against overcrowding in schools permitted only one student out of every 100 to be Jewish. To show their ethnicity, students had to produce family trees and official birth records.[55]

At first, it seemed that Nazis just wanted Jews to leave Germany, not necessarily to kill them. But emigration was very difficult at the time; there was nowhere to go. The U.S., a popular destination for Europeans, was also experiencing a severe depression, and the government only allowed a few immigrants. Out of 505,000 Jews in Germany in 1934, about 1 percent of the population, about

37,000 Jews left Germany in 1933. Those who did leave left penniless, as the German government seized the émigrés' property and money.[56]

The German quest for *Lebensraum*—living space for its "pure" Aryan population—started when Hitler annexed Austria in 1938. Hitler quickly put in place anti-Semitic policies. The quest for *Lebensraum* continued when the German army invaded Poland on September 1, 1939. Great Britain and France decided that Hitler had to be stopped and declared war on Germany. World War II was underway. Shortly thereafter, the Nazis defeated Denmark, Norway, France, Belgium, Holland, Luxembourg, and marched into the Soviet Union in 1941. It looked very bleak for the Allies until the U.S. joined them after the Japanese attacked Pearl Harbor on December 7, 1941.

Poland had the largest Jewish population in Europe, over 3 million. In order to separate them from the general population, they were required to wear badges on their chests with the yellow star of David prominently displayed. The Nazis herded Jews into walled ghettos in Warsaw and other cities, where overcrowding, lack of sanitation, disease, and starvation killed thousands. In the Warsaw ghetto the food allocation was only 181 calories a day.[57] They either smuggled in food or died.

Mid-1941 to 1942 marked the implementation of the "Final Solution to the Jewish question," as Hitler termed it. Although mass killings of about one million Jews took place before the "Final Solution" was fully put in place in 1942, the solution was to do away with the entire Jewish population. Nazis commenced building extermination camps to carry out the industrialized mass slaughter. Under the direction of Heinrich Himmler, the chief architect of the plan, the eastern territories of Germany were to get rid of "undesirable" peoples—especially Jews. Once cleared, German settlers would be encouraged to move in and occupy the territory, changing it into their so-called "Garden of Eden."[58]

A Survivor of the Babi Yar Massacre

Dina Pronicheva was one of those ordered to march to the ravine at **Babi Yar**. She was forced to undress, and then shot. Badly wounded, she played dead, lying in a pile of corpses, and eventually managed to escape. One of the very few survivors, she later told her horrifying story to writer Anatoli Kuznetsov.[60]

"It was dark already…They lined us up on a ledge which was so small that we couldn't get much of a footing on it. They began shooting us. I shut my eyes, clenched my fists, tensed all my muscles and took a plunge down before the bullets hit me. It seemed I was flying forever. But I landed safely on the bodies. After a while, when the shooting stopped, I heard the Germans climbing into the ravine. They started finishing off all those who were not dead yet, those who were moaning, hiccupping, tossing, writhing in agony. They ran their flashlights over the bodies and finished off all who moved. I was lying so still without stirring, terrified of giving myself away. I felt I was done for.

I decided to keep quiet. They started covering the corpses over with earth. They must have put quite a lot over me because I felt I was beginning to suffocate. But I was afraid to move. I was gasping for breath. I knew I would suffocate. Then I decided it was better to be shot than buried alive. I stirred but I didn't know that it was quite dark already. Using my left arm I managed to move a little way up. Then I took a deep breath, summoned up my waning strength and crawled out from under the cover of earth. It was dark. But it was dangerous to crawl because of the searching beams of flashlight and they continued shooting at those who moaned. They might hit me. So I had to be careful. I was lucky enough to crawl up one of the high walls of the ravine, and straining every nerve and muscle, got out of it."

Special mobile killing units made up of German soldiers began to round up and murder Jews, Poles and Soviets; thousands were herded to areas outside towns and forced to dig their own graves. German soldiers forced them to undress and then ruthlessly shot them, flinging them into the pits or graves they had just dug. In just two days in September 1941, the Nazis massacred 35,000 Jews and tossed them into a ravine at Babi Yar, outside Kiev, Ukraine. In the following months the number killed grew to over 100,000. Within a week of the German invasion of the Soviet Union, more Jews were murdered than had been killed in the entire eight years of Nazi rule in Germany.[59]

To murder such a large number of people required a great deal of planning. The Nazis decided to use killing techniques that they had first used on mentally and physically disabled Germans and Poles: gas. One method of execution was to place the victims in a sealed chamber on a truck and pump poisonous gas fumes into the chamber until all inside were dead. Using this as a model, the Final Solution took a more ghastly turn when the Nazis began to construct special killing centers with gas chambers in Poland that were used solely for mass murder. All the Jews of Europe were to be rounded up and sent to six main extermination camps in Poland—Belzec, Chelmno, Treblinka, and Sobibór, while Auschwitz-Birkenau and Majdanek were both extermination and work camps. To get to the death or work camps, the Nazis forced the victims onto transport trains that criss-crossed the Polish landscape. The railway system moved its human cargo thousands at a time with clockwork efficiency. Victims were told they were being "resettled" to a new area because if they suspected what was about to happen to them they may have revolted. The victims brought their suitcases filled with food

Hungarian Jews being selected by Nazis to be sent to the gas chamber at Auschwitz concentration camp, 1944

and belongings. The train's passengers arrived at the camps exhausted, hungry, and thirsty, not having eaten or had water for days on end.

Once the victims arrived at the Treblinka camp, they handed over all their valuables. Next, younger adults, mainly men and some women were selected for work, while others, including mostly children and their mothers, pregnant women, and the elderly, were sent directly to the gas chambers. The guards ordered those headed to the gas chambers to undress. Naked, they were lined up in rows and forced to run down a fenced-in path called the "tube" or "funnel" with a large chamber labeled showers at the end. They were told they were going to be disinfected. Some victims knew what awaited them, and they resisted their fate. According to observers, the pushing, shoving, crying, howling and shouting was deafening and agonizing. The guards pumped deadly carbon monoxide inside the closed chamber until everyone expired. Then a Jewish work crew unceremoniously removed the bodies and buried them in giant, anonymous trenches.[61] In some camps, special-detail men extracted everything useable from the corpses, even gold from their teeth and their hair. The fate of

83

those selected to work, was not much better than those gassed; thousands died from overwork. For over three years, this horrible scenario was repeated every day. Through a combination of luck and determination a few did manage to survive.

In 1942, the Nazis constructed **Auschwitz,** their largest concentration camp. Unlike Treblinka, Auschwitz had a large working population, along with the notorious gas chambers. There, the Nazis

Not Only Jews - More Nazi Genocides
The Disabled

The Nazis wanted to have a pure Aryan race. To reach this goal they passed a law in 1933 that forced the sterilization of people with so-called hereditary diseases, since they thought only those who were "perfectly" healthy should have children. The law sterilized those who were deaf, mentally and physically disabled, as well as alcoholics and those with epilepsy. All told, 300,000 - 400,000 people, who were mostly living in institutions, were sterilized.[62]

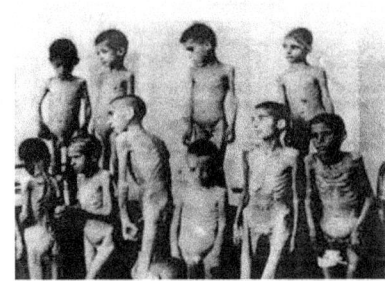

Romani children in Auschwitz, victims of medical experiments

In 1939, Hitler instituted "mercy killings," where doctors could kill what they considered to be "incurable patients" under the euthanasia program. However, there was no mercy in the killings, since the patients did not ask to die and the killing was done in secret. At first the method of killing was performed with a lethal injection; later carbon dioxide was used, a technique that would soon be used in the gas chambers.[63] From 1939-1945, 250,000 mentally and physically disabled people were murdered.

The Roma

The Roma, commonly known as Gypsies, had a long history of persecution in Germany. The 1935 laws for the "Protection of German Blood and Honor" prohibited their marriage to Germans. In 1938, Henrich Himmler drew up the document: "The Final Solution to the Gypsy Question." The Nazis rounded up the Roma, and they were sent to work and to death camps. They wore black triangles as identification labels. The Roma genocide was overlooked after the war, and it was many years before the whole story was told. An estimated 500,000 Roma were killed during the Holocaust.[64]

Gay Men

The Nazis, concerned about the falling birth rate, targeted gay men for persecution. They established the Office for Combating Homosexuality and Abortion in 1935, in which informers of all kinds, even school children, were encouraged to tell authorities if they thought certain men to be gay. They arrested the men, and they were sent to concentration camps. Gay men wore pink triangles for identification in the concentration camps, where they were harshly treated and used for medical experiments, which few survived. The Nazis generally did not target lesbians. The number of gay men killed ranged from 10,000 to 15,000.[65]

Other Holocaust Victims

Considered impure, the Nazis also attacked Poles, Russians and other Slavs. They killed 3 million Christian Poles, and 3.3 million prisoners in German concentration camps died in captivity. All together about 25 million citizens of the Soviet Union died during the German invasion of their country. The Nazis also selected Communists, Afro-Germans, and Jehovah's Witnesses for persecution. Although they were not gassed, many were killed or died in horrible conditions in the camps. Even before Hitler, the few people of African origin in Germany were targets of discrimination. Some were sterilized and others used in medical experiments. The number who died is unknown.

perfected their killing methods. They built large underground gas chambers with fake showerheads. The victims were told to undress in a large dressing room. Once in the air-tight gas chamber, the insecticide, Zyklon B gas crystals, was dropped through ventilation ducts that pumped out the deadly gas. Once the gas dispersed, Jewish work crews moved the bodies to one of five specially built crematoriums designed to burn the bodies. The dead were placed in these ovens and cremated. Ashes from the bodies were dumped in a nearby pond or river. More than 20,000 people could be gassed and cremated each day. Those deemed fit to work were used as slave labor at industrial factories. From 1940-1945, at the Auschwitz complex, 405,000 prisoners became slaves and of these, about 340,000 died through executions, beatings, starvation, and sickness.

LIBERATION

In early 1945, the Nazi regime was tottering. The Soviets pummeled them from the east, and the Allied armies thrashed them from the west. Hitler ordered many of the prisoner camps to relocate from occupied Poland to the deep forests in interior Germany. The prisoners unable to keep up with the evacuation were shot, and many died. Their bodies were left unburied. Some of those who managed to survive the marches were left to starve by German troops, who attempted to escape as Allied troops closed in.

As Allied troops moved across Europe against the Nazis in the spring of 1945, they encountered tens of thousands of concentration camp prisoners. The prisoners who had somehow survived the forced marches were suffering from starvation and disease. Soviet forces were the first to approach a major camp, reaching Majdanek near Lublin, Poland, in July 1944. The rapid Soviet advance surprised the Germans, who demolished the camp in an attempt to hide the evidence of mass murder. Camp staff set fire to the large crematorium, but in the hasty evacuation the gas chambers were left standing. In the summer of 1944, the Soviets also came across the sites of the Belzec, Sobibor, and Treblinka killing centers. The Germans had dismantled these camps in 1943, after most of the Polish Jews had already been killed. The Soviets liberated Auschwitz but found only several thousand gaunt prisoners alive when they entered the camp. There was abundant evidence of mass murder in Auschwitz. The retreating Germans had destroyed most of the warehouses, but in other buildings the Soviets found the victims' personal belongings, such as 348,820 men's suits, 836,255 women's outfits, and 14,000 pounds of human hair.[66]

Liberators confronted unspeakable conditions in the Nazi camps, where piles of corpses lay unburied. Only after the liberation of these camps was the full scope of Nazi horrors exposed to the world. The small percentage of inmates who survived resembled skeletons, the demands of forced labor, lack of food, and months and years of maltreatment took their toll. Many were so weak that they could hardly move. Disease remained an ever-present danger; many camps had to be burned down to prevent the spread of epidemics. Survivors of the camps faced a long and difficult road to recovery.

STORY OF ANNE FRANK: A HOLOCAUST VICTIM

Over one million Jewish children died in the Holocaust, **Anne Frank** was one of them. She gained international fame with publication of her diary after her death. Her diary chronicles her experiences hiding from the Nazis during their occupation of the Netherlands. The following is her story.[67]

Anne was born on June 12, 1929, in Frankfurt, Germany, and lived there for the first five years of her life with her father, Otto, mother, Edith, and older sister, Margot. After the Nazis came to power in 1933, the Frank family fled to Amsterdam in the Netherlands. The Nazis easily conquered the

Netherlands, and occupied Amsterdam in May 1940. For her 13th birthday on June 12, 1942, Anne received as a gift a book she had shown her father in a shop window a few days earlier. Although it was an autograph book with a small lock on the front, Anne decided she would use it as her diary. Anne had dreams of becoming a writer, and that day she began writing in her diary.

In July 1942, German authorities and their Dutch collaborators began to round-up Jews in the Netherlands to send to Auschwitz-Birkenau and Sobibor killing centers in German-occupied Poland. Terrified by this news, the Frank family went into hiding in a secret attic apartment behind the office of the family-owned business at 263 Prinsengracht Street. Anne referred to this place of refuge in her diary as the Secret Annex. Otto Frank's friends and employees had helped to prepare the hiding place and smuggled food and clothing to the Franks at great risk to their own lives. Anne wrote of their dedication and of their efforts to boost the family's morale during the most dangerous of times. All were aware that if caught they could face the death penalty for hiding Jews.

Anne Frank, school photo 1940

Anne spent most of her time reading and studying, but she regularly wrote in her diary. She wrote a narrative of the daily events, and personal entries about her feelings, beliefs and ambitions. As her confidence in her writing grew, she wrote about her belief in God and her thoughts about human nature.

On the morning of August 4, 1944, the Nazis discovered their hiding place after an unknown Dutch caller tipped them off. That same day, they arrested the Franks and soon after they were sent to a transit camp. In September 1944, the Franks boarded a train for a three-day journey to the Auschwitz concentration camp. After unloading from the train, the Nazis forcibly separated the men from the women and children. Anne, her sister and mother were separated from Otto Frank, who would never see his family again. Of the 1,019 passengers on the train, 549—including all children younger than 15—were sent directly to the gas chambers. Anne, who had turned 15 three months earlier, was one of the youngest people to be spared, at least for the time being. She soon realized that most people were gassed upon arrival. She thought that her father, in his 50s and not in very good health, had been killed immediately.

Along with her mother, sister, and the other females not sent to the gas chamber, Anne was forced to strip naked to be disinfected, her head was shaved and she was tattooed with an identifying number on her arm. Anne was assigned to hard labor; by day she hauled rocks and dug rolls of sod. At night, she and fellow female prisoners were crammed into overcrowded barracks. Witnesses later testified that Anne became withdrawn and tearful when she saw children being led to the gas chambers. However, other witnesses reported that more often than not she exhibited strength and courage, and that her outgoing and positive nature allowed her to get extra bread rations for Margot and herself. Disease in the tightly packed, unsanitary compounds was rampant and before long Anne's skin became badly infected by scabies. Guards moved Anne and Margot into a medical wing, which was constantly dark and infested with rats and mice. Edith Frank stopped eating to save every morsel of food for her daughters. She secretly passed food to them through a small hole at the bottom of the infirmary wall.

Anne encountered two long-time female friends who were confined in another part of the camp. The two women both survived the war and later discussed the brief conversations that they had with Anne through a wire fence. They described Anne as bald, gaunt and shivering. Margot at the time was severely ill. Neither of them saw Margot again as she was too weak to leave her bunk. Anne told them that she believed her parents were dead, and for that reason she did not wish to live any longer.

In October 1944, more than 8,000 women, including Anne and Margot, were selected for labor due to their youth and relocated to the Bergen-Belsen camp in northern Germany. Edith Frank was left behind and later died from starvation. In March 1945, tents were put up at the camp to house the new prisoners. As the camp population rose, disease swept through like wildfire. A deadly typhus epidemic killed around 17,000 prisoners. Both Margot and Anne contracted the disease. Witnesses later testified that Margot died from a fall from her bunk. A few days after Margot's death, in March 1945 Anne died from typhus, just a few weeks before British troops liberated the Bergen-Belsen camp on April 15, 1945. In order to prevent the further spread of disease, the British burned the camp. Anne and Margot, along with thousands of others, were buried in a mass grave, the exact whereabouts of which is unknown. Anne's father, Otto, survived the war. Soviet forces liberated Otto at Auschwitz on January 27, 1945.

One of the people who had helped hide the Franks found Anne's diary in the secret apartment after the family's arrest. Anne's father arranged for publication of the diary after the war. Published in many languages, it is read in thousands of middle and high schools in Europe and the Americas. Anne Frank has become a symbol for the lost promise of the children who died in the Holocaust.

Questions to Consider
1. How did you feel after reading about the horrific atrocities of the Holocaust?

RWANDA

"The people whose children had to walk barefoot to school killed the people who could buy shoes for theirs." — a Tutsi teacher

On April 6, 1994, a small private jet flew above Rwanda, a small nation in central Africa. The airplane carried two prominent African leaders—the president of Rwanda Juvenal Habyarimana, and President Cyprien Ntaryamira from the neighboring nation of Burundi. The airplane was about to land at the Kigali International Airport, the location of Rwanda's capital city, when suddenly two missiles streaked into the sky and blasted the plane. The craft shuddered, and then plunged into the presidential palace below. The two men, plus the entire airplane crew, died. The downing of the aircraft was the spark that lit the fuse of the powerful powder keg known as the Rwandan Genocide. The assassinations set in motion a whole chain of fast-paced events that shocked the world. Within an hour of the plane's crash Hutu extremists began carrying out detailed plans to kill the Hutu prime minister, other moderate members of the opposition, and the Tutsi. Over the course of approximately 100 days, from April 6 through mid-July, at least 500,000 people were killed. Most estimates point to a death toll between 800,000 and 1,000,000, as high as 20 percent of the total population.[70]

In 1994, **Rwanda**, a country of about 8 million people, was composed of two main ethnic groups: the Hutu 85 percent of the population and Tutsi 14 percent, while 1 percent included the Twa (or Batwa), one of the indigenous Pygmy groups of central and western Africa. Traditionally, the Hutus were peasant farmers and the Tutsis were cattle owners. As with all African countries, except Ethiopia, in the first part of the 20th century Rwanda was subject to European colonial rule. The Belgians harshly ruled over the country starting in 1918. The Belgians reinforced the idea, largely introduced by Roman Catholic missionaries, that the Hutus were native to Rwanda, and the Tutsis were a superior, more "civilized" people from the north. The Tutsi generally cooperated with the Belgians, who granted them privileges. Even though the Tutsis became the elite in Rwanda, they both shared the same language, Kinyarwanda and French, and intermarried. In Kinyarwanda, Hutu means "servant" and Tutsi means "rich in cattle."

Prior to the 1994 genocide, tension ran high between the Tutsi and Hutu. There were at least five previous mass killings, beginning with the Hutu Revolution in 1959, which changed the country's

Rwanda: The Victim's Story

Domina Nyirandayambaje, born in 1950, lost her husband and three of her children during the genocide. Her husband's killer, Pacifique Mukeshima, was recently released from prison and now lives only a short walk from her own hut. Nyirandayambaje says that she hopes to use the compensation for genocide victims promised by the government to pay her children's school fees.

Domina Nyirandayambaje, Rwanda

"The genocide started in April 1994. My husband and I were hiding, but we were discovered and brought back to our house. We were here three or four weeks and then they killed him on May 19, 1994, with our children. Three of our children died with my husband, and I remained with the other five. Another one fled and we still don't know if he was killed. We had a lot of problems. One day, I was even raped. After the genocide ended, I continued to think about my life, wondering about my physical situation. I went to take an HIV test to make sure that I wasn't infected and I realized things weren't good on that point. The men who raped me died in prison.

When I heard about this reconciliation program, I was convinced I had to forgive because the perpetrators were used by Lucifer. This young man you talked to (the killer of her husband) was strengthened by God and confessed his crimes, and I was no longer doubtful about who killed my husband and I forgave him from my heart. It's time for reconciliation. We can't want to take revenge. I can't wish for them to die. I really pray to God to make it possible for me to live with (the killers), because when I see them and think about my husband and my beloved children that I lost, I ask God to protect me from bad thoughts and for strength so that I can keep on living.

My husband's killer appeared before the *gacaca* and confessed. Before that, he'd already done it in front of the public prosecutors. He's not the only person who killed (my family members). He's the only one who confessed. Some of the others are still in prison, and others have been released. One was released and moved to another town in Rwanda, where he's working. He was released because there wasn't enough evidence, but the prisoner who confessed named him as helping him with the killing.

I don't know about the *gacaca* courts. Except for the man who confessed, the other (people in the community) don't take *gacaca* that seriously. Maybe some will be willing to participate. But a number of people, when they're asked about what happened; they just say they don't know. Maybe if the people who don't want the *gacaca* realize that peace is coming again, they'll change and will become honest and confess. And then by God's power, *gacaca* will reach this goal of reconciliation."

leadership, from Tutsi to Hutu. About one million Tutsis who had fled during these massacres, lived in refugee camps in the neighboring nation of Uganda. Eventually the Tutsi in exile built up an army called the Rwandan Patriotic Front (RPF). Inside Rwanda in the late 1980s and early 1990s, the Hutu-led government encouraged violence against the Tutsis and began training a military. In

Rwanda: The Perpetrator's Story

Pacifique Mukeshima, 20 years old during the 1994 genocide, admits that he killed two people during the bloodletting. After spending seven years in prison, he returned home to his village in May 2003 as part of a program that granted early release to prisoners who have confessed their crimes.[69]

Nyarubuye Church Massacre, Rwanda

"I participated in the genocide. I killed a man's wife—named Karuganda—with one other person. I hit her with a club and the other one with a knife. I also killed a man named Muzigura. I joined a crowd of people at around 2 p.m. These people were shouting loudly, and when I got there I realized they were holding Muzigura. I got a machete from one of the men who were there and then I hit Muzigura, cutting him on the thigh. Another man finally hit Muzigura on the head with a pickaxe and he died. I knew the people I killed. They weren't hidden. One was caught by a crowd of people and the other was sitting outside her house. I got involved, first of all, because of ignorance. Second, people got involved because of the temptation to loot the victims' belongings. Then finally, there were bad authorities who were teaching people that they had to kill their Tutsi enemies. Most people participated. I believe it was because the government kept on encouraging people to kill. Most of my friends were involved.

At the end of the genocide, I fled to Congo. I came back with the help of the UN High Commission for Refugees. They brought me back to Kigali and I was arrested there. There were people who knew me and they denounced me. I was in prison for seven years. I want to thank the organizations, such as the National Unity and Reconciliation Commission, which taught us the importance of confessing. I was convinced that it was important to confess because I became a Christian.

Reconciliation is not possible if there is no truth. Rwandans were the source of this genocide. I killed my fellow Rwandans and so the solution has to come from Rwandans. On April 15, 2000, I decided to confess and apologize for what I did. I was released and sent to the solidarity camp. What they taught us in the camp was wonderful. We were taught how one should behave with those he hurt. One has to go and apologize for the things he did. One has to know how to behave in the presence of survivors. Some don't want to forgive, others forgive easily, and others are still angry. One has to know how to behave in front of these different kinds of people and show in his behavior that he's completely changed.

I came home in May. I appeared before the *gacaca* court, confessed and asked pardon from the victims' relatives. They forgave me. I encouraged other people to confess because reconciliation will not be possible without recognizing one's crimes. Some people claimed reparations for their things, and my parents sold part of our farm in order to pay back what I destroyed. I have no vision for the future. To prepare for the future, you need a foundation or a base. We can ask for aid from the National Unity and Reconciliation Commission to restart our lives. I really hope for nothing.

Human Rights Violations

1990 the RPF, a group composed mostly of Tutsi refugees, invaded Rwanda. The Rwandan Civil War, fought between the Hutu government, with support from other African nations and France, and the RPF, increased ethnic tensions in the country. The Hutu believed that the Tutsi intended to enslave them and, thus, resisted. The Hutu built up stashes of assault rifles, guns, and grenades, along with farm instruments, such as machetes and axes. Egypt and France supplied arms to the Hutu, and they continued to train troops and advise the government on military matters. The Hutu prepared the names and addresses of Tutsis to be targeted in advance. Identity cards indicating ethnicity were issued. Schools separated children, Hutu on one side and Tutsi on the other. The economy was faltering because of low coffee prices, their main export, and corruption, but the Hutu government blamed all the country's ills on the Tutsi.

To peasant farmers with a long memory of past Tutsi misrule, the hysterical propaganda had a powerful effect. The local print and radio news media played a central role in fanning the hatred leading to the genocide, while the international media either ignored or seriously misinterpreted events on the ground. Due to high rates of illiteracy, radio was an important way for the government to deliver messages to the public. Two key radio stations stirred up violence before and during the genocide. One of the stations, Radio Rwanda, repeatedly broadcast a message warning that Tutsi would attack Hutu, a message local officials used to convince Hutu they needed to protect themselves by attacking first.

News of the airplane crash spread quickly. UN commander Lieutenant General Romeo Dallaire was watching television in his residence in Kigali when he was alerted to the crash. Dallaire was in Rwanda to help negotiate the peace accords between the Rwandan government and the RPF. Dallaire rushed to a local military barracks, where a group of Hutu generals had already claimed authority over the country. Dallaire reminded the generals that the lawful leader of Rwanda was the prime minister. They laughed.[71]

In the next 24 hours, the Hutu generals gunned down specific moderate politicians, many of them Hutu, who favored the peace accords with the RPF. Hutu assassins surrounded the Hutu Prime Minister, Uwilingiyimana and her family in an UN compound, then shot them. They next took ten Belgian soldiers, who were part of her escort, prisoner and hacked them to death with machetes. The Belgian government pulled out its remaining peacekeepers, just as the perpetrators had planned. Western nations removed their nationals from Kigali and abandoned their embassies in the initial stages of the violence, leaving Dallaire's meager UN force alone to face the genocide.[72]

Samuel Ndagijimana worked as an orderly in a brick hospital connected to a church complex in the countryside of Rwanda. He recalled the horrible events he witnessed there. As tensions mounted many Tutsi sought refuge in the church. More than 2,000 refugees crowded onto the church grounds with Hutu soldiers forming a tight ring around them. Many of the refugees had just fled horrifying massacres and knew their upcoming fate. The Tutsi ministers sent notes to the Hutu leaders begging for mercy. The Hutu leaders callously responded "You will be eliminated. You must die." Another message announced that the killings would begin the next day promptly at nine o'clock. The Hutu killers kept their word. At the appointed hour soldiers piled out of trucks and began firing guns and flinging grenades into the gathered crowd of Tutsis. Some of the Tutsi had collected rocks, bricks, and sticks in a feeble attempt to fend off the attackers. "But they proved useless," remembered a survivor.[73]

Another massacre occurred at the countryside village of Nyarubuye. On April 12, 1994 more than 1,500 Tutsis sought refuge in a Catholic church. Local militia acting with the priest and other local authorities used bulldozers to knock down the church building. People who tried to escape were hacked to death with machetes or shot. Local priest Athanase Seromba was later found guilty of the crime of genocide and sentenced to life in prison for his role in the atrocities.

Journalist Fergal Keane and a news crew visited the church in Nyarubuye, which served as a gathering place for hundreds of Tutsi just weeks before. Keene described seeing a white marble statue of Christ and fluttering above a banner celebrating Easter, but below the bodies of the victims rotted in the heat. He described the remains of men, women, and children strewn along the paths of the grounds, either hacked to death by machetes or exploded by grenades. He painted a picture of horror, fear, pain, and abandonment etched onto the dead faces. "Here the dead have no dignity" he wrote. Other Tutsi had fled into the church where bodies lay between pews and another pile lay at the foot of the statue of the Virgin Mary. The dead were left unburied at Nyarubuye as a memorial.[74] Their bodies, now skeletons, are a vivid reminder of unspeakable crimes humans have inflicted upon fellow humans.

You are probably asking yourself: "How could the killers commit such acts?" One witness later described how groups cleverly pressured and then forced others to join them: "Everyone was called to hunt the enemy," the witness said. "But let's say someone is reluctant. Say that guy comes with a stick. They tell him, 'No, get a *masu*' (a stick studded with nails). So, he does, and he runs along with the rest, but he doesn't kill. Everyone must help to kill at least one person.' So this person who is not a killer is made to do it. And the next day it's become a game for him. You don't need to keep pushing him."[75]

Once the killing began, the troops encouraged or forced other Hutus to take part, even to kill members of their own families. Even though some Hutus hid their Tutsi relatives, friends and neighbors, hundreds of thousands joined in the butchery. Many of the perpetrators were members of the militia and unemployed youth, but all members of society, including teachers, journalists, priests, ministers, and doctors took part in the carnage. The message was: "Either you took part in the massacres or you were massacred."[76]

Human skulls at the Nyamata Memorial Site, Rwanda

The killing took place everywhere and openly—in people's houses, on the street, at roadblocks, and some of the worst massacres took place in churches. In a church north of Kigali, 1,200 people were slaughtered in a single day. The method of killing people sheltered inside buildings was to toss in grenades and then shoot or hack people to death as they ran out. The perpetrators used the Kagera River as a place to dump corpses. They killed thousands on the banks and then heaved the bodies into the swift currents. Grisly photographs show the bloated corpses washed into shallows or caught in reeds or rocks.

The Hutu especially targeted Tutsi women during the genocide. They portrayed the Tutsi women as sexual weapons that the Tutsi men would use to weaken and ultimately destroy the Hutu men.

Gender-based propaganda included cartoons printed in newspapers depicting Tutsi women as sex objects.[77] The perpetrators of war rape were mainly members of the Hutu militia, military soldiers of the Rwandan Armed Forced (RAF), including the Presidential Guard, and civilians. Perpetrators did not spare pregnant women from sexual violence. Men who knew they were HIV positive raped many women, possibly with the intention to pass on the HIV virus to Tutsi women and their families.[78] Rwanda is a patriarchal society, where children take the ethnicity of the father. Therefore, the social disgrace attached to rape meant that some husbands left wives who had been raped, or that potential husbands considered the rape victims unsuitable for marriage. The long-term effects of war rape for the victims included social isolation, unwanted pregnancies and babies. Some women felt they had to perform self-induced abortion. Sexually transmitted diseases were also widespread, including syphilis, gonorrhea and HIV/AIDS. Estimates show that 2,000 – 5,000 pregnancies resulted from war rape.[79]

Scholar Jared Diamond in his book *Collapse: How Societies Choose to Fail or Succeed* offers an interesting theory as to why the genocide took place in Rwanda. He accepts some of the factors that helped lead to the genocide including the Hutu fears of the Tutsi that grew out of the long history of Tutsi domination, various Tutsi-led invasions of Rwanda, Tutsi mass killings of Hutu, and the murder of individual Hutu political leaders in neighboring Burundi. Those Hutu fears increased in 1993.[80] But Diamond has added another factor to the list of causes that contributed to genocide. Diamond states that the usual reasons for the genocide in Rwanda do not answer the question: "How, under those circumstances, were so many Rwandans so readily manipulated by extremist leaders into killing each other with the utmost savagery? If it was just ethnic hatred, why did Hutus kill other Hutus, an estimated 5 percent of the Hutu population had been killed by its own members."[81] Diamond argues that population pressures, a factor ignored by most sources, was one of the important contributors to the genocide.

Rwanda and neighboring Burundi are the two of the most densely populated countries in Africa, and among the most densely populated in the world. In 1990 the average population in Rwanda was 760 people per square mile, higher than that of the United Kingdom at 610 and approaching that of the Netherlands at 950. But, unlike the Netherlands, Rwanda has carried on its traditional agricultural methods and failed to institute effective family planning. To feed a growing population, farmers cleared forests and drained marshes to gain new farmland, while also adding an extra two or three consecutive crop plantings in fields within one year. Forest clearance led to drying-up of streams and more irregular rainfall. In 1989 there were severe food shortages resulting from a drought brought on by a combination of regional and global climate change plus effects of deforestation.[82] High population densities translated into very small Rwandan farms that continued to decrease in size as the population grew. The average-size farm in one of the farming districts was .72 acre. Farmers further divided each farm on average into 10 separate parcels, so that they were tilling absurdly small parcels averaging only .07 acre in 1993.[83]

Since all the farmland was already tilled, young people found it difficult to marry, leave home, acquire a farm, and set up their own household. Increasingly, young people postponed marriage and continued to live at home with their parents. For example, in the 20-25 year old age bracket, the percentage of young women living at home between 1988 and 1993 rose from 39 percent to 67 percent, and the percentage of young men rose from 71 percent to 100 percent. By 1993, not a single man in his early 20s lived independently of his parents, contributing to the deadly family tensions that erupted in 1994.[84] Not surprisingly, it proved impossible for most people in Rwanda to feed themselves on so little land. The percentage of the population consuming less than 1600 calories per day, considered below the famine level, which was 9 percent in 1982 and 40 percent in 1990. Conflict between families escalated. The most painful and socially disruptive land disputes were those pitting fathers against sons. These conflicts over land harmed family ties, and turned close relatives into competitors and bitter enemies.[85]

The situation of constant and growing conflict forms the background against which the 1994 killings took place. But even before 1994, Rwanda experienced rising levels of violence and theft, committed especially by hungry, landless young people without off-farm income. High population densities and worsening starvation were associated with more crime.[86] Not surprisingly, many victims of violence were large landowners, a majority of them men over the age of 50. Another victim category was young men and children, particularly those from poor backgrounds, who were driven by fear to enlist in the warring militias. The largest number of victims were half-starved people or very poor people with little or no land. The 1994 events provided a unique opportunity to settle scores or to reshuffle land properties, even among Hutu villagers. Diamond observes that "It is not rare, even today, to hear Rwandans argue that a war is necessary to wipe out an excess population and to bring numbers into line with the available land resources." Gerard Prunier, a scholar of East Africa, points out: "The decision to kill was made by politicians, for political reasons. But at least part of the reason why it was carried out so thoroughly by the ordinary rank-and-file peasants in their family compound was the feeling that there were too many people on too little land, and that with a reduction in their numbers, there would be more for the survivors."[87]

Diamond is quick to point out that population pressure was not the single cause of the Rwandan genocide. Other factors did contribute. Those other factors included Rwanda's history of Tutsi domination of Hutu, Tutsi killings of Hutu, outside Tutsi invasions of Rwanda, Rwanda's economic crisis, especially falling coffee prices, drought, desperate young Rwandan men displaced as refugees into settlement camps, and competition among Rwanda's rival political groups willing to stoop to anything to retain power.[88] All of these factors, including population pressure, interacted to contribute to the horrific genocide.

The Rwandan government published the official figure for the number of victims of the genocide at 1,174,000 in 100 days (10,000 murdered every day, 400 every hour, 7 every minute). Other sources put the death toll closer to 800,000, 20 percent of whom were Hutus. About 300,000 Tutsis survived the genocide. Thousands of widows, many of whom were raped, are now HIV-positive. There are about 400,000 orphans and nearly 85,000 of them have become heads of families.[89]

When the genocide spent its furor and refugees returned, the government began the long-awaited genocide trials at the end of 1996. In 2001, the government began implementing a participatory justice system, known as *Gacaca*, in order to address the enormous backlog of cases. In these courts, the convicted are invited to admit their guilt in exchange for significant reductions in their sentences. In the meantime, the UN set up the International Criminal Tribunal for Rwanda (ICTR). In 1998, the ICTR made the landmark decisions that rape warfare is, in fact, a crime of genocide. It was an important addition to the term's legal definition and a judgment that could be important in future ICC actions.[90]

The U.S. government was reluctant to become involved in the "local conflict" in Rwanda and refused to label the killings as "genocide," a decision which then-president Bill Clinton later came to regret. In March 1998, on a visit to Rwanda, U.S. President Bill Clinton spoke to the crowd assembled on the tarmac at Kigali Airport: "We come here today partly in recognition of the fact that we in the United States and the world community did not do as much as we could have and should have done to try to limit what occurred" in Rwanda. Four years after the genocide, Clinton issued the "Clinton apology," acknowledging his failure to efficiently deal with the situation in Rwanda, but not formally apologizing for inaction by the U.S. government or the international community. In an interview Clinton stated that he believes if he had sent 5,000 U.S. peacekeepers, more than 500,000 lives could have been saved.[91]

Questions to Consider
1. If Jared Diamond's theory has merit, how would you have solved the problem of population pressures in Rwanda in order to avoid the genocide?
2. Why do you think the international community didn't become involved in the Rwanda genocide?

As Martin Nielmoeller stated at the beginning of this chapter, being aware of human rights violations is the first step in helping to stop these atrocities. If we are more aware of the abuses, as in those examined in this chapter, we are more likely to take a stand in preventing outbreaks of human rights violations.

Chapter Four

Case Studies of Human Rights Abuses

"Truth resides in every human heart, and one has to search for it there, and to be guided by truth as one sees it. But no one has a right to coerce others to act according to his own view of truth."

— *Mohandas Gandhi*

Cases Studies of Human Rights Abuses

This chapter presents different case studies of human rights abuses. They range from 19th century events to recent abuses. They are arranged in a loose chronological order and different geographic locations.

The Zulu of South Africa

The **Zulu** is the largest South African ethnic group, with a population of 10-11 million people living mainly in a province in South Africa. Their language, Zulu, is a Bantu language. **Shaka** (c.1787-1828), a powerful and controversial leader in Zulu history, took over the Zulu Empire in 1816 and has been called a military genius, innovator and reformer, but has also been condemned for the brutality of his reign. The Zulu king still continues to cast a long shadow over the history of southern Africa.

I have included Shaka in this section of case studies of human rights abuses because some historians accuse him of carrying out genocide. But genocide is a difficult accusation to make. While some would claim that Shaka at the time was guilty of genocide, others would claim that he was a brave warrior. What is the truth? One's perspective certain bears heavily on how events are interpreted.

Between 1810 and 1828, the Zulu kingdom under the leadership of Shaka waged a determined campaign of expansion and annihilation in the region. Zulu armies laid waste to huge swathes of present-day South Africa and Zimbabwe. Central to Shaka's power was the army in which young men from across the kingdom served under Shaka's direct command. By carefully building a warrior culture, he purposely created a climate of discipline and obedience. He rewarded individuals who displayed exceptional courage but executed those accused of weakness. He directed the military reviews that followed successful campaigns, in which the "cowards" were publicly stabbed to death. Executions for breaking rules of etiquette were a feature of daily life in Shaka's court. He immediately condemned individuals for offenses such as sneezing when he was talking, or making him laugh when he wanted to be serious. Victims were often clubbed to death and their bodies left for the vultures, which came to be known as "the king's birds." Although the number of individuals killed in this manner was probably small, it served to intimidate the opposition and to show the king had terrifying power.[1]

Zulu armies aimed at totally destroying their enemies. Those exterminated included whole armies, as well as prisoners of war, women, children, and even dogs. His armies used the especially brutal method of impaling their enemies. According to a foreign witness, Shaka was determined not to leave alive even a child, but to wipe out the whole tribe.[2]

In 1827, Shaka's mother Nandi died. The king used his personal grief to launch an extensive political purge and even personally attacked and killed those who broke the mourning rules or were deemed insufficiently grief-stricken. In this mourning period Shaka ordered that no crops should be planted the following year, no milk (the basis of the Zulu diet) was to be consumed, and any woman who became pregnant was to be killed along with her husband. Even cows were slaughtered so that their calves would know what losing a mother felt like. One contemporary British observer estimated that during the mass panic at the funeral ceremonies alone, as many as 7,000 people died from dehydration and exhaustion, although this is probably an exaggeration.[3] Following Shaka's erratic behavior after his mother's death, his half-brothers made at least two assassination attempts; one succeeded in 1828.

At the time of his death, Shaka ruled over 250,000 people and could quickly assemble more than

50,000 warriors. His 10-year-long kingship resulted in a huge number of deaths, many of which occurred during mass tribal migrations to escape rival armies. The European invasion of these regions, which began shortly after, was greatly assisted by the upheaval and depopulation caused by the Zulu assault.

Little historical evidence was left to bear testimony to the terror. But it remains alive in the oral tradition of the people whose ancestors were subjugated, slaughtered, or fled the Zulus. It appears that Shaka practiced a gender-selective killing plan that is rather unusual. When Shaka conquered the Butelezi clan, for example, he utterly demolished them as a separate tribal body by bringing all their men into his own clan. But he also destroyed women, infants, and the elderly, whom he deemed useless for his expansionist purposes.[4]

The question remains: were the policies of Shaka genocide? At first glance, the answer seems to be yes, but looking more deeply it may not be so clear. One thing our study of genocide teaches us is that events are not always black or white; there are usually shades of gray. The theory of the **Mfecane** makes the case that the forceful expansion of Shaka's armies caused a brutal chain reaction of widespread chaos and warfare among indigenous communities across southern Africa during the period between 1815-1840, as homeless tribes turned on their neighbors in a deadly cycle of violence and conquest. Scholars note that stories of cannibalism, raiding, burning of villages or mass slaughter were based on the clearly documented accounts of hundreds of victims and refugees. But why did this violence occur? According to the evil man theory, Shaka was the monster responsible for the devastation. Zulu sources are sometimes critical of Shaka, and numerous negative images abound in Zulu oral history.

King Shaka's reputation has undoubtedly suffered at the hands of the European colonials and apartheid regimes that displaced Zulu authority—and for whom Shaka became a symbol of savagery, indirectly justifying European interference in the region. But some scholars claim the evil man theory must be treated with caution. They say the discrediting of Shaka is based on the need of apartheid era historians to justify the apartheid regime's racist policies. Many agree that he certainly was dictatorial, ruthless, and used terrorist tactics; however, the popular image of Shaka as personally bloodthirsty, mentally unstable and a perpetrator of genocide is not supported by contemporary evidence.[5] Some scholars hold that it generally neglects several other factors, such as the impact of white settlers expanding into Zulu territory, slave trading and environmental factors. These scholars say this twisting of the historical record by apartheid supporters was a way to cover their exploitative tracks.[6]

Artist's drawing of King Shaka

Historian Julian Cobbing challenged the theory of the Mfecane in the 1980s. He did not deny that major upheavals had taken place over much of southern Africa in the 1820s and 1830s. Yet, his argument was that the wars and migrations of the period had primarily been caused by the impact of European colonial settlement expansion, European slave traders, and commerce in southern Africa, not solely by the ravages of Zulu armies. Cobbing went on to say that the Mfecane theory was simply wrong.[7] One critic of Cobbing's theory is historian Elizabeth Eldredge, who claims that Cobbing ignored the key roles played by forceful leaders like Shaka. She challenged Cobbing's theory on the grounds that the European slave trade was not dominant enough at the time of the Mfecane to have had any meaningful influence. She argues that placing the fault entirely on the Zulus was instead a result of heavily biased analysis.

Other historians challenge the suggestions that Zulu aggression caused the Mfecane, citing archaeological evidence which shows that drought and environmental decline led to increased competition for land and water, which forced the migration of farmers and cattle herders throughout the region. The population increased in Zululand with the introduction of maize (corn) from the Americas. Although maize produced more food than indigenous grasses on the same land and helped sustain a larger population, it also required more water. By the end of the 1700s much of the farmable land was in use. Declining rainfall and a 10-year drought in the early 1800s meant that a battle for land and water resources began. The tribal warfare of the Mfecane was highly successful in areas weakened by overpopulation and overgrazing.[8] I would argue that a balanced view of the Mfecane is needed. The Zulu expansion was a major factor; it seems clear that aggressive Zulu military activities sparked a tremendous uproar of change. But other factors need to be added into the mix, such as environmental decline, population pressures, new corn crops, and European colonial advances and some slave trading.

The figure of Shaka still sparks interest not only among contemporary Zulu. But his legacy remains unclear; he defies simplistic portrayal. Currently, popular film and other media glorify him and have certainly contributed to his appeal. There is even a theme park called Shakaland in South Africa. Against this glorification must be balanced the devastation and destruction that he wrought.[9]

> **Questions to Consider**
> 1. Do you think that Shaka was guilty of genocide? Explain.
> 2. What impact does bias contribute to determining if genocide has been committed?

THE DEMOCRATIC REPUBLIC OF THE CONGO

The **Democratic Republic of the Congo** (DRC) is a country located in Central Africa with a population of just over 66 million people. The capital is Kinshasa, and the official language is French. It is often confused with its neighbor, the Republic of Congo. Through its history it has been known as Zaire, the Congo Free State, and the Belgian Congo. The country is a vast territory, which if superimposed on a map of the U.S. would stretch from the Atlantic Ocean to the Mississippi River. The Congo straddles the equator and receives annual rainfall in some areas as high as 80 inches (2,032 mm) or more. It has the highest frequency of thunderstorms in the world. Thus, it is able to sustain the second largest rain forest in the world, after that of the Amazon.

This story of the DRC starts with European exploration of the region that took place from the 1870s until the 1920s. Sir Henry Morton Stanley, an Englishmen, first undertook exploration of the region under the sponsorship of **King Leopold II** of Belgium. On several expeditions Stanley explored the Congo River and laid the groundwork for a commercial state. Desperate for a colony, Leopold set his sights on the huge land mass in central Africa, what would become the Congo. From the 1870s onward, Leopold schemed his way to dominating the Congo River basin. He formally acquired rights to the territory at the Conference of Berlin in 1885, where the European colonial powers staked their claims to African colonies—of course, without input from Africans. He made the land his private property and ironically named it the Congo Free State, which he ruled until 1908.[10]

Leopold was motivated by a desire to add wealth and luster to Belgium's dynasty and by extension to Belgium itself. He stated that Belgium must have a colony, but the country lagged behind Great Britain, France, Germany, Spain, and the U.S. in the colonial acquisition race. He regarded colonies as essential for two reasons. First, colonies would be a source of cheap raw materials that would lower the costs of production and make Belgian industry more competitive. Second, colonies would support middle class investment and careers in the form of clerks, administrators, and military officers.

The exploitation of the Congo began in earnest with the take-off of the ivory and rubber trades after 1889. The booming demand for rubber and soaring prices sealed the fate of the Congolese people. Europe consumed all the rubber Congo produced. To aid production, the Belgian government began various infrastructure projects, such as construction of a railway that ran from the coast to the capital of Leopoldville (now Kinshasa). It took years to complete. The goal for Leopold and his associates in nearly all the projects was to increase the money they could extract from the colony. Leopold even extracted the vast mineral resources of the Congo to add to his own personal jewelry box. Arguably, King Leopold II subjected the Congolese people to the worst excesses and exploitation of modern European colonialism.

The colonists brutalized the Congolese people to produce rubber. The milky latex sap found in rubber trees grew wild in the Congo River basin, and the Belgians wanted lots of rubber, which was primarily used in the manufacture of bicycle and automobile tires. Although rubber was plentiful, the problem was how to harvest it cheaply. Slavery was outlawed; therefore, a system to coerce native people to work to collect rubber was needed. Since no one in their right mind wanted to work long, difficult hours under harsh conditions just to get rubber for the Belgians, the plan would have to be brutally and rigidly enforced. The plan imposed a general tax on the Congolese people. On the surface, this plan seems nonthreatening; after all, we all pay taxes. But it proved to be more sinister as the details unfolded. First, to pay taxes the Congolese people needed money. Since most of the people were subsistence farmers who lived in self-sufficient villages, they had no need for Belgian money or no way to obtain it. Therefore, they had to pay the taxes with their labor or in certain goods. Conveniently, the Belgian government had them pay their taxes with the rubber they collected. The government also conscripted their labor for special infrastructure projects, such as road building, harbor construction and general maintenance of transportation networks. Often these taxes were levied on chiefs or village headmen who supplied slaves (although supposedly illegal) to the Belgian state. The Belgians shipped the rubber to Europe to be molded into new products for the insatiable consumer market.

Armed with police powers and the profit motive, the rubber industry devised ways to acquire even more rubber. The government hired agents to set collection quotas for villages. The agents rounded up and transported workers to rubber vine regions where they collected almost nine pounds of dry latex every two weeks, an almost impossible task. As latex supplies dwindled from reckless over-harvesting, enforcement agents resorted to even harsher methods to meet their quotas. The agents forced men to bring their wives and children to work alongside them. The agents also kidnapped and held hostage women and children in order to force the men to work without pay as rubber-harvesters. The hostages would not be released until the men brought in the required rubber quota. Failure to meet the quota meant flogging, jail, or, in extreme cases, execution.

The agents implemented even harsher techniques to get more rubber. The most scandalous practices were limb amputations—cutting off hands and feet. Evidence mounted that agents slashed the workers' bodies as punishment for failing to meet rubber quotas or other infractions. Even more common was a whipping with the fearsome *chicotte*, a thick whip made of hippopotamus hide fashioned into a corkscrew shape with edges as hard as wood and as sharp as knives.

The Congolese population declined appreciably during Leopold's rule. A shocking number of people died—approximately 10 million, more than in the Holocaust during World War II. Estimates vary but some put it at 60 percent or more in certain areas. Famine, pestilence, diseases, crop destruction, overwork, hunger, and unsanitary conditions killed millions. During these years of intense rubber harvesting, the area was stripped of much of its exposed natural resources and thousands of Africans were conscripted into a monstrous system of forced labor. Leopold's rule resulted in a deterioration in the conditions of daily life for the Congolese. Author Joseph Conrad wrote *The Heart of Darkness* in 1902 about conditions in central Africa. Under King Leopold, the Congo became the heart of imperial darkness.

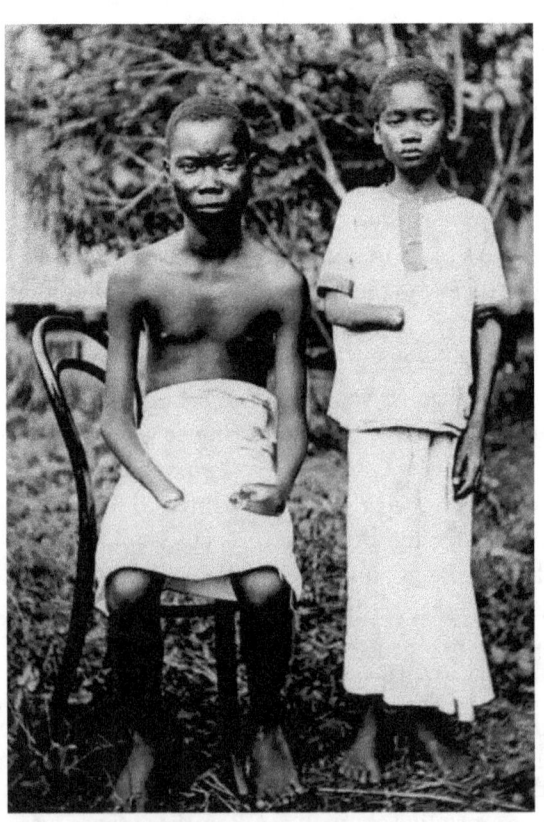
Child victims of Belgian atrocities

Despite initial reluctance, finally the Belgian parliament in 1908 responded to international pressure, especially from Great Britain, to end the atrocities of King Leopold II. It took over the area they called the Belgian Congo, and the elected Belgian government administered it.

The Belgian Congo achieved independence on June 30, 1960, and it became the Republic of Congo. Patrice Lumumba led the Congo independence movement and became the new Prime Minister. But shortly after he was sworn into office, he was overthrown in a military coup, and then in 1961 kidnapped and executed. The U.S. and Belgium both supported the coup. The Congo has vast mineral wealth, in particular copper and diamonds, and both countries wanted a hand in obtaining its wealth. Also, the U.S. at the time was supporting very questionable leaders, usually unelected military dictators, around the world as long as they took a stand against communism.

For five tumultuous years, leadership changed hands in the Congo until **Joseph Mobutu** strong-armed his way to power in a bloodless military coup in 1965. Because of his staunch anti-communist stance, Mobutu had the support of the U.S. for his 31½ year reign. In 1971 he renamed the country the Republic of Zaire. While in office he formed a totalitarian regime and regularly tortured or murdered rivals. He notoriously mismanaged the country's economy and diverted money from the sale of natural resources for his own and his supporters' personal enrichment. He presided over three decades of using the revenue from the state's mining monopoly as his own personal piggy bank. Mobutu almost single-handedly destroyed his country's economy, which was one of Africa's best in the 1960s. In 1984, his personal fortune amounted to $5 billion (US), stashed in safe Swiss bank accounts. He owned a fleet of Mercedes-Benz cars that he traveled in between his numerous palaces, while the nation's roads crumbled and many people starved. While his impoverished citizens looked on, he bragged to *60 Minutes* (US news program) in 1984 that he was the world's second-richest man. Two years later, at the White House, President Reagan praised Mobutu as a useful Cold War ally, "a voice of good sense and goodwill." Many Congolese will never forget those words.[11]

During his reign Mobutu regularly met and had the support of U.S. presidents, but relations cooled after the collapse of the Soviet Union in 1991. Through the 1990s a cry for democratic reform swept the country. Although Mobutu promised reform and free elections, he failed to carry through with his promises. By 1996, Mobutu's rule was weakening and tension with his neighbors was mounting. He essentially replaced the country's formal, mineral-based economy with an utterly corrupt machine. When Mobutu resigned, the network of graft he left behind easily shifted into a minerals-based war economy run by its own army, invaders, rebels, and warlords.[12]

The First Congo War (1996 to 1997) claimed more than 200,000 causalities, mostly civilians, although it got little world news coverage. The war ended when rebel forces backed by foreign powers such as Uganda and Rwanda overthrew Mobutu. Rebel leader Laurent-Désiré Kabila declared himself president and changed the name of the nation back to Democratic Republic of the Congo. However, Kabila also failed to carry out democratic reforms, and charges of corruption against him were allegedly comparable to those committed by Mobutu. Pro-democratic reformers turned against him and in 2001 he was assassinated. His son, Joseph, became president ten days later, elected in 2006 and reelected in 2011 for a second term. He continues to preside over the country at the time of this writing.[13]

Following the First Congo War was the more deadly **Second Congo War** (1998-2003). The war, known as the African World War or the Great War of Africa, devastated the country and involved seven foreign armies. Despite peace accords in 2003, fighting continues in eastern Congo where the prevalence of rape and other sexual violence is beyond description.[14] The war is the largest in modern African history and directly involved eight African nations—Rwanda, Zimbabwe, Uganda, Burundi, Angola, Chad, Sudan, and Namibia—as well as about 25 armed groups. By 2008, the war and its aftermath had killed 5.4 million people, mostly from disease and starvation, making the Second Congo War the deadliest world conflict since World War II.[15] The war drew in Congo's neighbors, as foreign armies and rebel groups fought for control of the country's rich natural resources. The conflict wrecked infrastructure already weakened by decades of neglect and displaced millions more from their homes or they sought asylum in neighboring countries. A 2003 peace agreement brokered a transitional government, and multi-party elections were held in 2006, won by Joseph Kabila.[16]

The Congo is a resource rich country. The Belgian Royal Institute of Natural Sciences in Brussels houses about a thousand of Congo's mineral varieties. Congo's soil has every mineral known to humankind: 10 percent of the copper; 30 percent of the cobalt; and 80 percent of the coltan. From 1998 – 2001, coltan was the most desired mineral and the U.S. was the world's number one importer—until China took that number one spot in 2002. Engineers use coltan in everything from PlayStations and iPods to magnets, cutting tools, and jet engines. Congo has untold quantities of

CASE STUDIES OF HUMAN RIGHTS ABUSES

bauxite and zinc, cadmium and uranium, gold and diamonds. Cassiterite, a derivative of tin that is also used by the electronics and computer industries, has become the most coveted Congolese mineral (ironically it makes devices more eco-friendly). Additional minerals that are in high demand include tin, tantalum and tungsten used in cell phones, iPods and digital cameras.[17] Tin is used to solder circuit boards in cell phones and laptops. Tantalum, derived from coltan, is an ingredient in batteries in cell phones, videogame consoles and laptops. Tungsten, from wolframite, vibrates cell phones.[18]

What has caused this horrible crisis that most people in the Western world know very little, if anything, about? Although the most obvious answer is corruption, graft, and greedy repressive dictators, the reason goes beyond misrule. The Congo's treasure trove of valuable minerals is the country's greatest blessing and most lasting curse. The Congo should be one of the world's richest countries if the government honestly distributed all the mineral wealth to its citizens evenly. But it doesn't.

Rebels have occupied two entire eastern provinces, where the bulk of minerals are mined. Congo's national army has become a partner in treachery and cooperates in the illegal trade. Local forced laborers, many of whom the rebels hold at gunpoint, extract the minerals. There are approximately 1.5 million "diggers" in the Congo, black-market miners, many of them indentured to Chinese middlemen and financiers. These diggers currently produce about 75 percent of the minerals exported, mostly by clawing for nuggets with pickaxes or their bare hands. The minerals are loaded onto 30-ton flatbed trucks and smuggled to China on cargo ships via South African or Tanzanian ports or through trading houses through Rwanda and Burundi and on to Western or Asian buyers.[19]

Gold mining in the Congo

This trade in minerals is fueling the conflict in eastern Congo. Armed groups control many of the mines and force individual miners to pay "taxes" on the minerals they mine. Illegal mining funds militias who purchase weapons used to kill, loot and rape their way across eastern Congo.[20] Ongoing, rampant smuggling and corruption continue at all stages of the mining process, while the state took in a paltry $32 million in 2006.[21] Without a strong central government or professional army, illegal operations have treated Congo's riches as an all-you-can-eat buffet.

Following the "blood diamonds" campaign in Sierra Leone, there is an effort underway to show how the minerals or diamonds have been mined. A Congolese representative pointed out that while blood diamonds might be better known, there was also "blood copper," "blood gold," and "blood cobalt."[22] If all such exports were properly sourced and monitored, corporations and state enterprises would not buy "blood minerals" and there would be no reason for militias to go to war to acquire them. Human rights activists are encouraging U.S. companies selling products using columbite-tantalite, cassiterite, wolframite or derivatives of these minerals to disclose the country of origin of these minerals.[23]

Few people in the Democratic Republic of the Congo (DRC) have been unaffected by the armed conflict. A survey conducted in 2009 by the International Council of the Red Cross (ICRC) shows that 76 percent of the people interviewed have been affected in some way—either personally or due to the wider consequences of armed conflict.[24] The long and brutal conflict has caused massive suffering for civilians with frequent breaches of humanitarian and human rights law. Even though the UN supports a 17,000-strong peacekeeping mission, it is spread very thin across the vast territory.[25] In 2009 people in the Congo were dying at a rate of 45,000 per month, and 2,700,000 people have died since 2004 due to widespread disease and famine. Children under the age of five are the hardest hit, accounting for nearly half of all deaths despite making up 19 percent of the population. They are especially susceptible to diseases like malaria, measles, dysentery, and typhoid, which can kill when medicine is not available.[26]

Rape has been a tool of war throughout human history, but rarely in modern times has its practitioners been so brutal and random. Sexual assault victims as young as 3 and as old as 67 turn up in clinics to seek medical treatment from vicious attacks. Five-year-old Antoinetta Borauzema peeked out from behind her hands as she told visitors at the Heal Africa's Children program of her recent abduction and rape by an armed man. "They dragged two of us into the bush. He lay on top of me. It hurt." A doctor at the shelter said Antoinetta likely would need surgery and plenty of psychological counseling to help her grow into a secure, loving and confident adult. Doctors say girls and boys have survived appalling violence, attacks that will affect them for the rest of their lives. Some rebel groups prey upon children when they are alone in the fields or even snatch them from the arms of screaming parents. Children who survive traumatic sexual experiences have problems in adulthood. Boys are more likely to become sexual predators, while girls may turn to prostitution even before they have grown into adults.[27]

Gang rape has replaced looting and pillaging as the chosen weapon of social terror because it demoralizes families, villages and tribes. Throughout the area, women are afraid to work in the fields or gather firewood from the jungle, even in a group. Soldiers have even carried away women and girls to be used as sex slaves.[28] Ugenimana Dometile, 65, has bad eyes and a deeply wrinkled face. She should be commanding respect in her community, where the life expectancy is just 48. Instead, two militiamen raped her and left her for dead. In an interview at a shelter she told her story: "They broke into our house and looted everything. I tried to run away, but I fell and so they caught me." She now mostly sits on the front porch of the shelter or looks after abandoned children who are the unwanted results of rapes.[29]

The damage done to the victims is far more than physical. Like in Darfur, the victim is blamed in rape cases, and many Congolese men shun their wives for being raped, saying they must send them away because the women have been "unfaithful." Many rape victims are afraid to return to their villages for fear of being shunned or sent away, a near death sentence in a culture where family is of central importance.

The lack of punishment is a big problem, but the Congo's police force and national army face great obstacles in catching the perpetrators, let alone bringing them to justice: evidence is rarely gathered, judges are bought off, and courts are delayed in backlog cases. In a country where more than 80 percent live below the poverty line, many women simply cannot afford the time or $40 court fee for a trial. In addition, women must be able to name and identify their attackers, which is often impossible if the rapist was a soldier or rebel. Victims also risk public shaming by merely discussing sex and violence. Meanwhile, scores of women and children gather at places of refuge, such as those run by Heal Africa, a Christian group that provides medical and social recovery at seven centers in eastern Congo. Although no one knows for sure how many women are rape victims, the UN estimates that 200,000 women have been raped in the past decade and that 40 are raped each day, just in the eastern region of the Congo.[30]

The aftermath of the war has gutted the country. Paradoxically, over a century of exploitation of this mineral-rich laden country has left the Congolese people one of the poorest in the world. About 80 percent of Congo's inhabitants live on 50 cents a day. The gross domestic product per capita is about $300, or less than a dollar a day.[31] The Congo remains a humanitarian tragedy and a place of gross human rights violations.

> **Questions to Consider**
> 1. What is the responsibility of the international community in solving the multiple problems in the Congo? Who needs to be involved? Why hasn't more been done already?

ARMENIA

The glorious Ottoman Empire in the 1500s stretched along the coast of North Africa, into southern Europe, and across the heart of the Middle East to the Persian Gulf. Its capital was Istanbul (formerly Constantinople), an ancient city on the Bosporus Strait that stood as a gateway between Europe and Asia. Generally, the Ottoman Turks were tolerant of the many different people they ruled; each had its own culture and language. There were Jews, Christians, and Muslims, which was the predominate religion in the empire. The Christian **Armenians** had lived for over 2,000 years in the rugged mountains of central Asia, in what is now eastern Turkey. Because the harsh landscape and long winters isolated the Armenians from outside invaders, they were able to keep their language, culture, and identity intact.[32]

Armenia prospered over time, and a middle class emerged that played a role in commerce and trade. Even though they were officially second-class citizens, the Ottoman Turks both envied and distrusted the Armenians because they held so much commercial power. As the Ottoman Empire declined in the 1800s, the distrust grew. Nationalism swept through the empire, as it did in many parts of the world. The border regions of Greece and parts of the Balkans broke away and formed their own independent nations. As Armenia grew stronger, Armenians began to clamor for reforms. They resented the sultan who ruled their region and when they demanded regional autonomy and other human rights, the Ottoman Turks retaliated. From 1894-1896, the Ottoman Turks massacred 200,000 – 300,000 Armenians.[33]

Filled with nationalistic fever, a rebel group called the Young Turks seized power from the sultan in the early 1900s. At first they wanted to reform and modernize the empire, but soon they took on the same views as the sultan they had replaced. The Turks thought of minorities, such as the Armenians, as enemies from within, taking away energy and strength from the empire. The Armenians were proud of their culture and their tight-knit communities and worried what the militant nationalists had in store for them. The Turks called the "problem" with Armenia the Armenian Question.[34]

The Armenian Question was soon answered when, under the cover of World War I, the genocide against the Armenians began in earnest. In 1914 the world was engulfed in World War I (1914-1918).

The Ottoman Turks joined the war on the side of Germany and Austria-Hungary, fighting against Great Britain, France, Russia, and later the United States, which entered the war in 1917. The Armenians pleaded with the Turks not to go to war with Russia. Many Armenians lived across the Ottoman border in Russia, and tens of thousands enlisted in the Russian army. When the Turks asked them to launch an insurrection against the Russians in the Caucasus Mountains, the Armenians refused. The Turks then accused the Armenians of supporting the Russians and branded them as part of the enemy. The Turks would later cite this fact to defend their view that the Armenians were a traitorous enemy.[35]

Armenian quarter of Adana left pillaged and destroyed after the massacres in 1909

To the Turks the Armenian Question took on new importance. The Turks believed that the Armenians would help the Russian army invade their homeland. The Ottoman army stripped Armenian men of their weapons and herded them into forced labor camps. Those who had not died from overwork, illness, or starvation were shot, falling into graves they had just been forced to dig. In 1915, the Ottoman Turks ordered the resettlement of the Armenian people. On the night of April 24, 1915, the Turks told 600 Armenian men—community leaders, intellectuals, professionals and businessmen—that they were to be resettled, and the government intended no harm. Instead, once the men had reported, they were marched out of the village to a remote place and shot. With the men (even those as young as 12 years old) out of the way, the Turks marched women, children, and elderly into barren desert regions, where they were forced at bayonet point to walk for weeks without

Edward Racoubian: The Armenian Genocide

We walked for many days, occasionally running across small lakes and rivers. After a while we saw corpses on the shores of these lakes. Then we began seeing them along the path: twisted corpses, blackened by the sun and bloated. Their stench was horrible. Vultures circled the skies above us, waiting for their evening meal. At one point, we came upon a small hole in the ground. It was a little deeper than average height and 25-30 people could easily fit in it. We lowered ourselves down into it. There was no water in it, but the bottom was muddy. We began sucking on the mud. Some of the women made teats with their shirts filled with mud and suckled on them like children. We were there for about a half hour.

Many days later we reached the Euphrates River, and despite the hundreds of bodies floating in it, we drank from it. We quenched our thirst for the first time since our departure. They put us on small boats and we crossed to the other side. From there we walked to Ras-ul-Ain.

Of a caravan of nearly 10,000 people, there were now only 300 of us left. My aunt, my sisters, my brothers had all died or disappeared, only my mother and I were left. We decided to hide and take refuge with some Arab nomads. My mother died there under their tents. They did not treat me well—they kept me hungry and beat me often and they branded me as their own.[37]

food or water. Those who did not die from exposure died of starvation. The girls and women were tortured, raped, and often killed. Many women committed suicide by throwing themselves and their children off cliffs and into rivers. Many desperate Armenian parents gave their children to Turkish and Kurdish families who raised them as Muslims.[36]

World War I raged on for four years. Along with a staggering death toll of 15 million, the treaties after the war dismantled the German, Austrian, Russian, and Ottoman empires. The war victors installed a new Turkish government in part of the area of the former Ottoman Empire, and the victors, mainly the French and British, carved up and placed into protectorates the rest of the empire. The new Turkish government was aware of the Armenian slaughter. The British and French launched an investigation, but failed to finish it. Turkish leaders blamed the murders on "uncontrolled elements"— soldiers who had disobeyed orders and acted more cruelly than necessary. The Turkish government held a trial, and seven leading perpetrators were tried, found guilty, and sentenced to death. But they did not carry out the sentences, and the guilty individuals fled. Turkey was determined to start anew and from their point of view did not want to dwell on what happened to the Armenians.[38] To them, the case was closed.

By the end of the genocide, the Armenian population had been decimated. While there is no consensus as to how many Armenians lost their lives, nearly 2 million Armenians were alive at the start of the war, and estimates range from over 500,000 to 1.8 million Armenians died between 1914 and 1918. Of those who lived, about 250,000 escaped, another 200,000 were forced to convert to Islam, and about 400,000 somehow survived.[39] The Ottoman Empire similarly attacked other ethnic groups during this period: about 500,000 Assyrians (Syria) and about 300,000 Pontic Greeks died.[40] Some scholars consider those events to be part of the same policy of extermination.[41]

The Armenian Genocide is the second most-studied case of genocide after the Holocaust.[42] But was it genocide? There are different sides to the issue. Even today, Turkey does not accept the word genocide as an accurate description of the events. In recent years, it has faced repeated calls to accept the events as genocide. The majority of Armenian diaspora communities were founded as a result of the genocide.[43]

Questions to Consider
1. Do you think the Turks committed genocide against the Armenians?
2. If not, why wouldn't it be called genocide?

UKRAINE

Today Ukraine is an independent nation in Eastern Europe, and Kiev serves as its capital and largest city. Ukraine has a long and notable history dating back to the 9th century when it was home to the eastern Slavic people (an ethnic group). It was known at the time as the state of Kievan Rus, a Golden Age in Ukrainian history in which it was the largest and most powerful nation in Europe. However, it disintegrated in the 12th century, and in 1240 the Mongol invasion totally devastated Kievan Rus. After a period of political integration and a brief republican form of government, a number of regional powers divided it up. By the 19th century, Russia integrated the largest part of Ukraine into its empire, and the rest fell to Austro-Hungarian control. Ukraine attempted to declare its independence following World War I (1917–21) and the Russian Civil War (1917-1923), but it failed. Instead, it became part of the new nation of the Soviet Union in 1922. The Soviet revolution devastated Ukraine. It left over 1.5 million people dead and hundreds of thousands homeless. Soviet Ukraine faced a famine in 1921, in which 5 million Ukrainians and Russians died of starvation. Ironically, Ukraine has some of the most fertile soil in the world and grows wheat and many other crops, but peasant farmers did not plant crops amidst the disruptions of war and political instability.

The founder of Soviet Communism, Vladimir Lenin, ruled the Soviet Union until his death in 1924, followed by the dictatorship of **Joseph Stalin**, who ruled until his death in 1953. Early in his rule Stalin launched Five Year Plans. His goal was to increase industrialization, which lagged behind the rest of Europe, and to make agriculture more productive through **collectivization**. With collectivization, peasant farmers handed over ownership of their land and control of production to large-scale, industrial, state-owned farms. The goal of collectivization was to increase agricultural output, to bring the peasantry under more direct political control, and to make tax collection more efficient. These changes were drastic. In fact, changes on this scale had not been seen since the abolition of serfdom (unfree peasants) in 1861. Peasants experienced a severe drop in their living standards. Stalin's unrealistic goals for increased agricultural production were not met, and peasants mounted a fierce resistance to his plans. Stalin blamed the wealthy Ukrainian farmers known as *kulaks* for the lack of cooperation. The *kulaks*, considered wealthy by the standards of the time, actually only owned no more than ten hectares (24 acres) of land and employed only a few other workers. But Stalin ruthlessly reacted and commanded 5 million kulaks to be sent to the Russian Artic, where it was impossible to farm, placed into Gulag (prison) labor camps, or shot. With so many farmers killed or imprisoned, the agricultural production goals were unmet; still Stalin pressed remaining farmers to produce food. By 1932, the collective farms had virtually stopped producing food, and peasants were left to starve. To ensure that they didn't take grain, the death penalty for stealing food was imposed. Starving people who were caught with even a fistful of grain were shot on the spot.

Meanwhile, much of the production that was still going on had shifted from subsistence crops to growing wheat, which was exported to pay for Soviet industrial projects and the military.[44]

Ukrainian communist leaders protested the situation but to no avail. Instead, the Soviet military moved in Russian soldiers to seal the borders to prevent the escape of starving peasants. People ate anything they could find—leaves from trees and bushes, birds, cats, dogs, and in some cases, they resorted to cannibalism. Still, the Soviet state refused to send food to the area, and denied the starvation. Even uttering the world "famine" was against the law, and those who did could be arrested and killed.[45]

Relief was finally sent in the summer of 1933, but it was too late for many. An estimated 7 million people, including 3 million children—almost all of them peasants—died in the winter of 1932-33, 25

Chicago American's front page

percent of all Ukrainians. The Soviets had destroyed the *kulak* resistance.[46] The state denied the forced famine until the Soviet leader Mikail Gorbachev opened up the country's records in the mid-1980s. In 1991, Ukraine became an independent nation upon the dissolution of the Soviet Union.

Was the elimination of 25 percent of the Ukrainian population considered genocide? Although they were certainly not the only ethnic group to suffer under Stalin's repressive actions, many argue that the ethnic Ukrainians were undeniably treated differently. During the late 1920s there were mass arrests, deportations and executions of politicians, teachers, priests, intellectuals and others to suppress Ukrainian national identity. From 1932 the military closed Ukraine's borders to prevent journalists and others from traveling freely; an internal passport system prevented starving peasants from leaving their villages to search for food; death certificates were falsified so that deaths from starvation were not recorded; and offers of aid from Western charities were not allowed into Ukraine. Recent documents from Ukrainian state archives clearly show that famine was used as an instrument of Stalin's policies and that no humanitarian considerations were given in his ambitions. A name has been given to Stalin's crimes against humanity targeted at the Ukrainian people: the **Holodomor**.[47]

Questions to Consider
1. Do you think the elimination of 25 percent of the Ukrainian population by Stalin is genocide?

CAMBODIA

Cambodia lies in the southeastern part of Asia, neighboring the countries of Vietnam, Laos, and Thailand. Cambodia was once part of the powerful Hindu and Buddhist Khmer Empire, which ruled most of the Indochina Peninsula between the 11th and 14th centuries. The Khmer Empire's center of power was Angkor, which is the site of one of the largest pre-modern religious temples in the world: Angkor Wat. The well-preserved temple is the destination for many tourists around the world and symbolizes the importance of Cambodia's past as a regional power. More than 90 percent of its population is of Khmer origin and speaks Khmer, the country's official language. Introduced around the 13th century, the dominant religion is a form of Theravada Buddhism practiced by 95 percent of the 14 million people.[48]

Cambodia was a protectorate of France from 1863 to 1954, and administered as part of their colony of French Indochina. According to international law, a **protectorate** is different from a colony in that it is a self-governing territory protected diplomatically or militarily against third parties by a stronger state. It retains a measure of independence and remains a state under international law. During most of World War II, 1941 to 1945, the Japanese Empire occupied Cambodia and the rest of French Indochina. Cambodia gained independence from France in 1953, but France was unwilling to give up its colony of Vietnam. The French waged war against the rebellious Vietnamese, Cambodia's neighbor, but fared badly in the conflict. They met an inglorious defeat in a remote Vietnamese mountainous garrison called Dien Bien Phu in the winter of 1954. The United States, alarmed by the defeat of France and always fearful of communist expansion around the world, decided to step in to "protect" Vietnam from communism. Many Vietnamese, especially in the north, didn't want to be protected from communism, while others sided with the U.S. Thus, the long and costly Vietnam War started on a small scale in 1954, and finally came to a humbling close for the U.S. in 1975.

Cambodia was the setting for much of the ground and air war between the U.S. and Vietnam. American bombs killed about 150,000 Cambodian peasants from 1969-1973. Others fled the unsafe countryside to settle in the capital city of Phnom Penh. The U.S. supported the military government in Cambodia until its withdrawal from Vietnam on April 17, 1975, when U.S. support ended. Amidst the chaos of American withdrawal from Vietnam, Pol Pot and his Khmer Rouge army, most of whom were teen age peasant boys, swept into the capital and took control of the country. The leader of **Khmer Rouge** was a shadowy and mysterious figure, Saloth Sar, who changed his name to **Pol Pot**. He was determined to remake Cambodia into his twisted vision of an ideal society. Although a declared communist, he believed deeply that Cambodia should return to the power and glory it had enjoyed between the 11th and 14th centuries. He sought to eliminate outside influences and anyone who was not "pure" Cambodian.[49]

The Khmer Rouge believed that Western ideas corrupted Cambodians. Instead, they tried to create a society in which no one competed against each other and all people worked for the common good. This meant, in theory, that no rich could exploit the poor, and people would not starve or be left without a livelihood. The Khmer Rouge thought that illiterate peasants in the countryside were more pure than urban dwellers. Their aim was to purify society by eliminating the people who were holding it back, either "reeducating" people about their faults or getting rid of them altogether. Stephen Solarz, who traveled to Southeast Asia after the Khmer Rouge took control of Cambodia recalled that "They were killing anyone who wore glasses, because if they wore glasses it suggested they knew how to read, and if they knew how to read, it suggested they had been infected with the *bourgeois* [capitalist middle class] virus."[50]

Pol Pot wanted to turn back the clock and shut the country off from all foreign influences, including foreigners, newspapers, radio, television, mail, and even money. There were no human rights: no free speech and no freedom to travel. Pol Pot organized the whole society according to a system of schedules and rules, and people were killed for the slightest violation of the most insignificant rule.[51] In a country where 95 percent of the people were Buddhist, the Khmer Rouge decided the religion was incompatible with its program. They ordered the murder of Buddhist monks throughout the country and destroyed their monasteries. A Khmer Rouge official later explained that the Cambodian people had just stopped practicing Buddhism and that the monks then deserted the temples and monasteries. They also methodically identified other groups in Cambodia for elimination: Chinese, Vietnamese, and Muslims. From 1975-1979, anyone who was not a "pure" Cambodian lived an uncertain life.[52]

The Khmer Rouge ruthlessly strove to purify their nation. They forced two million people to leave the cities for the countryside, with about 20,000 dying during the evacuation. Those who survived the forced march were required to work in rice fields and on agricultural projects. Thousands died of starvation, overwork, and disease.[53] The Khmer Rouge rounded up and killed former government officials, army officers and soldiers, Buddhist monks, the educated and the well-off, such as doctors, teachers and lawyers, as well

Skulls of Khmer Rouge victims

as their peasant relatives. Only 2,000 of the country's 70,000 Buddhist monks survived. The Khmer Rouge targeted all those who opposed the regime.

Finally some of the Khmer Rouge forces mutinied, and the rebels crossed the border to ask the Vietnamese to help them. The Vietnamese invaded in early 1979 to drive the Khmer Rouge from power. Pol Pat fled into the jungles of southwest Cambodia and then sought exile in Thailand. The Khmer Rouge government limped along with aid from the U.S. until 1997.[54]

News of the events in Cambodia had been circulating through the international community for years. But the U.S. was still recovering from its painful defeat in Vietnam, and the idea of sending soldiers back into the region, which some argued for, would not garner much, if any, support. Most Americans wanted to forget the whole region. However, when Vietnam invaded Cambodia, the U.S. sided with the Khmer Rouge, because it still considered Vietnam an enemy. The U.S. also hoped to keep favor with China, which supported the Khmer Rouge. From 1979-1997, Pol Pot and a number of the old Khmer Rouge carried out operations from the border region of Cambodia and Thailand, where they clung to power. Despite evidence of genocide, the U.S. and China supported the Khmer Rouge as it fought against the new Cambodian government. They continued to sit in the UN as the representative of Cambodia.[55]

Pol Pot died in 1998, perhaps by poisoning. He and other Khmer Rouge leaders, unlike many of the top Nazi officials in Germany, faced little prosecution for their crimes. From 1.7 to 2.5 million people had been either murdered or starved to death during the Khmer Rouge reign of terror, approximately 21 percent of the population.[56] Thousands of bodies were found in mass graves, the individuals either shot or beaten to death. The invading Vietnamese soldiers uncovered a prison, Tuol Seng, a former high school in Phnom Penh where 16,000 Cambodians had been tortured and killed for allegedly plotting against Pol Pot's regime. The prison now serves as the Tuol Sleng Genocide Museum.[57]

Was the Khmer Rouge guilty of genocide? Some say it was not genocide because the perpetrators and the victims were both of the same ethnic and national group. Those who died were not specifically targeted for destruction for who they were. It was Cambodians killing Cambodians. Others argue that the Khmer Rouge did commit genocide by murdering many groups simply for who they were—ethnic Chinese, Buddhist monks, and Vietnamese. They cite the fact that the UN determined that the Cambodians were killed because of their political beliefs, and this fell under the definition of genocide.

Questions to Consider
1. In your analysis of this case study: Did Pol Pot and the Khmer Rouge commit genocide?

GUATEMALA

Guatemala is an independent country located in Central America just south of Mexico. It has a long and interesting history, in particular, the impressive Mayan civilization that built countless sites that are still standing in Guatemala and throughout Central America. During the Classical period of the Mayans (250-900 CE), the civilization reached its heights and was characterized by cities including temples, astronomical observatories, and sports arenas. When the Classical Mayan civilization collapsed around 900 CE, the Mayans abandoned many of the cities. Different theories are given for the collapse of the great Mayan civilization; one is that they experienced a drought-induced famine.[58] Because the population had exceeded the carrying capacity of the area, it could no longer support such a large urban population, and people took refuge in smaller farming villages. Although the Classical Mayan civilization collapsed, the Mayan people survived and merely resettled into a simpler, small-village way of life.

From the 1500s onward, the Spanish colonized the region, including the area of Guatemala today. As in the rest of the Americas, perhaps as many as 90 percent of the area's indigenous people died during colonization, mainly due to deadly European diseases. The Spanish mercilessly suppressed the Mayan people, destroying many of their ancient books called codex and attempted to destroy their language, culture, and traditions. Yet in spite of the oppression, each generation of Mayans in Guatemala has continued to retain its language and culture. Today, of Guatemala's 14 million people, 60 percent are of Mayan descent.[59]

The United States has had a rather complicated relationship with Guatemala . From the 1950s through the 1990s, the U.S. government directly supported Guatemala's army with training, weapons, and money, supposedly to fight communism, and it also supported the largest American corporation in Guatemala: United Fruit Company (now Chiquita Brands). United Fruit owned an enormous amount of land and hired peasants to take care of their vast plantations. In a democratic election in 1951, Jacobo Árbenz Guzmán (1913-1971) was elected President. In 1952 his government enacted a popular agrarian reform agenda that gave the government the authority to buy up uncultivated portions of large plantations, and the landowners would be paid a fair price. The land would be distributed to impoverished peasant families. As expected, the largest land-owner—United Fruit—refused the government's fair rate offer for the 85 percent of their land that was uncultivated. The U.S. Central Intelligence Agency (CIA), at the urging of the United Fruit Company, staged a Guatemalan coup d'état in 1954 in which Arbenz was overthrown, and a president who was friendly to the U.S. and supportive of United Fruit was installed.

In response to the coup and the increasing communist influence in the region, several **guerrilla** (rebel) organizations, who allegedly represented impoverished peasants, self-organized to fight the U.S.-friendly military regimes. The **Guatemala Civil War** (1960-1996) ensued, the longest civil war in Latin American history. The decades-long conflict pitted the right-wing, Guatemalan military government against leftist (communist) and indigenous guerilla movements. The U.S. supported the military regimes during the 36-year war, with the purpose of preventing Guatemala from adopting communism. Without U.S. support, the military would not have been such a vital force in the civil war.

The civil war was long and complicated. In the early part of the war (1960s), urban-based middle-class intellectuals and students primarily led the guerilla groups. The Guatemalan army, trained by American advisors and the CIA, easily defeated these groups. During the late 1970s, the war shifted to fighting on both the urban and rural fronts, especially in the mountainous regions of the Mayan Highlands. The defining event of the Guatemalan Civil War happened on the morning of January 31, 1980 when a group of indigenous peasant farmers occupied the Spanish Embassy in Guatemala City to protest the kidnapping and murder of Mayan peasants by the Guatemalan army. The police responded to the emergency, and a fire resulted, destroying the embassy and leaving 36 people dead. The funeral of the victims included Rigoberta Menchu's father, Vicente Menchú, attracted hundreds of thousands of mourners, catalyzing the formation of a new guerilla group: Popular Front of 31 January.[60] After this event, the war entered its most violent stage, as the army targeted mostly unarmed indigenous civilians, resulting in thousands of deaths (see chapter 5). Although the rebels committed excesses, a great deal of evidence gathered by Amnesty International, Americas Watch and observers,

Ixil people carrying their loved ones' remains after an exhumation in the Ixil Triangle in 2012

found that the Guatemalan army carried out the vast majority of the killings.[61] U.S. support peaked in the early 1980s under the Reagan administration, when the military practiced a "scorch the earth" policy, destroying hundreds of Mayan villages and massacring thousands of villagers who were accused of supporting the rebels.[62] In 1983, indigenous activist Rigoberta Menchú wrote a testimonial account, *I, Rigoberta Menchú, An Indian Woman in Guatemala*, which gained worldwide attention and caused outrage about the atrocities in Guatemala. But for the most part from 1986-1995, the army ruled from behind the scenes.[63]

The Guatemalan Civil War finally ended in 1996 when the UN negotiated a peace accord between the guerillas and the government. Both sides made major concessions. The guerrilla fighters disarmed and received land to farm. In 1999, according to the UN-sponsored Truth Commission, government forces and state-sponsored militias were responsible for over 93 percent of the human rights violations during the war, and 83 percent of the violence was directed against Mayans. During the first 10 years, the victims of the state-sponsored terror were primarily students, workers, professionals, and opposition figures, but in the last years the victims were thousands of mostly rural Mayan farmers and non-combatants.[64] More than 450 Mayan villages were destroyed, over 200,000 Guatemalans had been killed or "disappeared," (they were kidnapped and never seen again), and over 1 million people became refugees. The majority of the Guatemalan diaspora—ranging from 480,000-1 million people—is located in the United States.[65]

The Truth Commission stated that the Guatemalan state engaged in an intentional policy of genocide against specific ethnic groups in the Civil War.[66] Some argue that the violence was not just directed against Mayans as an ethnic group but against Mayans as political rebels. The perpetrators of genocide also targeted those who were fighting for land reform, basic civil rights and an end to oppression.[67] In 1999, President Bill Clinton stated that the United States was wrong to have provided support to the Guatemalan military that took part in the brutal civilian killings. In 1992, the Nobel Peace Prize was awarded to Rigoberta Menchú for her efforts to bring international attention to the government-sponsored genocide against the indigenous population and for her work in favor of broader social justice.

Questions to Consider
1. What human rights violations do you think the Guatelmalan army committed during the civil war?

BOSNIA AND KOSOVO

Yugoslavia, a former nation in southeastern Europe, was carved out of the defeated Ottoman Empire at the end of World War I in 1918. Yugoslavia was composed of various ethnic and religious groups that had been historical rivals, even bitter enemies, including the Serbs (Orthodox Christians), Croats (Catholics), ethnic Albanians (Muslims), Macedonians (Orthodox Christians), Montenegrins (Orthodox Christians), Slovenes (Roman Catholic, Protestants), and Bosnians and Herzegovinians (mix of all). All these different ethnic minorities with different languages, religions, and customs were shoveled into one country.[68] The dye was set for conflict in the future.

During World War II, Nazi Germany invaded and partitioned Yugoslavia. Joseph Tito, a fervent nationalist and communist, led a fierce resistance movement. Following Germany's defeat, Tito, a strong leader, reunified Yugoslavia under the slogan "Brotherhood and Unity," merging together Slovenia, Croatia, Bosnia, Serbia, Montenegro, Macedonia, along with two self-governing provinces, Kosovo and Vojvodina. Although Tito was a communist, he remained friendly with both the Soviet Union and the United States during the Cold War, playing one superpower against the other and getting financial aid from both. Tito ruled Yugoslavia with an iron fist but was able to keep the different factions together until his death in 1980. Without his iron rule, Yugoslavia plunged into political and economic chaos.

By the late 1980s, a new leader emerged from Serbia: **Slobodan Milosevic**, a former communist who fanned nationalistic pride and religious hatred to gain power. But he was unable to keep Yugoslavia together after the fall of the Berlin Wall in 1990, when political instability rocked many areas that had once been under Soviet influence. Along with the Soviet Union, the nation of Yugoslavia began to fall apart. Memories of ethnic and religious tensions, identities, and rivalries that stretched back for centuries began to resurface once again.[69] Milosevic wanted to create a Greater Serbia out of the former Yugoslavia, in which Serbs and Orthodox Christians were separate from Muslims and other ethnic groups. Serbian nationalism was on the march.

Ethnic tensions quickly turned violent. In June 1991, Slovenia and Croatia both declared their independence from Yugoslavia, which sparked a civil war. The national army of Yugoslavia, now made up of Serbs controlled by Milosevic, stormed into Slovenia but failed to subdue their independence movement and withdrew after only ten days of fighting. Since Slovenia had almost no Serbian population, Milosevic turned his armies to Croatia, a Catholic country where Orthodox Serbs made up 12 percent of the population. Aided by Serbian guerrillas in Croatia, Milosevic's forces invaded in July 1991 to supposedly "protect" the Serbian minority. The Serbs began the first mass executions of the conflict, killing hundreds of Croat men and burying them in mass graves.[70]

The response of the international community was guarded. U.S. President George H.W. Bush recognized the independence of both Slovenia and Croatia but chose not to get involved militarily. The UN imposed an arms embargo for all of the former Yugoslavia; however, the Serbs under Milosevic were already the best armed force and, thus, maintained a big military advantage. By the end of 1991, the Serbs and Croats fighting in Croatia agreed to a U.S. sponsored cease-fire agreement.[71]

Bosnia and Herzegovina, typically called **Bosnia**, seceded from Yugoslavia in 1992, and the Serbian army invaded shortly thereafter. In April 1992, the U.S. and European Community recognized the independence of Bosnia. The Bosnian Serbs were armed and ready to assist the Serbian forces led by Milosevic in joining greater Serbia. They used former Yugoslavian military equipment to attack non-Serbian Bosnia, which was far superior to the ill-equipped weaponry Bosnians used to defend themselves. The Serbs justified the war in terms of race and religion. The Orthodox Christian Serbs declared that they were coming to the aid of fellow Serbs living in Bosnia who, they said, were being abused by Muslim forces. Bosnia at the time was a mixture of ethnic groups (Serb 37.1 percent,

Bosniaks (Bosnian Muslims) 48 percent, Croat 14.3 percent) and religious minorities (Muslim 40 percent, Orthodox Christian 31 percent, Roman Catholic 15 percent, and other 14 percent).[72]

Serbian forces surrounded and besieged Bosnia's predominantly Muslim capital city of Sarajevo, along with other cities. The siege lasted for more than three years. Serbian artillery fire battered buildings in Sarajevo, the once proud city of the 1984 Winter Olympic Games, reducing the cosmopolitan city to ruins. Snipers gunned down helpless civilians, including children, walking in the streets, eventually killing over 3,500 children. The world community reacted with shock and disbelief. Just hours from the comfortable capitals of Western Europe, people were killing one another with intense savagery.[73]

Bosnian Muslims (Bosniaks) were hopelessly outgunned. As the Serbs gained ground, they began to methodically empty their villages and destroy their mosques. In some scenarios mass shootings of Bosniaks resulted in the depopulation of entire towns. In other instances, the Serbs began to systematically roundup Bosniak men and boys and forced them into make-shift concentration camps. The Serbs also terrorized Muslim families into fleeing their villages by using rape as a weapon against women and girls. These repeated atrocities were eerily similar to those committed by the Nazis during World War II. The actions of the Serbs were labeled as "ethnic cleansing," a name which quickly took hold among the international media. Some observers of ethnic cleansing accused the Serbs of committing genocide. This is a charge the Serbs disputed vigorously, then and now.[74]

The Srebrenica Genocide Memorial in Potočari

Rumors began to circulate to the outside world that the Serbs had constructed a number of camps for captured Muslims. Escapees described the horror of the camps: murders, starvation, and the mistreatment and rape of women. In the summer of 1992, Western journalists gained entry into the camps and questioned inmates and recently released prisoners who told horrible stories of torture and executions. But the images were even more shocking: listless prisoners stood behind barbed wire, their skin drawn tight over their ribs, shoulder blades, and cheekbones. The resemblance between these images and those of the Nazi concentration camps at the end of WWII was clear.[75]

Many Western leaders loudly expressed sympathy and resolved to act, but despite media reports of the secret camps and mass killings, the world community remained mostly indifferent. The UN imposed economic sanctions on Serbia and sent its troops to protect distribution of food and medicine to homeless Muslims. But the UN did not act militarily against the Serbs. Throughout 1993, Serbs in Bosnia freely killed Muslims, confident that the UN, U.S., or the European Community would not take military action. Radovan Karadzic, president of the illegitimate Bosnian Serb Republic, once told journalists, "Serbs and Muslims are like cats and dogs. They cannot live together in peace. It is impossible."[76]

The U.S., the world's lone superpower, was reluctant to get involved in a bloody conflict that many believed was a nasty civil war based on centuries of divisions and hatred. Politicians deplored the massacres, and editorial pages expressed outrage, but the killings, shootings, and ethnic cleansing continued. Although the U.S. did not send soldiers to the region, President Bill Clinton, who had promised during his election campaign in 1992 to stop the ethnic cleansing in Bosnia, issued a warning through the North Atlantic Treaty Organization (NATO) demanding that the Serbs withdraw their weaponry from Sarajevo. The Serbs quickly complied, and NATO imposed a cease-fire (truce) in Sarajevo. In May 1993, the UN established six "Safe Havens," Muslim towns in Bosnia that would be under UN peacekeeper supervision.[77] But Bosnian Serbs were not deterred; they not only attacked the Safe Havens but the UN peacekeepers as well. NATO forces responded by launching limited air strikes against Serb ground positions. The Serbs retaliated with impunity; they captured hundreds of UN peacekeepers as hostages and turned them into human shields, chained to military targets. At this point, some of the worst genocidal activities of the four-year-old conflict occurred in Srebrenica.[78]

About 60,000 Muslim refugees had fled into the city of Srebrenica to escape the hostility and advancing Serbian forces. A French UN commander bluffed his way through Serbian lines surrounding the town and witnessed thousands of starving, sick people in Srebrenica. He immediately declared that the town's refugees were "under the protection of the UN." The Serb forces reluctantly stopped. Just a month later, the UN declared that Srebrenica and 30 square miles (78 kilometers) around it was a "safe area"—the first one in UN history. However, the city was in an unstable situation, deep in eastern Bosnia within 10 miles (16 km) of the Serbian border and surrounded by Serbian forces.[79]

The worst massacre of the genocide took place at Srebrenica from July 11 to 16, 1995. There in the Safe Haven city under the eyes of international peacekeepers, the Serbian forces systematically separated the city's men, between ages 11 and 65, from the women. As the UN peacekeepers stood by helplessly, the men and boys were loaded onto trucks or buses and driven to execution sites in isolated locations where they were shot—8,000 of them. It was the worst mass murder in Europe since World War II.[80]

The Serbs continued to engage in mass rapes of Muslim females. They captured and transported 50,000 Muslim women to schools or community centers where they were gang-raped and continually abused for days to months at a time. According to Jane Springer, "The rapists told the women that they wanted to impregnate them so they would have Serb babies. Once pregnant, the women were often kept imprisoned until it was too late for them to have safe abortions."[81]

Over the next few years, Srebrenica and two other "safe areas" in eastern Bosnia led a tenuous existence. The war had exhausted both the Serbs and Bosnians, and there had been little hope for a resettlement. The UN forces, equipped with sky blue helmets and driving in white armored vehicles, tried to preserve some kind of control. But they were unable to mount any kind of sufficient defense with the larger Serb forces surrounding them. Their only real deterrent was the North Atlantic Treaty Organization (NATO) warplanes based in nearby Western Europe.

On August 30, 1995, in response to the killings at Srebrenica, military intervention finally began as the U.S. led a massive NATO bombing campaign targeting Serbian artillery positions throughout Bosnia. The pinprick bombing offensive continued into October. Serb forces also lost ground to Bosnian Muslims who had received arms shipments from the Islamic world. As a result, Muslim-Croat troops eventually retook half of Bosnia. Faced with the heavy NATO assault and a series of ground losses to the Muslim-Croat coalition, Serb leader Milosevic was finally ready for peace talks. On November 1, 1995, leaders of the warring factions, including Milosevic, traveled to Dayton,

Ohio in the U.S. for peace talks. After three weeks of negotiations, disputants agreed to the Dayton Peace Accords. Among other things, the agreement called for democratic elections and stipulated that war criminals would be handed over for prosecution. NATO deployed over 60,000 soldiers to preserve the cease-fire. Slobodan Milosevic, the architect of war, had reinvented himself as the Man of Peace. He signed the Dayton Peace Treaty on behalf of the Bosnian Serbs.[82] But Milosevic had overseen the systematic murder of over 200,000 Muslim civilians; more than 20,000 were missing, while 2,000,000 had become refugees. It was, according to U.S. Assistant Secretary of State Richard Holbrooke, "the greatest failure of the West since the 1930s."[83]

Milosevic, the so-called man of peace, had another trick up his sleeve. He inflamed long-standing tensions between Serbs and Muslims in the independent province of Kosovo. Orthodox Christian Serbs in Kosovo were a minority of only 10 percent, but they considered Kosovo the cradle of their culture, religion, and national identity. It had been an area of contention throughout the 20th century. The Serbs, in a familiar refrain, claimed the Albanian Muslim majority were mistreating them. Eventually, Serbian-instigated political unrest in Kosovo led to its loss of independence and domination by Milosevic and the Serbs. With three wars already fought and lost (Slovenia, Croatia, and Bosnia), Milosevic started planning his fourth: Kosovo. Over the 10 years leading up to the war, conditions in Kosovo had worsened.

The ethnic Muslim Albanians did not like Serbian rule and demanded a return of their independence. They organized the Kosovo Liberation Army (KLA), an Albanian guerrilla organization, to defend their province and ethnic heritage from Serbian rule. By the summer of 1998, ethnic Albanians of Kosovo were staging mass protests against Serbian rule. Serbian police and army reinforcements were sent in to crush the KLA. Peace talks in France were resumed but went nowhere. NATO was again called up to bomb Serbian military targets in Kosovo and Serbia in March 1999. Meanwhile, Serbian forces launched a campaign of ethnic cleansing against Kosovo Albanians. Some 750,000 refugees fled to neighboring Albania, Macedonia and Montenegro. The international tribunal in The Hague said its investigators had found at least 2,000 bodies. After 11 weeks of NATO bombing, Milosevic withdrew his troops and police, the ethnic Albanian refugees returned home and about 100,000 Serbs—roughly half the province's Serbian population—fled. The UN sent a peacekeeping force to monitor the region.[84]

In May 1999, the international war crimes tribunal in The Hague indicted Milosevic as the first-serving head of state indicted for crimes against humanity. According to the indictment, Milosevic and a number of his colleagues bore direct responsibility for crimes that are alleged to have included the deportation of almost 750,000 Kosovo Albanians and the murder of 600 individually identified ethnic Albanians. But this time, Milosevic's responsibility was clear; his grip on power was beginning to slip.

In the presidential election of September 2000, the opposition leader, Vojislav Kostunica, clearly defeated Slobodan Milosevic. When the Milosevic's government called for a second ballot, the people spontaneously organized a general strike and widespread demonstrations. The opposition supporters captured Belgrade's parliament building and the headquarters of state television. Milosevic and his wife fled the country. Thirteen years of brutal rule ended in 12 breathtaking hours.[85]

Six months later officials arrested Milosevic outside his mansion. He would stand for trial on charges of genocide and crimes against humanity. The trial got under way in early 2002 at the International Criminal Tribunal for the former Yugoslavia in The Hague. Investigations by the Organization for Security and Co-operation in Europe, including the interview of some 3,000 witnesses or survivors, uncovered a grim tale of murder, mutilation and rape. It found that Serbs had carried out human rights abuses on an enormous scale—but had also suffered atrocious revenge attacks following the war. The trial continued but Milosevic's recurrent ill-health frequently interrupted the defense. Milosevic died in March 2006. The prosecution had completed its case but the defense continued. The court ultimately established what had happened in Kosovo. Many ethnic Albanians felt that Milosevic's untimely death robbed them of a verdict. However, in the long-run they prevailed; the international community recognized Kosovo's declaration of independence in 2008. Since the 1990s, the Balkans has been relatively peaceful.[86]

> **Questions to Consider**
> 1. Do you think that Milosovic was guilty of genocide or other human rights violations? Explain.
> 2. Do you think NATO, the U.S. or other organizations/nations should have acted earlier in the conflict?

THE TALIBAN

Every street of Kabul is enthralling to the eye
Through the bazaars, caravans of Egypt pass
One could not count the moons that shimmer on her roofs
And the thousand splendid suns that hide behind her walls
   —a stanza from the poem **Kabul** by the 17th-century Persian poet Saib-e-Tabriz

The streets of Kabul, the capital of Afghanistan, are no longer enthralling to the eye. The 20th century conflicts, especially since 1979, have taken a toll on the war-ravaged city and countryside. Afghanistan's location, sandwiched between the Middle East, Central Asia and the Indian subcontinent along the ancient Silk Road, means that the country has long been a place fought over, despite its rugged and forbidding landscape. The landlocked country has recently suffered from instability and conflict that has left its economy and infrastructure in ruins, and many of its people are refugees.

In some of the previous case study sections, we have examined human rights abuses in a particular nation that have been carried out by strong centralized governments against ethnic minorities or "undesirables." The situation in Afghanistan today is different. The central government of Afghanistan is very weak and unable to effectively govern the vast, mountainous territory and the tribal groups that make-up the nation. Various factions inside

Taliban flag

and outside Afghanistan vie for control of the government in order to impose their idea of rule on the nation of 28 million people. One of the factions is the Taliban.

The word **Taliban** means "student" in the Pashto language, one of the official languages in Afghanistan. Most of the Taliban belong to the Pashtun ethnic group, a tribal society with over 60 tribes and 400 clans and a population of over 42 million. Tribal societies have been a form of political and social organization for thousands of years in human history and continue in certain areas of the world. They are often patriarchal (male dominated) and practice a traditional code of strict conduct and honor. A common ancestry and ethnic customs and traditions unite tribes together. For over 250 years, the Pastuns have been the dominant ethnic group in Afghanistan and the 2nd largest in Pakistan.[87] The Taliban, a religious and political movement, were predominantly a Pashtun militia, and imposed their ethnic customs onto non-Pashtuns. They belong to the Sunni branch of Islam but follow a particularly narrow interpretation of Islam. Most observers label their interpretation of Islam as extremist or radical, which means that they do not follow mainstream tenets of Islam but interpret the religion to suit their political motives. Only a minority of Muslims practice this extreme version of Islam.

The Taliban governed Afghanistan from 1996 until 2001 when its leaders were removed from power by North Atlantic Treaty Organization (NATO) forces after the 9/11 attacks in the U.S. The Taliban has regrouped since 2001, and from 2004 onwards it has been a strong insurgency (rebel) movement governing at the local level and fighting a guerrilla war against the governments of Afghanistan, Pakistan, the U.S., and allied NATO forces. Although displaced by more extremist groups in 2014, such as ISIS (ISIL), the Taliban continues to operate in Afghanistan and tribal areas of northwest Pakistan. The Taliban does not follow a modern type of political organization as do most independent countries. Yet, they have been able to rule, at one time or another, a country such as Afghanistan.

During the 19th and early 20th centuries, Afghanistan was a pawn of Russia (its neighbor) and Britain, as they expanded their empires at the expense of Afghanistan. When Russia was diverted during its civil war (1917-1922), the British recognized Afghanistan as a fully independent monarchy in 1921. The monarchy ruled from 1933 until a 1973 coup overthrew it.

Afghanistan entered a period of continuous civil conflict from 1973 forward. In 1978, a pro-communist faction in Afghanistan staged a coup and set out to transform the country's tribal society into a modern, communist nation. The Soviet Union invaded Afghanistan to support the Communist faction in 1979. The U.S. was alarmed at this aggression and President Jimmy Carter protested the Soviet invasion by boycotting the 1980 Olympic Games held in Moscow, Soviet Union. Muslims generally do not like communism, since it is against religion; therefore, many radical Muslims from around the world provided arms or soldiers to help the Afghans fight against the Soviets. Muslims fighting the Soviet Union were called the ***mujahideen*** guerilla forces. One of the key players in organizing training camps for the foreign Muslim volunteer fighters was Osama Bin Laden, a member of the Saudi Arabian royal family. Since the U.S. did not want to see communism in central Asia, it financed and supplied arms to the *mujahideen* forces. By 1987, 65,000 tons of U.S.-made weapons and ammunition had been used each year in the war.[88] The Soviet Union spent a vast amount of money in the war, but met a humiliating defeat in 1989 when they were forced to withdraw.

The *mujahideen* guerrilla factions overthrew the communist government in 1992, and the country descended into a civil war as different groups fought for control. In 1994, the Taliban made gains against the other factions, including the Northern Alliance. The civil war was basically an ethnic conflict between the Pashtun Taliban and the non-Pashtun Northern Alliance, with both sides believing in an extreme form of Islam. By 1995, the civil war killed more than 25,000 civilians in Kabul. In 1996, the Taliban emerged victorious in the civil war; seizing Kabul and establishing control over most of the country. The Taliban initially enjoyed enormous good will among the Afghans, who were weary of the corruption, brutality, and the continuous fighting of the *mujahideen*.

At first the United States and other foreign governments supported the Taliban in hopes that they would be able to restore order in war-ravaged Afghanistan and rein in corrupt, lawless tribal leaders. However, these hopes began to fade as the Taliban began to expel thousands of girls from schools, restrict women's rights, and abuse ethnic groups, primarily the Hazaras.[89] In 1996, Osama bin Laden moved from his hiding place in Sudan to Afghanistan. At first the Taliban did not welcome him, since he was a foreigner, but later he was able to forge an alliance between the Taliban and his al-Qaeda organization. The civil war in Afghanistan continued even after the Taliban captured Kabul in 1996, with the Northern Alliance feebly attempting to oust the Taliban from power from 1996 to 2001. However, the Northern Alliance's efforts proved largely unsuccessful, as the Taliban continued to make gains and eliminated much of the Alliance's leadership. Russia, Turkey, Iran, India, and eventually the United States supported the Northern Alliance, while Saudi Arabia, Pakistan and the United Arab Emirates supported the Taliban.

Since this book focuses on human rights, let's turn to the Taliban's human rights violations from 1996 to 2001. The Taliban implemented one of the strictest interpretations of Islamic law in recent times. Their ideology is severe and anti-modern, combining Pashtun tribal codes and radical interpretations of Islam. The Taliban banned a wide variety of activities that had previously been lawful. One Taliban list of prohibitions included: eating pork, using pig oil, keeping pigeons, hanging pictures in homes, using anything made from human hair, installing satellite dishes, clapping during sports events, flying kites, playing pool and chess, wearing masks, consuming alcohol, using computers, watching television and movies, drinking wine, eating lobster, using nail polish, lighting firecrackers, collecting statues, trimming beards, looking at sewing catalogs, sending Christmas cards, and producing music. Men had to wear their hair short with a head covering, and have a beard extending farther than a fist clamped at the base of the chin. The Taliban forbade displaying pictures, paintings, portraits, photographs, stuffed animals or dolls. They closed movie theaters and banned music and dancing. They outlawed Western hairstyles, gambling, and not praying at specific times.[90] The Taliban punished those accused of theft by amputating a hand, while they publicly executed those guilty of rape and murder. The Ministry for the Promotion of Virtue and Suppression of Vice (PVSV) made up these rules that the "religious police" judiciously enforced. When the Taliban conquered new towns, hundreds of religious police beat with long sticks offenders, typically men without beards and women who were not dressed properly.[91]

The Taliban targeted women in particular for strict control. Women could not be employed, educated or participate in sports. They were prohibited from wearing clothing regarded as "stimulating and attractive," including the Iranian *hijab*, which was viewed as insufficiently complete in its covering since the face was revealed. They required women to wear the **burqa**, a traditional all black bulky robe covering the entire body except for a small screen at eye level. Taliban restrictions became more severe as they took control of more areas. In 1998 the religious police in Kabul forced all women off the streets and issued new regulations ordering "householders to blacken their windows, so women would not be visible from the outside."[92] The Taliban did not allow women to take a taxi without a close male relative as an escort, wash clothes in streams, nor have their body measurements taken by tailors. They forbade home schooling for girls. Since almost all the teachers in primary schools in Kabul were women, the Taliban closed down the schools for girls and boys. The Taliban did not permit females to attend co-educational schools; this prevented the vast majority of young women and girls in Afghanistan from receiving even a primary education. The Taliban restricted women's jobs to the medical sector, since they did not allow male medical personnel to examine women. In June 1998, the Taliban stopped all women from going to general hospitals in Kabul, leaving only one functioning all-women's hospital. There were many reports of the Taliban publicly beating Muslim women for violating their version of Islamic law.[93]

The Taliban destroyed hundreds of cultural items and traditions that they regarded as anti-Islamic, including artifacts at museums and private art collections. In 2001, the Taliban wielded sledgehammers to destroy works of art at the National Museum of Afghanistan.[94] They carried out a senseless desecration in March 2001 when they ordered the demolition of two Buddha statues carved into cliffsides at Bamiyan—one 38 meters (125 ft) tall and carved in 507 CE, the other 53 meters (174 ft) tall and carved in 554 CE. It was a UN Educational, Scientific and Cultural Organization (UNESCO) protected site, and many countries around the world roundly condemned the act. However, the Taliban claimed that all representations of humans and idols, including those in museums, must be destroyed in accordance with Islamic law which, they say, prohibits any form of idol worship. Even the countries that supported the Taliban—Pakistan, Saudi Arabia and the United Arab Emirates—denounced the act as savage.[95]

Taliban religious police beating a woman in Kabul on August 26, 2001

The Taliban banned local festivities, even the traditional Afghan New Year's celebration of Nowruz, since it was regarded as anti-Islamic. No cultural celebrations for the Afghan people were allowed if women were present. If only men were at the celebration, the Taliban would allow it to go forth, as long as it did not go past the 9:00 (21:00) curfew time. Even at the Kabul zoo, the Taliban killed most animals or left them to starve.[96]

The Taliban are of Pashtun ethnicity, which makes up about 40 percent of the Afghan population. At first the Taliban stated that they were willing to share power with other ethnic groups, but as their control increased, they refused to share power with the other 60 percent. In fact, the Taliban received extensive support from Pashtuns across the country, who thought that the movement might restore their national supremacy. Critics of the Taliban complained that their dominance made it appear as if they were an occupying force. Also, many Muslims claimed that many of the Taliban prohibitions had no validity in the Qur'an (Koran) or Islamic law.[97]

The Taliban, who are Sunni, do not consider Shias (these are the two largest branches of Islam) to be "real" Muslims. They also declared that the Hazara ethnic group, which total over 10 percent of Afghanistan's population, were not Muslims.[98] The worst attack on innocent civilians came in summer 1998 when the Taliban swept into predominantly Hazara cities and for two days drove their pickup trucks up and down the narrow streets, shooting indiscriminately—shop owners, cart pullers, women and children shoppers, and even goats and donkeys. They reportedly killed more than 8,000 noncombatants.[99] During the following years, groups such as Human Rights Watch documented rapes and massacres of the Hazara people by Taliban forces.[100]

The devastation and hardship of the war against the Soviet Union and the civil war that followed was a factor influencing the ideology of the Taliban. The young Taliban soldiers were often barely literate, and did not know the finer points of Islamic law and history. Although many attended Islamic religious schools in Pakistan, *madrasas*, their teachers were not well-educated in the details of Islam or Islamic law. They were brought up in a male society and had sub-standard knowledge of their tribal and clan history and no traditional skills, such as farming, herding, handicraft-making. In such an environment, war meant employment and peace meant unemployment. Domination of women showed manhood. For the Taliban, rigid Islamic belief was not merely out of principles, but out of political survival.[101]

Peace did not bring economic prosperity to Afghanistan. Opium poppies, used to produce the addictive drug heroin, have been grown in Afghanistan and, with the war shattering other parts of the economy, opium again became the number one export. But in 2000 the Taliban banned opium production, which still accounted for 75 percent of the world's supply. Others claimed that the Taliban cut back opium production to shore up its price, and increase the income for poppy farmers and revenue for Afghan tax collectors, not to prevent its use.[102] When the Taliban vacated power in 2001, opium cultivation increased in the provinces taken from Taliban control. By 2005, poppy production was 87 percent of the world's opium supply, rising to 90 percent in 2006.[103] As of 2009, the Taliban were supporting the opium trade and getting money from it.

The Taliban did not cooperate with the UN and NGOs (non-governmental organizations) to receive much needed relief. Infrastructure and the economy were decimated, there was no running water, little electricity, few telephones, few paved roads or regular energy supplies. Basic necessities like water, food and housing were in desperately short supply. In addition, the clan and family structure that provided Afghans with a social and economic safety net was in tatters. Afghanistan's infant mortality rate ranked the highest in the world. A full quarter of all children died before they reached their 15th birthday.[104]

On September 9, 2001, al-Qaeda carried out a suicide bombing attack killing the military leader of the Northern Alliance (the opposition to the Taliban). Al-Qaeda was planning the 9/11 attacks on the U.S. and its members wanted to eliminate opposition in Afghanistan, since they knew that the attacks would provoke serious U.S. retaliation against them. In response to the terrorist attacks on September 11, 2001, the U.S. launched a military campaign to topple the Taliban regime and eliminate Osama bin Laden's terrorist network, Al-Qaeda. The earlier assassination left the Northern Alliance leaderless, but they held together and worked with the U.S. and its allies in the campaign called Operation Enduring Freedom.[105]

A new Afghan government took office to replace the ousted Taliban. Despite charges of corruption, Hamid Karzai won democratic elections to become the new president. His job was a tough one: to assert central government authority while curbing the power of local, tribal strongmen. The Northern Alliance mainly fought the ground war against the Taliban, while the U.S. and its allies conducted an aerial attack. Although the coalition was able to force the Taliban from power, coalition forces were never able to entirely destroy it. An insurgency movement, a Taliban guerrilla war, continues. Its operation is based in the mountainous and largely lawless tribal area on the Pakistan-Afghanistan border. As the U.S. military diverted its attention from Afghanistan to the invasion and occupation of Iraq, the Taliban regrouped and began to extend its influence in the southern part of Afghanistan. The resurgence of the opium trade helped fill the group's coffers. As the fighting continued, foreign soldiers from neighboring countries filled the Taliban ranks.[106]

Cases Studies of Human Rights Abuses

The Taliban expanded its control into the Swat valley of northwestern Pakistan, once called the "Switzerland of Pakistan" since it is a beautiful and a popular tourist destination for skiers. Taliban fighters have taken over valuable emerald mines in the valley, a source of income for their operations. The following is a story of a family fleeing the Taliban's takeover of the Swat valley.

A Refugee Family in the Swat Valley

In May 2009 Hanifa and her four children fled their home in Mingora, in the Swat valley, where fighting has intensified heavily over the past month. Hanifa's eyes filled with tears when she talked about Gul Shah, 17, and Zeenat, 15, whom she hasn't seen since they left to visit family in another village. "I am very worried about my children and desperately want to go back to Swat and find them, but the younger children do not let me go," she says. "They are afraid that if I go I will be killed like their father." Hanifa and her children fled after her husband, Bahadur Khan, was killed in crossfire. "We didn't even have time to give my husband a proper burial, and we had to leave his body with the men in our neighborhood, because it was too dangerous for women and children to stay," she said.

Walking out of the war zone Hanifa and her children walked for days over extremely difficult mountain terrain to escape. The trip left Palwasha, age five, with blistered feet. "I was exhausted and wanted to sit down but my mother kept on walking and forced us to walk," she said. "It was too dangerous to stop. There was shelling and bullets were flying over our heads, and I desperately wanted to get my children to a safer place," explained Hanifa.

Despite the deep sorrow of losing her husband and the separation from her eldest children, Hanifa is grateful for the shelter and basic provisions they have received in Jalozai refugee camp. The largest camp in the area, Jalozai is home to almost 90,000 people. Almost 50,000 have arrived within the last three weeks. Only a small minority of those displaced by the fighting live in the camps—the rest are staying with friends, family or have found other forms of shelter. The majority of those in the camps are women and children—many of the men have stayed in their homes to protect their property. The Pakistani government and UNICEF established the camps for the displaced people fleeing the Taliban. The family is provided basic services at the camp, as well as help for children who have recently been severely traumatized, orphaned or separated from their families.[107]

Questions to Consider

1. Do you think the Taliban is guilty of human rights violations? If so, which ones?
2. Do you think that the Taliban should be left alone to govern as they see fit or should the UN, US or other international organizations intervene in Afghanistan? Explain.

The Crisis in Darfur

"In this country with its diverse population, if you give guns to one group you're pitting brother against brother and that's volatile and it's not good. And who is it that's done that? The Sudanese government has done that."[108] —The chief of the village of Harraza in Darfur

Darfur is a large province that is part of the nation of the Republic of Sudan, the largest country in Africa and the tenth largest in the world; the capital city is Khartoum. It is located in the northeast part of Africa just south of Egypt, and east of the Sahara Desert, the Nile River bisects Sudan in two. Great Britain administered Sudan as its colony until it became an independent nation in 1956. In

2011, South Sudan declared its independence from the Republic of Sudan.

Civil wars stemming from ethnic, religious, and economic conflict between northern Sudan with Arab roots and Southern Sudan with Christian and native African religious roots have plagued Sudan's modern history. Since the 1980s, civil war pitting the central government in Khartoum against rebels in the southern region has torn Sudan apart. One of the key reasons for the recent conflict was oil, which is concentrated in the south and controlled by rebel groups. In 2003, the U.S. pushed peace talks between the two groups that made some progress. Both sides decided how to divide the oil revenue. But as one conflict appeared to be settled, another related conflict broke out in Sudan's western region: Darfur.

Darfur is huge, roughly the size of Texas, and is divided into three large states that have a collective population of about 6 million people. Geographically Darfur is a semi-arid plain, which makes it difficult to sustain a large population. A famine in the mid-1980s led to the first significant fighting in Darfur. A low level conflict has continued since that time. The fighting reached a peak in 2003 with the beginning of what is known as the Darfur Conflict. Darfur is a multi-ethnic society, with 40 to 80 different ethnic groups living in small villages. The people of Darfur are typically either farmers or nomads. The farmers tend to be more African and the nomads more Arab. However, this is a place where most people are Muslims and most also have dark skin; therefore, foreigners find it difficult to distinguish between Arabs and Africans. Both groups have lived in the region for centuries.[109]

Camp of Darfuris internally displaced by the War in Darfur

The traditional conflict between the Arabic nomads and African farmers has been more of an economic conflict than an ethnic one. But since the mid-1990s, friction between the two groups has increased. The nomads moved about the country with their herds, often trampling farmers' fields. Some farmers, who also owned animals, competed for food and space with the nomads' animals. The farmers have also resented how the government and President Omar al-Bashir have treated Darfur; they feel the Sudanese government is encouraging hatred against one another. The farmers say the top local government positions go only to candidates with Arab backgrounds, and there is little government money for roads, hospitals, and schools. Aggravating the situation, the population has grown dramatically, and a drought has contributed to the scarcity of pasture land.[110] Scarce resources have contributed to the tragedy.

The spark that set off the wave of shocking atrocities was ignited in early 2003 when the Khartoum government in the north made peace with the southern rebels. Some farmers in Darfur thought that they could use armed rebellion to make the government address some of their concerns. In early 2003, a small rebel movement of African villagers in Darfur confronted the largely Arab government of Sudan. The rebels, called the Sudanese Liberation Army (SLA), had taken up arms to protest the critical shortage of resources in Darfur and alleged discrimination by the government in Khartoum. The uprising shocked the government, which moved quickly to crush the rebels. To carry out this task the government gave weapons to local Arab nomadic militia groups; among the most feared were the ***Janjaweed*** (the word comes from Arabic jan meaning evil and jawad meaning horse). Adding volatility to the situation, the Arab nomads were already in conflict with the African farmers over land and cattle.[111]

The government ordered the Janjaweed nomads to massacre the farmers and forced the survivors to flee their homes. Without warning, Sudanese airplanes bombed villages, and then trucks loaded with soldiers and Janjaweed militia on camels and horses surrounded and attacked the villagers. In some cases, the villagers fled and only lost their food, animals, and homes. In other cases, the soldiers and Janjaweed slaughtered the men and boys and raped the women. The attackers then looted the villages and set fire to wooden huts. They repeated this scorched-earth policy over and over again. From the air, it looked as though over 400 villages were mere black smudges across the stark landscape.[112]

Arab Janjaweed tribes have been a major player in the conflict

The UN condemned the government in Khartoum for atrocities in 2004, but officials insisted that the stories of rapes and murders were greatly exaggerated. Eventually, the government promised it would halt and disarm the Janjaweed, but reports only grew worse. Darfur survivors gathered in camps, while humanitarian groups helped them as much as possible. The Paris-based Doctors Without Borders sent medicine and doctors to the area, but the need for food and medical care was overwhelming. In September 2004, President George W. Bush declared the crisis in Darfur genocide. There was much outrage in the United States over the suffering in Darfur, but little action was taken. In December 2005, the U.S. Congress rejected a last-minute plea from U.S. Secretary of State Condoleezza Rice to send $50 million to support groups trying to secure peace in the region. The Sudanese government also barred UN investigators from entering the country to collect evidence on possible war crimes.[114]

By 2004, details of what actually happened in Darfur finally got the attention of human rights

A Janjaweed Attack...as told by the village chief of Torora in Darfur

"On March 3, 2006, at about 5 a.m., the *Janjaweed* attacked [our] cattle camp. After their previous looting we decided to store our cattle together between the three villages: N'Djamena, Moukchacha, and Modaina. When other neighboring villagers heard the fighting they came running to the cattle camp. But the *Janjaweed* had set up ambushes between the camp and the villages. Many of us were killed and we had to let the cattle go and return to our villages. When we came back we heard shooting near the villages we had come from. While we were gone the Janjaweed had encircled our villages and when we tried to get back in they shot at us. Inside the villages they killed all the men. Over the next days they came back over and over again, each time taking more things till we had nothing worth taking anymore."[113]

The Crisis in Darfur

Rape in Darfur...as told by a resident of the Djawara village in Darfur

"One Sunday after the attack on Djawara, some girls from our village went to gather firewood in the wadi and came across some Janjaweed. One of them managed to escape to warn us. When we, parents and other villagers arrived in the wadi, the Janjaweed shot at us. Four girls were raped. Here girls have a duty to get married—there are hardly any single people—but none would marry these girls now that this has happened. The four girls are 13, 10, 12 and 9 respectively."[116]

groups and the international press. Hundreds of thousands of refugees who fled the region told horrific stories of burned villages, husbands and sons slaughtered before their eyes, and women and girls brutally raped. The refugees, many of them starving, gathered in wretched refugee camps in neighboring countries of Chad and Libya, also badly affected by drought. The refugees and some Western observers said there was a deliberate attempt to drive black Africans out of Darfur.[115]

In May 2006, the Sudanese government signed a peace agreement with one of the rebel groups. But the government continued to fight the two other groups that refused to sign the agreement. The rebels also fought amongst themselves, making the conflict in Darfur even more confusing and complex.

One of the weapons of war in Darfur, as in Rwanda, was rape. Physicians for Human Rights interviewed for a study as many as 40 percent of the women who had been raped or sexually assaulted in Darfur. They found that rape victims suffer physical, psychological and social scars. In Darfur, a conservative Muslim society, rape victims suffer from dishonor and shame. Husbands often disown their wives who are raped, while unmarried rape victims may never marry because society considers them to be "spoiled."[117] Fearing social isolation, many rape victims do not tell anyone about their suffering, even health care workers. A 20-year-old woman from a small village in Darfur did tell Physicians for Human Rights investigators, "They saw me and it was too late to run. They took me inside my house and raped me several times. They beat me, then they left me to die." Fortunately,

Arielle Wisotsky and Help Darfur Now[123]

Think high school field trips don't change lives? Think again. Back in 2005, Arielle Wisotsky visited the Holocaust Museum in Washington, DC with her high school class. There she learned of the genocide going on in Darfur for the first time. It deeply affected her, and she realized she couldn't just stand there letting another tragedy happen (her grandmother is a Holocaust survivor). So, Arielle decided to take action. Educating herself on Darfur, she then started to educate others by forming the non-profit Help Darfur Now with two of her friends, David and Eric Messinger.

"I had done some community service before, but nothing to this extent," says Arielle. Help Darfur Now is basically an organization of high school and middle school students. Our main goal is to raise awareness of what's going on in Darfur and raise money. When we started out, we thought we'd raise $1,000. We sent fundraising letters to family members and family friends, but then we started getting press, because people thought it was interesting that we were so young."

Now, three years later, Arielle is a student at Tufts University, and Help Darfur Now has raised over $400,000 aiding the relief of Darfur, giving its money to organizations like Doctors Without Borders and the International Rescue Committee. "I know it sounds cliché," she admits, "but one person can make a difference, three people can make a difference. People think you can't, but you can."

local women found her and helped her recover, but it took months for her to heal from the physical injuries. She later rejoined her husband in Chad, but she cannot bring herself to tell her husband, her relatives, or anyone in the refugee camp about being raped.

In addition to feeling isolated, many victims of rape do not receive necessary medical attention and psychological counseling. Those who report rape to authorities but cannot find four male witnesses to corroborate their charges may be prosecuted for adultery, whipped and imprisoned. The attackers who sexually assault women also beat them, leaving them with broken bones and internal and external bleeding. A woman who becomes pregnant from the rape must confront a difficult dilemma—whether to abandon her baby or risk community rejection by keeping the baby. Thus, the Janjaweed use rape as a way to "pollute" blood lines and undermine family bonds.[118]

Oil is another factor in the Darfur crisis, as mentioned above. Even though there is no oil in Darfur itself, the Sudanese government uses it to pay for its enormous military expenditures. Sudan sells oil to China, who, in turn, sells it weapons, including tanks, aircraft, medium-sized weapons and small arms. China has even helped Sudan set up its own small and medium-sized weapon production factories. The Western media often describe the crisis in Darfur, and in other African conflicts, as a "tribal conflict;" however, other factors such as the Sudanese government's desire to control land and regional resources and to consolidate its power, are important.[119]

An immense humanitarian crisis occurred in Darfur. Despite the world's outcry, the violence continued in Darfur, and the number of dead and displaced increased. From direct attacks and the deterioration of living conditions, many experts estimated that 200,000 to 400,000 people died through 2009, mostly through starvation and disease, while more than 2.5 million were displaced.[120]

The International Criminal Court (ICC) issued an arrest warrant for al-Bashir on March 4, 2009, on counts of war crimes and crimes against humanity, but ruled that there was insufficient evidence to prosecute him for genocide.[121] Al-Bashir is the first sitting head of state ever indicted by the ICC. He responded to the arrest warrant by stating that it would "not be worth the ink it is written on" and then danced in front of thousands of cheering supporters. The African Union, League of Arab States, and the governments of Russia and China opposed the ICC's decision.[122] Al-Bashir won the 2010 Sudanese presidential election, and continues as the president as of this writing in 2015.

Despite these atrocities, is the Darfur crisis a genocide? Countless individuals, NGOs and even some governments recognize the Darfur situation as genocide. Yet others say the intent of the al Bashir government in Khartoum to eliminate black Africans is not persuasive enough.[124]

Questions to Consider
1. From the examples included here, how would you describe the causes of genocide in Darfur?

There are many more case studies on human rights violations and genocide that could have been included in this chapter. One is unfolding at the time of this writing in Syria, where over 200,000 people have been killed and another 4 million are refugees fleeing the conflict. I hope this chapter has sparked interest in learning more about the human rights abuses that have occurred in the past and that are continuing today.

CHAPTER FIVE

HUMAN RIGHTS ACTIVISTS

"Each time a man stands up for an ideal or acts to improve the lot of others or strikes out against injustice, he sends forth a tiny ripple of hope, and crossing each other from a million different centers of energy and daring, those ripples build a current that can sweep down the mightiest walls of oppression and resistance."

— *Robert F. Kennedy, United States*

An Introduction to Human Rights Activists

This chapter on human rights activists is a hopeful chapter. Following some very bleak topics, this chapter highlights the open-minded and compassionate part of our human behavior. I am writing about six remarkable humans rights activists, although thousands more could be noted. I wanted to give a cross section of backgrounds, geographic locations, and causes that motivate these dedicated individuals to work for the dignity of all human beings. Wangari Maathai from Kenya championed human rights through the environmental movement. Shirin Ebadi from Iran, a woman and a lawyer, fought against the denial of human rights to women and children by the Islamic Republic. Aung Sui Kyi from Burma (Myanmar) worked to establish human rights in a military dictatorship. Rigoberta Menchu, an indigenous woman from Guatemala, struggled for indigenous rights during the Guatemalan Civil War that targeted indigenous people. Mohamed Yunus from Bangladesh worked to establish human dignity through championing economic rights for all, including poor, powerless women. The Dali Llama from Tibet, a Buddhist monk, has been a tireless spokesperson for human rights, despite their religious calling.

Wangari Maathai, Kenya

"It is evident that many wars are fought over resources which are now becoming increasingly scarce. If we conserved our resources better, fighting over them would not then occur...so, protecting the global environment is directly related to securing peace...those of us who understand the complex concept of the environment have the burden to act. We must not tire, we must not give up, we must persist."
— Wangari Maathai on receiving the news of being awarded the Nobel Peace Prize, 2004

Wangari Maathai (1940-2011) founded the **Green Belt Movement** (GBM) in Kenya in 1977. The movement is a grassroots non-governmental organization (NGO) that focuses on environment conservation and development through a nationwide grassroots tree-planting campaign. Kenyans manage the campaign using local capacity, knowledge, wisdom and expertise. Most members, primarily women, live in rural areas. Maathai became internationally known in 2004 when she was awarded the Nobel Peace Prize for her efforts in the GBM. Despite Maathai's untimely death in 2011, the GBM continues.

Maathai was born April 1, 1940, in the Ihithe tribe of Kenya. Because of her keen intellect, she was able to pursue higher education in the U.S., a rarity for girls in rural areas. She earned her biology degree from Mount St. Scholastica College in Kansas and a master's degree at the University of Pittsburgh. When she returned to Kenya, Wangari Maathai worked in veterinary medicine research at the University of Nairobi, and eventually, despite resistance from male students and faculty, she earned a Ph.D. She worked her way up through the academic ranks, becoming head of the veterinary medicine faculty, a first for a woman at that university. In 2003, she ran for a seat in Kenya's Parliament, and she won with 98 percent of the vote and served until 2007; this was the country's first free and fair election in decades.[1]

Kenya is located on the eastern coast of Africa and is slightly smaller than the state of Texas or the country of France. The capital and largest city is Nairobi. The equator runs across the country and divides it into two nearly equal parts. Currently, forests cover less than 2 percent of Kenya; scrub and semi-desert vegetation covers the largest area, followed by savanna grassland. The population has grown rapidly in recent decades. Each person belongs to one of the country's 42 communities; although there are many similarities, each community has its own unique culture. A few of the communities are the Luo, Kikuyu, Kamba, Luhya, Maasai, Meru, Embu, Somali and Turkana. Maathai was of Kikuyu ethnicity.[2]

The British colonized and ruled Kenya and the surrounding area known as East Africa. After the end of World War II there was a rallying cry in Africa for liberation from European colonial rule and the establishment of free and independent countries. Kenyan peasants formed the Mau Mau Movement (1952–1960), an armed struggle against the British. Members of Maathai's Kikuyu ethnic group formed the core of the resistance. Although the uprising failed militarily, it hastened Kenyan independence and motivated other Africans to fight for independence. Kenya finally gained independence in 1963.

The period of colonization was very difficult for the Kenyan people. Their cultural values and indigenous ways of living were considered inferior to those of the British and the West. Their traditional values were eroded, trivialized and deliberately belittled with colonization, while modern values were praised.

Wangari Maathai, Kenya

Maathai states, "Even after colonization, it is unfortunate that [indigenous] cultural values still continue to be suppressed today in the name of modernization, civilization and Christianity. As a result, many people are less appreciative of the environment because they now perceive it as a commodity to be privatized and exploited." She compared the ways in which her grandparents, parents, and her generation looked upon outstanding members of their society and observed that her generation had marginalized heroes of the past and disregarded their great achievements. She thought that this too was "partly as a result of colonialism, which condemned our heroes and role models and instead praised those who collaborated with them (colonialists)."[3]

Maathai's most notable achievement was the organization of the Green Belt Movement that she founded in the 1970s. But it didn't happen overnight. In 1972, the environmental movement

Maathai on Tree-Planting

"In many parts of the less industrialized and less-consuming world, more than 90 percent of the rural population are poor and depend on inexpensive and readily available forms of fuel (grain stalks, wood fuel, cow dung, etc.) for cooking and warming their homes. In places where wood fuel is gathered but not replenished, the sources near the homesteads are quickly exhausted. This forces the gatherers, who are mostly women, to trek increasingly longer distances to gather the fuel, an exhausting and time-consuming exercise. Furthermore, in areas where wood fuel is gathered from forests, local biodiversity is threatened. This tree-planting project encourages communities to plant trees to replenish what they cut in order to maintain a consistent supply and also to use energy-saving technologies."[5]

took a major step forward when the UN established an Environment Program (UNEP) in Nairobi. This helped fuel her passion for the environment. She next formed Envirocare, a small organization headquartered in her home that planted trees in distressed areas. She ran into difficulties because she lacked support at home and in the community, but her fellow members of the National Council of Women of Kenya (NCWK) encouraged her efforts. She proposed a project in which the organization would plant trees. The purpose of the project was to inexpensively meet many of the rural members' need for wood fuel, building and fencing materials and soil conservation. In 1977, the group adopted her project.[4]

The women adopted the NCWK tree-planting project in the *Harambee* spirit, which means "Let us all pull together!" Many communities used and still use the word to boost the morale of participants during communal work. The first tree-planting ceremony took place in Nairobi on World Environment Day in 1977. True to her word, to pay respect to previous generations, Maathai and the women's group dedicated the first ceremony to honoring deceased Kenyans who had made outstanding contributions at the community or national level.[6]

At first the Kenyan forestry department was very supportive of the women's work. But over time, the women established direct relationships with farmers, and their project became more effective than the forestry department. This resulted in hostility from the forestry department and even the President of Kenya. Some farmers were intimidated and discouraged from planting trees. Therefore, NCWK decided to encourage women's groups to join Save the Land *Harambee* and establish their own tree nurseries where members could obtain seedlings. They launched a fund-raising campaign to raise money for the tree project. One of the few local companies that donated to the campaign was Mobil Oil of Kenya.[7]

The women organized seminars where government foresters taught the basics of tree nursery management to the women but used many technical terms. Since most of the women were illiterate, a less formal approach was needed. Then came the agricultural revolution! The modern way of farming used scientific knowledge, chemical fertilizers, large machinery, and lots of irrigation, while encouraging growing cash crops (crops sold to the world market) and management by men. Traditional farming was much different: women farmed, indigenous crops were grown, and diverse techniques suited to the environment were used. The women decided to do away with the professional foresters and instead relied on their traditions and common sense. After all, they had successfully cultivated crops on their farms for a long time. They decided to apply this strategy to tree planting, which encouraged women to use their traditional skills and wisdom. As a result, many women become foresters without a formal diploma.[8]

With community support, the women expanded tree planting to public lands. They planted seedlings in rows of at least 1,000 to form green belts of trees. These "belts" had the advantages of providing shade and windbreaks, conserving the soil, beautifying the landscape and protecting habitats for birds and small animals. They named the project of planting these belts of trees the Green Belt Movement. GBM defines a "green belt" as a woodlot established by planting several trees on a piece of land that can either be public or private. A public green belt aimed to plant a least 1,000 trees, while a private green belt planted at least 100 trees. They issued the seedlings free of charge, since many of the farmers could not afford the additional expense for tree planting. As interest and dedication grew in various communities, so did the Green Belt Movement, and by 1999, volunteers had established 6,000 tree nurseries in 26 districts.[9]

Maathai explained why communities embraced the idea of tree planting. In traditional times, both women and men farmed, though they grew different crops. The women cultivated annual crops, which they stored in granaries, while men grew perennial crops like yams, cassava and bananas, which were stored on the farm. With the colonial system, women gradually took over the men's farming roles. When the women planted trees, the men wanted to join in. And it was easy for them to do so because tree-planting was in keeping with their traditional responsibilities, since it provided the household with wood and building materials.[10]

As the GBM grew some of the managerial duties, such as record keeping, tree nursery management, organizing activities and providing leadership were handed-over to tree-nursery members. Community members gained experience and skills.[11] Tree-planting became an income-generating activity that supplemented incomes; therefore, the women's groups gained financially. All community members who planted trees benefited from an increased wood fuel supply and enriched soil.

Green Belt Movement

Maathai addressed several problems that resulted from decades of colonial rule and the imposition of modern farming methods. Known as the **African crisis**, it was the distressed state of affairs in many areas of African society that resulted in poverty, unemployment, disease, environmental degradation, political corruption, population pressures, malnutrition/starvation, and the subjugation of women. Maathai was aware of the complex and entrenched root causes of the African crisis and worked to correct the problems as much as she could with the tree planting program. The program encouraged subsistence farming and soil conservation, promoted the status of women, and reduced malnutrition and disease.[12]

One of the problems in Kenya, and Africa in general, was that since the 1970s many farmers had gradually turned to cash-crop farming, which meant that farmers grew crops to sell on the world market for prices determined by supply and demand. Since independence, Kenyan farmers had increased cash-crop farming at the expense of subsistence farming (growing crops for the household's consumption) because they thought that the money earned from cash-crops would generate an income to support their families. But because of mismanagement, high costs for seeds and fertilizers, and fluctuating prices for their crops, many farmers were left without enough money to purchase food. This resulted in unbalanced diets and malnutrition.[13] Instead, GBM encouraged farmers to practice both cash and subsistence farming so as to ensure enough food for the household. They also encouraged farmers to plant indigenous food crops—roots, cereals, legumes, yams, cassava, and vegetables—since these foods were high in nutritional value and contributed to local biological diversity.[14]

Malnutrition and disease, Maathai found, was an epidemic in Kenya. For example, farmers with moderate incomes replaced healthy, traditional unprocessed foods such as sweet potatoes, yams, cassava, and indigenous green vegetables with diets similar to urbanites. These foods had a high cost and were generally unhealthy, since they were high in carbohydrates but poor in proteins and vitamins. This left many families malnourished. Also, about 90 percent of the people living in rural areas were unable to cook their food properly because of lack of cooking fuel, which contributed to malnutrition.[15]

Maathai found that over the years food production in Kenya and Africa in general had gradually decreased in yield, which contributed to regular famines. In addition, the number of malnourished adults and children was increasing. Among the leading causes of poor crop yields were over-farming land, excessive use of chemical fertilizers and loss of topsoil. In response to these problems, GBM established a pilot project and urged farmers to adopt soil conservation, top-soil rebuilding and water-harvesting practices. To ensure that the project reached community members, it was conducted at the household level.[16] Maathai noted that over the years many farmers ignored organic and other sustainable methods of farming because they were convinced that chemical fertilizers were more beneficial. She believed these notions were misplaced and that many farmers were unaware that chemical fertilizers actually harmed soil fertility over the long term. GBM promoted organic farming techniques that inexpensively increased soil fertility, reduced fertilizer and pesticide costs and increased yields. They promoted the use of animal manure as fertilizer, mulching, composting, crop rotation and planting trees.[17]

Since agriculture was an important export in Kenya, Maathai claimed that the land's fertile topsoil was one of Kenya's most valuable national resources, and farmers should treat it as such. However, she found that farmers attached little economic value to the soil. During the rainy season, engorged rivers swept away thousands of tons of topsoil from Kenya's countryside to the ocean and lakes. Wind erosion denuded the land of vegetative cover, causing the loss of more soil. Soil erosion was caused by random deforestation, clearing vegetative cover, and planting along riverbeds, slopes and marginal lands. GBM trained community members to use inexpensive techniques to combat soil loss, such as planting indigenous species of trees, maintaining vegetative cover on the land, creating windbreaks, digging trenches, constructing terraces and protecting forests.[18]

It is a well-known fact that many politicians and decision makers in the developing world are the rich and powerful; Kenya is no exception. Unfortunately, many of the leaders ignore the issue of conservation, since they are usually involved, directly or indirectly, in the plundering of the country's natural resources.[19] Rich countries and businesses prefer to work with corrupt African leaders who will grant them concessions to their country's natural resources at a very cheap price, as long as the African leaders get their cut of the profit. The ones that suffer in this corrupt bargain are the impoverished and exploited citizens of Africa. Maathai understood this unfair practice and worked to change the system for the benefit of the poor. The Kenyan government was a major detractor and a source of harassment and violent obstruction to many of her noble efforts.[20]

The women of Kenya tell stories of the difficult past, when they walked long distances to fetch or purchase wood fuel and then slowly walked home carrying backbreaking loads. They also talk of the times when they had to change their diets because there was not enough fuel to cook with. But with the tree planting project things have changed for the better for many rural people. Today, they proudly tell how they can quickly obtain sufficient supplies of wood fuel, since it is now available on their farms. They also acknowledge a decline in soil erosion, the return of wildlife (especially birds and small mammals), and the benefits of cleaner air and shade. The men are grateful and full of praise for the women because of the wonderful work they have done for the community.[21]

GBM has also promoted awareness of the importance of the environment in schools. So far, over 3,000 schools have wood-lots that students helped to establish. When green belts are planted on school compounds, teachers are encouraged to fully involve students in the planting and nurturing processes.[22]

Maathai said deforestation is the main environmental challenge in Kenya. Even though GBM has planted millions of trees, forest cover has still been reduced to about 1.7 percent, while the UN Environment Program recommends a minimum of 10 percent. Two-thirds of Kenya is arid, semi-arid, and desert and it is vulnerable to the encroaching Sahara Desert. Always the optimist, Maathai summed up her life's efforts: "For many of us, because we are driven by idealism rather than politics, we have to train ourselves to be patient and realize that governments are not run by idealists. For those of us who come from that perspective you have to be patient and know that we're not going to change the big landscape; [but] perhaps we can change the landscape of a forest."[23]

Questions to Consider
1. Why do you think Wangari Maathai was so successful in establishing the GBM in Kenya?

SHIRIN EBADI, IRAN

"Any person who pursues human rights in Iran must live with fear from birth to death, but I have learned to overcome my fear." — Shirin Ebadi, 1999 interview

Shirin Ebadi is a human rights and democracy activist, a lawyer and founder of the Center for the Defense of Human Rights in Iran. She was awarded the 2003 Nobel Peace Prize for her significant and pioneering efforts for democracy and human rights, especially women's, children's, and refugee rights. She was the first Iranian and the first Muslim woman to receive the prize.[24]

Ebadi was born in 1947 in Hamadan, Iran, which is situated in the northwestern part and is believed to be among the oldest Iranian cities and one of the oldest cities in the world. She and her family were practicing Muslims and academics. Her father, Mohammad Ali Ebadi, was the city's chief notary public and professor of commercial law. Her mother devoted her time to her husband and four children. Ebadi's two sisters and one brother are highly educated, which is exceedingly respected in Iran. She spent her childhood in a family, as she says, "filled with kindness and affection." At the age of one, she and her family settled in Tehran, the capital, and she has since lived in the city. She attended Tehran University and gained a place at the Faculty of Law in 1965. After she completed her law degree, she started

Shirin Ebadi, Iran

a 6-month apprenticeship at the Department of Justice. She officially began to serve as a judge in March 1969, while continuing her education. She earned a doctorate with honors in private law in 1971 and in 1975, she became the first woman judge in Iran.[25] She is married, and her husband is an electrical engineer; they are the parents of two adult daughters.

The year 1979 marked a profound change in the life of Shirin Ebadi and millions of other Iranian citizens—the Iranian Revolution, later known as the **Islamic Revolution**. A brief background of this pivotal event will shed light on the life and work of Shirin Ebadi.

Mohammad Rezā Shāh Pahlavi, the Shah (emperor) of Iran, ruled the country from 1941 until his overthrow in the 1979 revolution. He inherited the office from his father Shah Reza Pahlavi (r. 1925-1941), whom the Allied powers of Great Britain and the Soviet Union unceremoniously deposed during World War II for his support of Nazi Germany. The Shah's father ushered in sweeping modern changes that the conservative tribal peoples and Islamic clerics strongly resented. For example, he replaced Islamic laws with Western ones, outlawed traditional Islamic clothing, forbade the veiling of women (hijab), and refused to separate the sexes in public spaces. Police forcibly removed and tore chadors from women who resisted his ban on public hijab.[26] The Shah continued the modernization trends his father ushered in, but he switched his allegiance to the U.S. and remained a staunch ally until the end of his reign.

During the early part of the Shah's reign, the U.S. became alarmed with the programs advanced by the popular Prime Minister Mohammad Mosaddeq (1882-1967), who won a democratic election in 1951. He proposed to nationalize (bring under national ownership) the Iranian oil industry, which had been under British ownership since 1913 (later called British Petroleum or BP). Since the U.S. purchased a great deal of oil from Iran, it feared that if the Iranian government controlled its own oil industry, shortages or price increases would result. The U.S. had a cozy relationship with the Shah which allowed them to trade military hardware made in the U.S for Iranian oil. Also, the U.S. was fearful that Mosaddeq would become too friendly with the Soviet Union, Iran's communist neighbor to the north; thus, Cold War fears played a part in U.S. actions. Before most Iranians knew what was happening, Mosaddeq was quickly removed from power in a coup d'état (overthrow) on August 19, 1953. The U.S. Central Intelligence Agency (CIA), at the request of the British, organized and carried out the coup. The Shah, who had fled the country, was reinstalled as the ruler. Iranians still remember the illegal interference by the U.S. in the affairs of their government and its hand in ousting a popular political leader.[27]

Like his father's regime, the Shah was known for his ruthless rule, focus on modernization, close ties with the West, disregard of democratic measures in Iran's constitution, contempt for traditional religious customs and disdain for clerical leaders. Communist, nationalist and Islamic groups criticized him for political corruption and violating the constitution. These groups largely criticized the Shah from outside Iran, as they were violently suppressed within the country. The Shah's secret police force—SAVAK—controlled the dissident groups. Also, many Iranians criticized the Shah's close ties with the U.S.

The conservative Islamic clerics, one of the dissident groups, opposed the Shah. The leader of this group, and ultimately of the Iranian Revolution, was the Shia (a branch of Islam) cleric **Ayatollah Ruhollah Khomeini**. He first came to political prominence in 1963 when he led the opposition to the Shah's program to breakup large landholdings, grant women the right to vote and provide equality in marriage, allow religious minorities to hold government office, and encourage friendly relations with Israel. Authorities arrested him for his protests and sent him into exile in France for 14 years. It was during his time of exile that the budding Islamic revival began to take shape, with followers rejecting modernization, shunning ties to the West, especially the U.S., and loathing the Shah's secular regime. Khomeini once called the Shah a "wretched miserable man" who had "embarked on the destruction of Islam in Iran." He preached that revolt and martyrdom against injustice and oppression was the Shia Islamic tradition, and that Muslims should reject the influence of both capitalism and communism.[28]

While in exile, Khomeini created the idea of *velavat-e faqih* (guardianship), which required that everyone have guardianship or supervision by leading Islamic jurists (judges). This supervision would protect Islam from deviating from traditional Islamic law, and in so doing it would eliminate poverty, injustice, and the plundering of Muslim land by foreign non-believers.[29] He believed that the Islamic jurists would be like an overprotective father, controlling every aspect of his child's life. Modernity had rejected the idea that fathers should be the undisputed ruler of the family; mothers and children should have rights and responsibilities as well. This paternalistic guardianship is what Ebadi would crusade against as a human rights lawyer in Iran.

Not everyone agreed with Khomeini's ideas. Opposition groups formed—students, democratic groups, communists, small businessmen (most were men at this time), secularists, and even some clergy. But cleverly Khomeini worked to unite this opposition behind him by focusing on the economic problems and unequal income under the Shah's corrupt regime, while sidestepping the idea of clerical rule that might divide the general public. He also relentlessly attacked the West and the U.S. specifically, as a cause of all Iranian problems. As we have seen in other human rights cases, blame targeted against an enemy is a way to distract the public from understanding a problem's real causes.

In the late 1970s, demonstrations against the Shah's regime increased, and the SAVAK responded with their customary heavy hand. Those killed by the secret police were martyred, which helped to fuel even more demonstrations. The Shah finally realized that he was facing a revolution and turned to his long-time ally for support. President Jimmy Carter offered his full commitment to the Shah's regime, despite his significant human rights violations. Anti-Shah demonstrations increased, drawing millions of demonstrators throughout the country. In one massive demonstration in December 1978, more than 10 percent of the country marched against the Shah's rule. Knowing his fate, the Shah arranged for his and the Empress Farah's departure on January 16, 1979. Scenes of spontaneous joy erupted throughout Iran, and crowds of exuberant demonstrators destroyed almost every sign of the Shah's dynasty within hours. The government installed a new politically moderate prime minister, and he immediately disbanded the hated SAVAK, freed political prisoners, ordered the army to allow mass demonstrations, promised free elections, and allowed Khomeini to return to Iran from exile.

Followers asked Khomeini to create a religious government in Qom, the religious center of Iran. On February 1, 1979, Khomeini triumphantly returned to Tehran from France. A crowd of several million screaming Iranians greeted him as a semi-divine figure at the airport. Now the unquestioned leader of the revolution, Khomeini promptly replaced the government's moderate leadership and installed his own government, as he stated "with the support of the nation."[30] He ordered that it was a religious duty for all Iranians to support their government. As the revolutionary movement gained momentum, soldiers flocked to Khomeini's side. The revolutionaries exuberantly took over police stations, military installations, government buildings, TV and radio stations, and the Shah's palaces. The revolution, essentially bloodless, was complete on February 11, 1979, which is celebrated as "Islamic Revolution's Victory Day," a national holiday. On April 1, the Islamic Republic of Iran was an official new nation.

As in most revolutions, tremendous emotion and energy is focused on removing the hated regime, but little thought is given to the replacement government. As in the case of Iran, the different factions united in their opposition to the Shah, but once the Shah was gone, these diverse factions would fight among themselves for control of the government. From 1979 to 1982, Iran was in a crisis. The economy and the daily workings of the government had collapsed, and military and security forces were in disarray. By 1982, Khomeini and his supporters had crushed the opposition factions and consolidated power. Their first task was to write a new constitution, and they declared that the new government should be 100 percent Islamic. In addition to a popularly elected president, the new constitution included an even more powerful post of unelected guardian jurist ruler. This post was intended for Khomeini, who would control the military and security services and had the power to appoint several top government officials. It increased the power and number of clerics on the Council of Guardians and gave it control over elections, as well as laws passed by the legislature. Khomeini's *velavat-e faqih* was being carried out.[31]

One of the events that helped to ensure Khomeini's rule was the **Iranian Hostage Crisis**. In late October 1979, the exiled Shah was dying from cancer and needed urgent medical treatment. Other countries refused to admit him but President Jimmy Carter extended an invitation to his

Iranian Revolution. protesters around Shahyad Square, 1979

old ally to come to the U.S. for medical care. In Iran there was an immediate outcry against Carter, and Khomeini demanded that the Shah be returned to Iran for trial and execution. On November 4, 1979, young Muslim students stormed the U.S. embassy compound and seized as hostages 53 American diplomats and staff. The hostages were hooded, handcuffed and paraded through the embassy to the delight of millions of Iranians who were expressing their anger at the U.S. They shouted "death to America" and other derogatory slurs. The diplomats in the embassy were called a "nest of spies." The holding of the hostages was very popular in Iran and continued for months even after the death of the Shah in July 1980. The hatred directed towards the Shah was now pointed directly at the Americans. Khomeini skillfully used the public outcry against the Americans to unite the Iranian people, suppress moderate voices and pass his radical constitution.[32] The prestige of Khomeini and the hostage takers was further enhanced when the Carter administration authorized a rescue attempt, which failed in dramatic fashion when two helicopters collided in the desert. America looked inept. A master at gaining publicity, Khomeini seized upon the collision to claim that the failure was due to divine intervention. The 53 hostages were held for 444 days and released on January 20, 1981, when Ronald Reagan was sworn in as President. Reagan's defeat of Carter in the

1980 election capped a series of humiliating events attached to the Carter administration.

The already shell-shocked Iranian people faced another traumatic event in September 1980, when the regime of Saddam Hussein in neighboring Iraq invaded Iran in an attempt to take advantage of the chaos in the country and destroy the revolution in its infancy. Iranians rallied behind their new government helping to stop and then reverse the Iraqi advance. The war lasted until 1988, and although both sides claimed victory, the war ended in a virtual stalemate. Both sides suffered over half a million deaths and many more causalities. Like the hostage crisis, the war served as an opportunity for the Khomeini regime to strengthen Islamic revolutionary fervor and quell fractious debate and dispute in Iran.

After the end of the Iraq War in 1988 and Khomeini's death in 1989, many evaluated the tumultuous decade in Iranian history. When Khomeini and his supporters carried out the policy of *velayat-e faquih* and installed an Islamic Republic, many, including Ebadi, became disillusioned. They thought that what began as a popular revolution against the Shah was soon transformed into an Islamic fundamentalist power-grab. Many thought that Khomeini would be more of a spiritual guide than an actual political ruler.[33] Those that did disapprove of the Khomeini regime were severely suppressed. The number of protesters and revolutionaries killed during the Iranian Revolution appear to be about 3,000, although many more were imprisoned or physically and emotionally threatened.[34]

The revolution brought an increase in education and health care for the poor, promotion of Shia Islam as the only religion, an end to secularism, and a halt to American influence in governmental affairs. But the revolution did not bring about more political freedoms, governmental honesty and efficiency, or economic equality. There developed a deep rift between the revolutionary generation and younger Iranians; those under 35 make up 70 percent of the population. They could not understand all of the revolutionary passion at the time. Since the revolution, the number of women in the civil service and higher education has risen, women make-up over 66 percent of the university's student body, a cause of concern among some of the clerics. Several women have been elected to the Iranian parliament.[35] Even though there have been improvements in many areas for women, the ideology of the revolution opposes equal rights for women. Within months of the founding of the Islamic Republic the 1967 Family Protection Law was repealed, female government workers were forced to observe the Islamic dress code (hijab), women were barred from becoming judges, beaches and sports were sex-segregated, the marriage age for girls was reduced to 13, and married women were barred from attending regular schools. Although the government has reversed some polices restricting women's activities, segregation of the sexes from schoolrooms to ski slopes to public buses to wedding parties, is strictly enforced.

Iran's economy has stagnated in recent years. There is still an over-reliance on petroleum exports for government income. Per capita income fluctuates with the price of oil—reportedly falling at one point to 25 percent of what it was prior to the revolution—and still has not reached pre-revolution levels.[36] Unemployment among Iran's young population has steadily risen as job creation has failed to keep up with the population surge of young people. There are also strict restrictions on travel to Iran from the U.S; in 2007, there were only 500 travelers to Iran from the U.S.[37]

The story of the revolution serves as backdrop for the life and work of Shirin Ebadi. She was an important opposition figure in the Islamic Revolution and its aftermath. Following the victory of Khomeini, his supporters believed that according to Islamic law women could not serve as judges. When conservative Islamic clerics took control of the country, they dismissed Ebadi and other female judges from their posts. They introduced severe restrictions on the role of women, calling them "too emotional" to hold a high ranking position in the judicial system. Instead, they gave Ebadi the job of a clerk in the very court in which she once presided over. Women protested these unfair changes to no avail. Ebadi could not tolerate this demotion and requested retirement, which was granted. During the aftermath of the revolution, the judiciary department was in a great deal of flux; officials even turned down her application for practicing law. She found herself unemployable and housebound for many years.

She used her time of unemployment to write several books and published many articles in Iranian journals. Finally, she received her lawyer's license in 1992 and set up her own practice. As a lawyer, Ebadi took on many controversial cases of dissident figures that had been critical of the conservative clerics. In one case she defended the families of murdered victims who were killed during an attack on the university dormitory. In another case two of her clients, liberal intellectuals Daryoush and Parvaneh Forouhar, were mysteriously stabbed to death at their home in 1998. The couple was among several dissidents who died in a wave of grisly murders that terrorized Iran's intellectual community. Suspicion fell on extremist hardliners who were determined to stop the more liberal climate fostered by President Khatami, who allowed freedom of speech during his presidency (1997-2005).[38] But Khomeini had set up the Council of Guardians to wield power over the president; therefore, Khatami's reforms were met with intense clerical resistance. In 2000, the hardliners accused Ebadi of distributing a videotaped confession of a right-wing thug who claimed that high up conservative leaders encouraged physical attacks on pro-reform gatherings and figures. She received a suspended jail sentence and a ban on practicing law (which was later lifted). The case brought increased focus on Iran from human rights groups abroad.

Ebadi's outspoken campaigns for democracy and greater rights for Iranian women and children often brought her into conflict with conservative clerics. She led a movement for strengthening the legal status of children and women and took on a number of social cases that included child abuse.[39] She was a driving force behind the reform of family laws in Iran that changed divorce and inheritance legislation to be more beneficial for women. She also defended women's rights activists in the courts.

In 2001, Shirin Ebadi established a non-governmental organization in Iran, the Center for the Defense of Human Rights. She wrote academic books and articles calling for greater legal protection for Iranian children and showing alleged human rights violations by Iranian authorities.[40] Human rights groups across the world admire her for refusing to be silenced and her willingness to take on politically sensitive legal cases. She is a popular figure in the Iranian reformist movement. But her outspokenness has also led to her harassment by the conservative forces that control the judiciary. In 1996, Human Rights Watch honored Ebadi as a leading human rights defender for her contribution to the cause of human rights in Iran, and in 2003 she won the prestigious Nobel Peace Prize. A statement by the Nobel award committee said of Ebadi, "As a lawyer, judge, lecturer, writer and activist, she has spoken out clearly and strongly in her country, Iran, and far beyond." The Nobel committee also paid tribute to her courage, noting that she had "never heeded the threat to her own safety."[41]

Ebadi wrote a fascinating memoir of her life in 2006: *Iran Awakening: A Memoir of Revolution and Hope*. She now lectures in law at the University of Tehran. Each year, students from inside and outside Iran flock to attend her human rights training courses.[42]

Questions to Consider

1. What do you think was Shirin Ebadi's greatest obstacle in her human rights work in Iran?

Aung San Suu Kyi, Burma

"The struggle for democracy and human rights in Burma is a struggle for life and dignity. It is a struggle that encompasses our political, social and economic aspirations." — Aung San Suu Kyi

Aung San Suu Kyi (pronounced Ong San Soo Chee) is a non-violent pro-democracy activist and chairperson of the National League for Democracy (NLD), a Burmese political party. A Theravada Buddhist, she won the Rafto Prize and the Sakharov Prize for Freedom of Thought in 1990 and 1991, and was awarded the Nobel Peace Prize in 1991 for her non-violent struggle to restore democracy to Burma.

Suu Kyi was born on June 19, 1945 in Rangoon, Burma. Her father, Aung San, founded the modern Burmese army and was the hero of Burma's independence movement from the British, which ended in 1948. When Suu Kyi was only two years old, her father's rivals assassinated him in 1947. She grew up with her mother, Khin Kyi, and two brothers in Rangoon. Her favorite brother, Aung San Lin, died when he accidentally drowned in an ornamental lake by their home. Her elder brother immigrated to San Diego, California, and became a U.S. citizen. For much of her childhood Suu Kyi was educated in English Catholic schools, where she had a talent for learning languages.

Aung San Suu Kyi, Minister of Foreign Affairs, Burma, as of March 2016

In 1960, the newly formed Burmese government appointed Khin Kyi, Suu Kyi's mother, as the Burmese ambassador to India and Nepal. Suu Kyi lived with her mother in New Delhi, India and graduated from Lady Shri Ram College in the city in 1964. She continued her education at Oxford University in Britain, obtaining a degree in 1969. While studying at Oxford, she met her future husband Dr. Michael Aris, a scholar of Tibetan culture. After graduation, she lived in New York City with a family friend and worked at the UN for three years, primarily on budget matters. Her years at the UN made a deep impression on Suu Kyi. In 1961, U Thant, Burma's UN representative, was elected Secretary-General of the UN; he was the first non-Westerner to head any international organization and would serve at that post for 10 years. Among other Burmese to work at the UN at the time was a young Suu Kyi. She married in 1972 and the following year gave birth to their first son, Alexander Aris, in London; their second son, Kim, was born in 1977. She earned a Ph.D. at the University of London's School of Oriental and African Studies, in 1985. She also worked for the government of Burma.

Let's turn to a brief history of Burma, since developments in that country have played a significant role in the life of Aung San Suu Kyi and her human rights campaign. But first, is the country named Burma or **Myanmar**? It all depends. In 1989, the military government in Burma officially changed the English translations of many colonial-era names, including the name of their country from Burma to "Union of Myanmar." The UN recognized the country's name change 5 days after the junta announced it. The U.S., Canada, the United Kingdom (UK) and other countries still refer to the country as Burma; however, Germany, Japan, China, Russia, and others use the name Myanmar. In light of the fact that a corrupt military rules the country and was responsible for the name change, I will use the name Burma.

Burma is the largest country by geographical area in mainland Southeast Asia, or Indochina with a population of around 47 million. Over many centuries, traditional kingships and local governments ruled the Burmese peoples until Great Britain's 19th century conquest largely stripped away their authority. The British colonial administration continued with limited local self-government until Burma achieved independence in 1948. The new state came into being as a parliamentary democracy and, despite ethnic conflict, survived as a representative government until an army coup toppled the government in 1962.[43]

The Burma Socialist Program Party (BSPP), a military-dominated government, held power for the next 26 years. The government denied free elections and freedom of expression and association. Authorities brutally crushed student and worker demonstrations in the 1960s and 1970s. Human rights abuses, such as torture and random imprisonment, were common. Under the BSPP the country's economy steadily deteriorated, and by mid-1988, rice shortages and popular dissatisfaction reached a crisis point. The police slaying of a student sparked wide-spread demonstrations who demanded that an elected civilian government replace the BSPP regime. Soldiers fired on crowds of unarmed protesters, killing thousands. Finally, the army announced a coup, during which they opened fire with machine guns on demonstrators in Rangoon killing 5,000 people and jailing thousands.[44]

In 1988 Aung San Suu Kyi returned to Burma from England to nurse her dying mother and was immediately plunged into the country's democracy uprising. She joined the newly-formed National League for Democracy (NLD), the most popular opposition party, and gave many rousing speeches calling for democracy. Although the military regime responded to the uprising with brute force, it was unable to maintain its grip on power. The regime pledged to call a general election in 1990; instead they placed Suu Kyi, leader of the NLD, under house arrest in 1989 and jailed many others. To the surprise of most observers, a free vote did take place in 1990 with the NLD winning a staggering 82 percent of the parliamentary seats. It was a resounding rejection of military rule but the military refused to recognize the results of the election. They arrested many pro-democracy supporters and imprisoned them without trial. Some have died in prison. Others fled into exile. Despite condemnation from world leaders, the military consolidated its power and rule of Burma. Suu Kyi remained under house arrest.

During her first house arrest period (1989-1995), Suu Kyi was awarded the Nobel Peace Prize in 1991. The publicity of the prize brought attention to her situation and the military's suppression of the Burmese people. After 6 years of house arrest, she was finally released in July 1995. In 1999-2000, the military widened its campaign of intimidation against the grass roots NLD, as well as its leadership. In early 2001, she served her second stretch under house arrest until her release in May 2002. During a tour of northern Burma in May 2003, the government militia mob attacked Suu Kyi and her supporters. They killed 100 people in the attack and arrested over 100 people, including Suu Kyi. She entered her third house arrest period (2003-2010), and the military closed all the country's pro-democracy offices.[45]

It was during the time of Suu Kyi's first house arrest that her husband Michael Aris died of cancer on his 53rd birthday in London on March 27, 1999. Since 1989 when Suu Kyi was first placed under house arrest, he had seen her only five times, the last of which was a Christmas visit in 1995. Doctors diagnosed Michael with terminal prostate cancer in 1997. He petitioned the Burmese authorities to allow him to visit Suu Kyi one last time, but they rejected his request. Despite appeals from prominent figures and organizations, including the U.S., UN Secretary General Kofi Annan and the Catholic Pope John Paul II, the Burmese government would not grant Aris a visa. The government urged Suu Kyi to join her family abroad when she was not under house arrest, but she was unwilling to depart the country, fearing that she would be refused re-entry. She also remained separated from her children, who lived in the UK.[46]

In October 2006, the military government set up a roadmap that would lead to a democratic state; however, pro-democracy organizations within and outside Burma called the plan a sham. The plan sought to legitimize an authoritarian government and establish the military as above the constitution and the law. Currently the regime has a military force of 500,000 for a country of only 47 million people. It has one of the largest armies in Asia, yet has no external enemies. Pro-democracy and human rights groups have identified many grave human rights abuses by the Burmese military.[47]

The International Labor Organization (ILO), a UN agency, charged Burma's regime with a crime against humanity for its widespread and systematic use of forced labor. The ILO described how the military forced men, women, children and the elderly to labor on roads, railways and other construction projects. They also faced punishments such as "money demands, physical abuse, beatings, torture, rape and murder."[48] In 2000, after the junta failed to end forced labor, the ILO urged all its members, including governments, labor unions and employers, to sever their ties to the regime. Some of the worst forced labor abuses have been reported from southeastern Burma, where forced labor has been used on tourism development projects. The Burma Campaign UK, a human rights group, and other campaigns have pressured a long list of companies to withdraw from Burma, including British American Tobacco, Texaco, Levi Strauss, Triumph International, Premier Oil, Total Oil (France) and Chevron (US).[49]

Flag of National League for Democracy

The international community has sought to pressure Burma to allow more democratic policies. The U.S. has imposed tough economic sanctions on Burma, such as a ban on new investment, an asset freeze, and prohibition on most Burmese imports. Amnesty International, a human rights organization, has found that "torture has become an institution" in Burma. They, along with the UN, Human Rights Watch, and other groups, have repeatedly detailed a gruesome list of abuses, including murder, torture, rape, detention without trial, massive forced relocations, and forced labor. Even before 1988, Burma's army has committed human rights abuses, especially in its actions against ethnic groups along the country's borders. Children have been particularly targeted. Hundreds of thousands of people have fled their homes to avoid abuse by the military; many remain internally-displaced persons.

There is ongoing suppression of other fundamental freedoms in Burma today. The generals do not respect the most basic of globally recognized civil and political rights, despite the fact that Burma has signed several important international human rights treaties. There is no freedom of expression; the military authorities must even approve art exhibitions. The few independent publications that survive, besides sports and romance magazines, are subject to severe censorship. Articles even mildly critical of official actions are inked over or torn from offending issues, while state newspapers are filled with vicious attacks on democratic forces. The military closely controls broadcast, as well. State-monopoly radio and television broadcast images of the military's generals cutting ribbons and making speeches. But the Burmese people want reliable news, such as the British Broadcasting Corporation, the Voice of America, the Democratic Voice of Burma, and Radio Free Asia, which estimate that their Burmese audience is probably greater per capita than anywhere else in the world.[50]

Aung San Suu Kyi's Agenda

- Stop the widespread use of forced labor.
- End over 1 million people being forced from their homes.
- Free 2,200 political prisoners, many of whom are tortured.
- Halt the use of 70,000 child soldiers, more than any other country.
- Cease using rape as a war weapon against ethnic women and children.
- Terminate nearly half the government's military budget.
- Help the one in ten babies who die before their 15th birthday.

The military repressed religious expression. Burma is a predominantly Buddhist country, and the military regime demands that Buddhist clergy support its rule. Troops have invaded monasteries to remove Buddhist leaders who support human rights and the democracy movement. Burma also has large Muslim and Christian communities. The army repeatedly attacks Muslims in southwestern Burma and has instigated dozens of attacks on mosques which were ransacked and destroyed. The army also closely monitors and restricts Christian churches. In some border areas, soldiers have deliberately wrecked churches and promoted discord among minority ethnic groups. Despite the repression, the NLD, ethnic nationalities, students and monks continue to resist the regime.[51]

The campaign for a democratic Burma has become an international cause and continues to grow in strength, thanks in part to Aung San Suu Kyi's simple message. She says, "Only by fighting fear can you truly be free." A message Burma's military fears and aims to silence.

In a bizarre incident on May 3, 2009, an American man, identified as John William Yettaw, swam, univited, across the lake that abuts Suu Kyi's house. Authorities arrested him when he made his return trip three days later. It is unknown what his motives were. On May 13, Suu Kyi was arrested for violating the terms of her house arrest because the swimmer, who pleaded exhaustion, was allowed to stay in her house for two days before he attempted the swim back. The military later imprisoned her. She pleaded innocent at her trial. On August 11, 2009, Suu Kyi was sentenced to imprisonment for three years with hard labor. The military rulers later commuted her sentence to further house arrest of 18 months.[52]

On October 1, 2010 the government unexpectedly announced that Suu Kyi would be released from house arrest in November 2010 so she could organize her party, although she could not run in upcoming elections. But she did run in the 2012 elections and won the vote for a seat in Parliament. The same year she announced that she wanted to run for the presidency in 2015. But the current Constitution, which came into effect in 2008, bars her from the presidency because she is the widow and mother of foreigners. The government seems to have written these measures to prevent her from being eligible.

For Aung San Suu Kyi dedication to her country's freedom she has been awarded numerous international honors, including the Nobel Peace Prize and others mentioned above. She has also been awarded the Sakharov Prize from the European Parliament and the United States Presidential Medal of Freedom. A military machine of 500,000 soldiers denies a whole nation its most basic rights. She symbolizes the struggle of Burma's people to be free. She has called on people around the world to join the struggle for freedom in Burma, saying, "Please use your liberty to promote ours."

Questions to Consider
1. How would you describe the significance of Aung San Suu Kyi in Burma's fight for freedom?

RIGOBERTA MENCHU, GUATEMALA

"We Indians never do anything which goes against the laws of our ancestors." — Rigoberta Menchu

Rigoberta Menchu belongs to the Quiche people (a branch of the Mayans), one of the largest of the 23 ethnic groups in Guatemala, each having its own language. She was born on January 9, 1959 in the hamlet of Chimel on the Altiplano (highlands) to a poor peasant family who lived in a village in the northwestern Guatemalan province of El Quiche. She was immersed in the Mayan culture. Her interesting story spans her childhood growing up poor in a poor country as an indigenous person with a culture different from modern culture and as a global activist fighting for the rights of indigenous peoples. In a sense, she speaks for all indigenous peoples of the American continent. The cultural discrimination she has suffered is something that all the continent's indigenous peoples have been experiencing since the Spanish conquest. Her voice allows indigenous peoples to speak. She is a witness who has survived the violence aimed at destroying her family, community and culture, and she is stubbornly determined to break the silence and to confront the systematic extermination of her people.[53]

Rigoberta Menchu, Guatemala

In her biography, Menchu tells the story of the Guatemalan people and her personal experiences, which are, in essence, the reality of a whole people. Colonial powers have historically oppressed her people, and she is determined to make sure that the sacrifices her family and community have made to fight this oppression will not have been in vain. She makes it clear that "Latin Americans are only too ready to denounce the unequal relations that exist between ourselves and North America, but we tend to forget that we too are oppressors and that we too are involved in relations that can only be described as colonial. In countries with a large Indian population, there is an internal colonialism which works to the detriment of the indigenous population."[54]

As a child Rigoberta Menchu lived in the village of Chimel where she was born. To her, it was a paradise that had no big roads and no cars. People could only reach it by foot or horseback. Her parents moved to Chimel in 1960 and began cultivating the land. No one had lived there before because it was very mountainous, but they were determined to stay no matter how hard the life. They had been forced to leave their previous hometown because *ladinos* (Guatemalans of mixed Spanish and Indian ancestry) settled there and gradually took control. Her parents spent all they earned and accumulated so much debt that finally they had to leave their house to pay the *ladinos*. She said "The rich are always like that. When people owe them money they take a bit of land or some of their belongings and slowly end up with everything. That's what happened to my parents."[55]

Rigoberta's father had a very hard life as a child. His father died when he was a child, leaving his wife with three small boys to raise. Her grandmother went to work as a servant for the town's only wealthy family. The boys did small jobs around the house, such as carrying wood and water and tending animals. As they grew into young men, her employer didn't want to keep feeding them, so her grandmother had to give away her eldest son, Rigoberta's father, to a man who fed and worked him. He didn't get paid because he had been given away. Her father soon left that situation and found a job on a plantation growing coffee, cotton, and sugar cane. He sent for his mother and brothers to live with him. Things were very hard, they earned very little money but were able to finally save enough to move to the high country. Shortly after the move, her grandmother became ill and died. The brothers decided to split up to find work in different parts of the country. The army forcibly recruited her father where, as he said, he learned "some very bad things."[56]

Her father served a difficult year's stint in the army, after discharge her mother and father met and soon after married. Her mother also came from a very poor family who lived in the Altiplano. They moved about looking for work in the area and were hardly ever at home. Her parents got permission from the government and scraped together enough money to pay a fee to cultivate land in the Altiplano. Since it took many long, hard years for the land to finally produce crops, her parents had to travel down to the coastal region to work on the plantations. The family grew rapidly; Rigoberta was the sixth of nine children. Like other indigenous families, the children suffered from malnutrition. Most children didn't reach the age of 15 years old. When she was a little girl she remembered spending only 4 months in the family's house in the Altiplano and the rest of the year working on the coastal plantations. Only a few families owned the vast plantations producing cash crops that were sold abroad. Poor families like the Menchu's tended the crops, a harsh life that her parents and others endured for many years.[57]

In Rigoberta Menchu's community there was a highly respected elected representative who acted as a father to the whole village. Her mother and father were the village's representatives and the mother and father for all the children of the village. The birth of a baby is very significant for the community, as it belongs to all, not just the parents. Her mother, a midwife, helped women give birth at home; villagers considered it a scandal to have a child in the hospital. The community baptized a newborn before the parents took the infant to church. The newborn's hands were tied for eight days, which symbolized that one should not accumulate things the rest of the community does not have. On the eighth day the child's hands were untied; the open hands meant s/he knew how to share and be generous. The family teaches each child to live like fellow members of his/her community; no one had more than others.[58]

Rigoberta's fellow villagers were Catholic, but they saw the religion as just another channel of spiritual expression. They didn't totally trust all the priests, monks, and nuns of the church. They believed that the sun was the father, and our mother was the moon; they were the pillars of the universe.[59] Rigoberta felt that the Catholic Church has tried to "keep her people in their place," but as Christians they gradually acquired an understanding of their rights and dignity. She thinks "that unless a religion springs from within the people themselves, it is a weapon of the system."[60]

Wrapped in a shawl and placed on her mother's back, Rigoberta started going to the plantations with her mother shortly after she was born. They took all the necessities for their stay on the plantations—bedding, cooking utensils, and clothing. Sometimes employers paid them by the day and sometimes for the amount of work done. Children who did not work did not earn any pay and were not fed. The little ones who worked got a ration of tortillas. Rigoberta's mother had to share her ration of food with her. The plantations had a cantina owned by the landowners that sold food, alcohol, and sweets. The children always pestered their parents for sweets, cakes and soft drinks. The prices were marked up on an account, and at the end of the work period when the workers were paid, they had to settle their debt, which was always a lot. For example, if a child accidentally broke a branch of a coffee bush, the worker had to work to make it up. Every plantation had a cantina where workers got drunk and piled up huge debts. They often spent most of their wages just paying off the debt. Rigoberta sadly remembered her father and mother going to the cantina out of despair. She commented, "But he hurt himself twice over because his money went back to the landowner. That's why they set up the cantina anyway."[61]

Rigoberta remembered her first visit with her father to the capital, Guatemala City. It was a big step in her life; for the first time she traveled in a truck with windows. They brought some mimbre, a type of willow used in furniture making, to sell. She was fascinated with all she saw. She remembered her father telling her "When you're old enough, you must travel; you must go around the country." They stayed in the city for three days but were very hungry because they did not have enough money to eat.[62]

Rigoberta worked from the time she was small. She helped her mother, who had to carry her little brother on her back as she picked coffee. When she was 8 she started to earn money on the plantation by picking coffee, and when the family returned to their mountain home, she worked in the fields growing maize (corn). The plantation work was very hard and her parents were usually exhausted. She noted that most of the women who worked picking cotton and coffee had 9 or 10 children. Of these, 3 or 4 were healthy and would survive, but most of them had swollen bellies from malnutrition and the mother knew that 4 or 5 of her children would die. Even Rigoberta's brother died from malnutrition. She also observed that men who had been in the army often abused young girls. Many girls had no families and turned to prostitution. She was sad to see this happen since prostitution did not exist in Indian culture. As she saw it, "In the eyes of our community, anyone who doesn't dress as our grandfathers, our ancestors, is on the road to ruin." She saw suffering everywhere.[63]

Rigoberta celebrated her 10th birthday in the Altiplano. Her parents explained to her that she was now an adult and what her future life would be like, although she had seen enough to know what it would probably be like. They explained her responsibilities and that soon she would be a woman who could start having children.[64] On her 12th birthday, it was the custom to receive a gift of a small animal to raise; her father gave her a pig. She sold weavings that she did in her spare time, after working in the fields all day, to get enough money to buy food for her pig.[65]

Rigoberta's community respected many things connected with the natural world. For example, water was sacred to her community. She explained, "Water is pure, clean, and gives life to humans. The same is true for the earth. The earth is mother of humans, because she gives us food. Her people eat maize, beans and vegetables; they cannot eat things made with equipment or machines. That is why they ask the earth's permission to sow maize and beans." Copa, the resin of a tree, was a sacred ingredient in candles for her people. The candles gave off a strong, smoky, delicious aroma when burned, and they were used in ceremonies to represent the earth, water and maize. They prayed to their ancestors and recited ancient prayers. Their grandfathers said they must ask the sun to shine on all its children: the trees, animals, water, man and enemies. To them, an enemy was someone who steals or goes into prostitution.[66]

A happy moment in village life was when the farmers planted maize (corn). They had a fiesta in which they asked the earth's permission to cultivate her. They lit candles and offered prayers and then blessed the seeds for sowing. According to the ritual, they honored the seed because they buried it in the sacred earth and by the next year it would multiply and bear fruit. Rigoberta said, "We do it mainly because the seed is something pure, something sacred. For us the word seed is very significant." They did the same with beans. When the maize started growing on their farms, they went back down to work on the plantations. When they came back, the maize had reached maturity. Maize was the center of their culture; they believed they were made of maize. They had a ceremony before harvesting, celebrating the harvest and asking the earth's permission to cultivate her. They thanked mother earth for the harvest. After they harvested their crops, they all gathered together for a feast.[67]

Indigenous people in village

Every village had a community house where they all assembled to celebrate their faith, to pray, and to enjoy special ceremonies and fiestas. They all worked communally to clear bush in the mountains, and when sowing time came, the community met to discuss how to share the land, whether each one would have his own plot or if they would work it collectively. Everyone joined in the discussion. In her village, they decided to have their own plots of land but also to keep a common piece of land shared by the community. If anyone was ill or injured, s/he would have food to eat from the communal land. It mostly helped widows. Each day of the week, someone would work the communal land.[68]

Rigoberta saw a stark difference between indigenous and modern education. To indigenous people, nature was their teacher. Her father was very suspicious of modern schools and said that once people learned to read and write, they weren't any use to the community anymore. They moved away and were indifferent toward their community. Rigoberta wanted to go to school to learn to read and write. Her father said she would have to learn on her own since he had no money for her education. He thought she was trying to leave the community and was concerned that she would forget her heritage. She still insisted she wanted to learn. Despite her father's misgivings, she sporadically attended a Catholic school.[69]

As she was becoming a woman, her parents told her that she had to be a mother. They also warned her not to not wait too long before getting married, although the community did not shun childless couples. Unlike the *ladinos*, her community did not reject the *huecos*, what they called homosexuals. They saw all different ways of life as part of nature. They also said that whatever her ambitions were, she had no way of achieving them. That's just how life was.[70]

When Rigoberta turned 14 many of the villagers went as a group to work on the plantations. She and a friend, Maria, were assigned to pick cotton that was being sprayed with chemicals. Maria died from the poisoning and was buried on the plantation. Rigoberta was mad with grief. She hated the people who sprayed the crops, holding them responsible.[71] Rigoberta decided, against her parents' warnings, to take a job as a maid in the capital city. The maid's job was a disaster, as she described it, she was treated worse than the owner's dog. She worked for a couple months then left, vowing never again to take such an insulting position. Her job as a maid left her with the impression that the rich were un-Christian, lazy and mean.

After she left the maid's job she was distressed to find that her father was in prison. Big landowners had come to their village to take away the land that her father and other villagers had cultivated for over 22 years. The peasant farmers, like her father, were at a disadvantage because they did not speak Spanish and did not understand their rights. The big landowners had started to threaten her father when he began getting involved with the unions, which were helping the peasants keep their cultivated land. The most upsetting thing for her was not being able to communicate; therefore, she vowed to learn Spanish. After a year and a great deal of trouble, her father was finally released from prison. Everyone in the community helped to get her father out of prison by contributing to the legal fees needed for his case.[72]

The landowners were furious that her father had been released. Shortly after his release, the landowner's guards kidnapped him near the village. Her brother immediately mobilized the whole village to get him back. The villagers cut off the kidnappers' escape path, and they used their weapons—machetes, sticks, hoes, and stones—to fight the kidnappers. They found her father, who the kidnappers had abandoned, beaten and tortured but was still alive. The villagers carried him to the nearest health center, but the landowner's guards had gotten there first and paid the doctors not to treat him. Her mother had to call an ambulance to take him to a hospital in the next city. He arrived at the hospital half dead. Her father remained in the hospital, and her mother had to work in the city to pay for his care.[73] While still in the hospital, they received another threat that said her father would be kidnapped from the hospital. The family decided he needed a safer place to stay. With the help of some priests and nuns, they transferred him to a secret place where the landowners could not find him. After a year in the hospital and in hiding, he returned to his home in the village, but, according to Rigoberta, he was not the same.

When her father was in the hospital he talked to many people in the region and found that indigenous peoples in other areas were also being treated badly and faced eviction from their land. He continued to work with the unions, traveling and fighting for his community. Rigoberta traveled with her father learning about the things he was doing. She was also learning Spanish from the nuns and priests who were helping them. Some Europeans were sending money to help support their cause.[74]

Then in 1977, authorities arrested him again and put him in prison, charged as a political prisoner and sentenced to life imprisonment. But her father was not alone; priests, nuns, the unions, and the community supported him in his fight. The unions pressed for his release. After imprisonment for only 15 days, he was suddenly released. While in prison, he met a fellow prisoner who told him the peasants should unite and form a Peasants' League to reclaim their lands. Upon his release, her father joined with other peasants and started the Peasant Unity Committee (CUC). They all started thinking about the roots of their problems and came to the conclusion that everything stemmed from the ownership of land. The best land was not in the peasants' hands but belonged to the big landowners. Every time these landowners saw that the peasants had new land, they tried to throw them off of it and steal it from them.[75]

It was at this point that Rigoberta began to learn about politics. She wanted to find out about the problems indigenous people faced in the rest of Guatemala. The CUC started to grow and spread like wildfire among the Guatemalan peasants. She began to see that the root of her people's problems was exploitation. The rich got richer because they exploited the labor of the poor. She also saw that the *ladinos* were culturally oppressing her people by taking away their traditional way of life and preventing them from unifying. She started to work as an organizer and continued to learn Spanish. She joined the CUC in 1979 and traveled to different areas of Guatemala. But a main barrier in her interaction with different people in her country was that they couldn't understand each other. She couldn't speak their indigenous language, other than Quiche, and they couldn't speak Spanish. So, along with Spanish, she began to learn three other indigenous languages. One of the issues that she worked on was the barrier between the *ladino* and indigenous communities. The *ladinos* were a minority in Guatemala, since indigenous people made up 60 percent of the population. She found, to her surprise, that not all *ladinos* were rich; many were very poor, but they felt superior to indigenous people. This sense of superiority prevented the two groups of poor people from unifying together to solve their common problems.[76]

In 1979, the government began a crackdown on her family and other members of the CUC. Government soldiers accused her little brother, who was doing organizing work as well, of being a communist. The soldiers took him away and beat and tortured him for over 16 days. They cut off his fingernails and then his fingers, cut off his skin, burned part of his skin, and then cut off the fleshy part of his face. Twenty men with him had also been tortured and one woman had been raped and then tortured. They died a horrible death. No one was held responsible for their deaths. On January 31, 1982, security forces killed her father when he and other peasants occupied the Spanish Embassy in the capital to protest the plight of Guatemalan Indians (see chapter 4). Rigoberta's father, Vicente Menchu, had become a national hero and led the protest. In this same span of time, high-ranking army officers kidnapped, raped, and tortured her mother, who also died a horrible death.[77] The Guatemalan government wanted Rigoberta, but after her mother's death she fled to Mexico.

While in Mexico, she dictated her autobiography, *I, Rigoberta Menchu* (1984), telling the world not only about her own story, but also about the lives of her fellow indigenous people. Her book and her social justice campaign brought international attention to the conflict between indigenous peoples and the military government of Guatemala. In 1992, she was awarded the

Nobel Peace Prize and used the $1.2 million cash prize to set up a foundation in her father's name to continue the fight for human rights of indigenous peoples. Due to her efforts, the United Nations declared 1993 the International Year for Indigenous Populations. Menchú now serves as a UNESCO Goodwill Ambassador and is a figure in indigenous political parties. She unsuccessfully ran for President of Guatemala in 2007 and 2011.

> **Questions to Consider**
> 1. What do you think was Rigoberta Menchu's biggest contribution to promoting human rights for indigenous peoples?
> 2. How was her struggle different from others described in this chapter?

Muhammad Yunus, Bangladesh

"My greatest challenge has been to change the mindset of people. Mindsets play strange tricks on us. We see things the way our minds have instructed our eyes to see." — Muhammad Yunus

Defending human rights takes many forms. **Muhammad Yunus** took the path of defending the human rights of some of the poorest women in the world through economic empowerment. His strategy of lending money to poor women and requiring them to pay it back with interest enhanced not only their own lives but that of their families' as well.

Muhammad Yunus was born June 28, 1940 in one of the poorest and most densely populated places on earth. He was the third of nine children, born to a Muslim family in the village of Bathua. In 1944, his family moved to the large port city of Chittagong in what was the Bengal Province of British India, which is now Bangladesh. His father was Hazi Dula Mia Shoudagar, a jeweler, and his mother, Sofia Khatun, cared for the children. By 1949, a severe psychological illness afflicted his mother; however, his father cared for her until her death in 1982.[78] Mohamad attended primary school and later attended Chittagong Collegiate School, where he was an active Boy Scout. He stated, "Aside from the fun, scouting taught me to be compassionate, to develop an inner spirituality, and to cherish my fellow human beings." He vividly recalled a train trip across India to the First Pakistan National Boy Scouts Jamboree in 1953, and

Muhammad Yunus, Bangladesh

he also traveled to Canada with the Boy Scouts in 1955. Young Yunus had many talents; painting, graphic design, photography, and he won awards for drama acting.[79]

In 1957, he enrolled in the department of economics at Dhaka University, completing his undergraduate degree in 1960 and graduate degree in 1961. He always thought of himself as a teacher, and immediately out of college at the age of 21 his alma mater Chittagong College offered him a teaching position in economics. At the same time, he also tried his hand at private business. After obtaining a loan, he started a successful business that produced packaging and printing materials and made a healthy yearly profit. Despite his business success, he still wanted to study and teach.

When he was offered a Fulbright scholarship to get a Ph.D. in the United States, he jumped at the chance.[80]

While in the U.S., Bangladesh, once a colony of British India, was experiencing significant political events. After the end of World War II, Mahatma Gandhi and others worked to gain India's independence in 1947. Shortly after India's independence, the western portion of the country, Pakistan, established a separate country after a violent civil war with India. The eastern portion of India decided to be part of Pakistan and became known as East Pakistan (1947-1971). Over one thousand miles separated East and West Pakistan, which proved to be a major separation. In the early 1970s a civil war between East and West Pakistan broke out, resulting in the formation of the independent nation of Bangladesh in 1971. Yunus' was very happy that his country was now an independent nation in charge of its own destiny.

With Ph.D. in tow, Yunus returned to Bangladesh in 1972. After a short stint in the new government's Planning Commission, he returned to Chittagong University as a professor of economics and head of the department. One of the many things that bothered him as a professor was the gap between the economic theory taught in universities and the wretched poverty around him. He became more curious about the villagers whom he could see from the "ivory tower" of his college office. In thinking about the problem he said, "Analyses of the causes of poverty focus largely on why some countries are poor rather than on why certain segments of the population live below the poverty line. Most economists believe that poverty and hunger will cease when economic prosperity increases." He found that "economists spend all their talents detailing the processes of development and prosperity, but rarely reflect on the origin and development of poverty and hunger. As a result, poverty continues."[81]

In 1976, he started to visit the poorest households near his university. Since there were Muslim, Hindu and Buddhist sections, he visited them all. One day as he and a female colleague were making the rounds, they stopped at a run-down house with crumbling mud walls and a low thatched roof pocked with holes. As he made his way through the scavenging chickens, beds of vegetables, and children running naked in the yard, he saw a woman squatted on a dirt floor of the porch weaving a half-finished bamboo stool. She was totally absorbed in her work. They called out a greeting to the women, who sprang to her feet and scurried inside the house. Finally, after reassurances that they meant no harm, she peered out from the window, since traditions did not allow women to talk to men face-to-face when another male was not at home. Since he could not talk to her, his female colleague began to ask her some questions. Her name was Sufiya and she was 21 years old with 3 children. Since Sufiya did not have enough money to buy bamboo to make the stool, she bought the bamboo from a middleman for 5 taka (about 22 cents at the time). She then sold the finished stool back to the middleman for a profit of about 2 cents. Yunus, through his colleague, asked her if it would be cheaper to borrow the cash from a moneylender to buy her own raw materials. She replied "Yes, but the moneylender would demand a lot. People who deal with them only get poorer." Sufiya said that the moneylender charged 10 percent interest a week, and sometimes 10 percent per day! Yunus wondered how Sufiya and her children would ever break the cycle of poverty. She earned barely enough to feed herself, let alone feed or provide shelter for her children. Yunus felt that millions of situations like Sufiya's were hopeless.[82]

He was angry that Sufiya only earned 2 cents a day, yet university economic courses theorized about sums in the millions. He asked, "Why did my university courses not reflect the reality of Sufiya's life and millions of other women just like her?" He decided this was a problem he wanted to tackle, and he did.

Yunus decided that he would ask the local bank to make loans to the poor villagers. The bank manager laughed at his request, replying that the poor do not have collateral or cannot read and write or fill out loan forms. It simply cannot be done. Yunus stubbornly refused to give up, but he did recognize that the poor remained poor because they had no access to capital, no collateral for loans, and their borrowing requirements were so modest that it was not cost-effective for large banks to lend them money. Finally he decided to secure a $300 loan for himself. He would be the banker to the poor!

Yunus studied all the details of his new banking venture. In structuring the credit program for the poor, he decided to do things differently from the traditional banks. For one, he decided that conventional banks usually demanded repayment in one lump sum, which is often a psychological barrier for borrowers since they have to come up with a large amount all at once. Instead, he decided that under his program borrowers would make daily repayment of the total loan amount. The sum repaid would be so small that borrowers would barely miss the money. He would require that the loans be fully repaid in one year.

Yunus and his team started experimenting with small collateral-free loans to landless rural peasants and impoverished women. The loans would be for a wide variety of projects ranging from buying a cow or chicken and selling milk and eggs, to buying raw materials such as willow for making baskets for sale in the marketplace, or buying a cell phone for communication. In developing their program, the new bankers discovered that support groups were crucial to the success of the operation. Thus, they required each applicant to join a group of like-minded people living in similar economic and social conditions. Each client who wanted to borrow a sum of money had to find four friends who also wanted to borrow money. If any of the five group members defaulted on their loan, the bankers held all accountable. This group support would build commitment and provide community support. The bankers were convinced that solidarity would be stronger if the groups self-organized, and they refrained from micro-managing them. Group membership created support and protection but also smoothed out erratic behavior and made each borrower more reliable. Shifting supervision to the group reduced the work of the bank and also increased the borrower's self-reliance. Because the group approved each member's loan request, they assumed moral responsibility for the loan. If any member got in trouble, the group usually helped out.[83]

Initially, Yunus wanted half of the borrowers to be women. This was a challenge. At first, women were reluctant to accept loans. They said, "No, no, I have never touched money in my life. You must go to my husband. He understands money. Give the money to him." But Yunus was patient and explained why a loan would benefit her family. But the more he tried to approach women, the more they ran away. Yunus and his banking colleagues worked hard to come up with a way they could build trust in women so that they would accept loans from men. They included more women, since this trust-building took time.[84]

Yunus wanted to loan money to women because their first priority was their children. They wanted their children to have better lives. A woman's second priority was the household. She wanted to buy utensils, build a stronger roof, or find a bed for herself and her family. Men had an entirely different set of priorities, and they were looser with money. They wanted to enjoy it right away, not wait for tomorrow. When a poor father earned extra income, he focused more attention on himself. Yunus began to see something very remarkable happening; when money entered a household through a woman, it brought more benefits to the family than the same amount of money going to men. Perhaps it was because women had learned how to manage with scarce resources. And women had a long-term vision; they could see a way out of poverty and had the discipline to carry out their plans. Women suffer more from poverty than men; perhaps that is why they are more motivated to escape it. The bankers decided to make a determined effort to attract women clients because they got better results from the same amount of money.[85]

In 1983, after 7 years of experimenting, Yunus officially started the **Grameen Bank**. The word Grameen, is from the word gram or village, and means "of the village" in the Bengal language. This revolutionary bank is still going strong today with 2.4 million families with loans, and more than 1,050 branches serving 35,000 villages in Bangladesh; 94 percent of the clients are women. Its rules are strict. Initial loans are as little as $10 dollars and must be repaid with 20 percent interest; 98 percent of Grameen's borrowers repay their loans in full, a rate of return far higher than other banks.[86]

Grameen Bank logo

Yunus was able to overcome two major obstacles when he started the Grameen program. First, commercial banks discriminated against women. He overcame this obstacle with trust-building and designing a system that built on women's support groups. Secondly, commercial banks had blocked credit to the poor by demanding collateral, something no poor person had. He found that the poor do have an intangible type of collateral. They will probably need a second or third loan; therefore, their collateral is to be timely and responsible in their payments so they can establish a good credit record.[87]

According to Yunus, Grameen Bank has worked in ways not initially anticipated. For instance, some women borrowers decided to commit themselves to a set of promises that they called the "sixteen decisions." These are commitments that the women borrowers agreed upon to help improve

---

A Typical Woman Getting a Loan from Grameen Bank — Mohammad Yusuf

"A typical initial loan is around $35. The night before a woman is going to accept the money from the bank she will be tossing and turning to decide whether she is really ready for it. She is scared that maybe something terrible will happen to her. And finally in the morning her friends will come over and they will try to persuade her. Let's go through with it. If you don't go, we can't. We can't always worry. It was not easy coming to this point. And finally, with their encouragement, she will come to the bank.

When she holds that money, it is such a huge amount in her hands, it is like holding the hope and treasure that she never dreamt she would achieve. She will tremble, tears will roll down her cheeks, and she won't believe we would trust her with such a large sun. And she promises that she will pay back this money, because the money is the symbol of the trust put in her and she does not want to betray that trust.

And then she struggles to pay that first loan, that first installment, which is due the following week, and the second installment, which is payable the following week, and this goes on for 50 weeks, and every time that she repays another installment she is braver! And when she finishes her 50th installment, the last one, and she has now paid in full, she wants to celebrate. It is not just a monetary transaction that has been completed; it is nothing less than a transformation of that person. Now she is a woman who feels like she is somebody. She finds self-worth, self-esteem. Proving that she can take care of herself."[89]

themselves and their families above and beyond the loans. They decided to maintain discipline, to create unity, to act with courage, and to work hard in all of their endeavors. They agreed to keep their families small and to send their children to school, to plant as many tree seedlings as possible, and even to eat vegetables. These are some of the resolutions the women created; the bank did not impose them.[88]

Grameen is involved in transformation. The clients are transforming their lives from powerless and dependent to self-sufficient, independent, and politically aware. The next generation will reap the benefits; a generation with better food, education, medication, and the firsthand satisfaction of taking control of their lives. The 16 decisions are an example of the transformation. Yunus has found that Grameen children attend school in record numbers because their mothers really take that commitment seriously. Now many of the children are continuing in colleges, universities, and going to medical schools. Grameen Bank recently came up with another loan product to finance higher education for all Grameen children in professional schools.[90]

Yunus points to a Scientific American study in Bangladesh showing that children in Grameen families were healthier than other children. They also did a study of population growth in Bangladesh and found that the average number of children per family 20 years ago was 7, but now it has been reduced to 3. Although all these changes may not be due to the bank program, as women make economic progress, they make decisions about their personal lives and how many children they choose to have. The bank is not a population program, but it has had a beneficial side effect.[91] Another beneficial side effect of the program is that women have participated in voting. In the 1996 election in Bangladesh, voter participation was 73 percent, the highest percentage ever, and women voted more than men. In some of the elections, Grameen members were elected to local posts, as well as seats in Parliament.[92]

Yunus cited resistance to his program from husbands who felt insulted, humiliated, and threatened that the bank gave loans to their wives and not them. Sometimes the tension within the family led to violence against the women. In response to this problem, the bankers decided to start meeting with the husbands and explained the program in a way that they could see how it would benefit their family. They also arranged to meet with husbands and wives together so everyone understood the expectations. Easing the husband's concerns reduced their initial resistance. Some neighborhood men opposed the program because of religious objections. The bank carefully examined whether the program was in some way anti-religious but found that these critics actually cloaked their opposition to women's independence in religious trappings instead of admitting that they felt threatened. According to Yunus, "It was the male ego speaking in religious terms. We found that it was best to give the program some time. It soon became clear that the women borrowers were

Grameen Bank building Dhaka, Bangladesh

still attending to their religious duties, at the same time earning money and becoming confident."[93] Women even started confronting the religious critics.

Yunus pointed out that the Grameen Bank program received some of the strongest criticism from development professionals. Grameen bankers never expected opposition from the development quarter, but it happened and became controversial. Development has traditionally been multi-million dollar loans from the World Bank or other big Western and Chinese banks for large infrastructure development projects, such as dams, highways, ports, irrigation projects, and airports. The money for these projects would go to a large Western multi-national corporation or Chinese state enterprise that would employ a few local laborers (men). The profits mostly would go to the upper level management of the multi-national corporation or state enterprises and little if any would "trickle down" to poor local people. The large development projects would have no positive effect on women's lives. The development projects were just the opposite of what Yunus and his bank were doing. Critics insisted that giving tiny loans to women who do not have knowledge and skills does not bring about real change in the country or the village and is not true development.[94] The real issue was Yunus and the Grameen Bank offered a different kind of development that challenged the powerful. Their grassroots method threatened profits for multi-nationals and the kickbacks to local officials; therefore, critics ridiculed and dismissed their program.

Yunus adds, "What we do is not in the development professionals' or academics' book. It does not fit into their universe. If you are an academic, you wander around in your abstract world, and decide microcredit programs are silly because they don't fit your ideas." But Yunus forcefully claims, "I work with real people in the real world. So whenever academics or [development] professionals try to draw those conclusions, I get upset and go back and work with my borrowers—and then I know who is right."[95]

Yunus has garnered world-wide attention and praise for his grassroots, ground-breaking strategy of working to alleviate world poverty. In 2006, Yunus and the Grameen Bank were jointly awarded the Nobel Peace Prize "for their efforts to create economic and social development from below." He is one of the founding members of Global Elders, a group of public figures noted as elder statesmen, peace activists, and human rights advocates. The goal of the group is to solve global problems with over 1,000 years of experience among individual members. Yunus said he would use part of his share of the $1.4 million award money to create a company to make low-cost, high-nutrition food for the poor. The rest would go toward setting up an eye hospital for the poor in Bangladesh. The food company, Social Business Enterprise, will sell food for a nominal price.[96] Yunus has taken his Boy Scout motto to heart, showing compassion for all, in all of his endeavors.

Questions to Consider

1. What are the reasons for the success of Yunus's bank? In what ways is it totally unique?

His Holiness The Dalai Lama, Tibet

"Such human qualities as morality, compassion, decency, wisdom and so forth have been the foundations of all civilizations. These qualities must be cultivated and sustained through systematic moral education…, so that a more humane world may emerge." — His Holiness the Dalai Lama

Lhamo Döndrub (the Dalai Lama) was born on July 6, 1935, to a farming and horse trading family in the small village of Takster in northeastern Tibet. He was the fifth of 16 children, but only 9 survived childhood. The **Dalai Lama** is a line of religious leaders in Tibetan Buddhism. "Lama" is a general term referring to Tibetan Buddhist teachers. The title, Dalai Lama, means "Ocean of Wisdom." The current Dalai Lama is the 14th in the line of religious leaders who have chosen to be reborn in order to enlighten (inform) others. Tibetan Buddhists believe the Dalai Lamas is the reincarnation of the Bodhisattva of Compassion and the patron saint of Tibet. Bodhisattvas are enlightened beings who have postponed their own nirvana (heaven) and chosen to be reborn in order to serve humanity. Religious leaders chose him to be the head of state and the spiritual leader of the Tibetan people.

Dalai Llama, Tibet

After the death of the 13th Dalai Lama in 1933, a search began for the 14th Dalai Lama. A search party, following omens and visions, began the process of locating the next spiritual leader. One member of the search party had a vision of a sacred lake indicating Amdo as the region to search, and specifically a one-story house with distinctive guttering and tiling. Finally, the Döndrub family house, with its features resembling those in the vision, was found. His eldest brother had been recognized at the age of 8 as the reincarnation (rebirth) of the high Lama Taktser Rinpoche. Now, the search party identified a little two-year old boy as the possible future Dalai Lama. As part of the test to determine if he was the future Dalai Lama, they presented to the boy various relics, including toys, some of which had belonged to the 13th Dalai Lama and some of which had not. According to the story, the boy correctly identified all the items owned by the previous Dalai Lama, exclaiming, "That's mine! That's mine!"[97] The child was recognized formally as the reincarnated Dalai Lama and renamed Thubten (or Tenzin) Gyatso. In 1939, at the age of four, the religious leaders took the boy in a formal procession to Lhasa, the political and spiritual capital of Tibet. His followers call him His Holiness the Dalai Lama or simply His Holiness.

The Dalai Lama began his monastic (religious) education at the age of six. The curriculum consisted of five major subjects—logic, Tibetan art and culture, Sanskrit, medicine and Buddhist philosophy—and five minor subjects—poetry, music and drama, astrology, phrasing and synonyms. At the age of 11, while peering through his telescope, the boy spotted the Austrian mountaineer Heinrich Harrer, who was visiting the area. He became one of the young Dalai Lama's tutors, teaching him about the outside world. The two remained friends until Harrer's death in 2006. Even before he finished his formal education at the age of 15, he was enthroned formally as the Dalai Lama. He became the region's most important spiritual leader and political ruler. At the age of 23, he took his final examination in Lhasa and passed with honors. He was awarded the highest-level degree equivalent to a doctorate of Buddhist philosophy.[98]

The Dalai Lama assumed full political power at such a young age because of a crisis: China invaded Tibet in 1950. The Chinese Communist party under the leadership of Mao Zedong had won a long and brutal civil war against the Nationalist Party of China (supported by the US). Mao was anxious to flex his muscle and bring under Chinese control surrounding territories that had historical links to China; Tibet was one of these areas. The Chinese government regarded the Dalai Lama as the symbol of an outmoded theocracy (religious rule) in need of modernization. In October 1950, the Chinese army invaded the country, moving through Tibetan defenses with ease. Shortly after the invasion, the 15-year-old boy was enthroned as ruler of Tibet. In the aftermath, Chinese occupiers brutally repressed and executed thousands of Tibetans, while thousands were imprisoned or starved to death in prison camps. They pillaged and demolished hundreds of Buddhist monasteries, temples and other cultural historic buildings. The Chinese purposely tried to wipe out Tibetan culture and identity; for example, they instructed the Tibetans to dress like Chinese, and profess atheism (no belief in God or religion). They forced Tibetans to burn their sacred books, and condemn, humiliate and kill their elders and teachers.[99]

A Tibetan resistance movement formed, but it was no match for the overwhelming Chinese troops. In 1951, the Chinese military pressured the Dalai Lama to ratify a 17-point agreement which dictated rule by the Chinese central government and the Tibetan government. In 1954, the Dalai Lama attempted to work with the Chinese government; he and a Tibetan delegation went to Beijing for peace talks with Mao and other Chinese leaders. However, the talks did not lead to Chinese troop withdrawal from Tibet. When Tibetans took to the streets in 1959, demanding an end to Chinese rule, troops crushed the revolt and killed thousands of protesters. With the Chinese troops' brutal suppression of the Tibetan national uprising and the effective collapse of the Tibetan resistance movement, the Dalai Lama had good reason to believe that the Chinese government was planning to kill him. He decided to flee on foot across the mountain passes of India to establish a government-in-exile. Over 80,000 Tibetans, also fleeing persecution, followed him. It was later revealed that the U.S. Central Intelligence Agency (CIA) had assisted the Dalai Lama's escape and had supported Tibet's initial resistance to the Chinese Communists.[100] Since 1959, he and other exiled Tibetans have been living in Dharamsala, northern India; the seat of the Tibetan political administration in exile. It is often referred to as "Little Lhasa."

While in exile, the Dalai Lama began the task of preserving the culture of the Tibetan people and publicizing their plight on the world stage. Since the Chinese invasion, he repeatedly appealed to the UN on the question of Tibet. In 1959, 1961 and 1965, the UN General Assembly adopted three resolutions on Tibet that required China to respect the human rights of Tibetans and their desire for self-determination. However, China has virtually ignored these resolutions. During 1963, the Dalai Lama helped to form a democratic constitution for Tibet based upon the Universal Declaration of Human Rights. In the 1970s, he helped to open the Library of Tibetan Works and Archives in Dharamsala, which houses over 80,000 manuscripts and important resources related to Tibetan history, politics and culture. Tibetans consider it one of the most important institutions for Tibetan works and archives in the world.[101]

Meanwhile, new waves of repression erupted in the 1980s and, continue today. The Dalai Lama proposed the Five Point Peace Plan for Tibet in September 1987 as the first step towards a peaceful solution to the worsening situation in Tibet. Characteristic of his Buddhist teachings, the Dalai Lama has advocated a "middle way" to resolve the status of Tibet—genuine self-rule for Tibet within China. He envisions that Tibet would become a sanctuary, a zone of peace at the heart of Asia, and he called for the end of ethnic Han Chinese immigration into Tibet. The peace plan also called for "respect for fundamental human rights and democratic freedoms" and "the end of China's use of Tibet for nuclear weapons production, testing, and disposal." His Holiness continues today in his quest to secure autonomy for Tibet and to preserve its indigenous culture. To date, the Chinese

The Dalai Lama on Compassion

"When I visited the Nazi death camps of Auschwitz, I found myself completely unprepared for the deep revulsion I experienced at the sight of ovens where hundreds of thousands of human beings were burned....And while it is necessary to have legislation and international conventions in place to prevent such disasters, these atrocities happen in spite of them. What of Stalin and his pogroms? What of Pol Pot, architect of the Killing Fields? And what of Mao, a man I knew and once admired. All three had a vision, a goal, with some social agenda, but nothing could justify the human suffering they caused. So, you see it all starts with the individual, with asking what the consequences are of your actions. An ethical act is a nonharming act. And if we could enhance our sensitivity to others' suffering, the less we would tolerate seeing others in pain, and the more we would do to ensure that no action of ours ever causes harm. In Tibetan we call this *nying je*, translated generally as compassion. A great Tibetan scholar, who spent more than 20 years in prison enduring terrible treatment, including torture, wrote letters during his confinement and smuggled them out—and they were acclaimed by many as containing the most profound teachings on love and compassion ever heard."[105]

Lhasa's Potala Palace, today a UNESCO world heritage site

government has murdered, massacred, tortured, or starved to death over one million Tibetans, one-fifth of the population.[102]

Conditions in Tibet and its repression under the Chinese government have in more recent years sparked an international protest movement, including the attempted disruption of the 2008 Summer Olympic Games held in Beijing, China. One of main issues that concerns China is the Tibetan independence movement, which is working to establish historical Tibet as an independent state. The movement, often called "Free Tibet," is largely led by Tibetans in exile with the support of some individuals and organizations outside of Tibet. Among these supporters are a number of American and European celebrities, including Richard Gere and Brad Pitt, and some non-Tibetan followers of Tibetan Buddhism. The goals of the Tibetan independence movement are different from the goals of the Dalai Lama, who has consistently called for greater autonomy for Tibet within China, not full independence, which he described as "out of the question."[103]

Tensions between China and the Tibetan government-in-exile worsened in the wake of unrest in Tibet in March 2008, the worst in over 20 years. The Dalai Lama asked for an international investigation into China's treatment of Tibetan people, which he said amounted to cultural genocide. China responded by hardening its position and denouncing the Tibetan proposal for autonomy as a bid for "disguised independence." The Dalai Lama is also facing challenges from within the exile community. Some young Tibetan activists believe pacifism does not work and, although most approve of the Dalai Lama's leadership, a growing number are calling for a tougher stance on the Tibetan question. But the Dalai Lama has restated his life-long commitment to a peaceful resolution. He stated, "It goes without saying how much admiration I have for the enthusiasm, determination, and sacrifice of the Tibetans in Tibet. However, it is difficult to achieve a meaningful outcome by sacrificing lives. The path of non-violence is our irrevocable commitment and it is important that

The Dalai Lama on the Value of Life

"I realize that being the Dalai Lama serves a purpose. If one's life becomes useful and beneficial for others, then its purpose is fulfilled. I have an immense responsibility and an impossible task. But as long as I carry on with sincere motivation, I become almost immune to these immense difficulties. Whatever I can do, I do; even if it is beyond my ability. Of course, I feel I would be more useful being outside government administration. Younger, trained people should do this, while my remaining time and energy should concentrate on the promotion of human value. Ultimately, that is the most important thing. When human value is not respected by those who administer governments or work on economic endeavors, then all sorts of problems, like crime and corruption, increase. The Communist ideology completely fails to promote human value, and corruption is consequently great. The Buddhist culture can help to increase self-discipline, and that will automatically reduce corruption. As soon as we can return to Tibet with a certain degree of freedom, I will hand over all my authority. Then, for the rest of my life, I will focus on the promotion of harmony among the different religious traditions."[106]

---

there be no departure at all from this path."[104]

Along with his decades-long political work as leader of the Tibetan government in exile, he has expanded his role as spiritual leader of Tibet to spiritual leader and inspiration to the world. His Holiness has been at the forefront of important global issues. In this section, the Dalai Lama explains his views on compassion, the value of life and the art of happiness. He states, "My call for a spiritual revolution is thus not a call for a religious revolution. Nor is it a reference to a way of life that is somehow other-worldly, still less to something magical or mysterious. Rather, it is a call for a radical re-orientation away from our habitual preoccupation with self towards concern for the wider community of beings with whom we are connected, and for conduct which recognizes others' interests alongside our own."

Despite over 50 years in exile, the reach of the Dalai Lama has extended far beyond his community, and he is now recognized as one of the world's leading religious figures. He is a noted and engaging public speaker and a charismatic and charming individual, who is invited to share his words of wisdom and inspiration around the worldwide. In 2009, he traveled to more than 62 countries spanning 6 continents. He is the first Dalai Lama to travel to the West, where he seeks to spread teachings of compassion and non-violence and to promote ethics and interfaith harmony. He has met with presidents, prime ministers and crowned rulers of major nations and has held dialogues with many well-known scientists. He has met with different religious leaders throughout the world and visited the late Pope John Paul II on several occasions.[108]

Since 1959 the Dalai Lama has received over 100 major awards, honorary doctorates, prizes,

---

The Dalai Lama and the Art of Happiness

"The Dalai Lama says the purpose of life is happiness. We can train our human outlook that focuses on the individual self to shift our perception to focus on compassion and love for others. Then happiness can be found. Happiness is determined more by the state of one's mind than by one's external (outside) conditions, circumstances, or events—at least once one's basic survival needs are met. Thus, happiness can be achieved through the systematic training of our hearts and minds, through reshaping our attitudes and outlook; happiness is in our own hands."[107]

and other recognitions for his message of peace, inter-religious understanding, universal responsibility and compassion. He has authored more than 72 books, been given honorary Canadian citizenship in 2006, and been awarded the U.S. Congressional Gold Medal in October 2007. In 1989 he was awarded the Nobel Peace Prize for his consistent opposition to the use of violence in his quest for Tibetan self-rule. He has consistently advocated policies of non-violence, even in the face of extreme aggression. He also became the first Nobel Laureate to be recognized for his concern for global environmental problems.

President Barack Obama and Dalai Llama

The Dalai Lama announced his semi-retirement on December 17, 2008. He said that the prime minister of the elected parliament-in-exile will decide the future course of the movement he had directed for over five decades. He underwent minor gallstone surgery in 2008, and his doctors advised him to cut down on long travel and to get more rest. He told reporters in Dharamsala, "I have grown old.... It is better if I retire completely and get out of the way of the Tibetan movement."[109]

The Dalai Lama is truly a global citizen, but he humbly describes himself as a simple Buddhist monk. This quote from the Dalai Lama is an appropriate end to this chapter on human rights activists: "It is my belief that whereas the 20th century has been a century of war and untold suffering, the 21st century should be one of peace and dialogue. As the continued advances in information technology make our world a truly global village, I believe there will come a time when war and armed conflict will be considered an outdated and obsolete method of settling differences among nations and communities."

Questions to Consider

1. Looking at the early years of the 21st century, do you think the Dalai Lama's dream of peace and dialogue will come true? What will it take to make it come true?

The last chapter, Chapter 6, explores Human Rights Today by studying the different treaties and organizations, local, national, and global, which work towards implementing and ensuring human rights today.

CHAPTER SIX

HUMAN RIGHTS TODAY

"There is so much each one of us can do to make a difference. We are at a dangerous juncture in the history of mankind... We need to defend our principles and values, human rights, civil liberties and the rule of international law. If we don't our world will further descend into a state of chaos."

— Bianca Jagger

The study of human rights can be a depressing topic for many of us. The atrocities have been horrific, and the pain and suffering inflicted by humans on other humans has been disheartening. Yet, our human behaviors are like a double-edged sword; they cut both ways. As we know, humans are capable of great horror and cruelty and also great compassion and caring. We have examined our cruel side in several of the chapters, but our compassionate side shines through in the last two chapters.

This last chapter looks at several treaties, organizations, institutions, people and groups that are committed to defending and upholding human rights. People who administer these organizations have, in many cases, dedicated their lives to the cause of promoting human rights. It is an uplifting chapter, especially in contrast to the earlier chapters. Hopefully, some of you will be inspired to take up the cause of human rights and lend your talents, treasure, and time to a cause you feel committed to.

THE ROLE OF THE UNITED NATIONS IN PROTECTING HUMAN RIGHTS

I introduced the United Nations in the first chapter, and it is such an important and active world institution that it has been mentioned in every chapter. When a government violates the human rights of its residents, the victims may be able to appeal to their country's laws or bill of rights and get a court to order to stop the violations. But appropriate national laws and bills of rights may be unavailable. If this is the case, the victims of human rights violations may seek help from international organizations and laws.

In the past, international law did not provide rights and protections for individuals; its concern was the rights and duties of countries or states. There were no international organizations working to enforce legal rights of individuals. After World War I the League of Nations had some success in protecting minority rights, but its noble effort ended with the rise of Nazi Germany and the beginning of World War II in 1939. After the horrific atrocities that were committed during World War II, nations decided that an international organization was desperately needed to promote international peace and to secure human rights in all countries. Many felt this was necessary in order to lessen the dangers of falling back into another terrible war. The United States was instrumental in helping to create the United Nations in 1945. The UN Charter established goals of protecting future generations from the "scourge of war" and promoting "fundamental human rights" and the "dignity and worth of the human person."[1]

Emblem of the United Nations

Chapter 1 explained how human rights for everyone was included in the Universal Declaration of Human Rights, ratified in December 1948. The Universal Declaration was a set of recommended standards rather than a binding treaty. Now, however, almost all of the norms in the Universal Declaration have been incorporated into widely-ratified UN human rights treaties. The Universal Declaration has been very successful in setting a template for later human rights treaties and in encouraging countries to include this list of human rights in national constitutions and bills of rights. The Universal Declaration, and the treaties that followed it largely define what people today mean when they speak of human rights.[2]

The Universal Declaration was born, unfortunately, at a time that limited its success. The Cold War—a conflict between capitalist and communist countries—was beginning and any form of cooperation between the two factions was met with resistance from both sides. The United States led the capitalist countries and the Soviet Union led the communist countries, but Western Europe, which had been ravaged by two world wars, followed a middle way and were leaders in passing the UN Declaration and ratifying their own conventions. They also provided ways to enforce these conventions through the European Court of Human Rights, whose job is to receive, evaluate, and investigate complaints, interpret the law, mediate disputes, and issue judgments. All countries in Western Europe were bound to their human rights declarations. Regional arrangements, similar to those in Europe, exist in the Americas and Africa. Efforts to protect human rights through international law have obviously not been totally successful; many human rights violations still occur around the world, but international human rights law is a work in progress. The human rights agenda has advanced much farther than anyone would have expected in 1950 or even in 1975.[3]

THE UNITED NATIONS HUMAN RIGHTS TREATIES

International law contains many human rights treaties that transform lists of human rights into legally binding state obligations. This section sketches the development of international measures to promote and protect human rights. Some of these treaties we have already introduced in previous chapters, but it is also helpful to remember them all listed together.

The first United Nations treaty was the Genocide Convention, approved in 1948, just one day before the Universal Declaration of Human Rights. The Convention defines genocide and makes it a crime under international law. The Convention requires states to enact national laws prohibiting genocide, to punish those who commit genocide, and to allow persons accused of genocide to be transported to countries capable of carrying out the charges. It also calls for the UN to prevent and suppress acts of genocide.

The UN has seven separate treaties known as the Human Rights treaty bodies that monitor compliance and implementation. Although the UN system for implementing human rights is very powerful, its tools are largely limited to consciousness-raising, persuasion, mediation, and exposure of violations to public scrutiny. The following are the seven human rights treaty bodies.

1. and 2. **The International Covenant on Civil and Political Rights** and the **International Covenant on Economic, Social, and Cultural Rights** are two treaties ratified in 1966. The UN's Human Rights Commission wanted to create treaties that would make the rights in the Universal Declaration into norms of international law accepted by all nations. However, the Cold War tensions between the United States and the Soviet Union hampered the implementation of these treaties. There was a deep division between those who believed in the importance of social rights and those who thought that these rights could not be enforced in the same way as civil and political rights. Thus, the Commission decided to create two separate treaties, and drafts of the two international covenants were submitted to the General Assembly for approval in 1953, but agreement was delayed until 1966, when the UN General Assembly finally approved the Civil and Political Covenant, which contains most of the civil and political rights found in the Universal Declaration, and the Social Covenant, which contains the economic and social rights found in the second half of the Universal Declaration. These treaties became operative in 1976 and have now become the most important UN human rights treaties. As

of 2006, about 75 percent of the world's countries have ratified these two treaties.[4]

3. **The International Convention on the Elimination of All Forms of Racial Discrimination** is a second-generation human rights treaty which encourages its members to eliminate racial discrimination and promote understanding among all races of people. The UN General Assembly adopted the convention on December 21, 1965, and it entered into force on January 4, 1969.[5]

4. **The Convention on the Elimination of All Forms of Discrimination Against Women** was adopted in 1979 by the UN General Assembly. It is often described as an international bill of rights for women. Consisting of a preamble and 30 articles, it defines what constitutes discrimination against women and sets up an agenda for national action to end such discrimination.[6]

5. **The Convention on the Rights of the Child** is popularly known as **UNICEF**. Perhaps you went trick-or-treating for UNICEF as a child. Adopted in 1989, its mission is to advocate for the protection of children's rights, to help meet their basic needs and to expand opportunities for them to reach their full potential. The provisions and principles of the Convention on the Rights of the Child guide UNICEF's agenda. In 1989, world leaders decided that children needed a special convention just for them because people under 18 years old often need special care and protection that adults do not. The leaders also wanted to make sure that the world recognized that children have human rights too.[7]

Logo for UNICEF

6. **The Convention Against Torture and Other Cruel, Inhuman or Degrading Treatment or Punishment** passed in 1987. It requires states to take measures to prevent torture within their borders, and forbids states to return people to their home country if there is reason to believe they will be tortured.[8]

7. **The Convention on the Protection of the Rights of All Migrant Workers and Members of Their Families** is an international agreement, signed on December 18, 1990.

United Nations Human Rights Agencies

Human Rights treaties are only one part of the UN's human rights program. The UN has several agencies and courts to address continuing human rights abuses. Three notable agencies are the High Commissioner for Human Rights (OHCHR), which serves as a full-time advocate for human rights; the Human Rights Council, which address gross human rights violations; and the Security Council, which has the authority to impose diplomatic and economic sanctions, sponsor peacekeeping missions, and authorize military interventions in cases of human rights emergencies.

In 1993, the United Nations General Assembly established the office of the **High Commissioner for Human Rights**. The OHCHR coordinates the many human rights activities within the UN, working closely with the 7 treaty bodies, and other UN agencies such as the Human Rights Council. The High-Commissioner assists in the development of new treaties, sets the agenda for human rights agencies within the UN, and provides advisory services to governments. Most importantly, the High Commissioner serves as a full-time promoter for human rights within the UN and has field offices throughout the world.[9]

Established in 2006, the Human Rights Council consists of 47 members, elected directly and individually by the General Assembly with membership based on equitable geographic distribution.

Its responsibilities include "promoting universal respect for the protection of all human rights," addressing gross human rights violations, making recommendations to the General Assembly, and "responding promptly to human rights emergencies."[10]

The **Security Council**'s mission is to maintain international peace and security. The 15-member body consists of 5 permanent and 10 elected members. Nine votes are needed to approve any measures. Any of the five permanent members (China, France, Russia, the United Kingdom, and the United States) can exercise their veto power to prevent any given action. The permanent membership of 5 countries, with their veto power, reflects their economic and military power within the Security Council.

Three other UN agencies are indirectly involved in promoting human rights: UN High Commission for Refugees (UNHCR), World Health Organization (WHO), and World Food Program (WFP).

Established on December 14, 1950, the **Office of the United Nations High Commissioner for Refugees (UNHCR)**, is also known as the UN Refugee Agency. Headquartered in Geneva, Switzerland, the agency leads and coordinates international action to protect refugees worldwide. Its primary purpose is to safeguard the rights and well-being of refugees. It strives to ensure that everyone can exercise the right to seek asylum and find safe refuge in another state, with the option to return home voluntarily, integrate locally or resettle in a third country. It also has a mandate to help stateless people. Since 1950, the agency has helped tens of millions of people restart their lives. With a staff of more than 9,300 people in 123 countries, the agency continues to help and protect millions of refugees, returnees, internally displaced and stateless people. The UNHCR has won two Nobel Peace Prizes in 1954 and 1981.[11]

The **World Health Organization** (WHO), a specialized UN agency, is concerned with international public health. Established on April 7, 1948, now celebrated every year as World Health Day, the agency has played a leading role in the eradication of smallpox. With 7,000 people working in 150 country offices and in 6 regional offices, its current priorities include communicable diseases, in particular HIV/AIDS, Ebola, malaria and tuberculosis. Headquartered in Geneva, Switzerland, the agency is also working to ease the effects of non-communicable diseases; sexual and reproductive health, development, and aging; nutrition, food security and healthy eating; occupational health; and substance abuse.[12]

The **World Food Program** (WFP) is the world's largest humanitarian agency fighting hunger worldwide. WFP was first established in 1961 when American George McGovern, director of the U.S. Food for Peace Program, proposed establishing a global food aid program. The UN General Assembly formally established it in 1963 on a three-year experimental basis and in 1965 they permanently extended it and established headquarters in Rome, Italy. In emergencies, the agency gets food to where it is needed,

World Health Organization

saving the lives of victims of war, civil conflict and natural disasters. After the emergency has passed, food continues to flow to the communities in order to help rebuild shattered lives. WFP pursues "a vision of the world in which every man, woman and child has access at all times to the food needed for an active and healthy life." On average, the WFP reaches more than 90 million people with food assistance in 80 country offices each year. About 13,500 people work for the organization, most of them in remote areas directly serving the hungry and poor. The European Union is a permanent observer in the WFP and, as a major donor, participates in the work of its Executive Board. The agency is voluntarily funded.[13]

REGIONAL HUMAN RIGHTS ORGANIZATIONS

Regional Human Rights Systems assist the UN by promoting and protecting human rights in particular parts of the world. Five regions—Europe, the Americas, Africa, Asia, and the Middle East—have their own declarations and conventions. Because of their locations, regional agencies and courts have better chances of investigating alleged violations promptly and securing relief for victims. Regional agencies are also likely to be more attuned to the culture and identity of the region and may accordingly have a deeper understanding of problems and reforms.[14] The 5 organizations are listed in order of establishment.

1. **The European Convention for the Protection of Human Rights** (1950) is an international treaty to protect human rights in Europe. The Council of Europe drafted the convention in 1950 and it entered into force on September 3, 1953. All 47 Council of Europe member states are party to the Convention and new members are expected to ratify it. Based on the Universal Declaration of Human Rights, the European Convention establishes human rights norms, legally binds member states to respect these norms, and creates a system of negotiation and enforcement. The European Convention was formed in response to Europe's role in the atrocities of World War II as well as the human rights abuses of communism.[15]

The Convention has established the European Court of Human Rights, based in Strasbourg, France, to enforce human rights standards. Countries that accept the European Convention agree to a list of rights and also approve the investigation and settlement of human rights complaints. The Court hears applications alleging that a state has breached human rights provisions set out in the Convention. An individual, a group of individuals or one or more states can lodge an application. Besides judgments, which participating governments almost always accept, the Court can also issue advisory opinions.

2. **The Inter-American Commission on Human Rights** (IACHR) (1959) is an independent agency of the Organization of American States (OAS), the oldest regional organization of states. In 1948, 21 states signed the OAS Charter, establishing the OAS and affirming their commitment to democracy, liberty, and equality before the law. One OAS principle is the "fundamental rights of the individual without distinction as to race, nationality, creed, or sex." The mission of the IACHR is to promote and protect human rights in the American hemisphere and to investigate individual complaints and prepare reports on countries with severe human rights problems. All 35 of the countries in the Americas currently comprise the OAS.[16] Created by the OAS in 1959, the Commission has its headquarters in Washington, D.C.

3. **African Commission on Human and Peoples' Rights** (1987) is tasked with promoting and protecting human rights and collective (peoples') rights throughout Africa. The Commission reports to the African Union (formerly the Organization of African Unity). The Commission was based for the first two years in Addis Ababa, Ethiopia. In November 1989, it relocated to Banjul, Gambia. The Commission came into existence with the enactment of the African Charter on Human and Peoples' Rights on October 21, 1986. One of the purposes of the Commission is oversight, interpretation and consideration of individual complaints in violation of the Charter. In 1998, the Commission

adopted the African Court on Human and Peoples' Rights and it came into effect in 2005.

The African Charter on Human and Peoples' Rights (also known as the Banjul Charter) is an international human rights agreement charged with promoting and protecting human rights and basic freedoms in Africa. In addition to recognizing individual rights, the Charter also recognizes collective or group rights, or peoples' rights and third-generation human rights. The Charter recognizes group rights to a degree not matched by the European or Inter-American regional human rights documents. The idea of drafting a document establishing human rights protection in Africa was first thought about in the early 1960's. Although there was a call on African governments to adopt an African convention on human rights with a court and a commission, most governments were more concerned with political and economic rights. Yet, African governments have continued to create governmental institutions to promote basic rights in Africa. One of these institutions is the African Union.

African Commission on Human and Peoples' Rights

The African Union covers the countries of the African continent. One of its objectives is the promotion and protection of human rights; explicitly it supports group rights—the rights of peoples—such as the right of a group to freely dispose of its natural resources in the exclusive interest of its members and the right of a colonized or oppressed group to free themselves from domination. The African system has enormous human rights problems to address, frequently facing non-cooperation by governments without adequate resources to implement its objectives. Despite its limited legal and economic resources, the African Union seems to be slowly constructing international ways to promote and protect human rights.[17]

4. **The Arab Charter on Human Rights** (ACHR) (2004), adopted by the Council of the League of Arab States on May 22, 2004, affirms the principles contained in the UN Charter, the Universal Declaration of Human Rights, the International Covenants on Human Rights and the Cairo Declaration on Human Rights in Islam. Included are a number of traditional human rights: the right to liberty and security of persons, equality of persons before the law, protection of persons from torture, the right to own private property, freedom to practice religious observance and freedom of peaceful assembly and association. On September 15, 1994 a first version of the Charter was presented to the members for ratification; however, no state ratified it. An updated version of the Charter was presented in 2004, and the amended version came into force in 2008 when seven members of the League of Arab states had ratified it. As of November 2013, the Charter has been ratified by Algeria, Bahrain, Iraq, Jordan, Kuwait, Lebanon, Libya, Palestine, Qatar, Saudi Arabia, Syria, the UAE (United Arab Emirates) and Yemen. The Arab Human Rights Committee is the treaty body established to supervise implementation of the Charter.[18]

Arab Charter on Human Rights

In 1945, Egypt, Jordan, Iraq, Lebanon, Syria and Saudi Arabia signed the Pact of the Arab League States and created the League of Arab States. The countries formed the League to strengthen ties between the Arab states on the basis of respect for their independence and promotion of their common interests. There were 22 League members in 2011. The League of Arab States is separate from the Organization of the Islamic Conference, which was the second largest inter-governmental organization in 2011 with 57 member states, just below the UN in membership. The Organization has a permanent delegation to the UN and supports the Cairo Declaration on Human Rights in Islam, which serves as a guide for member states in human rights matters to insure compatibility with Sharia Law.[19]

5. The **ASEAN Intergovernmental Commission on Human Rights** (AICHR) (2009) was inaugurated in October 2009 as an agency of the Association of Southeast Asian Nations (ASEAN). Its human rights commission promotes and protects human rights, and regional co-operation on human rights in its member states: Brunei Darussalam, Cambodia, Indonesia, Lao PDR, Malaysia, Myanmar, Philippines, Singapore, Thailand and Viet Nam. The Commission drafted the ASEAN Human Rights Declaration in 2012 and ASEAN members adopted it unanimously at its meeting in Phnom Penh, Cambodia. The Declaration detailed ASEAN nations' commitment to human rights for its 600 million people.

Association of Southeast Asian Nations (ASEAN) emblem

The Declaration itself has been criticized by ASEAN civil society, international human rights organizations such as Amnesty International, Human Rights Watch, the U.S. Department of State, and the UN High Commissioner for Human Rights. Human Rights Watch described it as a "declaration of government powers disguised as a declaration of human rights." ASEAN civil societies have noted that "the Declaration fails to include several key basic rights and fundamental freedoms, including the right to freedom of association and the right to be free from enforced disappearance." Further, the Declaration contains clauses that could be used to undermine human rights, such as "the realization of human rights must be considered in the regional and national context." or that human rights might be limited to preserve "national security" or a narrowly defined "public morality."[20]

Promotion of Human Rights by States

Perhaps the most important role that states play in international human rights law is in creating and ratifying human rights treaties. Executive and legislative bodies ratify treaties by consent at the national level. For a treaty to be passed in the U.S., for example, it needs passage by a two-thirds vote of the members of the Senate. Once a treaty is established, states help give it life by creating laws to implement it and use it as a standard for evaluation. The United Kingdom Human Rights Act of 1998 is an example of how international norms have been incorporated into domestic law. The act protects rights similar to the ones in the European Convention on Human Rights, including the right to life, liberty, security and a fair trial, and the prohibition of torture, slavery, and forced labor.

States often take actions, alone or together with other states, to promote and protect human rights in other countries. For example, in the late 1990s Australia led the military effort to restore peace and respect for human rights in East Timor. Another crisis erupted in 2006 and Australia, Portugal,

New Zealand, and Malaysia again sent troops to suppress the violence. States use diplomacy, limit trade or aid, impose economic sanctions, or even intervene militarily to promote human rights in other countries.

Humanitarian intervention is the use of force by one state to prevent or stop severe human rights violations and other humanitarian disasters in another state. There is always the risk of a state pursuing its own foreign policy goals under the guise of humanitarian intervention. The United States' invasion of Iraq in 2003 exemplifies this concern. War can easily be rationalized by calling it humanitarian intervention and emphasizing high-minded motives.

Unfortunately, there are situations in which military intervention is the only possible means of ending severe human rights violations. For example, international organizations have been widely criticized for not intervening during the genocide in Rwanda. Efforts by states help to add real power to the international human rights system. The countries of Western Europe, Canada, Australia, and the United States, have been the historic pillars of the human rights establishment, but other non-Western countries, such as South Korea, are becoming more involved. Although states have human rights problems of their own and have not always met the challenge of human rights emergencies, they have sometimes provided military and peacekeeping forces at considerable cost to themselves in money and lives. States do not have a legal commitment to support human rights beyond basic principles, but commitment by many states to the UN Human Rights Charter guides their resolve.[21]

NON-GOVERNMENTAL ORGANIZATIONS

Non-governmental organizations (NGOs) are extremely active at the international level in the areas of implementing human rights, dispensing humanitarian aid, and monitoring human rights violations. The term is widely accepted as referring to a legally constituted organization created by natural or legal persons with no participation or representation of any government. In the cases where governments totally or partially fund NGOs, it maintains its non-governmental status and excludes government representatives from membership in the organization. NGOs are often referred to as civil society organizations, third sector, the independent sector, the non-profit sector, the voluntary sector, or by other names. Estimates of the number of NGOs throughout the world vary so widely, perhaps as a result of varying definitions. Estimates at the low end specify around 26,000 while other estimates say 1-2 million organizations are working toward ecological sustainability and social and economic justice.[22]

Nongovernmental organizations (NGOs) are different from institutions such as the UN because they allow for collaboration between local and global efforts for human rights by "translating complex international issues into activities to be undertaken by concerned citizens in their own community." The functions of international NGOs include investigating complaints, advocacy with governments and international governmental organizations, and policy making, while local activities include fundraising, lobbying, and general education.[23]

Although they do not have the authority to put into practice or enforce international law, NGOs have several advantages over governmental bodies in the human rights system. Much of their work includes information processing and fact finding so NGOs can educate people about their human rights and gather information regarding human rights abuses in violating countries. Once they gather information, NGOs can design campaigns to educate the international community of these abuses. A key function of NGOs is **advocacy**—urging support for human rights and attempting to influence governments or international groups with regard to specific actions. Advocacy involves education, persuasion, public exposure, criticism and provoking specific responses to human rights abuses.[24]

Representatives of NGOs are seen everywhere in the international human rights community. Many representatives attend and often participate in the meetings of UN human rights bodies. They provide information about human rights situations through their reports and testimony. They help to shape the agendas, policies, and treaties of the UN through their participation and lobbying.

NGOs range in size and scope from large organizations with affiliates around the world to small NGOs with perhaps only one person running the organization. Some of the larger NGOs committed to human rights include Amnesty International, Human Rights Watch, the International Commission of Jurists, International Red Cross, Carter Center, the International Federation of Human Rights, Lawyers Committee for Human Rights, Minority Group Rights, Physicians for Human Rights, Freedom House, Save the Children, Medicins san Frontieres (Doctors without Borders), Robert F. Kennedy Justice and Human Rights, and Oxfam. Besides these high profile NGOs there are thousands of local and national organizations working on human rights issues. The following section describes a few of the well-known human rights NGOs and their missions. They are listed in alphabetical order.

AMNESTY INTERNATIONAL

"The candle burns not for us, but for all those whom we failed to rescue from prison, who were shot on the way to prison, who were tortured, who were kidnapped, who disappeared. That's what the candle is for."
— Peter Benenson, founder of Amnesty International

Amnesty International is a worldwide non-governmental organization whose mission is "to conduct research and generate action to prevent and end grave abuses of human rights and to demand justice for those whose rights have been violated." Amnesty draws public attention to human rights abuses and campaigns in order to enforce compliance to international standards. It works to mobilize public opinion which puts pressure on individuals who perpetrate abuses. It is an internationally recognized organization with more than 3 million members and subscribers in more than 150 countries and regions around the world. They have offices in more than 80 countries and campaign for human rights and justice on a wide range of issues. In the field of international human rights organizations, Amnesty has the longest history and broadest name recognition, and many say it sets standards for the movement.[25]

Amnesty International

English labor lawyer Peter Benenson founded Amnesty International in London in July 1961 in response to reading about torture. According to his own account, he read of the Portuguese government sentencing two students to 7 years of imprisonment in 1961 for having drunk a toast to liberty. He wrote his famous newspaper article *The Forgotten Prisoners* describing his reaction: "Open your newspaper any day of the week and you will find a story from somewhere of someone being imprisoned, tortured or executed because his opinions or religion are unacceptable to his government ... The newspaper reader feels a sickening sense of impotence. Yet if these feelings of disgust could be united into common action, something effective could be done."[26] Benenson worked with his friend Eric Baker, a Quaker, who had been involved in the

Seven Areas of Amnesty Focus

Women's Rights
Children's Rights
Ending Torture
Abolition of the Death Penalty
Rights of Refugees
Rights of Prisoners of Conscience
Protection of Human Dignity

Campaign for Nuclear Disarmament, as well as head of Quaker Peace and Social Witness. In his memoirs Benenson described him as "a partner in the launching of the project."[27] What started as a short action soon became a permanent international movement working to protect those imprisoned for non-violently expressing their views. Since Amnesty International has supported thousands of campaigns in its long and successful history, a few in each decade are highlighted.

By the mid-1960s, Amnesty International's global presence was growing, and the organization established a committee to manage their growing number of national organizations, called Sections. The international movement was starting to agree on its mission and implementation. It was helping prisoners' families, sending observers to trials, presenting information to governments, and finding asylum or overseas employment for prisoners. Amnesty was also gaining recognition among intergovernmental organizations and would consult with the United Nations, the Council of Europe and UN Education, Scientific, and Cultural Organization (UNESCO).

During the 1970s, Amnesty's actions widened to include opposition to long-term prison detention without a fair trial and to the torture of prisoners. They were concerned that the Central Intelligence Agency (CIA) in the U.S. and other nations, where torture was against the law, sent prisoners to "client states" that carried out the torture for them. They mounted a public campaign "Abolition of Torture" for several years. The organization was awarded the Nobel Peace Prize for its campaign against torture in 1977 and the UN Prize in the Field of Human Rights in 1978. In its Nobel Lecture following the awarding of the peace prize, the Amnesty spokesman had these moving words: "[An] irony often mentioned by our members is that at times they have gained more from the prisoner they sought to help than the prisoner has gained from them: much of courage, of the value of human dignity and freedom, of the durability of the human spirit."[28]

Through the decade of the 1980s, Amnesty International continued to campaign for prisoners of conscience and torture. They were also concerned about refugees, particularly those who were forced to flee because of human rights violations. It started a campaign to make governments address the human rights violations which were forcing people into exile. In 1988, on the 40th anniversary of the Universal Declaration of Human Rights, Amnesty launched the 1988 Human Rights Now! Tour, which was designed to widen awareness of human rights. Aided by some of the most famous musicians and bands of the day, such as Bruce Springsteen and Sting, they played a series of 20 concerts on 5 continents over 6 weeks to bring public attention to the issue of human rights.

In the 1990s, Amnesty International's membership grew to over 2.2 million in over 150 countries and territories. It took action during armed conflict and human rights violations in areas such as Angola, East Timor, the Persian Gulf, Rwanda, Somalia and the former Yugoslavia. Its position was that action, even the use of force, should be employed to prevent human rights problems from becoming human rights catastrophes. Amnesty favored the creation of a UN High Commissioner for Human Rights, established in 1993 and the International Criminal Court (ICC), established in 2002.[29]

After 2000, Amnesty International turned its attention to the challenges arising from economic globalization. This was a major shift in their policy, as activists widened the scope of their work to include economic, social and cultural rights, an area that they had not worked on in the past. Amnesty worked against the growing power of corporations and the detrimental effects they had in undermining the authority of many nation states.

During the decade Amnesty International turned its attention to violence against women and ways to control the world's arms trade. One of its campaigns in 2015 was maternal health. Around the world, one woman dies every 90 seconds from complications of pregnancy or childbirth—more than 350,000 per year. Amnesty believed that many of these deaths were preventable. It worked to make sure that all women have the right to access quality maternal health care, regardless of race, ethnicity or income.[30]

If you live in the United States, there is an Amnesty International USA organization with local Amnesty chapters in cities throughout the U.S. Amnesty provides new members with an Activist Toolkit. It has information to help new groups get started, useful tips on running an existing group, and ideas for planning events and activities. It also provides a crash course on how Amnesty operates.[31] A local Amnesty chapter is a great and easy way to get involved in the issue of human rights!

THE CARTER CENTER

"At the Carter Center, we believe all people are entitled to basic human rights. When people have these rights, they feel a sense of justice and self-worth. These are the seeds of peace."

— Founder, President Jimmy Carter

Nestled in a park-like setting surrounded by the skyline of Atlanta, Georgia, the **Carter Center** looks more like a relaxing retreat center rather than a vibrant hub of human rights activity. Former U.S. President Jimmy Carter, who served one term in office from 1977 to 1981, founded the Carter Center in 1982. This short description of the Carter Center is not about whether you agree with his policies as president but about what he and his wife Rosalyn have done since he served as president. Its Human Rights program is one of special interest to our study. In fact, Jimmy Carter was awarded the Noble Peace Prize in 2002 for his work "to find peaceful solutions to international conflicts, to advance democracy and human rights, and to promote economic and social development" through The Carter Center.[32]

Among President Carter's many humanitarian efforts was his strong support for establishing the post of High Commissioner for Human Rights

Carter Center, Atlanta, Georgia

at the U.N. in 1993, and since then the Carter Center has worked closely with each of the high commissioners. It has also endorsed the work of the International Criminal Court (ICC) and voiced concerns about torture and other critical human rights issues. Since its founding the Center has undertaken peace activities in more than 55 countries worldwide.[33] The Center also supports citizens who monitor and advance human rights at the grassroots level. For example, in the Democratic Republic of the Congo, it has provided training and networking resources to local human rights groups and, at the invitation of the Congolese government, it has assisted in a review of the fairness of national mining contracts.[34]

According to the Carter Center, wars produce the worst violations of human rights. Since the end of the Cold War, there have been more than 50 major armed conflicts over territorial boundaries, religious affiliation, national or ethnic identity, or access to natural resources. The Conflict Resolution Program works to resolve such conflicts and build long-lasting peace. As a non-partisan NGO, the Center has become a trusted broker for peace, serving as an alternative channel for dialogue and negotiation until official diplomacy at the state level can take place. Program staff and interns monitor daily many of the world's armed conflicts to better understand their histories, the underlying causes, the primary actors involved, disputed issues, and efforts being made for resolution. If invited, the Center will mediate among all major adversaries (enemies); President Carter has even traveled to some of the regions and remained in close touch with key leaders. The process is not instantaneous; it takes patience, persistence, and many steps to ease tensions while building consensus around shared goals, strengthening the rule of law, and bringing justice to victims.

I took a tour of the human rights program at the Carter Center and met with the director, Karin Ryan, in November 2009. She said that Jimmy and Rosalyn Carter have made a personal commitment to human rights for all people around the world; this was a founding principle of the Center. These rights include civil, political, social, economic, and cultural rights and freedoms as outlined in the Universal Declaration of Human Rights. Both of the Carters have personally supported thousands of human rights defenders by appealing through letters or in private meetings to heads of state on behalf of those who are persecuted for their work. Ryan said the Center supports human rights by holding governments accountable for their actions. It is the nature of most governments to want to hold on to and expand their power; therefore, governments need a check on their power. She said, "Governments hate human rights campaigns because it means that they have to be held accountable for their actions. It is much easier for governments to just ignore them." She continued, "That is why human rights campaigns are so important; people get involved and put pressure on the government through different tactics that they use."

Ryan highlighted two campaigns that the Carter Center was involved in at the time: the conflict in the Congo and in Israel and Palestine. She said that public awareness about the human rights abuses in the Congo gets very little attention, despite the fact that the number of deaths is far higher than in other human rights campaigns that get far more media attention such as Darfur or Israel/Palestine. I agreed. I asked her why that was the case and she thought that perhaps it was because the conflict in the Congo is very complicated (we like simple answers) and it covers a very large area in central Africa, a region Americans know very little about. Also, there are no clear good guys and bad guys. In addition, it is very rich in mineral resources that we need for all of our latest technological devices. If we look closely at the problems in the Congo, we may feel somewhat complicit in the atrocities, since our demand for consumer technology helps to fuel the competition and conflict over mining these valuable resources. Therefore, the media largely ignores the conflict. (see the

President Carter at a book signing, 2014

Congo in chapter 4)

In the Katanga Province in the Democratic Republic of the Congo (DRC), thousands of children spend their days digging for minerals, breaking stones, and transporting and washing minerals, risking exposure to dangerous levels of radiation, potential pulmonary diseases, and physical and sexual abuse by peers and adults. The Carter Center spearheads one project as part of a larger child protection campaign in which radio messages to mining communities tell of the dangers faced by children working in the mines.

One of Jimmy Carter's accomplishments during his presidency was his leadership in negotiations that led to the Camp David Accords. Two long-time rivals in the Middle East—Egyptian President Anwar El Sadat and Israeli Prime Minister Menachem Begin—signed the Camp David Accords on September 17, 1978. Carter was directly involved in 12 days of secret and intense negotiations at Camp David, the presidential retreat outside of Washington D.C. The Accords led directly to the 1979 Israel-Egypt Peace Treaty and took a significant step towards peace in the Middle East. It also resulted in Sadat and Begin sharing the 1978 Nobel Peace Prize. Since his presidency, Carter has taken a stand for Palestinian human rights in the face of much criticism from both Israel and certain groups in the U.S. The Carter Center has also worked with Israeli peace movements to help resolve the conflict in the Middle East.

Carter has been very active since leaving the White House. He has traveled extensively to conduct peace negotiations, observe elections, and advance disease prevention and eradication in developing nations. He also is a key figure in Habitat for Humanity and has participated in many building projects. Despite turning 90 years old on October 1, 2014, Carter is still very active at the Carter Center.

Freedom House

In 1941, Americans who were concerned with the mounting threats to peace and democracy founded **Freedom House** in New York City. Eleanor Roosevelt and Wendell Willkie (Republican presidential candidate in 1940) served as Freedom House's first honorary co-chairpersons. Today Freedom House is an independent watchdog organization that supports democratic change, monitors freedom, and advocates for democracy and human rights around the world. It describes itself as a "clear voice for democracy and freedom around the world." Freedom House has vigorously opposed dictatorships of the far left and the far right, including dictatorships in Latin America, apartheid in South Africa, Soviet domination of Central and Eastern Europe, and religiously-based totalitarian regimes such as those in Sudan, Iran and Saudi Arabia. It provides support to individuals working in the world's young democracies to overcome the legacy of dictatorships and political repression and bring about greater freedom and openness.

Freedom House is a non-profit organization with more than a dozen offices spread over 4 continents and an experienced staff of over 150 individuals. Along with its offices in Washington D.C. and New York City, it has offices in Hungary, Romania, Jordan, Kazakhstan, Kyrgyzstan, and South Africa. Freedom House works directly with democratic reformers on the front lines in their own countries. I recently took a tour of Freedom House at its Washington D.C. headquarters office situated on DuPont Circle. The office was alive with activity; student interns were bustling about meeting week-end deadlines, while two young men who had just returned from helping to launch a human rights program in Turkey were bubbling with enthusiasm over their successful initiative. It was inspiring to witness such enthusiasm and commitment for the cause of human rights among the staff at Freedom House. I interviewed Paula Schriefer, Directory of Advocacy, and Elizabeth Floyd, Editor of Special Reports for Freedom House's New York office. Elizabeth told me that the crown jewel of Freedom House's educational outreach is Freedom in the World; a project launched in 1973.

Freedom in the World is an annual survey of global political rights and civil liberties that rates every country in the world on a series of indicators basic to freedom as experienced by individuals in that country. The UN Universal Declaration of Rights serves as a guidepost. The survey measures freedom according to two broad categories: political rights and civil liberties. Political rights enable people to participate freely in the political process, including the right to vote easily in legitimate elections, compete for public office, join political parties and organizations, and elect representatives who are accountable to the electorate. Civil liberties allow for the freedoms of expression and belief, rights for associations and organizations, the rule of law, and personal autonomy without state interference. Freedom House assigns each country a rating—on a scale of 1 to 7—for political rights and civil liberties; a rating of 1 indicates the highest degree of freedom and 7 the lowest level of freedom. These ratings determine whether a country is classified according to the survey as Free, Partly Free, or Not Free. Freedom House publishes the survey annually and provides a comparison of the global state of freedom in individual countries. It is a fascinating and easy-to-use tool to find out the status of human rights in different countries.

HUMAN RIGHTS FIRST

Founded in 1978, **Human Rights First** (formerly known as the Lawyers Committee for Human Rights) is a nonprofit, human rights organization with headquarters in New York City and Washington, D.C. The organization has focused on protecting the rights of refugees, supporting human rights defenders, and pressing for the U.S. government's full participation in the international human rights system. Human Rights First has organized its work into five areas: human rights defenders, law and security, refugee protection and fighting discrimination. It also directs attention to what it regards as the erosion of human rights in the U.S. in the aftermath of 9/11, the rise in anti-Semitic, racist and anti-Muslim hate crimes in Europe and war crimes and crimes against humanity. Its mission "is based on the principle that core human rights protections apply universally, and thus extend to everyone by virtue of their humanity."

During the 1990s, Human Rights First reported on unjust legal systems around the world. The organization worked with pop singer Peter Gabriel in 1992 on an initiative called Witness, which was designed to provide frontline human rights defenders with video cameras to document abuses. Since that time, Witness, now a human rights non-profit organization based in Brooklyn, New York, has used uses video and online technologies to open the eyes of the world to human rights violations. It has worked with over 300 organizations in more than 70 countries.

In response to the Rwandan Genocide (1994) and the Balkan Wars (1991-1995) that followed the breakup of the former Yugoslavia, Human Rights First began focusing considerable attention on how to hold the perpetrators of mass atrocities legally responsible. Along with others, the organization called for a permanent international tribunal to try war crimes, crimes against humanity and genocide, and it has waged a successful campaign to create the International Criminal Court (ICC).

One of the more controversial stances by Human Rights First is the issue of how to address human rights violations committed by non-state actors, such as corporations. During the 1990s, Human Rights First took the then unpopular step of working directly with global apparel manufacturers to create a system of standards to ensure that workers had basic rights, including a safe workplace and fair working hours and pay. It was one of the founders of the Fair Labor Association, whose members include corporations, as well as human rights and other public interest organizations. Human rights activists, union leaders and the press have criticized Human Rights First for its engagement with those responsible for human rights abuses. However, the strategy of "engagement" has gained more credibility over time as an alternative way to challenge abusive practices.

What began as the Lawyer-to-Lawyer Network has evolved into the Human Rights Defenders Program. This program supports and advocates for international human rights defenders whose lives, and often the lives of their families, are at risk. They work with local human rights activists in Colombia, Cuba, Egypt, Guatemala, Iran, Indonesia and Thailand. I recently stopped by the Human Rights First office in Washington D. C., strategically located next door to the U.S. Supreme Court Building. I interviewed Julia Fromholz, Director of Crimes against Humanity Program and she told me the gripping and sad story of Munir Said Thalib.

Munir Said Thalib, Indonesia

Munir Said Thalib (1965-2004) was one of Indonesia's most famous human rights and anti-corruption activists. Affectionately known simply as Munir, he won the 2000 Right Livelihood Award, an alternative to the Noble Peace Prize. He was a notable human rights campaigner in Indonesia and faced intimidation, including death threats. He accused the Indonesian military of human rights violations in East Timor and other provinces, claiming they ran a criminal network in illegal tree logging and drug smuggling. On September 7, 2004, Munir flew from Singapore to Schiphol Airport in Amsterdam, Netherlands. On the flight he fell deathly ill and a doctor on-board treated him. However, he mysteriously died two hours before arrival. From his autopsy it was determined that he died of arsenic poisoning—in fact, his body contained a level of arsenic almost three times the lethal dose. During his trial, eye witnesses recounted that he took what looked like arsenic during his flight transit in Singapore or sometime near that time. The perpetrators of his death remain a mystery. Munir is survived by his wife, Suciwati and their two young children. She has campaigned tirelessly for justice for Munir, both in Jakarta and abroad at the United Nations, in Asia, and the United States. She has also helped bring together victims of other human rights violations to campaign for justice and reform. Human Rights First has hosted Suciwati in the U.S. and has lobbied the U.S. and Indonesian governments to push for progress in the case.[35] Munir was posthumously awarded the Train Foundation's Civil Courage Prize, which recognizes "extraordinary heroes of conscience." In 2013 a museum in Malang, East Java, Indonesia was opened in his honor.

A second Human Rights First program is called Law and Security. After the September 11, 2001 attacks, the U.S. government passed a number of measures in the name of counterterrorism. Human Rights First and others regarded these laws as restrictions on refugees and other immigrants, unlawful detention, and torture. Since 2003, Human Rights First has led an effort to mobilize and work closely with national security experts to challenge certain laws passed by the George W. Bush administration, especially the use of what it feels are coercive interrogations. Human Rights First recruited and has worked closely with a group of almost 50 retired U.S. generals and admirals who have taken a stand against torture and official cruelty. In January 2009, members of the group stood with President Obama as he signed three executive orders to ban torture, close the Guantánamo Bay detention camp, and end the CIA's use of secret prisons. This group of generals played an active role with Human Rights First in promoting the Congressional adoption of the Detainee Treatment Act of 2005, which prohibits all forms of cruel, inhuman or degrading treatment of detainees by any U.S. official. Also, Human Rights First created its Primetime Torture project to challenge television's depiction of cruel interrogations as being effective. The organization is working with Hollywood producers, writers and directors, experienced interrogators and military educators to limit the negative impact that popular culture has on the public debate and on soldiers' actions in the field.[36]

A third Human Rights First program is Refugee Protection. This program supports the rights of refugees and asylum seekers by providing pro bono (free) representation in courts. Human Rights First's asylum program currently represents more than 1,000 clients from more than 80 countries, obtaining a favorable outcome in 90 percent of these cases. In 2007, volunteer lawyers working with the program provided more than 85,600 hours of work annually, time worth more than $34.3 million in in-kind support. In 2007, the organization launched the Lifeline for Iraqi Refugees project in response to the refugee crisis as a result of the Iraq war. The project sought to resettle refugees and increase aid to the region. Human Rights First has been able to help increase the number of Iraqi refugees admitted into the United States to more than 15,000 as of October 2008.[37]

The fourth Human Rights First program is Fighting Discrimination. With anti-Semitic, racist, anti-Muslim and other violent hate crimes on the rise in Europe, activists have been working to strengthen the efforts of governments to track and prosecute such abuses. In its hate crime survey it examines anti-bias and nondiscrimination laws in European countries and documents hate crime violence, and evaluates government responses in a related report card.[38]

Human Rights Watch

Human Rights Watch is a visible presence in many areas of the world where human rights abuses are being committed. Its mission is "dedicated to protecting the human rights of people around the world." Its website indicates it is carrying out its mission. It is a non-profit NGO that focuses international attention on areas where human rights are being violated, gives voice to the oppressed, and holds the perpetrators accountable for their crimes. It has a staff of over 275 members consisting of human rights professionals, including country experts, lawyers, journalists, and academics of diverse backgrounds and nationalities. It is headquartered in New York City, and has offices in Berlin, Brussels, Chicago, Geneva, Johannesburg, London, Los Angeles, Moscow, Paris, San Francisco, Tokyo, Toronto, and Washington D.C.

Human Rights Watch logo

Helsinki Watch, the predecessor of Human Rights Watch, started in 1978 to monitor the Soviet Union's observance of the peace agreement called the Helsinki Accords. It adopted a strategy of publicly "naming and shaming" abusive governments through media coverage and through direct contact with policymakers. Americas Watch was founded in 1981 in response to the bloody civil wars in Central America. They used extensive on-the-ground fact-finding investigation to expose war crimes. In addition, Americas Watch also examined the role played by foreign governments, particularly the United States, in providing military and political support to abusive regimes. A number of additional "watches" were added to what was then known as "The Watch Committees"—Asia Watch (1985), Africa Watch (1988), and Middle East Watch (1989). In 1988, all the watch groups were united under one umbrella organization to form the Human Rights Watch.

Human Rights Watch is known for its accurate fact-finding and impartial reporting. Each year it publishes more than 100 reports and briefings on human rights conditions in over 90 countries. Local and international media use this information to broadcast human rights conditions to a wide audience. Because of its excellent reputation, the organization is able to meet with governments, the United Nations, regional groups like the African Union and the European Union, financial institutions, and corporations to press for changes in policies and practices that promote human rights and justice around the world.

There have been numerous success stories as a result of its actions. One campaign that activists have worked hard to raise awareness about is rape in the Congo. Juliane Kippenberg, senior children's rights researcher, interviewed one of the Congolese rape victims in the following moving story.

A Young Congolese Rape Victim

The 15-year-old girl, looking even younger than her years, lay on a mattress in a shelter in eastern Congo, her sleeping newborn son beside her. "I was just coming back from the river to fetch water," Regine sadly recounted. "Two soldiers came up to me and told me that if I refuse to sleep with them, they will kill me. They beat me and ripped my clothes. One of the soldiers raped me." Regine's parents brought her to the local army commander. "I recognized the two soldiers, and I know that one of them is called Edouard," she told Kippenberg. The commander said Regine was lying.

Sadly, Regine, whose name has been changed, is one of thousands of women and girls who were raped during the Congo's brutal conflict. The United Nations estimates that 200,000 women and girls have been the victims of sexual violence since 1998. In 2008 alone, nearly 16,000 rapes were reported in Congo. In the eastern part of the country, a battleground for government troops, militias, and foreign armies, many fighters systematically carry out sexual violence. Since January 2009, attacks on civilians have increased, with both government soldiers and militia fighters committing horrendous sexual crimes.

Regine still faces tough choices. Her family has told her she may come home but without her baby. If the army finally begins to take rape prosecutions seriously, other girls might not have to live through such horror as Regine.[39]

For the past five years, Human Rights Watch's researchers have helped raise awareness of sexual violence in the Congo by documenting rape, working with women's rights activists, and urging journalists to cover the issue. However, they became concerned that despite growing international awareness about sexual violence in the Congo, rape was not decreasing. Human Rights investigators found that broader problems contributed to sexual violence, including lax military control and poor living conditions for soldiers. Finally, in summer 2009 after years of campaigning, things began to change. Congo President Joseph Kabila agreed to meet with Human Rights officials and go forward with an anti-rape strategy. Human Rights Watch then held a press conference in the Congo city of Goma where activists loudly criticized the brutal abuses by all involved in the conflict, including the widespread rape by government soldiers. Soon after the press conference, Kabila and the military announced a zero-tolerance policy for sexual violence and other abuses. Since that time several rape trials have been opened, and one has led to the conviction of two high-level officers. Another officer has been arrested and is accused of raping a 28-year-old woman and persuading three other soldiers to rape her, too. Four other high-level officers are under investigation for related charges.[40]

In August 2009, Human Rights Watch briefed then U.S. Secretary of State Hillary Clinton's specialist on women's issues. The Human Rights Congo office helped to organize a meeting between Secretary Clinton and women's rights activists during her visit to Congo. Following these meetings, Secretary Clinton expressed serious concern at the lack of sexual violence prosecutions and pledged $17 million (US$) in aid for victims of sexual violence. After so many years of working on this issue, Human Rights Watch is cautiously encouraged by the new developments. It wants to make sure that prosecutions continue and that the military actually changes its policies.

Another of the many areas where Human Rights Watch has an active presence is Uganda, a smaller neighbor to the northeast of Congo. Uganda's violent history, rich mineral deposits, and location near countries involved in conflict have contributed to an unstable situation in the northern part of the country. Actually, the southern part of Uganda is relatively peaceful. I have included mention of Uganda in part because of Human Rights Watch's engagement in the area and also because of a very moving documentary called *War Dance*. The documentary takes place in the war-ravaged northern part of Uganda where a rebel group called the Lord's Resistance Army (LRA) is waging a brutal campaign against the government. At the time of this writing, the rebellion is now one of the longest running conflicts in Africa. The LRA is led by Joseph Kony, who claims he is a "spokesperson of God" and guided by the Holy Spirit. The group is intent on establishing a theocratic state based on the Bible's Ten Commandments and Acholi tradition (the region's tribal culture). However, the LRA is a perverse interpretation of these traditions and is accused of widespread human rights violations, including murder, abduction, mutilation, sexual enslavement of women and children, and forcing children to participate in hostilities for over two decades.[41] The U.S. has called the LRA a terrorist organization. The violence has displaced more than 1.6 million people and the rebels have killed or kidnapped tens of thousands of civilians. The UN estimates that the group has abducted 20,000 children.[42] Along with Human Rights Watch, the Carter Center has been involved in negotiations to stop the conflict.

The documentary *War Dance* takes place in this violent setting. It is a real-life story about a group of children attending school in a refugee camp who have been personally touched by the violence. The documentary shifts between the tragic brutality of the violent reality in the countryside of northern Uganda and the hope that music and dance provide for the children. The children are members of the Acholi ethnic group (tribe), whose total population numbers about 750,000. Their traditional houses are circular huts with a high straw peak. Most Acholi are Protestant, Catholic and, in lesser numbers, Muslim; however, they continue to infuse these religions with their traditional religious beliefs, such as the importance of the ancestor spirits. The children in the documentary perform their traditional tribal dance, the *Bwola*, in a nation-wide competition in the capital city of Kampala, in southern Uganda. As they practice for the competition, they express the joy, pride and hope that dancing, song, and music have brought to their otherwise dismal lives in the refugee camps.

On a lighter note, Human Rights Watch has a program called Youth Producing Change, a series of short films produced by young people. The Human Rights Watch International Film Festival in partnership with Adobe Youth Voices seeks youth-produced film, video and animated works on human rights issues made by youth ages 19 and under for its annual Youth Producing Change program. Young people across the globe are bravely exposing human rights issues faced by themselves and their communities, using digital cameras, computers and their own creativity. Youth Producing Change provides a platform for youth to share their perspectives with audiences worldwide.

INTERNATIONAL COMMITTEE OF THE RED CROSS

Flag of the ICRC

The official mission statement says, "The **International Committee of the Red Cross** (ICRC) is an impartial, neutral, and independent organization whose exclusively humanitarian mission is to protect the lives and dignity of victims of war and internal violence and to provide them with assistance." It also directs and coordinates international relief and works to promote and strengthen humanitarian law and universal humanitarian principles.[43]

Until the middle of the 19th century, organizations treating the wounded on the battlefield did not exist. However, that would change in June 1859, when Swiss businessman Henry Dunant decided to make a difference. As he was traveling to Italy to meet with the French emperor Napoléon III to discuss business affairs in Algeria, he arrived in the small town of Solferino where he witnessed the Battle of Solferino, an engagement in the Franco-Austrian War. The bloody battle and terrible aftermath shocked Henry Dunant, when in a single day about 40,000 soldiers on both sides died or were left wounded on the battlefield. Shaken by the suffering of the wounded soldiers and the lack of medical care, he completely abandoned his original business trip and for several days devoted himself to helping care for the wounded. He motivated the local population to aid in organizing relief assistance without discrimination. Upon Dunant's return to his home in Geneva, he wrote a book entitled *A Memory of Solferino,* which he published with his own money in 1862. The book described his experiences in Solferino and also advocated for the formation of national voluntary relief organizations to help nurse wounded soldiers in war. He sent copies of the book to leading political and military figures throughout Europe. In addition, he called for the development of international treaties to guarantee the neutrality and protection of those wounded on the battlefield, as well as medics and field hospitals.[44] This was the start of the ICRC.

On August 22, 1864, the first Geneva Convention issued the Amelioration of the Condition of the Wounded in Armies in the Field, and 12 states and kingdoms signed it. Although Dunant was forced to resign from the organization he founded in 1867 because of fraudulent business dealings in Algeria, he helped to inspire the founding of national societies in nearly every country in Europe. In 1876, the committee adopted the name "International Committee of the Red Cross" (ICRC), which is still its official designation today. Five years later, Clara Barton founded the American Red Cross.

The Red Cross today has a huge mission to alleviate suffering in conflict-torn parts of the world.

A few of the ICRC's missions that pertain primarily to human rights: stepping up efforts to prevent sexual violence in wars and help the victims; facilitates operations and raises awareness of the needs of people affected by conflict and violence; addresses the humanitarian needs of the most vulnerable migrants and their families; visits both prisoners of war and civilians interned during conflict with the aim to ensure humane treatment for detainees; works to prevent attacks on civilians and others not taking part in combat; and locates people, exchanges messages, reunites families and clarifies the fate of missing persons.

The ICRC works all over the world, although it is presently serving certain areas more intensely: Central African Republic, Iraq, South Sudan, Ukraine, Syria, Nigeria, Yemen, and Nepal. The following is a brief description of some of the issues in Syria, South Sudan, and Eastern Ukraine.

1. **Syria** An ongoing civil war since 2011 has ravaged the country. With a population of almost 23 million in 2013 and 18 million in 2014, according to the ICRC, it is in desperate need of humanitarian aid for 12 million people. There are a total of 6.5 million displaced people, and hundreds of thousands of refugees have flooded into neighboring countries of Turkey, Jordan, Lebanon, and Iraq. Emergency medical care is urgently needed for the 18,000 inhabitants of Yarmouk, a camp built for Palestinian refugees in southern Damascus. Humanitarian needs are growing in the camp, which has been hard hit by four years of conflict and cut off from outside help for long periods. "With the recent upsurge in fighting in and around Yarmouk the situation for civilians has deteriorated once again," said Marianne Gasser, the head of the ICRC in Syria. "People were already worn down by months of conflict and constant shortages of food, water and medicine and they need urgent help." Some families have managed to escape Yarmouk, fleeing to the nearby district of Yelda. Since April 2015, the ICRC and the Syrian Arab Red Crescent (SARC) have delivered 9,500 food parcels to families in Yelda, some of which had fled the camp. The ICRC has not been able to enter Yarmouk Camp since October 2014, when it delivered medical and water purification supplies in collaboration with the SARC and the Palestine Red Crescent Society.[45]

2. **South Sudan** The ICRC is extremely concerned for the wellbeing of tens of thousands of people who have reportedly fled fierce clashes in South Sudan's Unity State in May 2015. Amid ongoing fighting, humanitarian organizations, including the ICRC, have been forced to withdraw key staff from the area. The ICRC is calling on all parties to spare civilians and to allow the work of humanitarian organizations and medical personnel. "These communities face a fight for survival, hiding in the bush in unimaginably harsh conditions. The situation is alarming," said Franz Rauchenstein, who heads the ICRC's delegation in South Sudan. With the rainy season fast approaching, farming communities in Unity State need to plant their crops now to ensure decent harvests—something they cannot do due to the fighting. "Food is already scarce and many people have little choice but to depend on food aid. At the same time, aid groups are struggling to maintain a presence in the worst affected areas due to insecurity. It's a vicious circle that leaves thousands extremely vulnerable," added Mr. Rauchenstein. The ICRC works to promote respect of the laws of war through its dialogue with the fighting parties and to protect and respect civilians, and women and children in particular. The ICRC has been providing regular food rations to families in Leer County since the current crisis erupted in December 2013.[46]

3. **Eastern Ukraine** The second phase of humanitarian assistance to displaced civilians from eastern Ukraine started in the Rostov Region in April 2015. The ICRC has handed over to the local branch of the Russian Red Cross food parcels and hygiene materials for further distribution. In April alone, 12,000 displaced people received them. The ICRC will deliver similar aid every month.

Tens of thousands of people who fled hostilities in eastern Ukraine found refuge in southern Russia. Many are in need of such basic items as food, clothing and hygiene materials. "These people often stay with relatives and friends, but the resources of their hosts are limited," said the head of the ICRC Regional Delegation in Moscow, Pascal Cuttat. "This is where the ICRC comes in, providing assistance in cooperation with branches of the Russian Red Cross and complementing the efforts of local authorities." Last week, displaced people in Krasnodar Krai and Adygea began receiving aid provided by the ICRC. Families, the elderly and disabled people are receiving priority. The ICRC, supported by the local authorities, has also launched a public awareness campaign on the dangers of mines and unexploded weaponry in eastern Ukraine. In addition to relief efforts, the ICRC, together with the Russian Red Cross, is helping to restore contact between family members separated as a result of the conflict.[47]

The ICRC's budget is financed entirely by voluntary contributions which include donations from the nations party to the Geneva Conventions (governments), national Red Cross and Red Crescent societies, supranational organizations and public and private sources. Donations alleviate the suffering of conflict victims worldwide and are a source of encouragement to the ICRC in Geneva and its delegates in the field. All funding is voluntary and 93.5 percent of the donations are used directly for the ICRC's work in the field. The ICRC does not wait to receive funds before it responds to urgent needs in the field, and counts on the goodwill of its contributors to provide the funds as quickly as possible.[48]

Oxfam

Oxfam logo

Oxfam is an international confederation of 17 organizations working in approximately 94 countries worldwide to find solutions to poverty and what it considers injustice around the world. One person in three in the world lives in poverty. Oxfam's ultimate goal is to enable people to exercise their rights and manage their own lives. Oxfam works directly with communities and seeks to influence the powerful, to ensure that poor people can improve their lives and livelihoods and have a say in decisions that affect them. They campaign so that the voices of the poor influence local and global decisions that affect them. Each affiliate works together internationally to achieve a greater impact through collective efforts.[49]

The name "Oxfam" comes from the Oxford Committee for Famine Relief, founded in Britain in 1942. The group campaigned for food supplies to be sent through an allied naval blockade to starving women and children in enemy-occupied Greece during World War II. In 1995, a group of independent non-governmental organizations formed Oxfam International. Their aim was to work together for greater impact on the international stage to reduce poverty and injustice.

Oxfam International is a world leader in the delivery of emergency relief, implements long-term development programs in vulnerable communities and is also part of a global movement, campaigning with others, for instance, to end unfair trade rules, demand better health and education services for all, and to combat climate change. In 2015, there are 17 member organizations of the Oxfam International confederation based in Australia, Belgium, Canada, France, Germany, Great Britain, Hong Kong, Ireland, India, Italy, Japan, Mexico, The Netherlands, New Zealand, Quebec, Spain and the United States. The Oxfam International Secretariat is located in Oxford, UK. The Secretariat runs advocacy offices in Addis Ababa, Brasilia, Brussels, Geneva, New York and Washington DC. Volunteers play a key role in helping Oxfam achieve its mission, from office work to helping in shops or stewarding at events and concerts.

In November 2000, Oxfam adopted the rights-based approach as the framework for all the work of the Confederation and its partners. It recognizes the universality of human rights and has adopted overarching aims to express these rights in practical terms: the right to a sustainable livelihood, the right to basic social services, the right to life and security, the right to be heard, and the right to an identity.

Oxfam believes that poverty and powerlessness are avoidable and through human action and political will they can be eliminated. The right to a sustainable livelihood, and the right and capacity to participate in societies and make positive changes to people's lives, they believe, are basic human needs. According to their principles, peace and substantial arms reduction are essential conditions for development and that inequalities can be significantly reduced both between rich and poor nations and within nations.

Through programs like "Saving for Change," Oxfam is working to help communities become more self-sufficient financially. The Saving for Change initiative is a program whereby communities are taught how to form collective, informal credit groups. Through these groups, members who tend to be mostly women, pool their savings into a fund which is used to give loans for activities such as paying for medical care and school fees, in addition to using the loans to fund small-scale business ventures. Ultimately, the goal of the program is to leave the community with a self-sustaining organization where people who otherwise would not qualify for formal bank loans can go for financial assistance. In doing so, borrowers can start businesses which benefit not only themselves but also their communities. Oxfam also provides relief services during various global crises, including the Israeli–Palestinian conflict, North Korean famine, 2011 East Africa drought, 2012 Sahel drought and the 2015 Nepal earthquake.

One of the Oxfam International campaigns is called "The power of people against poverty." Although there are many compelling stories, I found one to be very uplifting—From grove to market: the Palestinian olive harvest in Farkha. In the Occupied Palestinian Territory—the West Bank, East Jerusalem, and the Gaza Strip—nearly a quarter of the people live below the poverty line. To help remedy this problem, Oxfam and local partners run the *From Grove to Market* program, helping Palestinian farmers improve the quality and quantity of their olive oil and assisting them to reach local and international markets. The annual olive harvest is one of the most important events of the year for Palestinian farmers. It brings families and communities together and provides an income for about 100,000 people. Olive farmers in the West Bank face enormous challenges. Israeli settlements, checkpoints and restrictions limit farmers' access to land, water and markets. Despite these challenges, olive farming has continued.[50]

From Grove to Market: Palestinian Olive Harvest in Farkha

We [Oxfam staff] spent a day harvesting olives with Baker, Amina and their family in the small village of Farkha. Baker is a founding member of the Farkha Cooperative, which now produces organic olive oil for sale in the Gulf. The day starts early. Amina wakes up at 4 a.m. to bake fresh bread, and then prepares food for the busy day ahead. She makes homemade labneh with zaatar (Arabic yoghurt with thyme), tomatoes, cucumbers, pickled olives, tomatoes and eggs, and packs it up to take with them to the fields. "The olive tree benefits us in so many ways. It helps us eat, and it symbolizes our culture and heritage," she says. By 7 a.m., the family packs up and heads out to the fields, loading up the mule with bags of food and bottles of water. "We freeze the water overnight so that it stays cold to drink," says Amina. Baker brings his portable radio so they can listen to the local news and music while they work.

Mohammed, 22 and the youngest of six sons and two daughters, heads to the fields to start the day's work. "We wait all year for the harvest season and all the family participates," says Baker. "We consider the harvest season as a celebration. The organic olive oil we produce brings enough income to cover the expenses of the family. We have benefited greatly from the *From Grove to Market* program," says Baker. He continues, "It has encouraged our cooperative to develop organic farming methods, which has helped us produce high quality oil that can be sold and compete in international markets. The training has developed our knowledge about olive trees and production. It trained us on the pruning process throughout the year, which has made our trees bear more fruit on a steady basis, instead of just one-off seasons." The younger you are, the higher up you have to climb the trees. Baker, Amina and the older members of the family pick from the lower branches, while their sons climb to pick the olives at the top.

Omar, 27, is normally a blacksmith in the village—and a part-time wedding DJ—but during the harvest he joins his family in the fields. "I raised my sons and daughters since they were young to love the olive tree because it benefits us and symbolizes hope for us," says Amina.

Picking olives is hard work, so by midday it's time to eat the food that Amina prepared. Amina and Mohammed set the food out while Baker makes a small fire to brew tea. Baker and his sons drop the olives and branches they pick onto a plastic sheet—among the equipment provided by *From Grove to Market*. Amina goes through the branches, picking any remaining olives. Once they are all removed, the branches are dried and used for firewood for cooking and heating back at home. "We use the wood to heat ourselves in winter," she says. Ghassan, a relative from the central West Bank town of Salfit, joins the family to help pick the olives. The harvest is the busiest time of the year for olive farmers, so they often take on extra labor—either relatives or paid casual laborers. For his work, Ghassan receives a share of the oil they produce, which he takes home to his family.

While Baker and his sons pick olives from the trees, Amina picks dry olives that have dropped to the ground early. These are kept aside in buckets so as not to mix them with the fresh ones from the trees—they are not high enough quality for olive oil, so they are pressed separately to make other olive oil products such as soap. The olives are put into sacks and taken home. The family's mule can only carry three sacks at a time, so when those are filled Omar heads home. Many farmers use plastic bags, but *From Grove to Market* has encouraged farmers to use cloth sacks to maintain a higher quality and meet international organic certification requirements.

Back at the house, Omar sorts the olives from the leaves and repacks them. Nothing goes to waste—the leaves are collected later and used to make compost. The olives are taken to the cooperative's office and weighed. They are put into crates that can be loaded into trucks. The cooperative then takes them to an olive press in the nearby town of Tubas, where they are pressed and turned into high quality olive oil.

The *From Grove to Market* program helps cooperatives across the West Bank to access new local and international markets. "Working together in a cooperative helps the farmers get better prices for their product," says Baker. "Sadly, years ago we produced a lot of olive oil but we had a problem marketing it. We had to sell the oil for half of what it cost to produce. So we formed a cooperative and set about getting international certification for organic olive oil. We stopped using chemicals to spray the trees. Now it is much higher quality."[51]

Robert F. Kennedy Center for Justice and Human Rights

An important human rights NGO was formed in memory of Robert F. Kennedy and has offices in Washington D.C., New York, and Italy. The mission of the RFK Center "strives to achieve Robert F. Kennedy's vision of a just and peaceful world by partnering with human rights leaders, teaching about social justice, and advancing corporate responsibility." I visited the Washington D. C. office a few years ago and spoke to Christine Hart. She was kind enough to explain the Center's programs and how the legacy of Robert Kennedy has inspired the work of so many people at the Center, as well as human right defenders around the world. She presented me with the beautiful book *Speak Truth to Power*, written and autographed by Kerry Kennedy, daughter of Robert Kennedy who now serves as president of the organization. For those of you who may not be familiar with Robert Kennedy, the following biography summarizes the man and his vision, highlighting his commitment to human rights.

The Short Life of Robert F. Kennedy

Born on November 20, 1925, in Brookline, Massachusetts, Robert Francis Kennedy was the seventh of nine children born to Rose and Joseph P. Kennedy. "I was the seventh of nine children," he later recalled, "and when you come from that far down you have to struggle to survive." His older brother was John F. Kennedy, president of the United States from 1961-1963. After wartime service in the Navy, he received his degree in government from Harvard University in 1948 and earned his law degree from the University of Virginia Law School three years later. Perhaps his best education came from the family dinner table. He recalls "I can hardly remember a mealtime when the conversation was not dominated by what Franklin D. Roosevelt was doing or what was happening in the world." On June 17, 1950, Robert Kennedy and Ethel Skakel married, and later had 11 children.

Robert F. Kennedy speaking on civil rights

In 1952, he made his political debut as manager of his older brother John's successful campaign for the U.S. Senate from Massachusetts. The following year, he served briefly on the staff of the Senate Subcommittee on Investigations, chaired by Senator Joseph McCarthy. Disturbed by McCarthy's controversial tactics, Kennedy resigned from the staff after six months. His later work as chief counsel for the Senate Rackets Committee, inspecting corruption in trade unions, won him national recognition for his investigations of Teamsters Union leaders Jimmy Hoffa and David Beck.

In 1960 Robert Kennedy worked tirelessly and effectively as manager of John Kennedy's presidential campaign. After the election, his brother appointed him Attorney General, where he won respect for his diligent, effective and nonpartisan administration of the Department of Justice. As Attorney General, Kennedy launched a successful drive against organized crime, increasing convictions by 800 percent during his term. He also became increasingly committed to the rights of African Americans, including voting rights, receiving an equal education, and using public accommodations. In September 1962, Robert Kennedy sent U.S. Marshals and troops to Oxford, Mississippi to enforce a Federal court order admitting the first African American student—James Meredith—to the University of Mississippi. Robert Kennedy saw voting as the key to racial justice and collaborated with President Kennedy when he proposed the Civil Rights Act of 1964, passed after President Kennedy was slain on November 22, 1963. Holding great admiration for his brother, he was devastated after his death.

Soon after President Kennedy's death, Robert Kennedy resigned as Attorney General and, in 1964, ran successfully for the United States Senate from New York. As New York's Senator, he initiated a number of projects in the state, including assistance to underprivileged children and students with disabilities and the establishment of the Bedford-Stuyvesant Restoration Corporation to improve living conditions and employment opportunities in depressed areas of Brooklyn. These programs were part of a larger effort to address the needs of the dispossessed and powerless in America—the poor, the young, racial minorities and Native Americans. He passionately sought to bring the facts about poverty to the conscience of the American people, journeying into urban ghettos, Appalachia, the Mississippi Delta and migrant workers' camps. He fervently stated "There are children in the Mississippi Delta whose bellies are swollen with hunger ... Many of them cannot go to school because they have no clothes or shoes. These conditions ... exist in dark tenements in Washington, D.C., within sight of the Capitol, in Harlem, in South Side Chicago, and in Watts. There are children in each of these areas who have never been to school, never seen a doctor or a dentist, or ...never read or even seen a book."

Robert Kennedy was also committed to the advancement of human rights abroad. He traveled to Eastern Europe, Latin America and South Africa to share his belief that all people have a basic human right to participate in the political decisions that affect their lives and to criticize their government without fear of reprisal. He also believed that those who strike out against injustice show the highest form of courage. In a 1966 speech to South African students he said, "Each time a man stands up for an ideal or acts to improve the lot of others, or strikes out against injustice, he sends forth a tiny ripple of hope, and crossing each other from a million different centers of energy and daring, those ripples build a current that can sweep down the mightiest walls of oppression and resistance."

On March 16, 1968, Robert Kennedy announced his candidacy for the Democratic presidential nomination. He sought to bridge the great divides in American life—between the races, between the poor and more affluent, between young and old, between order and dissent. He won critical primaries in Indiana and Nebraska and spoke to enthusiastic crowds across the nation. Robert Francis Kennedy was shot on June 5, 1968, at the Ambassador Hotel in Los Angeles, California, shortly after claiming victory in that state's crucial Democratic primary. He died in the early hours of June 6, 1968, at the age of 42. Although his life was cut short, Robert Kennedy's vision and ideals live on today through the work of his family, friends and the Robert F. Kennedy Memorial in Washington, D.C.[52]

Ethel Kennedy, the wife of Senator Robert F. Kennedy and the founder of the Robert F. Kennedy Center for Justice and Human Rights, received the Presidential Medal of Freedom, the nation's highest civilian honor, on November 25, 2014 in a ceremony at the White House. President Obama said at the ceremony, "As Bobby Kennedy's partner in life, she shared his commitment to justice. After his death, she continued their work through the Center she created in his name, celebrating activists and journalists and educating people around the world about threats to human liberty."

The Center is active in promoting human rights. A few of their programs include:
1. RFK Partners for Human Rights bolsters the efficacy of human rights defenders.
2. RFK Speak Truth To Power is a multi-faceted global initiative that uses the experiences of defenders from around the world to educate students and others about human rights and urge them to take action.

3. RFK Compass works with institutional investors to discuss the connections between investment performance and public interest issues to optimize rates of returns and address global challenges.
4. RFK Training Institute organizes training programs for high school teachers and increasingly engages with human rights leaders, executives, and nonprofit directors throughout Europe and other parts of the world to develop human rights and social justice strategies.
5. Health eVillages is a healthcare and human rights advocacy consortium, which aims to bring information and technology to clinicians fighting to save lives in underserved regions worldwide.
6. RFK Young Leaders are dedicated to empowering young human rights defenders.

Local Human Rights Organizations

I have described a few of the international non-governmental human rights organizations to give you a sampling of the work they are doing in the field of human rights. However, there are thousands of other organizations at the international, national, state and local levels that are doing outstanding work in promoting human rights. Unfortunately, I will not be able to list them all. But I would like to share with you a brief description of one local organization—the Albuquerque Center for Peace and Justice—in Albuquerque, New Mexico, where I live, that is involved in promoting human rights.

The Albuquerque Center for Peace and Justice (ACPJ)

Nestled on the corner of Silver and Harvard Streets, one block from the University of New Mexico campus in Albuquerque, New Mexico, is the **Albuquerque Center for Peace and Justice**. Housed in a sturdy brick building, it has a warm and inviting feeling, and there is always a hubbub of activity going on. ACPJ attracts a cross-section of people: senior peace and justice activists, enthusiastic student interns and volunteers, committed academics, faith-based workers, drop-ins from the university and people of diverse ethnic, racial, and class standing. The mission of ACPJ is to provide resources and space for organizations and individuals working on peace and justice issues to network with one another and share information. Through its programs and collaborations, its members work locally to support regional and global justice. They strive to create a world where collective needs are met sustainably and non-violently, and they value the interconnectedness of all life, emphasize cooperation and respect for diversity, commit to nonviolent conflict resolution and strive for peace within each person, while working towards creating peace in our community and in our world.

Albuquerque Center for Peace and Justice

ACPJ was founded in 1983. The initial focus of ACPJ was disarmament and conversion of the New Mexico economy that has been and still is devoted to armaments and war since the 1940s to an economy based on peaceful industries. APCJ's work broadened in the mid-1980s to include Central America solidarity movements, the Peace Education Project and the publication of news articles of local actions, campaigns, and commentary on peace and justice issues. In the 1990s, APCJ organized peaceful resistance to U.S. policies, including the 1991 Gulf War and the opening of WIPP (Waste Isolation Pilot Plant), a nuclear weapons waste dump in southeast New Mexico. In the 2000s, the work of APCJ greatly increased to support and implement projects that work to overcome challenges to peace and justice. One of the founding members, Sally Alice Thompson, who turned 91 in 2015, is still very active, and she attends almost every event. She recently walked 50 miles from Santa Fe to Albuquerque to protest the undue influence of money in political campaigns!

ACPJ serves as a training ground for many students involved in peace and justice issues. They host events, speakers, classes and religious services for interested parties. Their monthly calendar is always chockful of interesting events. For example, ACPJ hosted Ron Brenneman, the founder of the Amún Shéa School in El-Salvador in November 2014, as he toured New Mexico on a fund-raising and awareness campaign. I interviewed Ron for a blog on the school and attended his lecture at ACPJ. Another event I attended and blogged about was a group of interesting, committed and energetic women from NGOs in Africa who were learning about peacebuilding strategies on a whirlwind tour of the U.S. with the goal of implementing their new-found ideas in their respective African countries and communities. These are just two of the many programs that they host.

The community space at the ACPJ was alive with music, chatter, and lots of hugs and smiles during one of its newest programs, the Peace Café. Held weekly, the Café was successfully organized by a friend, Mollie Wilke, who is also a key organizer of the distribution of surplus food donations by local restaurants and grocery stores through the non-profit agency Desert Harvest and dispersed through ACPJ.

Our own non-profit organization, the Center of Global Awareness, is a member of their PAJOLA program. PAJOLA members support the APJC in initiating new projects and maintaining important ongoing services such as the monthly newsletter/calendar featuring local events and campaigns, lending video and print libraries, and community outreach programs. ACPJ is ably directed by Sue Schuurman.

I imagine that there are many organizations such as the Albuquerque Center for Peace and Justice in communities across the United States. I invite you to investigate the human rights organizations—large and small—in your local area to get a glimpse of what issues they are working on and what volunteer opportunities may be available to you and your friends.

Center for Global Awareness

THE FOCUS OF HUMAN RIGHTS IN THE FUTURE

Human rights is not a static issue; it is constantly changing and evolving. Although this book has given you a good overview of the topic, there are several issues that I believe will be important human rights issues in the future.

1. **Euthanasia** is the practice of intentionally ending a life in order to relieve pain and suffering. Euthanasia is legal in some countries. In some countries there is a divisive public controversy over the moral, ethical and legal issues of euthanasia. Those who are against euthanasia may argue for the sanctity of life, while proponents of euthanasia rights emphasize alleviating suffering, and preserving bodily integrity, self-determination and personal autonomy. Euthanasia or assisted suicide is legal in the Netherlands, Colombia, Switzerland, Japan, Germany, Belgium, Luxembourg, Estonia, Albania, the U.S. states of Washington, Oregon, Montana, and Vermont and, the Canadian Province of Quebec. I have included euthanasia as a topic of human rights importance, since a rapidly aging population in Western countries is demanding more rights over their quality of life and when to terminate their lives. The following is a law suit filed in California that personalizes the issue of euthanasia.

Euthanasia

Three California residents with advanced or terminal diseases, along with a doctor, filed a lawsuit against the state of California last week seeking the right to choose medical aid in dying. The suit—filed on behalf of the four plaintiffs by the nonprofit end-of-life advocacy organization Compassion & Choices—asserts that the California constitution and existing state laws should allow medical professionals to prescribe mentally competent patients with terminal illnesses medications "they can take in their final days to end their dying process painlessly and peacefully, ending unbearable pain and suffering," according to a news release.

The lead plaintiff in the case, and the only one whose illness is terminal, is Christy O'Donnell, a 46-year-old civil rights attorney, former Los Angeles Police Department sergeant and single mother. O'Donnell is a nonsmoker and vegetarian who was diagnosed with late-stage lung cancer in June 2014. The cancer had also spread to her brain. If the law allowed, she would choose to die peacefully in her bed with her 20-year-old daughter by her side, she told People magazine. "I am dying within the next few months, and I am going to die painfully. I am asking the courts for intervention to issue an order so that a doctor can legally prescribe a medication so that I don't have to die painfully, and so that every moment before I die, I don't have to spend afraid and worried about the painful manner in which I'm going to die."

In a video that was recorded in March 2015, she said the reason she became a lawyer was because she loves the law, "and the law is ever-changing. Our laws are set up to change with the needs of our society," she said. "This is an absolute need in our society that can't be ignored anymore."

Aid in dying, also referred to as death with dignity, is currently legal in five states: Washington, Oregon, Montana, New Mexico and Vermont. An end-of-life options bill modeled on Oregon's law is currently in committee in the California Senate.[53]

---

2. **Animal rights** is the idea that some, or all, non-human animals are entitled to the possession of their own lives and that their most basic interests—such as the lack of suffering—should be afforded the same consideration as humans. Although some surveys show the public is lukewarm in support of animal rights, I predict that it will become a more important issue in the future. Advocates of animal rights oppose the assignment of moral value and fundamental protections on the basis of species membership alone—an idea known since 1970 as speciesism. Advocates maintain that people should no longer view animals as property, nor should they be used as food, clothing, research subjects, entertainment, or beasts of burden. Multiple cultural traditions around the world—such as Hinduism, Buddhism, and Jainism, also support some forms of animal rights. One of the foremost and largest of the animal rights organizations in the world is the People for the Ethical Treatment of Animals, an American animal rights organization based in Norfolk, Virginia, and led by Ingrid Newkirk, its international president. A non-profit with 300 employees and 3 million members and supporters, its slogan is "Animals are not ours to eat, wear, experiment on, use for entertainment or abuse in any way."

PETA logo

3. **Right to Life** is a rhetorical device used in the abortion debate by those who wish to outlaw the intentional termination of a pregnancy. Pro-life advocates argue that prenatal humans are human

persons from the moment of conception and have the same fundamental "right to life" before birth as humans have after birth. Generally speaking, those identifying themselves as "right-to-life" believe abortion is morally unacceptable. Those on the other side say that a woman's right to control her own health, body and family size is also a human rights issue. Although this is not a new issue in the U.S., I predict that this hotly debated moral issue will continue to be a human rights issue.

One of the largest non-profit organizations supporting the right to life is the National Right to Life. Its mission is to promote respect for the worth and dignity of every individual human being, born or unborn, including unborn children from their beginning; those newly born; persons with disabilities; older people; and other vulnerable people, especially those who cannot defend themselves. Its areas of concern include abortion, infanticide, euthanasia, assisted suicide, and the killing of unborn children for their stem cells.[54] It has offices in all 50 states in the United States and many opportunities for involvement.

4. Human Rights and Multi-National Corporations

The issue of corporate responsibility has become serious because of some shocking examples of businesses' involvement in human rights abuses in various countries. Companies have the legal responsibility to maximize the return on shareholders' investment, and carrying out this charge may counter human rights compliance. On those rare occasions when companies do announce an intention to abide by human rights law, skeptics see it as a public relations move and not as a genuine response to some legal or ethical obligation. The issue is complicated because it lies at the intersection of the two results of globalization: the expansion and liberalization of international trade and commerce on one hand, and the universalizing effects of the human rights movement on the other. Intergovernmental organizations, including the Organization for Economic Cooperation and Development, the International Committee of the Red Cross, and the World Bank, have increasingly evaluated the human rights practices of private corporations.[55] With more sophisticated communication technologies and media outlets being used by human rights organizations, the issue of human rights, I predict, will be at the forefront of a corporation's public image. Yet, most corporations will continue to try to obfuscate their human rights record if it does meet international public standards.

5. Human Rights and the Environment

Since I think that environmental sustainability is the most important issue facing the human species today, I have included information about the close connection of human rights and the environment throughout this book. In a series of resolutions, the former United Nations Commission on Human Rights and the United Nations Human Rights Council have drawn attention to the relationship between a safe and healthy environment and the enjoyment of human rights. These resolutions have raised awareness of how fundamental the environment is as a prerequisite to the enjoyment of human rights.[56]

Concluding Insights: The Future of Human Rights

What will be the role of human rights in the future? In the first scenario, the protection of human rights is overwhelmed by environmental distress in which many people around the world are left to fight for scarce resources in order to survive. This continuing conflict overwhelms governments and non-governmental organizations that are unable to respond to human rights abuses, keep order and finally collapse from the strain. Lawless gangs roam freely to take what they can and inflict misery upon those who cannot compete. Are we destined to live in societies that must constantly use violence to quell dissent as our reptilian brains guide our governments? I am optimistic that we can create and choose another way.

The second scenario is much more optimistic and hopeful. Human rights expand as an accepted values system throughout the world. The global citizenry and organizations pressure authoritarian governments to institute human rights protections as outlined in this book. Even Western governments who support human rights, such as the United States, are constantly monitored and checked by non-governmental organizations to insure compliance with these values. Human rights becomes such a closely held value that a worldwide network of people and organizations work to enfold these values into their local, national, and global communities and way of life.

We must strive to rise above the petty cultural and historical differences and perspectives separating our religious traditions, cultural values, beliefs and ways of living, which have caused violent disagreements and untold conflict. We must arrive at a shared common purpose and understanding that unites us as a species. We are a meaning-seeking species, and the meaning of our existence has been spelled out to us in many different ways through different cultural and religious traditions spanning thousands of years of history. It is our obligation as global citizens of the 21st century to draw on these traditions that have been handed down to us by our ancestors and to shape them and make them meaningful for life today.

Understanding that our religious traditions have more similarities than differences is one step forward. Also recognizing that the underlying causes of conflict and violence emanate from competition over scarce resources, marginalization of less-powerful groups of people and lack of meaning and connection in our modern/globalized society instead of attributing all problems to the unsolvable differences in religious ideologies. This would be a start in creating a global society that focuses on compassion and sharing as its guiding principle.

As these human rights attitudes and values become more deeply embedded within our global citizenry, they become harder to abuse and thus become the global values system that we hope to achieve.

ENDNOTES

ENDNOTES: CHAPTER 1. HUMAN RIGHTS: AN INTRODUCTION

[1] Walter Kälin, Lars Müller, Judith Wyttenbach, *The Face of Human Rights*, (Italy: Lars Muller Publishers, 2004).
[2] Karen Armstrong, *Fields of Blood: Religion and the History of Violence*, (New York: Alfred A. Knopf, 2014) 7.
[3] James Nickel, *Making Sense of Human Rights, 2nd Edition*, (Oxford: Blackwell Publishing, 2006).
[4] Nickel, *Making Sense of Human Rights*.
[5] Nickel, *Making Sense of Human Rights*.
[6] Jane Springer, *Genocide: A Groundwork Guide*, (Toronto, CA: Groundworks Books, 2006).
[7] *United Nations*, "Universal Declaration of Human Rights." http://www.un.org/en/universal-declaration-human-rights/index.html, edited by the author.
[8] Henry Shue, *Basic Rights, 2nd Edition*, (Princeton: Princeton University Press, 1996).
[9] James Nickel, "Human Rights," *Stanford Encyclopedia of Philosophy*, (2006). http://plato.stanford.edu/entries/rights-human/#GenIdeHumRig
[10] Sonal Panse, "Ubuntu," *Buzzle.com*, (2006). http://www.buzzle.com/editorials/7-22-2006-103206.asp
[11] Desmond Tutu, *God Has A Dream: A Vision of Hope for our Time*, (New York: Doubleday, 2005).
[12] Dirk J. Louw, "Ubuntu: The Religious Other," *Philosophy in Africa*. http://www.bu.edu/wcp/Papers/Afri/AfriLouw.htm
[13] Stanlake and Tommie Marie Samkange, *Ubuntuism: A Zimbabwe Indigenous Political Philosophy*, (Salisbury: Graham Publishing, 1980) 106.
[14] Nelson Mandela, "What is Ubuntu, *YouTube*. http://www.youtube.com/watch?v=Dx0qGJCm-qU
[15] Dani W. Nabudere, "Ubuntu Philosophy: Memory and Reconciliation," *Research Documents International, Africa*, (2005).
[16] Panse, "Ubuntu," *Buzzle.com*.
[17] *Wikipedia*, "Ten Commandments," (2006). http://en.wikipedia.org/wiki/Ten_Commandments
[18] Elton L. Daniel, *The History of Iran*, (Westport, CT: Greenwood Publishing Group, 2000) 39.
[19] Reza Shabani, *Iranian History at a Glance*, (UK: Alhoda, 2005) 21.
[20] B.A. Robinson, "The Life of Buddha," *Ontario Consultants on Religious Tolerance*, (2007). http://www.religioustolerance.org/buddhism5.htm
[21] *Philosophy of Religion*, "Natural Law," (2008). http://www.philosophyofreligion.info/christian-ethics/natural-law-theory/
[22] *Wikipedia*, "Seneca."
[23] *Science*, "Human Rights: Stoicism." http://science.jrank.org/pages/9659/Human-Rights-Stoicism-Roman-Jurisprudence.html#ixzz0KUpzKkLJ&D
[24] *Colorado State University*, "Edicts of Ashoka." http://www.cs.colostate.edu/~malaiya/ashoka.html
[25] *Foreign Policy*, "The World's Fastest Growing Religions," (May 2007).
[26] *Wikipedia*, "Constitution of Medina." http://en.wikipedia.org/wiki/Constitution_of_Medina
[27] *United for Human Rights*, "Magna Carta," ret. May 15, 2015. http://www.humanrights.com/what-are-human-rights/brief-history/magna-carta.html
[28] *Wikipedia*, "Human Rights History."

ENDNOTES: CHAPTER 2. SOCIAL MOVEMENTS AND HUMAN RIGHTS

[1] *Academy of Achievement*, "Rosa Parks," interview, June 2, 1995. www.achievement.org/autodoc/page/par0int-2
[2] Charles Tilly, *Social Movements: 1768–2004*, (Boulder, CO, Paradigm Publishers, 2004) 262.
[3] Sidney Tarrow, *Power in Movement: Collective Action, Social Movements and Politics*, (Cambridge: Cambridge University Press, 1994).
[4] Herbert Blumer, "Collective Behavior," in Robert E. Park, *An Outline of the Principles of Sociology*, (New York: Barnes & Noble, 1939) 199.
[5] Luther P. Gerlach and Virginia H. Hine. *People, Power, Change: Movements of Social Transformation*, (Indianapolis: Bobbs-Merrill, 1970) xvi-xvii. I have edited the definitions to make them more understandable.
[6] Ralph H. Turner and Lewis M. Killian, *Collective Behavior*, (Englewood Cliffs, N.J.: Prentice Hall, 1987) 223.
[7] *Wikipedia*, "Social Movements." http://en.wikipedia.org/wiki/Social_movement
[8] Neil J. Smelser, *Theory of Collective Behavior*, (New York: Free Press, 1962).
[9] *Reference.com*, "Social Movements." http://www.reference.com/browse/social_movements
[10] Stacy J. Silveira, "The American Environmental Movement: Surviving through Diversity," *Boston College*, 9. http://www.bc.edu/bc_org/avp/law/lwsch/journals/bcealr/28_2-3/07_TXT.htm#BKMRK1
[11] St. John Barned-Smith, "How We Rage: This Is Not Your Parents' Protest," *Current*, (Winter 2007) 17-25.
[12] *PBS*, "Schools: Story of American Public Education: Horace Mann." http://www.pbs.org/kcet/publicschool/innovators/mann.html
[13] *PBS*, "Schools: Story of American Public Education: Booker T. Washington." http://www.pbs.org/kcet/publicschool/innovators/washington.html
[14] *Theodore Roosevelt Association*, "Conservationists." http://www.theodoreroosevelt.org/life/conservation.htm

[15] *Sierra Outlook*, "Theodore Roosevelt, John Muir: An Appreciation," Vol. 109 (Jan. 16, 1915) 27-28.
[16] Silveira, "American Environmental Movement," *Boston College*.
[17] Philip Foner, ed., *Mother Jones Speaks: A Working-Class Fighter*, (New York: Pathfinder Press, 1983).
[18] *U.S. Department of Labor*, "Union Members Survey." http://www.bls.gov/news.release/union2.nr0.htm
[19] Laura Del Col, "Life of the Industrial Worker in 19th Century England," *West Virginia Univ.: The Victorian Web*.
[20] Sharron Solomon-McCarthy, "The History of Child Labor in the United States," *Yale-New Haven Teacher Institute*, (April 1, 2008). http://www.yale.edu/ynhti/curriculum/units/2004/1/04.01.08.x.html#b
[21] Solomon McCarthy, "Child Labor," *Yale-New Haven Teacher Institute*.
[22] Miles Wolff, *Lunch at the Five and Ten*, (New York: Stein and Day, 1970).
[23] *Veterans of the Civil Rights Movement*, "March on Washington." http://www.crmvet.org/tim/tim63b.htm#1963mow
[24] William L. Van DeBurg, *New Day in Babylon: The Black Power Movement, 1965-1975*, (Chicago: University of Chicago Press, 1992) 195.
[25] Silveira, "American Environmental Movement," *Boston College*.
[26] Josie Glausiusz, "Better Planet: Can a Maligned Pesticide Save Lives?" *Discover Magazine*, (2007) 34.
[27] Mark Hamilton Lytle, *The Gentle Subversive: Rachel Carson, Silent Spring, and the Rise of the Environmental Movement*, (New York: Oxford University Press, 2007) 166-167.
[28] Lytle, *Rachel Carson*, 217.
[29] H. Patricia Hynes, *The Recurring Silent Spring*, (New York: Pergamon Press, 1989) 3 and 8-9.
[30] *Dictionary.com*, "Ecology." http://dictionary.reference.com/browse/ecology
[31] Eckardt C. Beck, "Love Canal Tragedy," *EPA Journal*, (Jan. 1979). http://www.epa.gov/history/topics/lovecanal/01.htm
[32] Denise Ames, *The Global Economy: Connecting the Roots of a Holistic System*, (Center for Global Awareness, 2013) 126.
[33] *You Tube*, "McLibel: When Two World Collide." http://www.youtube.com/watch?v=oqnNpEzYJ-Q&feature=channel
[34] *The Story of Stuff* (website).
[35] Benjamin Barber, *Consumed: How markets Corrupt Children, Infantilize Adults, and Swallow Citizens Whole*, (New York: W.W. Norton & Co., 2007).
[36] Barber, *Consumed*, 167.
[37] Silverira, "American Environmental Movement," *Boston College*, 8.
[38] *National Geographic Society*, "Peoples of the world."
[39] *University of Minnesota Human Rights Library*, "Study Guide: The Rights of Indigenous Peoples," (2003). http://www1.umn.edu/humanrts/edumat/studyguides/indigenous.html
[40] *University of Minnesota*, "Rights of Indigenous Peoples."
[41] *United Nations Permanent Forum on Indigenous Issues*, "Frequently Asked Questions: Declaration on the Rights of Indigenous Peoples." http://www.un.org/esa/socdev/unpfii/documents/FAQsindigenousdeclaration.pdf
[42] *International Forum on Globalization*, "Indigenous Peoples Program." http://www.ifg.org/programs/indig.htm
[43] *International Forum on Globalization*, "Indigenous Peoples Program."
[44] *United Nations*, "Overview of the issue of human rights of persons with disabilities," ret. May 15, 2015. http://www.un.org/esa/socdev/enable/rights/humanrights.htm#II
[45] *United Nations Treaty Collection*, "Convention on the Rights of the Child." http://treaties.un.org/Pages/ViewDetails.aspx?src=TREATY&mtdsg_no=IV-11&chapter=4&lang=en
[46] *UNICEF*, "Child Marriage is a Death Sentence for Many Young Girls," (2009). http://www.unicef.org/sowc09/docs/SOWC09-CountryExample-Mali.pdf
[47] *UNICEF*, "Child Marriage."
[48] *UNICEF*, "Child Marriage."
[49] *Coalition to Stop Child Soldiers*, "Child Soldiers." http://www.child-soldiers.org/childsoldiers/child-soldiers
[50] *UNICEF*, "Beyond Child Labor, Affirming Rights," (March 2001). http://www.unicef.org/ceecis/pub_beyond_en.pdf
[51] *UNICEF*, "Beyond Child Labor."
[52] Andreas Harsono, "Nike Accused of 'Slave' Child Labor," *Albion Monitor/News*, (1996). http://www.albionmonitor.com/9606a/nikelabor.html

Endnotes: Chapter 3. Human Rights Violation

[1] Niemoeller was a Protestant pastor who at first supported the Nazis, but later became openly critical of the Third Reich. He was imprisoned in concentration camps for seven years and freed in 1945, quoted in Jane Springer, *Genocide: A Groundwork Guide*, (Toronto, Canada: Groundwork Books/House of Anansi Press, 2006) 56.
[2] Springer, *Genocide*, 5-6.
[3] *Rome Statute of the International Criminal Court*. http://www.icc-cpi.int/NR/rdonlyres/EA9AEFF7-5752-4F84-BE94-0A655EB30E16/0/Rome_Statute_English.pdf
[4] *United Nations*, "International Criminal Court." http://www.icc-cpi.int/Menus/ICC?lan=en-GB and James Nickel, "Human Rights," *Stanford Encyclopedia of Philosophy*, (July 29, 2006). http://plato.stanford.edu/entries/rights-human/#GenIdeHumRig

[5] Claus Kreb, "The Crime of Aggression before the First Review of the ICC Statute," *International Criminal Court*, (2008) 5-7. http://law.case.edu/lectures/files/2008-2009/20080926_Kress_02clean.pdf

[6] George W. Bush, "President Discusses Beginning of Operation Iraqi Freedom," *White House Archives*, (Mar. 22, 2003). http://georgewbush-whitehouse.archives.gov/news/releases/2003/03/20030322.html

[7] Alex Callinicos, "Anti-war protests do make a difference," *Socialist Worker on-line*, (March 2005). http://www.socialistworker.co.uk/article.php?article_id=6067

[8] *Msnbc*, "CIA's Report: No WMD found in Iraq," (April 25, 2005). http://www.msnbc.msn.com/id/7634313/

[9] Ken Roth, "War in Iraq," *Human Rights Watch*, (Jan. 2004). http://www.hrw.org/legacy/wr2k4/3.htm

[10] John F. Burns, "How Many People has Sadam Hussein Killed?" *New York Times*, (Jan. 27, 2003). http://www.iraqfoundation.org/news/2003/ajan/27_saddam.html

[11] Frederick Taylor, "How Many Died in the Bombing of Dresden?" *Spiegel Online International*, (Oct. 2, 2008). http://www.spiegel.de/international/germany/0,1518,581992,00.html

[12] Geoffery York and Hayley Mick, "The Last Ghost of the Vietnam War," *The Globe and Mail*, (June 12, 2008). http://www.theglobeandmail.com/archives/article697346.ece

[13] *Department of the Army*, "Report of the Department of the Army Review of the Preliminary Investigations into the My Lai Incident, the Peers Report, Vol. I-III," (1970). http://www.law.umkc.edu/faculty/projects/ftrials/mylai/MYL_Peers.htm

[14] Hugh Thompson, "Moral Courage in Combat: The My Lai Story," *USNA Lecture*, (2003). http://www.usna.edu/Ethics/Publications/ThompsonPg1-28_Final.pdf

[15] *International Criminal Court*, "Rome Statute, Article 7".

[16] *Britannica Concise Encyclopedia*, "Trail of Tears."

[17] David M. Crane, "Case No. SCSL: The Special Court for Sierra Leone," *United Nations and the Government of Sierra Leone*, (Mar. 3, 2003).

[18] Susannah Price "UN pressed over Liberia's Taylor," *BBC*, (May 24, 2005). http://news.bbc.co.uk/2/hi/africa/4577547.stm

[19] *Associated Press*, "Liberia's Taylor," (2009). http://www.usatoday.com/news/world/2009-07-14-warcrimes_N.htm

[20] *American Scholar*, "Ralph Lemkin," Vol. 15, No. 2 (April 1946) 227-230.

[21] *United Nations*, "Prevention and Punishment of the Crime of Genocide." http://www.preventgenocide.org/genocide/officialtext-printerfriendly.htm

[22] Springer, *Genocide*, 20-21.

[23] *Genocide Watch*, 2002. http://www.genocidewatch.org/

[24] *Genocide Watch*, 2002.

[25] Gregory H. Stanton, "About Genocide," *Genocide Watch*. http://www.genocidewatch.org/aboutgenocide/8stagesofgenocide.html

[26] Springer, *Genocide*, 42.

[27] Springer, *Genocide*, 43.

[28] Springer, *Genocide*, 43.

[29] Springer, *Genocide*, 56-57.

[30] Springer, *Genocide*, 70-71.

[31] Springer, *Genocide*, 58.

[32] Springer, *Genocide*, 61.

[33] Springer, *Genocide*, 59.

[34] Springer, *Genocide*, 62.

[35] Springer, *Genocide*, 63.

[36] Springer, *Genocide*, 65.

[37] Springer, *Genocide*, 47.

[38] Springer, *Genocide*, 44-45.

[39] Springer, *Genocide*, 45.

[40] Leo Kuper, *Genocide: Its Political Use in the Twentieth Century*, (Harmondsworth: Penguin, 1981).

[41] Adam Jones, "Genocide a Comprehensive Introduction," *Genocide Text*, 4. http://www.genocidetext.net/gaci_excerpts.htm

[42] Jones, "Genocide," *Genocide Text*, 5.

[43] Jones, "Genocide," *Genocide Text*, 5.

[44] Jones, "Genocide," *Genocide Text*, 5.

[45] Jones, "Genocide," *Genocide Text*, 5.

[46] *Wikipedia*, "Crusades." http://en.wikipedia.org/wiki/Crusades

[47] Jones, "Genocide," *Genocide Text*, 3-6.

[48] *San Diego State University*, "Ibn Battuta's Trip: Persia and Iraq (1326 - 1327)." http://www.sfusd.k12.ca.us/schwww/sch618/Ibn_Battuta/Battuta's_Trip_Three.html

[49] *Wikipedia*, "Population history of American indigenous peoples." http://en.wikipedia.org/wiki/Population_history_of_American_indigenous_peoples#cite_note-hnn-29

[50] David Stannard, *American Holocaust: Columbus and the Conquest of the New World* (London: Oxford Univ. Press, 1992).

[51] Guenter Lewy, "Were American Indians the Victims of Genocide?" *History News Network*, (Nov. 11, 2004). http://hnn.us/articles/7302.html
[52] Lewy, "Victims of Genocide?" *History News Network*.
[53] Springer, *Genocide*, 34.
[54] Springer, *Genocide*, 35.
[55] Springer, *Genocide*, 38.
[56] Springer, *Genocide*, 38.
[57] Springer, *Genocide*, 50.
[58] Springer, *Genocide*, 50.
[59] *Associated Press*, "Ukrainian, Jewish leaders gather to mark Babi Yar anniversary," (Sept. 27, 2006). http://www.haaretz.com/hasen/spages/768009.html.
[60] Anatoli Kuznetsov, *Babi Yar: The Shattering Documentary Novel of Nazi Inhumanity*, (New York: Dell, 1967).
[61] Springer, *Genocide*, 47.
[62] Springer, *Genocide*, 53.
[63] Springer, *Genocide*, 53.
[64] Springer, *Genocide*, 54.
[65] Springer, *Genocide*, 55.
[66] Deborah Dwork and Robert Jan van Pelt, *Auschwitz: 1270 to the Present*, (New York: Norton, 1997) 10.
[67] Melissa Müller, Rita and Robert Kimber (trans.), *Anne Frank: The Biography*, (New York: Metropolitan Books) 194, and 246-271.
[68] *Frontline World*, "Fellows Project: Rwanda." http://www.pbs.org/frontlineworld/fellows/rwanda1103/portrait-2.html
[69] *Frontline World*, "Rwanda."
[70] *Wikipedia*, "Rwanda Genocide." http://en.wikipedia.org/wiki/Rwandan_Genocide
[71] Springer, *Genocide*, 81.
[72] Springer, *Genocide*, 81.
[73] Springer, *Genocide*, 83.
[74] Springer, *Genocide*, 83-84.
[75] Springer, *Genocide*, 85.
[76] Springer, *Genocide*, 87.
[77] *Wikipedia*, "Rwanda Genocide." http://en.wikipedia.org/wiki/Rwandan_Genocide
[78] *Wikipedia*, "Rwanda Genocide."
[79] *Wikipedia*, "Rwanda Genocide."
[80] Jared Diamond, *Collapse: How Societies Choose to Fail or Succeed*, (New York: Penguin, 2005) 315.
[81] Diamond, *Collapse*, 319.
[82] Diamond, *Collapse*, 319-320.
[83] Diamond, *Collapse*, 321.
[84] Diamond, *Collapse*, 321.
[85] Diamond, *Collapse*, 321 and 324.
[86] Diamond, *Collapse*, 325.
[87] Diamond, *Collapse*, 325-326.
[88] Diamond, *Collapse*, 327.
[89] *Wikipedia*, "Rwanda Genocide."
[90] Andrea Ford, "A Brief History of Genocide," *Time*, (Dec. 9, 2008). http://www.time.com/time/world/article/0,8599,1865217,00.html
[91] *Frontline*, "The Triumph of Evil," ret. April 9, 2009. http://www.pbs.org/wgbh/pages/frontline/shows/evil/

ENDNOTES: CHAPTER 4. CASE STUDIES OF HUMAN RIGHTS ABUSES

[1] *Enotes*, "Genocide: Shaka Zulu." http://www.enotes.com/genocide-encyclopedia/shaka-zulu/print
[2] Adam Jones, "Genocide a Comprehensive Introduction," *Genocide Text*, 8. http://www.genocidetext.net/gaci_excerpts.htm
[3] *Enotes*, "Genocide: Shaka Zulu."
[4] Jones, "Genocide," *Genocide Text*, 7
[5] *Enotes*, "Genocide: Shaka Zulu."
[6] Carolyn Hamilton, *Terrific Majesty: Powers of Shaka Zulu and Limits of Historical Invention*, (Cambridge: Harvard Univ. Press, 1998) 36-130.
[7] John Wright, "The Mfecane as Alibi: Thoughts on Dithakong and Mbolompo," *Journal of African History*, (Vol. 39 & 40, Sept./Oct. & Nov./Dec. 1995). http://web.uct.ac.za/depts/sarb/X0033_Wright.html
[8] *About.com*, "What was the Mfecane?" http://africanhistory.about.com/od/africanhistoryfaq/f/Mfecane.htm
[9] *Enotes*, "Genocide: Shaka Zulu."
[10] Adam Hochschild, *King Leopold's Ghost*, (New York: Mariner Books, 1999).

[11] Richard Behar, "Mineral Wealth of the Congo," *Fast Company Magazine*, (June 1, 2008). http://www.fastcompany.com/node/849680/print
[12] Behar, "Congo," *Fast Company*.
[13] *Wikipedia*, "First Congo War and Laurent-Désiré Kabila."
[14] Simon Robinson, "The Deadliest War in the World," *Time Magazine*, (May 28, 2006). http://www.time.com/time/magazine/article/0,9171,1198921,00.html
[15] Joe Bavier, "Congo war-driven crisis kills 45,000 a month," *Reuters*, (Jan. 22, 2008). http://www.reuters.com/article/worldNews/idUSL2280201220080122
[16] Behar, "Congo," *Fast Company*.
[17] Behar, "Congo," *Fast Company*.
[18] Gus Constantine, "Congo's mineral wealth lures exploiters," *Washington Times*, (Sept. 9, 2009). http://www.washingtontimes.com/news/2009/sep/08/congo-mineral-wealth-lures-exploiters//print/
[19] Behar, "Congo," *Fast Company*.
[20] Constantine, "Congo' Mineral Wealth," *Washington Times*.
[21] Behar, "Congo," *Fast Company*.
[22] Behar, "Congo," *Fast Company*.
[23] Constantine, "Congo' Mineral Wealth," *Washington Times*.
[24] *International Council of the Red Cross*, "Democratic Republic of the Congo," (2009). http://www.icrc.org/Web/eng/siteeng0.nsf/htmlall/views-from-field-report-240609/$File/Our-World-Views-from-DRC-I-ICRC.pdf
[25] Lydia Polgreen, "Congo's Death Rate Unchanged Since War Ended," *New York Times*, (Jan. 23, 2008). http://www.nytimes.com/2008/01/23/world/africa/23congo.html?pagewanted=1&_r=1
[26] Polgreen, "Congo's Death Rate," *New York Times*.
[27] Betsy Pisik, "Congo's shame: Rape used as a tool of war," *Washington Times*, (Sept. 8, 2009). http://www.washingtontimes.com/news/2009/sep/08/congos-shame-rape-used-as-tool-of-war//print/
[28] Pisik, "Congo's Shame," *Washington Times*.
[29] Pisik, "Congo's Shame," *Washington Times*.
[30] Betsy Pisik, "Congo: Men told not to shun raped women," *Washington Times*, (Sept. 9, 2009). http://www.washingtontimes.com/news/2009/sep/09/congo-men-told-not-to-shun-raped-women//print/
[31] Behar, "Congo," *Fast Company*.
[32] Jane Springer, *Genocide: A Groundwork Guide*, (Toronto, Canada: Groundwork Books/House of Anansi Press, 2006) 9.
[33] Springer, *Genocide*, 34.
[34] Springer, *Genocide*, 13.
[35] Springer, *Genocide*, 34-35.
[36] Springer, *Genocide*, 35.
[37] *Armenian Genocide Resource Library*, "Armenia." http://www.teachgenocide.org/i-witness/racoubian.htm
[38] Springer, *Genocide*, 19-21.
[39] Springer, *Genocide*, 35 and *Encyclopedia Britannica*, "Armenian Massacres." http://www.britannica.com/EBchecked/topic/35323/Armenian-massacres/35323suppinfo/Supplemental-Information
[40] *Armenian Genocide Resource Library*, "Patterns of Genocide." http://www.teachgenocide.org/files/Patterns_of_Genocide.pdf
[41] Dominik J. Schaller and Jurgen Zimmerer, "Late Ottoman Genocides," *Journal of Genocide Research*, (March 2008). http://www.informaworld.com/smpp/section?content=a790756628&fulltext=713240928
[42] R.J. Rummel, "Holocaust in Comparative and Historical Perspective," *Journal of Social Issues*, (Vol. 3, No.2. Apr. 1, 1998).
[43] *BBC News in Two Minutes*, "Armenian Genocide." http://web.archive.org/web/20070301211630/http://news.bbc.co.uk/2/hi/europe/6045182.stm
[44] Springer, *Genocide*, 38 and Hiroaki Kuromiya, *The Voices of the Dead: Stalin's Great Terror*, (New Haven: Yale Univ. Press, 2007) 2.
[45] Springer, *Genocide*, 39.
[46] Springer, *Genocide*, 39.
[47] Iryna Terlecky, "Ukraine's Holodomor," *Times Online*, (July 2008). http://www.timesonline.co.uk/tol/comment/letters/article4243813.ece
[48] Bureau of Democracy, Human Rights, and Labor, U.S. Department of State, "Diplomacy in Action, Cambodia, International Religious Freedom Report," (2005). http://www.state.gov/g/drl/rls/irf/2005/51507.htm
[49] Springer, *Genocide*, 66.
[50] Springer, *Genocide*, 65-66.
[51] Springer, *Genocide*, 66-67.
[52] Springer, *Genocide*, 70.
[53] Springer, *Genocide*, 67.
[54] Springer, *Genocide*, 67-68.
[55] Springer, *Genocide*, 73.
[56] *Yale University*, "Cambodian Genocide Program, 1994-2008." http://www.yale.edu/cgp/

57 Springer, *Genocide*, 69.
58 Richardson Gill, *The Great Maya Droughts*, (Albuquerque: University of New Mexico Press, 2000).
59 Springer, *Genocide*, 96.
60 Arturo Arias, *Taking Their Word: Literature and Signs of Central America*, (Univ. of Minnesota Press, 2007) 161.
61 Piero Gleijeses, afterword Nick Cullather, "Secret History: The CIA's Account of its Operations in Guatemala, 1952-1954," xxvii.
62 J. Patrice McSherry, "The Evolution of the National Security State: The Case of Guatemala," *Socialism and Democracy*, (Spring/Summer 1990) 133.
63 Susanne Jonas, "Democratization through Peace: The Difficult Case of Guatemala," *Journal of Interamerican Studies and World Affairs*, (Vol. 42, No. 4, Winter, 2000).
64 *Guatemalan Commission for Historical Clarification*, "Human rights violations, acts of violence and assignment of responsibility," (1999). http://shr.aaas.org/guatemala/ceh/report/english/conc2.html
65 The 2000 U.S. Census recorded 480,665 Guatemalan-born respondents; but later estimates have recorded more.
66 Springer, *Genocide*, 96 and *Guatemala Memory of Silence*, "Human Rights Violations."
67 Springer, *Genocide*, 97.
68 *CIA Fact Book*, "Guatemala Genocide." https://www.cia.gov/library/publications/the-world-factbook/
69 Springer, *Genocide*, 96.
70 *The History Place*, "Genocide 20th century, Bosnia Herzegovina." http://www.historyplace.com/worldhistory/genocide/bosnia.htm
71 *History Place*, "Genocide, Bosnia Herzegovina."
72 *CIA Fact Book*, "Bosnia."
73 Springer, *Genocide*, 98 and *History Place*, "Genocide: Bosnia Herzegovina."
74 Springer, *Genocide*, 96-97 and *History Place*, "Genocide: Bosnia Herzegovina."
75 Springer, *Genocide*, 100.
76 *History Place*, "Genocide: Bosnia Herzegovina."
77 Springer, *Genocide*, 99 and *History Place*, "Genocide: Bosnia Herzegovina."
78 *History Place*, "Genocide: Bosnia Herzegovina."
79 Springer, *Genocide*, 101.
80 Springer, *Genocide*, 73.
81 Springer, *Genocide*, 73.
82 *History Place*, "Genocide: Bosnia Herzegovina."
83 *History Place*, "Genocide: Bosnia Herzegovina."
84 *BBC One Minute World News*, "Flashback to Kosovo War," (July 2006). http://news.bbc.co.uk/2/hi/europe/5165042.stm
85 *BBC News in One Minute*, "Obituary: Slobodan Milosevic," (Mar. 11, 2006). http://news.bbc.co.uk/2/hi/europe/655616.stm
86 *BBC News in One Minute*, "Obituary: Slobodan Milosevic."
87 Olivier Roy, *Globalized Islam: The Search For A New Ummah*, (New York: Columbia University Press, 2004) 261.
88 Ahmed Rashid, *Taliban: Militant Islam, Oil, and Fundamentalism in Central Asia*, (New Haven: Yale Univ. Press, 2000).
89 Rashid, *Taliban*, 177 and 74-75.
90 Amy Waldman, "No TV, no Chess, No Kites: Taliban's Code, from A to Z," *New York Times*, (Nov. 22, 2001).
91 Rashid, Taliban, 105.
92 Rashid, *Taliban*, 114.
93 Rashid, *Taliban*, 71, 106, and 218-219.
94 Lawrence Wright, *The Looming Tower: Al Qaeda and the Road to 9/11*, (New York: Vintage, 2006) 337.
95 *CNN World*, "Pakistan and Japan plead for Afghan statues," (Mar. 9, 2001). http://edition.cnn.com/2001/WORLD/asiapcf/central/03/09/afghanistan.destruction/
96 Waldman, `No TV, no Chess, No Kites," *New York Times*.
97 Rashid *Taliban*, 100-102.
98 *Human Rights Watch Report*, "Afghanistan, the massacre in Mazar-e-Sharif," (Nov. 1998). http://www.hrw.org/legacy/reports/reports98/afghan/Afrepor0-03.htm
99 Rashid, *Taliban*, 73.
100 *Human Rights Watch*, "Massacres of Hazras in Afghanistan," (Feb. 2001). http://www.hrw.org/legacy/reports/2001/afghanistan/
101 Rashid, *Taliban*, 32.
102 Edith M. Lederer, "U.N. Panel Accuses Taliban of Selling Drugs to Finance War and Train Terrorists," *Associated Press*, (May 25, 2001).
103 Karen De Young, "Afghanistan Opium Crops Sets Record," *Washington Post*, (Dec 2, 2006). http://12.129.147.65/wp-dyn/content/article/2006/12/01/AR2006120101654.html
104 Rashid, *Taliban*, 71.
105 Wright, *Looming Towers*, 355.
106 Rashid, *Taliban*.
107 Shandana Aurangzeb Durrani, "Reaching out to families torn apart by fighting in Pakistan," *UNICEF*, (June 2009). http://www.unicef.org/infobycountry/pakistan_49925.html?q=printme June, 2009

[108] *Amnesty International, USA,* "Darfur Crisis: Testimonies from Eastern Chad." http://www.amnestyusa.org/document.php?id=ENGAFR200072006
[109] Springer, *Genocide,* 9.
[110] Springer, *Genocide,* 120-121.
[111] Springer, *Genocide,* 122.
[112] *Save Darfur,* "What Has Happened in Darfur? A Darfur Primer." http://www.savedarfur.org/pages/primer
[113] *Amnesty International,* "Darfur Crisis."
[114] Springer, *Genocide,* 130-131 and *BBC World News,* "Quick-Guide: Darfur," (Sept. 2006). http://news.bbc.co.uk/2/hi/africa/5316306.stm
[115] *BBC World News,* "Quick-Guide: Darfur."
[116] *Amnesty International,* "Darfur Crisis."
[117] *Physicians for Human Rights, Darfur Survival Campaign,* "Rape as a Weapon of War in Darfur." http://www.physiciansforhumanrights.org/sudan/rape/slide-show/
[118] *Physicians for Human Rights,* "Rape as a Weapon of War."
[119] Springer, *Genocide,* 10.
[120] *CIA Factbook,* "Sudan." https://www.cia.gov/library/publications/the-world-factbook/geos/su.html
[121] *International Criminal Court,* "Warrant of Arrest for Omar Hassan Ahmad Al Bashir," (Mar. 4, 2009).
[122] *BBC One Minute News,* "Warrant Issued for Sudan's Leader," (Mar. 4, 2009). http://news.bbc.co.uk/2/hi/africa/7923102
[123] *Help Darfur Now.* http://www.helpdarfurnow.org/index.php
[124] Springer, *Genocide,* 11.

Endnotes: Chapter 5. Human Rights Activists

[1] Wangari Maathai, *The Green Belt Movement: Sharing the Approach and Experience,* (New York: Lantern Books, 2006) 6.
[2] Maathai, *The Green Belt Movement,* 2-3.
[3] Maathai, *The Green Belt Movement,* 45 and 22.
[4] Maathai, *The Green Belt Movement,* 17.
[5] Maathai, *The Green Belt Movement,* 35.
[6] Maathai, *The Green Belt Movement,* 22.
[7] Maathai, *The Green Belt Movement,* 25-27.
[8] Maathai, *The Green Belt Movement,* 27.
[9] Maathai, *The Green Belt Movement,* 28-30 and 98.
[10] Maathai, *The Green Belt Movement,* 29.
[11] Maathai, *The Green Belt Movement,* 38 and 95.
[12] Maathai, *The Green Belt Movement,* 37.
[13] Maathai, *The Green Belt Movement,* 18.
[14] Maathai, *The Green Belt Movement,* 45.
[15] Maathai, *The Green Belt Movement,* 18-20.
[16] Maathai, *The Green Belt Movement,* 42.
[17] Maathai, *The Green Belt Movement,* 43.
[18] Maathai, *The Green Belt Movement,* 39-40.
[19] Maathai, *The Green Belt Movement,* 84.
[20] Maathai, *The Green Belt Movement,* 63.
[21] Maathai, *The Green Belt Movement,* 25.
[22] Maathai, *The Green Belt Movement,* 67.
[23] Maathai, *The Green Belt Movement,* 126 and 130.
[24] *Nobel Prize.org,* "Shirin Ebadi." http://nobelprize.org/nobel_prizes/peace/laureates/2003/ebadi-autobio.html
[25] *Nobel Prize.org,* "Shirin Ebadi."
[26] Sandra Mackey, *The Iranians: Persia, Islam and the Soul of a Nation,* (New York: Penguin, 1998) 184.
[27] Denise R. Ames, "Interviews of Iranian students at Tehran University," Iran, (June 5, 2007).
[28] Robin Wright, *The Last Great Revolution Turmoil and Transformation in Iran,* (New York: Alfred A. Knopf, 2000).
[29] Wright, *Last Great Revolution.*
[30] Ervand Abrahamian, *History of Modern Iran,* (Cambridge: Cambridge University Press, 2008) 161.
[31] Shaul Bakhash, *The Reign of the Ayatollahs,* (New York: Basic Books, 1984) 74-82.
[32] Moin, Baqer. *Khomeini: Life of the Ayatollah,* (New York: Thomas Dunne Books, 2000) 228.
[33] Moin, *Khomeini.*
[34] Moin, *Khomeini.*
[35] Wright, *Last Great Revolution.*

[36] Mackey, *Iranians*, 366.
[37] Ames, "Interviews, Iranian Students."
[38] *BBC One Minute World News*, "Shirin Ebadi," (Oct. 10, 2003). http://news.bbc.co.uk/2/hi/middle_east/3181992.stm
[39] *Nobel Prize.org*, "Shirin Ebadi."
[40] *Answers.com*, "Shirin Ebadi." http://www.answers.com/topic/shirin-ebadi
[41] *Nobel Prize.org*, "Shirin Ebadi."
[42] *BBC One Minute World News*, "Shirin Ebadi,"
[43] *Burma Campaign*, "About Burma." http://burmacampaign.org.uk/about-burma/
[44] *Burma Campaign*, "About Burma."
[45] *Burma Campaign*, "About Burma."
[46] *BBC News*, "Asia-Pacific: Obituary: A courageous and patient man," (Mar. 27, 1999). http://news.bbc.co.uk/2/hi/asia-pacific/305487.stm
[47] *Burma Campaign*, "About Burma."
[48] *Burma Campaign*, "About Burma."
[49] *Burma Campaign*, "About Burma."
[50] *Burma Campaign*, "About Burma."
[51] *Burma Campaign*, "About Burma."
[52] *Asia News It*, "Aung San Suu Kyi to be put under house detention," (June 9, 2009). http://www.asianews.it/index.php?l=en&art=15461
[53] *Asia News*, "Aung San Suu Kyi."
[54] *Asia News*, "Aung San Suu Kyi."
[55] Rigoberta Menchu, (trans. Ann Wright), *I, Rigoberta Menchu: An Indian Woman in Guatemala*, (New York: Verso Press, 1984) 2.
[56] Menchu *I, Rigoberta Menchu*, 3-4.
[57] Menchu *I, Rigoberta Menchu*, 5-6.
[58] Menchu *I, Rigoberta Menchu*, 8-9 and 15.
[59] Menchu *I, Rigoberta Menchu*, 8-9.
[60] Menchu *I, Rigoberta Menchu*, 134.
[61] Menchu *I, Rigoberta Menchu*, 24-25.
[62] Menchu *I, Rigoberta Menchu*, 31-32.
[63] Menchu *I, Rigoberta Menchu*, 36-37.
[64] Menchu *I, Rigoberta Menchu*, 48.
[65] Menchu *I, Rigoberta Menchu*, 51.
[66] Menchu *I, Rigoberta Menchu*, 57.
[67] Menchu *I, Rigoberta Menchu*, 54-55.
[68] Menchu *I, Rigoberta Menchu*, 55.
[69] Menchu *I, Rigoberta Menchu*, 1.
[70] Menchu *I, Rigoberta Menchu*, 60.
[71] Menchu *I, Rigoberta Menchu*, 88.
[72] Menchu *I, Rigoberta Menchu*, 111.
[73] Menchu *I, Rigoberta Menchu*, 111-114.
[74] Menchu *I, Rigoberta Menchu*, 114.
[75] Menchu *I, Rigoberta Menchu*, 115-116.
[76] Menchu *I, Rigoberta Menchu*, 118 and 167.
[77] Menchu *I, Rigoberta Menchu*, xiv.
[78] Muhammad Yunus, *Banker to the Poor: Micro Lending and the Battle Against World Poverty*, (New York: Perseus Books Group, 1999) 3-10.
[79] Yunus, *Banker to the Poor*, 7-12.
[80] Yunus, *Banker to the Poor*, 14-16.
[81] Yunus, *Banker to the Poor*, 35.
[82] Yunus, *Banker to the Poor*, 45-47.
[83] Yunus, *Banker to the Poor*, 62-63.
[84] Kerry Kennedy, *Speak Truth to Power: Human Rights Defenders Who are Changing Our World*, (New York: Umbrage Editions) 25.
[85] Kennedy, *Speak Truth to Power*, 26.
[86] Kennedy, *Speak Truth to Power*, 25.
[87] Kennedy, *Speak Truth to Power*, 25.
[88] Kennedy, *Speak Truth to Power*, 26.
[89] Kennedy, *Speak Truth to Power*, 26-27.
[90] Kennedy, *Speak Truth to Power*, 25 and 27.

⁹¹ Kennedy, *Speak Truth to Power*, 27.
⁹² Kennedy, *Speak Truth to Power*, 28.
⁹³ Kennedy, *Speak Truth to Power*, 28-29.
⁹⁴ Kennedy, *Speak Truth to Power*, 29.
⁹⁵ Kennedy, *Speak Truth to Power*, 29.
⁹⁶ *Associated Press*, "Yunus wins peace Nobel for his anti-poverty efforts," MSNBC, (Oct. 13, 2006). http://www.msnbc.msn.com/id/15246216/
⁹⁷ Patricia Cronin Marcello, *The Dalai Lama: A Biography*, (Westport, CT: Greenwood Press, 2003).
⁹⁸ *Dalai Lama Website*, "His Holiness the Dalai Lama: A Brief Biography." http://www.dalailama.com/page.105.htm
⁹⁹ Kennedy, *Speak Truth to Power*, 35.
¹⁰⁰ Kennedy, *Speak Truth to Power*, 35.
¹⁰¹ *Library of Tibetan Works and Archives*, "The government of Tibet in exile," (2008). http://www.tibet.com/ltwa.html
¹⁰² *Dalai Lama Website*, "Biography of Dalai Lama."
¹⁰³ *BBC News*, "Profile: The Dalai Lama." http://news.bbc.co.uk/2/hi/asia-pacific/1347735.stm
¹⁰⁴ *BBC News*, "Profile: The Dalai Lama."
¹⁰⁵ Kennedy, *Speak Truth to Power*," 35-36.
¹⁰⁶ Kennedy, *Speak Truth to Power*, 37.
¹⁰⁷ Kennedy, *Speak Truth to Power*, 37.
¹⁰⁸ *BBC News*, "Profile: The Dalai Lama."
¹⁰⁹ *Rediff India Abroad*, "Dalia Lama announces semi-retirement," (Dec. 17, 2008). http://www.rediff.com/news/2008/dec/17tibetrow-dalai-lama-announces-semi-retirement.htm

ENDNOTES: CHAPTER 6: HUMAN RIGHTS TODAY

¹ James Nickel, "Human Rights," *Stanford Encyclopedia of Philosophy*, (Jul 29, 2006). http://plato.stanford.edu/entries/rights-human/#GenIdeHumRig
² Nickel, "Human Rights," *Stanford Encyclopedia*.
³ Nickel, "Human Rights," *Stanford Encyclopedia*.
⁴ Nickel, "Human Rights," *Stanford Encyclopedia*.
⁵ *Human Constitutional Rights Documents*, "Elimination of All Forms of Racial Discrimination." http://www.hrcr.org/docs/CERD/cerd2.html
⁶ *United Nations*, "Convention on the Elimination of All Forms of Discrimination Against Women." http://www.un.org/womenwatch/daw/cedaw/
⁷ *United Nations*, "UNICEF." http://www.unicef.org/crc/
⁸ *United Nations*, "Convention against Torture and Other Cruel, Inhuman or Degrading Treatment." http://www.un.org/millennium/law/iv-9.htm
⁹ Nickel, "Human Rights," *Stanford Encyclopedia*.
¹⁰ Nickel, "Human Rights," *Stanford Encyclopedia*.
¹¹ *United Nations*, "Refugee Agency," ret. May 8, 2015. http://www.unhcr.org/pages/49c3646c2.html
¹² *United Nations*, "World Health Organization," ret. 5/8/15. http://www.who.int/about/en/
¹³ *United Nations*, "World Food Program," ret. 5/8/15. http://www.wfp.org/about
¹⁴ Nickel, "Human Rights," *Stanford Encyclopedia*.
¹⁵ Nickel, "Human Rights," *Stanford Encyclopedia*.
¹⁶ *Organization of American States* (OAS). http://www.oas.org/en/default.asp
¹⁷ *University of Minnesota Human Rights Library*, "African Charter on Human and People's Rights." http://www1.umn.edu/humanrts/instree/z1afchar.htm and Nickel, "Human Rights," *Stanford Encyclopedia*.
¹⁸ *Arab Charter on Human Rights*. http://www.humanrights.ch/en/standards/other-regions-instruments/arab-charter-on-human-rights/
¹⁹ *Arab Charter on Human Rights*.
²⁰ *Human Rights Watch*, "Civil Society Denounces Adoption of Flawed ASEAN Human Rights Declaration," ret. Jan. 17, 2013. http://www.hrw.org/news/2012/11/19/civil-society-denounces-adoption-flawed-asean-human-rights-declaration
²¹ Nickel, "Human Rights," *Stanford Encyclopedia*.
²² Paul Hawken, *Blessed Unrest*, (New York: Penguin Group, 2007) 2.
²³ Nickel, "Human Rights," *Stanford Encyclopedia*.
²⁴ Nickel, "Human Rights," *Stanford Encyclopedia*.
²⁵ Nickel, "Human Rights," *Stanford Encyclopedia*.
²⁶ Peter Benenson, "The forgotten prisoners," *The Observer*, (May 28, 1961). http://www.amnestyusa.org/about/observer.html
²⁷ *Amnesty International*, "Who we are." http://www.amnesty.org/en/who-we-are
²⁸ *Amnesty International*, "Who we are."

Endnotes

[29] *Amnesty International*, "Who we are."

[30] *Amnesty International*, "Who we are."

[31] *Amnesty International USA*, "Activist Toolkit," http://www.amnestyusa.org/get-activist-toolkit/page.do?id=103104

[32] *Norwegian Nobel Committee*, "2002 Nobel Peace Prize announcement," (Oct. 11, 2002).

[33] *The Carter Center*, "Peace Programs," (2009). www.cartercenter.org

[34] *Carter Center*, "Peace Programs."

[35] *Human Rights First*, "Human Rights Defenders program." http://www.humanrightsfirst.org/defenders/hr_defenders.aspx

[36] *Human Rights First*, "Human Rights Law & Security program." http://www.humanrightsfirst.org/us_law/us_law.asp

[37] *Human Rights First*, "Human Rights Protection program." http://www.humanrightsfirst.org/asylum/asylum.aspx

[38] *Human Rights First*, "Human Rights Fighting Discrimination." http://www.humanrightsfirst.org/us_law/us_law.asp

[39] *Human Rights Watch*, "Stopping Rape as a Weapon of War in the Congo." http://www.hrw.org/en/our-work

[40] *Human Rights Watch*, "Stopping Rape."

[41] *International Criminal Court*, "Warrant of Arrest unsealed against five LRA Commanders," (Oct. 14, 2005).

[42] *Human Rights Watch*, "Stopping Rape."

[43] *International Committee of the Red Cross*, "Who We Are," ret. May 15, 2015. https://www.icrc.org/en/who-we-are

[44] *International Committee of the Red Cross*, "Who We Are."

[45] *International Committee of the Red Cross*, "Syria," ret. May 15, 2015. https://www.icrc.org/en/document/syria-yarmouk-refugees

[46] *International Committee of the Red Cross*, "South Sudan," ret. May 15, 2015. https://www.icrc.org/en/document/south-sudan-tens-thousands-flee-fighting-face-critical-food-shortages

[47] *International Committee of the Red Cross*, "Ukraine," ret. May 15, 2015. https://www.icrc.org/en/document/russian-federation-icrc-steps-assistance-displaced-people-east-ukraine

[48] *International Committee of the Red Cross*, "Support Us," ret. May 15, 2015. https://www.icrc.org/en/support-us/where-does-your-money-go

[49] *Oxfam International*, ret. May 15, 2015. https://www.oxfam.org/en/about

[50] *Oxfam International*, "From grove to market: Palestinian olive harvest in Farkha." https://www.oxfam.org/en/occupied-palestinian-territory-and-israel/grove-market-palestinian-olive-harvest-farkha?utm_source=oxf.am&utm_medium=ZoXm&utm_content=redirect

[51] *Oxfam International*, "From grove to market."

[52] *RFK Center on Human Rights*, ret. May 15, 2015. http://rfkcenter.org/rfk?lang=en

[53] James Gerken, "California Lawyer With Terminal Cancer Sues State For Right To Die Peacefully," *Huffington Post*, (May 19, 2015). http://www.msn.com/en-us/news/us/california-lawyer-with-terminal-cancer-sues-state-for-right-to-die-peacefully/ar-BBjVOMK

[54] *National Right to Life*, ret. May 15, 2015. http://www.nrlc.org/about/mission/

[55] *Ethics and International Affairs*. http://www.ethicsandinternationalaffairs.org/2013/just-business-multinational-corporations-and-human-rights-by-john-gerard-ruggie/

[56] *United Nation*, "Environmental Protection," ret. May 15, 2015. http://www.unep.org/environmentalgovernance/Events/HumanRightsandEnvironment/tabid/2046/language/en-US/Default.aspx

GLOSSARY

abolitionist movement its goal was to end slavery and the Atlantic slave trade. (2)

addresses when a person has his/her human rights violated, instead, the violated person addresses his/her own government. (1)

advocacy urging support for human rights and attempting to influence governments or international groups with regard to specific actions. It involves education, persuasion, public exposure, criticism and provoking specific responses to human rights abuses. (6)

African Charter on Human and Peoples' Rights (Banjul Charter, 1981) promotes and protects human rights and basic freedoms for Africans. In addition to recognizing individual rights, it supports collective or group rights. (1)

African Commission on Human and Peoples' Rights (1987) promoting and protecting human rights and collective (peoples') rights throughout Africa, reports to the African Union.

African crisis distressed state of affairs in many areas of Africa resulting in poverty, unemployment, disease, environmental degradation, political corruption, population pressures, malnutrition/starvation, and the subjugation of women. (5)

ahimsa nonviolence in Sanskrit, an ancient Indian language, a practice characteristic of Buddhism. (1)

Albuquerque Center for Peace and Justice located in New Mexico, it provides resources and space for organizations and individuals working on peace and justice issues to network with one another and share information. (6)

American Federation of Labor (AFL) largest union in the U.S. for the first half of the 20th century, founded by Samuel Gompers in 1886 who served as president until his death. (2)

Amnesty International a worldwide NGO whose mission is "to conduct research and generate action to prevent and end grave abuses of human rights and to demand justice for those whose rights have been violated." (6)

animal rights non-humans are entitled to the possession of their own lives and that their most basic interests—such as the lack of suffering—should be afforded the same consideration as humans. (6)

anti-consumerism, a social movement that rejects certain kinds of consumerism, condemns modern corporations. (2)

Arab Charter on Human Rights (ACHR) adopted by the League of Arab States in 2004, affirms the principles in the UN Charter, the Universal Declaration of Human Rights, the International Covenants on Human Rights and the Cairo Declaration on Human Rights in Islam. (6)

Armenians lived for over 2,000 years in the mountains of central Asia, now eastern Turkey. Because the harsh landscape and long winters isolated the Armenians from outside invaders, they were able to keep their language, culture, religion (Christian) and identity intact. (4)

ASEAN Intergovernmental Commission on Human Rights (AICHR) inaugurated in October 2009 as an agency of the Association of Southeast Asian Nations. It promotes and protects human rights, and regional co-operation on human rights in its member states. (6)

Ashoka the Great ruled from 272 to 231 BCE the Maurya Empire in India. A contributor to human rights. (1)

Babi Yar massacre of Jews in the Ukraine, Soviet Union, in 1941, by Germans. (3)

Black Power movement was a defense against racial oppression and black separatism—promoted the establishment of separate social institutions and a self-sufficient, separate economy. (2)

Bosnia and Herzegovina, seceded from Yugoslavia in 1992, the Serbian army invaded shortly. Bosnian Serbs were armed and ready to assist the Serbian forces led by Milosevic in joining greater Serbia. (4)

Buddhism currently has 365 million followers and is the world's 4th largest religion, founder Siddhartha Gautama (563-460 BCE). (1)

burqa all black bulky robe covering the entire body except for a small screen at eye level, typically worn by traditional Muslim women. (4)

Cambodia lies in the southeastern part of Asia, it was once part of the powerful Hindu and Buddhist Khmer Empire, which ruled most of the Indochina Peninsula between the 11th and 14th centuries. (4)

Carson, Rachel (1907-1964) wrote *Silent Spring* in 1962, and it is widely credited with advancing the modern environmental movement. (2)

Carter Center founded by former U.S. President Jimmy Carter (1977 to 1981), its mission is "to find peaceful solutions to international conflicts, to advance democracy and human rights, and to promote economic and social development." (6)

collectivization peasant farmers in the Soviet Union reluctantly handed over ownership of their land and control of production to large-scale, industrial, state-owned farms. (4)

Confucianism a Chinese ethical and philosophical system that focuses on human morality and wrong action. (1)

Congress of Industrial Organizations (CIO) union organized in 1934 for assembly lines workers. (2)

conservation a social movement that sought to protect natural resources, including plant and animal species and their habitat. (2)

Constitution of Medina, drafted by Muhammad in 622, an early document that set out certain rights. (1)

consumerism consumption of particular material goods that support a specific life-style that society in general considers important. (2)

Convention on Elimination of All Forms of Discrimination against Women (CEDAW) (1979) an international bill of rights for women. (1)

Convention on the Rights of the Child (1989) extends children's human rights, more so than any other legal document up to that point. (1)

Convention on the Rights of All Migrant Workers (1990) a migrant worker is a person "engaged in a remunerated [paid] activity in a State of which he or she is not a national." (1)

crime of aggression (1974) the UN General Assembly defined it as the act of one nation against another. (3)

crimes against humanity particularly odious offences in that they constitute a serious attack on human dignity or grave humiliation or a degradation of one or more human beings. (3)

Cyrus Cylinder following the Persian conquest of Babylon in 539 BCE, emperor Cyrus the Great (600-530 BCE) issued a document describing how he had improved the lives of citizens of Babylonia, sent home lost peoples and rebuilt temples and shrines. (1)

Dalai Lama a line of religious leaders in Tibetan Buddhism. "Lama" refers to Tibetan Buddhist teachers. The current Dalai Lama is the 14th in the line of religious leaders who have chosen to be reborn in order to enlighten others. (5)

Darfur is a large province in the Republic of Sudan. It is located in the northeast part of Africa. Genocide took place in the province. (4)

Declaration on the Rights of Indigenous Peoples (2007) sets an important standard for the treatment of indigenous peoples. (2)

Democratic Republic of the Congo (DRC) located in Central Africa, a mineral-rich country and site of human rights abuses. (4)

Dewey, John (1859-1952) led the progressive education movement and is arguably the most influential educator in U.S. history. As an alternative to the drill-and-recitation methods Dewey said education should be grounded in experience. (2)

disability is the result of an impairment that may be physical, mental, sensory, emotional, developmental, or some combination of these. A disability may be present from birth or happen during a person's lifetime. (2)

Eastern worldview sees collective or group as more important than the individual. The significance of the family, group, clan, tribe, or nation overshadows individual achievements, desires, goals, or dreams. (1)

Ebadi, Shirin a human rights and democracy activist, lawyer and founder of the Center for the Defense of Human Rights in Iran, was awarded the 2003 Nobel Peace Prize for her efforts for democracy and human rights, especially women's, children's, and refugee rights. She was the first Iranian and the first Muslim woman to receive the prize. (5)

ecology is a branch of biology dealing with the study of living things, their environment, and the relationship between the two. When used in a cultural sense, it means the study of the detrimental effects of modern civilization on the environment. (2)

Edicts of Ashoka a collection of 33 writings on pillars, boulders, and cave walls scattered throughout northern India. The edicts spell out social and moral principles, that today we would call human rights. (1)

Eightfold Path in Buddhism includes right understanding, right thinking, right speech, right conduct, right livelihood, right effort, right mindfulness, and right concentration. (1)

Emancipation Proclamation signed by Abraham Lincoln in 1863, declaring slaves free within the bounds of the Confederacy. (2)

Enlightenment a 17th and 18th centuries philosophical movement in Europe that started to question the power of the kings and queens. They suggested a "social contract" between the rulers and the ruled, a concept similar to today's idea of human rights. (1)

Ethic of Reciprocity the Golden Rule, a worldwide ethical code stating one has a right to just treatment, and a responsibility to ensure justice for all. (1)

ethnic cleansing the maltreatment through imprisonment, removal, or killing of members of an ethnic minority by a local majority to achieve ethnic homogeneity in majority-controlled territory. (3)

euthanasia the practice of intentionally ending a life in order to relieve pain and suffering. (6)

European Convention for the Protection of Human Rights (1950) an international treaty to protect human rights in Europe. All 47 Council of Europe member states are party to the Convention and new members are expected to ratify it. (6)

European Social Charter (1961) revised in 1996, guarantees rights and freedoms which affect the daily lives of all individuals. (1)

evil man theory one man formulates genocide, too simplistic and does not explain why accomplices carry out genocide. (3)

first generation of human rights limits what others, including the government, can do to an individual and includes life, liberty, right of peaceful assembly, and freedom of thought, religion (worship), and speech. (1)

Five Pillars of Islam are faith, recited as "There is no God but Allah; Muhammad is His prophet," pray five times daily facing Mecca, almsgiving, or giving to the poor, fasting during the holy month of Ramadan, pilgrimage to Mecca, if possible, once a lifetime. (1)

Four Noble Truths of Buddhism suffering is real and has many causes, the cause of suffering is the desire to have and control things, there is an end to suffering which stops with final enlightenment, in order to end suffering, one must follow the Eightfold Path. (1)

Frank, Anne one of the million Jewish children killed during the Holocaust. She gained international fame with publication of her diary after her death which chronicles her experiences hiding from the Nazis during their occupation of the Netherlands. (3)

Freedom House founded in 1941 by Eleanor Roosevelt and Wendell Willkie (Republican presidential candidate in 1940). Today it is an independent watchdog organization that monitors freedom, and advocates for democracy and human rights around the world. (6)

Friedan, Betty wrote *The Feminine Mystique* in 1963, is often credited with igniting the second phase of the women's movement. (2)

genocide the deliberate and orderly massacre of a national, racial, political, or cultural group. (3)

Genocide Convention (1948) the UN Convention on the Prevention and Punishment of the Crime of Genocide (CPPCG). (1)

global justice movements are a loose collection of individuals and groups with the common theme of disapproval of the way that the world political-economy is functioning. (2)

God-given rights people are endowed by their Creator with certain inalienable rights that among these are "life, liberty, and the pursuit of happiness." These must be very general so that they can be applied across thousands of years of human history, not just recent history. (1)

Golden Rule see Ethic of Reciprocity (1)

Grameen Bank founded by Muhammad Yunus, this bank is still going strong today with 2.4 million families with loans, and more than 1,050 branches serving 35,000 villages in Bangladesh; 94 percent of the clients are women. (5)

Greek philosophers, Plato, Socrates, and Aristotle, thought that nature sets natural law and was everywhere. It provided the basis for rational systems of justice in order for humans to evaluate the moral authority of man-made laws. (1)

Green Belt Movement (GBM) founded by Wangari Maathai in Kenya in 1977. The movement is a grassroots NGO that focuses on environment conservation and development through a nationwide tree-planting campaign. (5)

Greensboro sit-in (1960), four African American college students staged a "sit-in" at a "white's only" lunch counter at a Woolworth's store in Greensboro, North Carolina. The lunch counter only had stools for whites, while blacks had to stand to eat. (2)

group rights protect ethnic groups from genocide and support ownership of their national territories and resources. (1)

Guatemala an independent country located in Central America just south of Mexico. Its history includes the impressive Mayan civilization that built countless sites that are still standing. (4)

Guatemala Civil War (1960-1996) the longest civil war in Latin American history, pitted the right-wing, Guatemalan military government against leftist (communist) and indigenous guerilla movements. The U.S. supported the military regime. (4)

Hammurabi's Code named after King Hammurabi of Babylon (Iraq and Syria today), which was etched onto a seven foot slab of basalt stone in 1780 BCE, one of the earliest legal codes. (1)

High Commissioner for Human Rights (1993), the UN established this office to coordinate its many human rights activities. (6)

Hitler, Adolph born in a small Austrian village, leader of Germany during World War II and main architect of the Holocaust. (3)

Holocaust is the classic case of genocide. The mass killings took place in Germany and Eastern Europe primarily during World War II (1939-1945). The main architect of the slaughter was the German leader Adolph Hitler. (3)

Holodomor name given to Joseph Stalin's crimes against humanity, targeted Ukrainian peasants for resisting agricultural collectivization. (4)

GLOSSARY

Human Rights First a nonprofit that focuses on protecting the rights of refugees, supporting human rights defenders, and pressing for the U.S. government's full participation in the international human rights system. (6)

Human Rights Watch a non-profit NGO that focuses international attention on areas where human rights are being violated, gives voice to the oppressed, and holds the perpetrators accountable for their crimes. (6)

humanism an educational and philosophical outlook that emphasizes the personal worth of the individual and the central importance of human values as opposed to only religious belief. (1)

indigenous peoples any ethnic group of people who inhabit a geographic region with which they have the earliest known historical connection. (1,5)

Inter-American Commission on Human Rights (IACHR) (1959) an independent agency of the Organization of American States (OAS), the oldest regional organization of states. (6)

Intergovernmental Panel on Climate Change (IPCC) winner of 2007 Nobel Peace Prize, a leading body for the assessment of climate change. Provides the world with the current state of climate change and its potential environmental and socio-economic consequences. (2)

International Committee of the Red Cross (ICRC) an impartial, neutral organization whose humanitarian mission is to protect the lives and dignity of victims of war and internal violence and to provide them with assistance. It also directs and coordinates international relief. (6)

International Convention on the Elimination of All Forms of Racial Discrimination (ICERD) (1965) promotes second-generation human rights in which signature-nations commit to do away with racial discrimination. (1)

International Criminal Court (ICC) (1998) the Rome Statute of the International Criminal Court. (3)

invasion of Iraq 2003 an example of the crime of aggression. U.S. led the invasion which marked the beginning of the Iraq War to disarm Iraq of weapons of mass destruction (WMD), to end Saddam Hussein's support for terrorism, and to free the Iraqi people. (3)

Iranian Hostage Crisis on November 4, 1979, students stormed the U.S. embassy compound in Tehran, Iran and seized as hostages 53 American diplomats and staff. They were held for 444 days and released on January 20, 1981. (5)

Islam one of the three monotheistic religions, along with Christianity and Judaism that trace their roots to the patriarch Abraham. The religion is based on the teachings found in the Qur'an (Koran), believed by followers to be the exact words of Allah (God) as revealed to the Arab prophet Muhammad through a messenger, the angel Gabriel. (1)

Islamic Revolution in Iran in 1979, revolutionaries overthrew the Shah and imposed an Islamic government. (5)

Janjaweed Sudanese government gave weapons to these local Arab nomadic militia groups who inflicted terror on farmers in Darfur. (4)

Jesus of Nazareth the central figure of Christianity, rebelled against the state control of the Roman Empire. For punishment of his acts of defiance and preaching of a more peaceful world, the Roman state crucified him on the cross. (1)

Judaism is one of the three monotheistic religions. Early followers believed each person can have a personal relationship with God and that he is both merciful and loving, as well as metes out punishment to those who disobey his commands. Also important is the idea of individual worth, which is different from the emphasis on the group. (1)

Khmer Rouge leader was Pol Pot, who sought to remake Cambodia into his vision of an ideal society. A communist, he believed that Cambodia should return to the power and glory of the past. He sought to eliminate anyone who was not "pure" Cambodian. (4)

Khomeini, Ayatollah Ruhollah a conservative Islamic Shia (branch of Islam) cleric, opposed the Shah. Leader of the Iranian Revolution. (5)

King Leopold II of Belgium, from 1870s onward, he dominated the Congo River basin. He formally acquired rights to the territory at the Conference of Berlin in 1885 and made the land his private property, which he ruled until 1908. (4)

King, Martin Luther Jr. leader of the American civil rights movement. (2)

Knights of Labor, organized in 1869, was the first successful national labor organization in the U.S. (2)

kulaks Ukrainian peasant farmers who resisted Stalin collectivization goals. Stalin carried out genocide against them in the 1930s. (4)

labor movement a social movement made up of workers, many have organized themselves into collective associations called unions. (2)

legal rights refer to all those rights found within existing legal codes. A legal right is recognized and protected by the law. (1)

Lemkin, Ralph fought tirelessly for acceptance of the term genocide to describe horrific crimes. (3)

Leopold, Aldo (1887-1948) an American ecologist, forester, and environmentalist, wrote *A Sand County Almanac*. Influential in the development of modern environmental ethics and championed wilderness preservation, introduced a new term: ecology. (2)

LGBT saw infrequent use in the U.S. until the 1990s when those within the movement spoke of gay, lesbian, bisexual and transgender people with equal respect. (2)

limbic system formed over the core brain and stimulated new behaviors, such as protecting others, nurturing the young, and sharing with other humans for survival. (1)

litigation or lawsuits are legal proceedings used to settle a dispute. (2)

lobbying practice of influencing decisions made by governmental legislators or officials for the benefit of its citizens. (2)

Locke, John (1632–1704) famous Enlightenment philosophers, contributed to the concept of natural rights, the notion that people are naturally free and equal. His ideas were important in the development of the modern idea of rights. (1)

Maathai, Wangari (1940-2011) founded the environmental group Green Belt Movement in Kenya in 1977. Awarded the Nobel Peace Prize in 2004. (5)

Magna Carta an English charter first issued in 1215 and written because of a disagreement about the rights of the king, the Catholic Church, and wealthy English landowners. Considered to be a contribution to body of human rights. (1)

Mann, Horace (1769-1859) a leading reformer from Massachusetts who worked for the expansion of public schools in 1837. (2)

materialist a person for whom collecting material goods is an important priority, and more specifically, refers to a person who primarily pursues wealth and luxury. In American society materialism is promoted as an important goal that we all should pursue. (2)

Maurya Empire (321 to 185 BCE) an empire in ancient India that established principles of civil rights in the 3rd century BCE under its ruler: Ashoka the Great. (1)

Menchu, Rigoberta belongs to the Quiche people (a branch of the Mayans), she has worked for the rights of indigenous peoples in Guatemala and throughout the world. For her work, she was awarded the Noble Peace Prize in 1992. (5)

Milosevic, Sloboban a former communist who fanned nationalistic pride and religious hatred to gain power in Serbia in the 1990s. (4)

Mobutu, Joseph came to power in a military coup in the Congo in 1965. The U.S. supported his 31½ year reign. In 1971 he renamed the country the Republic of Zaire. He diverted money from the sale of natural resources for his own personal enrichment. (4)

morals concerned with the principles of right conduct. (1)

moral rights these rights include the sense of decency and justice that each person has simply because they are human. (1)

Muhammad (570-632 CE) founder of Islam based on the teachings found in the Qur'an (Koran), believed by followers to be the exact words of Allah (God) as revealed to Muhammad through the angel Gabriel. Muhammad did not write the Qur'an, but his companions reportedly wrote down his recitations while he was alive. (1)

Muir, John (1838-1914), an American naturalist, scientifically studied plants and animals. His writings and philosophy strongly influenced the formation of the modern environmental movement. He was an early advocate of preservation of U.S. wilderness. (2)

mujahideen Muslim guerilla forces fighting the Soviet Union in Afghanistan in the 1970s. One of the key fighters was Osama Bin Laden. (4)

Myanmar in 1989 the military government changed Burma to "Union of Myanmar." U.S. does not recognize the name change. (5)

natural law is law that reflects the natural order of the universe, essentially the will of the gods who control nature. (1)

neoliberalism seeks to privatize services that the government provides. It supports the removal of regulations on corporate power and reduces government influence in businesses and personal lives. These and other policies took off in the 1980s and are continuing today. (2)

non-governmental organizations (NGOs) refers to a legally constituted organizations created by natural or legal persons with no participation or representation of any government. (6)

Office of the United Nations High Commissioner for Refugees (UNHCR) (1950), also known as the UN Refugee Agency, its primary purpose is to safeguard the rights and well-being of refugees. (6)

Oxfam an NGO, it is an international confederation of 17 organizations working in approximately 94 countries worldwide to find solutions to poverty and what it considers injustice around the world. (6)

Parks, Rosa (1913-2005) is credited with starting the American civil rights movement. (2)

perpetrators plan and recruit others to carry out genocidal killings. They may be the government, government collaborators, an army, mercenaries (private army), a militia (a band of soldiers), or ordinary citizens. (3)

Glossary

Pol Pot leader of Khmer Rouge, determined to remake Cambodia into his ideal society. Although a declared communist, he believed deeply that Cambodia should return to the power and glory it had enjoyed between the 11th and 14th centuries. (4)

Precepts in Buddhism followers are to practice non-violence, not commit theft, avoid sexual misconduct, always speaking truth, avoid intoxicating drinks, drugs, which lead to loss of mindfulness. (1)

preservationists wanted to protect resources in their natural state and did not believe that nature's purpose was to serve humans. Instead, they saw humans as part of nature enveloped in an interdependent web of life. (2)

protectorate different from a colony, self-governing territory protected against third parties by a stronger state. It retains a measure of independence. (4)

protest an objection, complaint or disapproval, reactions to events or situations, sometimes in favor, but most likely opposed. (2)

reptilian brain inherited from reptiles 500 million years ago, our self-centered survival behaviors—feed, fight, flee, and reproduce—direct us with no altruistic impulses. (1)

right to life those who wish to outlaw the intentional termination of a pregnancy. They argue that prenatal humans are human persons from the moment of conception and have the same fundamental "right to life" before birth as humans have after birth. They believe abortion is morally unacceptable. (6)

rightholders a person or agency having a particular right. (1)

RFK Center (Robert F. Kennedy) strives to achieve his vision of a just and peaceful world by partnering with human rights leaders, teaching about social justice, and advancing corporate responsibility. (6)

Roosevelt, Theodore (1901-1909) as president he permanently preserved some of America's most unique natural treasures. (2)

Rwanda central African country, site of genocide in 1994. (3)

St. Thomas Aquinas (1223-1274 CE) a Christian philosopher who expanded upon the idea of natural law, called for the rational guidance of creation by God the "Eternal Law." Humans understand this because of their powers of reason. (1)

Santa Clara County v. Southern Pacific Railway 1886 after the end of the Civil War railroad barons schemed to get the courts to give corporations the rights held by individuals. Citing the 14th amendment, they finally got their chance in this court case. (2)

Second Congo War (1998-2003), known as the African World War or the Great War of Africa, devastated the country and involved seven foreign armies. The war is the largest in modern African history and directly involved eight African nations—Rwanda, Zimbabwe, Uganda, Burundi, Angola, Chad, Sudan, and Namibia—as well as about 25 armed groups. By 2008, the war and its aftermath had killed 5.4 million people, mostly from disease and starvation, making the Second Congo War the deadliest world conflict since World War II. (4)

second generation rights include equality and nondiscrimination for women and minorities, the right to work, fair pay, safe and healthy working conditions, the right to form trade unions, social security, and sufficient food, clothing, housing, health care, and education. (1)

Security Council their mission in the UN is to maintain international peace and security. The 15-member body consists of 5 permanent and 10 elected members. Nine votes are needed to approve any measures. (6)

Shaka (c.1787-1828) a powerful and controversial leader in Zulu history, took over the Zulu Empire in 1816 and has been called a military genius, innovator and reformer, but has also been condemned for the brutality of his reign. (4)

social movement is about changing mainstream ideas, laws, policies, attitudes, and beliefs about a particular issue. (2)

sovereignty the modern world is organized into political units called nations; each nation is independent and allowed to run its own affairs without direct interference from other nations. (3)

Stalin, Joseph ruled the Soviet Union from 1924 until his death in 1953. He launched Five Year Plans to increase industrialization and to make agriculture more productive through collectivization. (4)

Stanton, Elizabeth Cady (1815-1902) co-organized the 1848 Seneca Falls convention, credited as the beginning of the American woman's suffrage movement. (2)

Stoicism, founded by the philosopher Zeno (333-263 BCE) in Athens, Greece, the Stoics provided a complete explanation of natural law. They argued that the universe is governed by reason, or a rational principle sometimes called God, mind, or fate. (1)

Stonewall Inn in Manhattan New York, an incident here in the early morning hours of June 28, 1969 sparked the LGBT movement. (2)

Suu Kyi, Aung San a non-violent pro-democracy activist and chairperson of the National League for Democracy (NLD), a Burmese political party. She was awarded the Nobel Peace Prize in 1991 for her non-violent struggle to restore democracy to Burma. (5)

Taliban an ultra conservative Muslim group who governed according to strict laws mainly in Afghanistan. (4)

Taylor, Charles born in 1948 in Monrovia, Liberia, found guilty in 2012 of 11 war crime charges against him. (3)

Ten Commandments moral foundation of Judaism and Christianity, also important in Islam. (1)

third generation rights include rights for women, minorities, and indigenous peoples. (1)

Thoreau, Henry David (1817-1862) wrote *Walden*, a study of wildlife, simple living, and self-sufficiency, lived what he called a "deliberate life." He wrote an essay, *Civil Disobedience*, individual resistance to civil government is a moral duty if the state is unjust. (2)

Trail of Tears (1830) U.S. President Andrew Jackson authorized the Indian Removal Act that relocated Native Americans from their homelands in the southeast to what was known as Indian Territory in present day Oklahoma in the west. (3)

Tutu, Archbishop Desmond was awarded the Nobel Peace Prize in 1984 for speaking out against apartheid in South Africa. (1)

Ubuntu meaning humanness in Africa, an African ethic that focuses on people's commitment and relations with each other. (1)

UNICEF a human rights treaty passed by the United Nations, the Convention on the Rights of the Child is popularly known as UNICEF. (6)

unions represent the interests of workers by campaigning for better treatment and benefits from employers, and for governments to pass laws granting workers certain rights. (2)

United Nations founded in 1945 at the end of World War II, the purpose is to assist in the cooperation among nations in the areas of international law and security, economic development, social progress, human rights, and achieving world peace. Located on international territory in New York City and has 192 member states. (1)

United Nations Convention against Torture and Other Cruel, Inhuman or Degrading Treatment or Punishment (1984) aims to prevent torture worldwide, requires states to take measures to prevent torture within their national borders, and prevents states from returning those to their home country who may face torture. (1)

United Nation's International Covenant on Economic, Social, and Cultural Rights (1966) Delegates work toward enjoyment of economic, social, and cultural rights (ESCR), including labor, health, education, and an adequate standard of living. (1)

Universal Declaration of Human Rights (UDHR) passed in 1948 under the leadership of Eleanor Roosevelt who served as the President and Chair of U.N. Commission on Human Rights from 1946-1952. A list of over two dozen specific human rights were outlined and passed by member states. Both civil and political rights and economic, social and cultural rights were included as basic human rights. The signatory countries pledged to respect and protect the dignity and rights of all humans across the globe. (1)

Vienna Declaration and Program of Action (VDPA) is a declaration adopted in 1993. It considers the promotion and protection of human rights a matter of high priority for the international community and repeats the universality of human rights as a standard for conduct. (1)

war crimes are violations of the laws or customs of war. The ICC tries war crimes that are violations of the laws in international and non-international armed conflicts. (3)

Washington, Booker T. (1856-1915) a leading voice for the educational and economic improvement of African Americans. He saw vocational education as a way to teach manual skills to African Americans that would help them work their way up the social and economic ladder. (2)

West a shortened term that describes the worldview and/or the specific nations of Western Europe and the United States that share a common history, heritage, and culture. (1)

Western worldview emphasizes individualism: individual accomplishment and responsibility, thinking of oneself as separate from one's family or others. (1)

Wollstonecraft Mary (1759-1797) wrote the Vindication of the Rights of Women (1792), in which she argued that women are not naturally inferior to men but appear to be only because they lack education. (1)

woman's suffrage supported the human rights goal of gaining suffrage for women 21 years and over. (2)

World Food Program (WFP) (1961) is the world's largest humanitarian agency fighting hunger worldwide, headquarters in Rome, Italy. (6)

World Health Organization (WHO), a specialized UN agency, is concerned with international public health. Established on April 7, 1948, now celebrated every year as World Health Day. (6)

worldview a collection of beliefs or the overall perspective from which one sees and interprets the world. (1)

Yugoslavia a former nation in southeastern Europe, was carved out of the defeated Ottoman Empire at the end of World War I in 1918. It was composed of various ethnic and religious groups that had been historical rivals, even bitter enemies, including the Serbs (Orthodox Christians), Croats (Catholics), ethnic Albanians (Muslims), Macedonians (Orthodox Christians), Montenegrins (Orthodox Christians), Slovenes (Roman Catholic, Protestants), and Bosnians and Herzegovinians (mix of all). (4)

Yunus, Muhammad took the path of defending the human rights of some of the poorest women in the world (Bangladesh) through economic empowerment. He won the Noble Peace Prize in 2006. (5)

Zulu is the largest South African ethnic group, with a population of 10-11 million people living mainly in a province in South Africa. Their language, Zulu, is a Bantu language. (4)

Index

A
abolitionist movement 29, 36-38, 40, 42
addresses 9
advocacy 59, 169, 175, 183, 187, 189
Afghanistan 117-122
African Charter on Human and Peoples' Rights 8, 166-167
African crisis 131
ahimsa 23
Albuquerque Center for Peace and Justice 187-188
American Federation of Labor 44
Amnesty International 61, 112, 141, 168, 170-172
animal rights 189
anti-consumerism 54-56
Arab Charter on Human Rights 167
Armenia 104-106
ASEAN Intergovernmental Commission on Human Rights 168
Ashoka 23

B
Babi Yar Massacre 82
Bangladesh 60, 128, 149-150, 152-154
Black Power 47, 51
"blood minerals" 102
Bosnia 112-116
Buddhism 12, 18-20, 23, 108-109, 155, 157, 189

C
Cambodia 75, 77, 108-110, 168
Carson, Rachel 48
Carter Center vii, 170, 172-174, 179
Carter, Jimmy 48, 50, 118, 135-137, 172-174
Carthage 78
child marriage 60-61
child rights movement 36
Christianity 10, 12, 17-19, 23-26, 79
civil disobedience 29, 34, 41, 45, 53
civil rights movement 9, 32-34, 45, 47
collectivization 107
Confucianism 20-21
Congress of Industrial Organizations 44
conservation 41-42, 48-49, 128, 130-132
Constitution of Medina 25
Convention Against Torture 8, 164
Convention on the Rights of All Migrant Workers 8, 164
Convention on the Rights of the Child 8, 60, 164
crime of aggression 62, 65-66
crimes against humanity 62, 65-66, 68-69, 73, 108, 116, 126, 175-176
Cyrus Cylinder 17-18

D

Dalai Lama 20, 154-159
Darfur 76, 103, 122-126, 173
Democratic Republic of the Congo (DRC) 98, 101-103, 173
Dewey, John 39
Diamond, Jared 92-94
disability 59
due process 5, 9, 26

E

Eastern worldview 11
Ebadi, Shirin 128, 133-138
ecology 48-49
Eightfold Path 18-19
Elimination of All Forms of Discrimination Against Women 8, 164
Emancipation Proclamation 29, 38
Enlightenment 4, 18-19, 22, 27-29, 36
Ethic of Reciprocity 12, 20
ethnic cleansing 69, 114-116
European Convention for the Protection of Human Rights 166
European Social Charter 7
Euthanasia 84, 188-190
"evil man" theory 75, 97

F

Five Pillars of Islam 25
Five Precepts 19
Four Noble Truths 18-19
Frank, Anne 85-87
Freedom House vii, 170, 174-175
Friedan, Betty 47

G

gacaca 88-89, 93
genocide 5, 7, 45, 57, 62, 65-67, 70-80, 84, 88-94, 96-98, 104-106, 108, 110, 112, 114-117, 124-126, 157, 163, 169, 176
Genocide Convention 7, 71, 163
global justice movements 52
God-given rights 10
Golden Rule 12, 20
Grameen Bank 152-154
Greek Philosophers 21-22
Green Belt Movement 128-131
Greensboro sit-in 46
group rights 4-5, 8, 10-11, 13-14, 167, 170
Guatemala 110-112, 128, 143-145, 148-149, 176
Guatemala Civil War 111
guerrilla 70, 111-113, 116, 118, 121

H

Hammurabi's Code 16
High Commissioner for Human Rights 164, 168, 171-172

Hitler, Adolph 72, 75, 80-82, 84-85
Holocaust vii, 6, 64, 75-76, 80, 84-85, 87, 100, 106, 125
Holodomor 72, 108
human rights iii, vii-vix, 2-30, 32, 36, 40-41, 43-45, 47, 51-55, 57, 59-60, 62, 64-69, 94, 96, 103-104, 109, 112, 117, 119, 124, 126, 128, 133, 135, 138-142, 149, 154, 156, 159, 162-191
Human Rights First 175-177
Human Rights Watch 66, 120, 138, 141, 168, 170, 177-180
humanism 27
Hutu 75-77, 87-93

I

indigenous peoples 4, 9, 11-13, 36, 56-58, 79-80, 143, 147-149
Inter-American Commission on Human Rights 166
International Committee of the Red Cross 180, 190
International Criminal Court (ICC) 64-65, 67, 74, 126, 172-173, 176
invasion of Iraq, 2003 66, 169
Iranian Hostage Crisis 136
Islam 10, 17-18, 24-26, 106, 115, 118-121, 128, 134-137, 167-168
Islamic Revolution 134-135, 137

J

Janjaweed 76, 124-126
Jesus 12, 23-24, 78
Judaism 10, 17, 24
Judeo-Christian tradition 17

K

Kennedy, Robert F. 127, 170, 185-186
Khmer Rouge 109-110
Khomeini, Ayatollah Ruhollah 134-138
King Leopold II 98-100
King, Martin Luther Jr. 32, 34, 42, 45, 47
Knights of Labor 43-44
Kosovo 112-113, 116-117

L

labor movement 43-44
legal rights 9, 26, 162
Lemkin, Ralph 70-73
Leopold, Aldo 48-49
LGBT movement 59
litigation 35-36, 54
lobbying 35, 37, 40, 50, 59, 73, 169-170
Locke, John 27-28
Love Canal 49-50

M

Maathai, Wangari 128-133
Magna Carta 26
Mann, Horace 38-39
"market women" in Liberia 71
McLibel Trial 54
Menchú, Rigoberta 111-112, 128, 143-149

Mfecane 97-98
Milosevic, Slobodan 70, 113, 115-117
Mobutu, Joseph 100-101
Mongols 79
moral rights 9, 40
morals 6, 10
Mother Jones 43
Muhammad 24-26
Muir, John 41-42
mujahideen 118
My Lai Massacre 68

N

natural law 21-23, 27-28
non-governmental organizations (NGOs) 58, 60-61, 121, 126, 128, 169-170, 173, 177, 182, 185, 188, 190

O

Ottoman Turks 104-105
Oxfam 170, 182-183

P

Parks, Rosa 32, 45
perpetrators 64, 71, 74-77, 88, 90-92, 103, 106, 110, 112, 176-177
Pol Pot 109-110, 157
preservationists 41-42
protectorate 106, 108
public education 36, 38-39

R

reptilian brain 3, 191
RFK Center for Human Rights 185
right to life 4, 5, 10, 168, 183, 189-190
rightholder 9
Roma 75-76, 80, 84
Roosevelt, Theodore 41-42
Rwanda 75-77, 80, 87-94, 101-102, 125, 169, 171, 176

S

Santa Clara County v. Southern Pacific Railroad 53
Second Congo War 101
Security Council 66, 164-165
Serbia 113-116
Shaka 96-98
six families of rights 4-5
social movements 30, 32-36, 45, 50-51, 58, 60, 62
St. Thomas Aquinas 23-24
Stalin, Joseph 107-108, 155
Stanton, Elizabeth Cady 40
Stoicism 22
Stonewall Inn 50-51
Sudan 8, 58, 76, 101, 119, 122-126, 174, 181
Suu Kyi, Aung San 139-143

T

Taliban 117-122
Taylor, Charles 68-71
Ten Commandments 17, 19, 179
Thalib, Munir Said 176
Thoreau, Henry David 29, 41-42
three generations of rights 4
Tibet 128, 154-159
Trail of Tears 68-69, 80
Tutsi 75-77, 87-93
Tutu, Archbishop Desmond 14

U

Ubuntu 14-16
Ukraine 72, 83, 106-108, 181-182
UNICEF 61-62, 122, 164
unions 4-5, 29, 43-44, 52, 54, 141, 147-148, 185
United Nations 6-8, 24, 30, 57, 59-60, 64, 149, 162-165, 171, 176, 178, 190
Universal Declaration of Human Rights 6-7, 12, 21, 24, 29-30, 156, 162-163, 166-167, 171, 173
universal rights 3

V

Vienna Declaration 8

W

war crimes 62, 65, 67-68, 70, 72, 76, 116, 124, 126, 175-176, 178
Washington, Booker T. 39
Western worldview 11-12
Wollstonecraft, Mary 28
woman's suffrage 29, 40
World Food Program 165
World Health Organization 165

Y

Yunus, Muhammad 128, 149-154

Z

Zulu 14, 96-98

ABOUT THE AUTHOR

Dr. Denise R. Ames is an educator with over 30 years teaching experience at secondary schools, universities, a community college, adult educational programs, and professional development workshops. She took her bachelor's degree in history education from Southern Illinois University, and master's degree and doctorate in history education with a focus in world history from Illinois State University. Her teaching topics range from academic subjects such as world history, global issues, United States history, Western Civilization, world humanities, cultural studies, and global business issues, to secondary social studies classes, pedagogy, and current topics such as global issues, the global economy, global education, and global awareness.

Dr. Ames is currently the founder and President of the Center for Global Awareness, a non-profit organization developing books and educational resources from a holistic approach and global perspective for students and educators in grades 9 through university. Her extensive travels, personal experiences, reflections, and scholarly research have all contributed to her common sense approach to the often overwhelming subjects she teaches and writes about. She is dedicated to working with educators, students, and the general public to foster a better understanding of the myriad of global issues we face, a holistic teaching model for world history, and the effects of the global economy on ourselves, the global community, and the environment.

Dr. Ames has presented numerous classes, workshops, and lectures on her holistic world history, the global economy, cross-cultural understanding, and global awareness locally, nationally, and internationally. In addition to her latest book *Human Rights: Towards a Global Values System*, she is the author of *Waves of Global Change: A Holistic World History* (2nd edition), *Waves of Global Change: An Educator's Handbook for Teaching a Holistic World History*, *The Global Economy: Connecting the Roots of a Holistic System*, *Connecting the Roots of the Global Economy: A Brief Edition*, and *Financial Literacy: Wall Street and How it Works*. She has also written numerous blogs, lesson plans, articles, and teaching units for the Center for Global Awareness.

World cultures and history have been Dr. Ames' life-long interest and study. Her extensive travels have taken her throughout the United States and to many international locations. Her destinations include (in order of most recent with year) Bahrain, United Arab Emirates, Qatar (2015), South Korea (2014), Germany (2014, 2013), China (2011, 1991), Turkey (2011), Iran (2007), Mexico (2007, 1974, 1967), Singapore (2006), Malaysia (2006), Spain, France, Italy (2006), Syria, Lebanon (2005), Costa Rica (2005, 2001), United Kingdom (2000), Israel, Palestine (1999), Galapagos Islands (1999), Ecuador (1999), Russia (1998), Slovenia (1996), Caribbean Islands (1996), Hong Kong (1991), Austria, Czech Republic, Slovakia, Hungary, former East Germany (1990), Soviet Union (Russia, Ukraine, Moldova, 1989), Brazil, Argentina (1988), Netherlands, Belgium, West Germany (1983), and Canada (many times). Most of her travel experiences focused on historical, economic and cultural developments in the particular country.

Along with her professional interests and work in history, global issues, and education, Dr. Ames has owned her own small retail business for eight years, constructed and remodeled eight houses, and exhibited and trained Arabian horses. She has two adult children, their spouses, and a granddaughter. She particularly enjoys traveling, hiking, yoga, reading, biking, gardening, and visiting with family and friends. She and her husband Jim currently reside near the campus of the University of New Mexico in sunny Albuquerque, New Mexico, USA.

www.ingramcontent.com/pod-product-compliance
Lightning Source LLC
Chambersburg PA
CBHW081742100526
44592CB00015B/2267